Uganda Now

EASTERN AFRICAN STUDIES

Abdul Sheriff
Slaves, Spices & Ivory in Zanzibar
Integration of an East African Commercial Empire
into the World Economy 1770-1873

Tabitha Kanogo
Squatters & the Roots of Mau Mau 1905–1963

David W. Throup
Economic and Social Origins of Mau Mau 1945–1953

David William Cohen & E. S. Atieno Odhiambo
Siaya
*The Historical Anthropology of an African Landscape**

Bruce Berman & John Lonsdale
Unhappy Valley
*Clan, Class & State in Colonial Kenya**

Bethwell A. Ogot & Christopher Ehret
*A History of Early Eastern Africa**

* forthcoming

This volume,
and the conference upon which it is based,
were sponsored by
the Danish Research Council for Development Research,
the Danish Social Science Research Council,
the Danish International Development Agency (DANIDA),
and the Institute of Commonwealth Studies, London University.
Thanks are also given to
the British Council and the Noel Buxton Trust
for assistance with travel expenses.
Thanks to the good offices of
the World Lutheran Federation
and Danchurchaid
copies are available for sale
in Uganda.

Uganda Now

Between Decay
& Development

EDITED BY
HOLGER BERNT HANSEN
& MICHAEL TWADDLE

WITHDRAWN

JAMES CURREY
London

OHIO UNIVERSITY PRESS
Athens

HEINEMANN KENYA
Nairobi

James Currey Ltd
54b Thornhill Square, Islington
London N1 1BE

Heinemann Kenya
Kijabe Street, P.O. Box 45314
Nairobi, Kenya

Ohio University Press
Scott Quadrangle
Athens, Ohio 45701, USA

Available in Uganda from
Uganda Bookshop
P.O. Box 7145
Kampala

British Library Cataloguing in Publication Data
Uganda now: between decay and development.
——— (Eastern African Studies)
1. Uganda. Social conditions
I. Hansen, Holger Bernt   II. Twaddle, Michael
967.6'104

ISBN 0-85255-315-3
ISBN 0-85255-316-1 Pbk

Library of Congress Cataloging-in-Publication Data
Uganda Now: between decay and development
edited by Holger Bernt Hansen and Michael Twaddle
p   cm
Bibliography: p
Includes index
1. Uganda ——— History ——— 1979
2. Uganda ——— Economic conditions ——— 1979
I. Hansen, Holger Bernt
II. Twaddle, Michael
DT433.285.U43 1988   967. 6'104 ——— DC19 88–5370

ISBN 0–8214–0896–8
ISBN 0–8214–0897–6 (Pbk)

Typesetting by Mikkel Hansen
in association with Saxon Printing Ltd
Printed in Great Britain
by Villiers Publications, London N6

CONTENTS

PART FOUR

Problems of identity and national integration

PART FIVE

Political perspectives

PART SIX

The way ahead

PART SEVEN

The continental context

LIST OF MAPS AND TABLES

CONTRIBUTORS

Deryke Belshaw is Professor of Agricultural Economics at the University of East Anglia, Norwich.

Hugh Dinwiddy was formerly Dean of Makerere.

Martin Doornbos teaches political science at the Institute of Social Studies at The Hague.

Keith Edmonds worked in the Uganda Ministry of Finance during the early 1980s.

Oliver Furley is Head of the Department of History and Politics at Lanchester Polytechnic, Coventry.

Holger Bernt Hansen teaches politics and religious studies at Copenhagen University.

George Kanyeihamba is presently the Ugandan Minister of Commerce.

Nelson Kasfir is Professor of Government at Dartmouth College, New Hampshire, USA.

D.A. Low is President of Clare Hall, Cambridge.

Ali A. Mazrui is Professor of Political Science at the University of Michigan, Ann Arbor.

Dan Mudoola is Director of the Makerere Institute of Social Research.

Dani Wadada Nabudere is presently teaching in Elsinore, Denmark.

Apolo Nsibambi is Professor of Political Science at Makerere University.

Christine Obbo is Professor of Anthropology at Wheaton College.

Anthony O'Connor is Reader in Geography at University College, London.

Louise Pirouet teaches at Homerton College, Cambridge.

John A. Rowe is Professor of History at Northwestern University.

Aidan Southall is Professor of Anthropology at the Madison campus of the University of Wisconsin.

Michael Twaddle teaches at the Institute of Commonwealth Studies at London University.

Michael Whyte is an economic anthropologist at Copenhagen University.

Peter Woodward is a political scientist at the University of Reading.

Christopher Wrigley is the author of *Crops and Wealth in Uganda*.

INTRODUCTION

It is now 25 years since Uganda ceased to be a British colonial dependency. In these years Uganda has come to symbolize Third World disaster in its direst form. Famine; tyranny; widespread infringements of human rights, amounting at times to genocide; AIDS; malaria; cholera, typhoid, and a massive breakdown of government medical services; corruption, black marketeering, economic collapse; tribalism, civil war, state collapse – think of any one current Third World affliction, and most probably Uganda will have suffered it with as much harshness as Afghanistan, Bangladesh, Cambodia, or any one of a score of other Third World countries.

Socially, this is appalling for Ugandans. Analytically, it is also confusing for outside analysts of the country's development – or rather arrested development – since independence 25 years ago. There seem to be just *too many* causes of the country's troubles. Which of them are of fundamental importance, which of only secondary significance?

At one time the answer to this question seemed pellucid: Idi Amin. It was because of *him* that there had been genocide, rampant inflation and widespread economic inefficiency, not to mention political decay, throughout the country. Milton Obote's years of power immediately after independence from Britain admittedly had had their drawbacks – the break-up of the initial alliance between his Uganda Peoples' Congress (UPC) and the Buganda-based Kabaka Yekka ('Kabaka only') movement; the declaration of a state of emergency in Buganda; abolition of the Buganda monarchy along with the smaller kingships in the western areas of the country; and the declaration of a one-party state that made Obote its president, and seemingly constitutionally irremovable. Or so it seemed, until Obote's military commander, Idi Amin, seized power on 25 January 1971 while Obote was attending a Commonwealth conference in Singapore.

Idi Amin's regime in Uganda soon revealed itself to be much

1

worse than Obote's, indeed one of post-colonial Africa's very worst. But how far Amin himself was the primary cause of its most appalling aspects is very debatable. Amin was a talented publicist. Before he seized power from Obote, he had a reputation amongst students at Makerere University as a political nonentity, and indeed featured in several end-of-term revues as such. This reputation was not entirely unjustified. Amin did lack certain educational skills at this time, and at least one of Obote's political henchmen boasted to an international gathering in 1969 that, whereas other African countries had had their civilian governments toppled by military interventions earlier in the 1960s, Obote had preempted this possibility by taking a number of countervailing measures – one of them being the appointment as military commander in Uganda of a complete nonentity, namely Amin. This was not a remark heard much again locally (so it would seem) after the Amin coup of 25 January 1971. For, whatever Amin's failings as President of Uganda between 1971 and 1979 may have been, and undoubtedly these were many, his being a political nonentity was clearly not one of them. Indeed, in more than one sense, Amin soon loomed larger than life. He was a compulsive talker to visiting journalists, and during the 1970s Uganda as a result was rarely out of the news. As Amin alternately amused and appalled his journalistic interviewers by his words as well as his deeds, Uganda received constantly sensational and superficial coverage in the international media until Amin's regime was finally overthrown by invading Tanzanian troops and Ugandan exiles in 1978–9.

Briefly there was then again popular euphoria at the overthrow of a tyrant (there had been popular euphoria also, initially, when Amin had toppled Obote from power). But relief again was short-lived. Famine, political violence, accelerating inflation and the evils emanating from that, all recurred both under the two short-lived post-Amin governments of Yusufu Lule and Godfrey Binaisa in 1979–80, and under the brief but murderous military regime that controlled the country until Milton Obote and the UPC again resumed power. This was after a highly controversial election in December 1980.

Morally, the Democratic Party (DP) claimed victory in this election. Insofar as it is possible to say at this distance, the DP would probably have won formally had Obote's allies not controlled the counting of votes; or rather re-counting, as the earlier counting was suspended by Obote's ally, Paulo Muwanga at the very moment when the DP appeared to be winning. But the Uganda Patriotic Movement (UPM) of the former defence minister, Yoweri Museveni, fared even worse in this election, Museveni himself not even being elected to parliament after the recount. A few weeks after this bitterly disputed election, Museveni and a few dozen other guerrillas took to the bush to fight the newly installed second Obote government, along with one or two bands fighting under other leaders. After concluding a tactical alliance with the Buganda-based fighters loyal to the first post-Amin president, Yusufu Lule, Museveni formed the National Resistance Army (NRA) and associated National Resistance Movement (NRM). Obote then ordered his troops to sweep all guerrillas out of Uganda. But they failed to do this. In the process of counter-insurgency Obote also appeared to alienate what little was left of popular tolerance for his second regime in Uganda, and for its IMF/World Bank-assisted plans for structural reconstruction of the country's economy.

By 1985 inflation in Uganda was again out of control. Human rights violations were by now so widespread that many local people were saying there had been fewer under Amin. Political support for central government was as elusive as ever. There was also considerable dissatisfaction within Obote's army that another member of Obote's Langi tribe had been appointed its commander after the death in a helicopter accident of Oyite-Ojok; a much younger and more junior man moreover than several other possible successors to Oyite-Ojok from Acholiland. In July 1985 Obote was suddenly toppled from power yet again by another military intervention in Ugandan politics, on this occasion led by Acholi army officers.

As well as being evidence of 'ethnic' distaste for Obote's promotion of yet another Langi commander, the Okellos' coup of July 1985 seems also to have been a pre-emptive action against the NRA guerrillas. These now controlled most of western Uganda, and seemed just about to seize the geographical centre of the country too. Hence the need for any third party that was able so to do, to act before the NRA itself did. However, in January 1986 Museveni's guerrillas successfully stormed into Kampala and installed the government that still rules there at the time of writing. Museveni also now became President of the country. The predominantly northern soldiery that had removed Obote from power just a few months before now took to its heels, and still continues to ravage parts of the far north of Uganda.

The material devastation and sheer scale of atrocities perpetrated by the second Obote government (1980–5) and its short-lived successor in late 1985 are now widely considered by Ugandans to have matched anything suffered under Amin's earlier murderous regime. As a consequence, at the time Museveni's NRA troops successfully seized control of the central organs of government at Entebbe–Kampala at the start of 1986, Uganda's reputation for malobservance of human rights, political disorder, and general economic collapse was even more terrible outside Uganda than it had been at the time of Amin's overthrow.

It had been very different at the start of the twentieth century. 'The East Africa Protectorate,' – present-day Kenya – Winston Churchill had written in 1908,

> is a country of the highest interest to the colonist, the traveller, or the sportsman. But the Kingdom of Uganda is a fairy tale. You climb up a railway instead of a beanstalk, and at the end there is a wonderful new world. The scenery is different, the vegetation is different, the climate is different, and, most of all, the people are different from anything elsewhere to be seen in the whole range of Africa. Instead of the breezy uplands we enter a tropical garden. In the place of naked, painted savages, clashing their spears and gibbering in chorus to their tribal chiefs, a complete and elaborate polity is presented. Under a dynastic King, with a Parliament, and a powerful feudal system, an amiable, clothed, polite, and intelligent race dwell together in an organized monarchy upon the rich domain between the Victoria and Albert Lakes. More than two hundred thousand natives are able to read and write. More than two hundred thousand have embraced the Christian faith. There is a Court, there are Regents and Ministers and nobles, there is a regular system of native law and tribunals; there is discipline, there is industry, there is culture, there is peace. In fact, I ask myself whether there is any other spot in the whole earth where the dreams and hopes of the negrophile, so often mocked by results and stubborn facts, have ever attained such a happy realization (Churchill, 1908).

Of course, this characterization of conditions in Uganda at the start of the British protectorate period was itself in part a fairy tale. It was written by a visiting British politician a few years after the signing of the Uganda Agreement of 1900 with the ruling chiefs of the Buganda kingdom, a treaty that had rewarded these chiefs for their 'discipline' and 'industry' in supporting British imperialism during a decade of earlier disorder and rebellions, with privileges as regards law enforcement, land tenure and tax collection that were most unusual in British colonial Africa. It was also a fairy tale written about only one part of the Uganda Protectorate – the Buganda kingdom – not those parts of it occupied by what visiting anthropologists would subsequently designate 'tribes without rulers'. And, as Christopher Wrigley points out in Chapter 2, the treaty of 1900 was to prove the foundation of subsequent British protectorate policy too, privileging Buganda to such an extent in the eyes of other Ugandans that Wrigley now sees this particular treaty as one of four tragic 'steps towards disaster' that made any kind of viable political independence for Uganda in the years after 1962 so much less likely than might have been otherwise the case.

'Uganda' was itself a British colonial creation, at first used ambiguously as both the name for the Buganda kingdom and the name of the wider Uganda Protectorate; later, just for the protectorate as a whole. Administratively, it was an amalgam of a number of peoples occupying a particular section of the East African interior and following widely differing political practices at the time of the European colonial partition at the end of the nineteenth century: some within African kingdoms, others within communities held together more by ritual authority than kingly power. As if these were not differences to cause difficulty enough in the newly independent African state that Uganda became in 1962, linguistically there were also basic problems of communication at the grass and banana roots of politics. There were major linguistic differences even within the Bantu family: for example, the Baganda living in the Kampala–Entebbe area spoke a language as different to that of the Bagisu occupying the easterly slopes of Mount Elgon as was English and Danish or Italian. Beyond this, though, there was a deeper divide between all such Bantu languages and others classified as 'Nilotic' by linguists – like Langi and Acholi – and another cleavage of comparable character between Nilotic and 'Sudanic' languages spoken in the West Nile area in the extreme north-west of Uganda. All three cleavages are comparable, in European terms, to the difference between Slavic and non-Slavic languages.

In his discussion of the 'dislocated polity' in Chapter 3, D.A. Low reflects upon the variety of alternative futures facing the 'thousand or so actual or latent political systems' that existed at the time of the European partition in black Africa, a number that had been reduced by the time of independence 'to a mere 50 or so'. Low suggests that after independence each colonial aggregation faced 'profound social and political difficulties as many new aggregations ... found themselves ensconced in an arbitrarily concocted new state'. Low's analysis of the resultant dilemma is a political and global one. He reviews the wide variety of 'methods by which the process of national aggregation in new states may be assisted', surveying South Asia and the Pacific for this purpose as well as Africa. His verdict upon Museveni's Uganda is cautiously optimistic. 'Skill, patience, a readiness to make the creative compromise, are all at a premium. But at least ... the structures underpinning the state look to be rather more promising than before'.

However, there are structures and structures. D.A. Low considers that, 'like most African countries Uganda was an artificial creation, comprising the northern interlacustrine Bantu along with the south-central Nilotes ... a large assortment of pre-colonial polities ... at its core it had the large kingdom of Buganda'. But Baganda failed to become 'Uganda's Prussians'. Successive attempts to create an alternative 'working majority' in Uganda also failed disastrously, both Amin and Obote finally resorting to populist policies that proved 'entirely useless and ... led them to the last resort of the politically bankrupt: terror'. Museveni's Uganda, on the other hand, 'comprises as credible a composed majority as Uganda has ever seen'. In some respects Low sees it resembling the political coalition of Obote's initial years of power (1962–6). But, unlike Obote's coalition, Museveni's is built upon 'Uganda's numerically preponderant Bantu southerners', with Baganda included at the coalition's political core, and it is backed up by a successful army.

In Chapter 4 Aidan Southall views the structural basis of Uganda's post-colonial nightmare very differently. He too is hopeful for the future of Museveni's regime, but sees political constituencies of whatever kind as less fundamental to its success than the adequate tackling of the global economic constraints impinging upon all independent African governments at the present time. Southall's basic question is therefore a rather different one. 'What kind of economic policy and what type of regime in the context of superpower confrontation and the severe constraints imposed by the international economy, can transcend ethnic conflicts and provide production incentives while avoiding the exploitation, corruption and inefficiency associated with excessive bureaucratic centralization?' There are two further questions that Southall poses in his chapter. Will 'Museveni's relatively small, hand-picked, highly trained and bush-hardened army be able to retain its standards and propagate them throughout the country, or will they be dragged down by the *magendo-mafutamingi* economy and way of life of the capital?' 'Secondly, will Museveni's government be able to reconcile the ethnic hatreds that have been continuously exacerbated for the past fifteen years and more?' Southall's discussion of these questions is basically Marxist, but old-time ethnicity ('ethnic conflicts ... reconcile the ethnic hatreds') remains very much part of his superstructure.

Christopher Wrigley is essentially sceptical about both Low's and Southall's approach. For him 'tribalism', underdevelopment theory, neocolonialism and the like are all 'general theories', and what is required is an approach that explains why Uganda and not its neighbours suffered a nightmare after independence from Britain. After all, as Wrigley points out, 'collapse into tyranny, anarchy and civil war is not the norm' after independence amongst Uganda's neighbours. He agrees that the colonial economic history of Uganda was important in shaping the character of post-colonial politics, but in a highly specific way. Uganda's economy was predominantly agricultural, and there was comparatively little foreign penetration of it under British protectorate rule. As a consequence, 'the capitalist class was small, and what there was of it, in the commercial and agricultural sectors, was also entirely alien, as was most of the proletariat'. Material advance for Ugandan Africans lay therefore essentially through state employment. Cultural cleavages were less important than either Low or Southall assume. The Bantu–Nilote split was not necessarily enormously important for Uganda after independence – 'such categories become politically significant only when politicians find use for them', as he rightly stresses – and the Langi–Acholi split in the army, which partly brought Obote's second presidency to an end in July 1985, had no cultural or linguistic resonance to it whatsoever. What *was* important was what happened in the state sector in Uganda. Hence the crucial importance in Uganda of four 'historical contingencies': first, making the Buganda kingdom the core of the British protectorate without creating countervailing administrative structures outside it; secondly, the 'Kabaka crisis' of the 1953–5 period, when the British governor deported the Ganda king and thereby set Ganda ethnic sentiment alight in an unusually virulent form; thirdly, fudging the constitutional character of Uganda as a unitary/federal state at the time of independence from Britain worsened the disparity between Buganda and other parts of this particular new state; and, fourthly, the army mutinies of 1964 throughout East Africa, to which Obote responded by basing his power thenceforth essentially upon armed force. Thereafter, it was inevitable that at some time the army itself would seek to seize power, and that this militarization of politics would have catastrophic effects. The task for Ugandans nowadays, Wrigley suggests, is nothing less than returning the army to barracks, reducing the pretensions of the state that had earlier set the country upon its tragic, downward course, and reconstituting civil society.

Christopher Wrigley's arguments provoked much thought when they were first presented for discussion in September 1985. Like the other papers presented on that occasion, Wrigley's paper is reproduced in this volume with such revisions as the author has wished to make in light of discussion of it in 1985 and what has happened since in Uganda – in Wrigley's case, none of substance. It hardly needs to be pointed out that the conference, which led to this book, itself took place at a highly inflammatory time. The coup that terminated Obote's second presidency in Uganda had taken place only two months before, and there were already many reports of disorders taking place under the succeeding Okello regime. NRA soldiers controlled Toro and much of the rest of western Uganda. Just over three months later NRA soldiers would also seize control of the Kampala region, and commence their armed takeover of eastern and northern Uganda. At the very time that one of the papers upon which an ensuing chapter in this book is based was first being presented and discussed at this conference, another delegate – with more than passing acquaintance with NRA activities in Uganda – burst into the conference with the news that 'Masaka has fallen'. Then another delegate distracted the discussion in another session with the revised report, 'No, Masaka has not fallen yet, but Mbarara *has* been captured'. It was a heady time at which to hold a conference discussing contemporary problems in Uganda.

The conference had been arranged to take place at Lyngby Landbrugsskole, a long-established but recently rebuilt Danish folk high school just outside the medieval city of Roskilde. It was an ideal setting in which to hold intensive interdisciplinary discussions amongst a multinational group of people concerned with Uganda from both the academic community and the aid agency world. Aid personnel concerned with Uganda were not initially invited to attend the conference as aid personnel, but when approached earlier for financial assistance had said in effect, 'Yes, but can one of our people attend too, for their education as it were?' Needless to say, the various academics attending the conference at Roskilde undoubtedly learned at least as much from the aid personnel also attending as did the latter from the former. The Lutheran World Federation representative in Kampala in September 1985 must also be mentioned as being most helpful in ferrying air tickets and information about the conference between the centre of Kampala and Makerere University in the confused situation then pertaining in Uganda. It is scarcely necessary to add that the conference at Lyngby Landbrugsskole, and the present symposium, would have also been much less informative had Ugandan scholars from Makerere not been able to contribute in person, and it took courage for them to attend any conference on 'Crises of Development in Uganda' in Europe at such a time.

Besides the unsettled situation in Uganda and the uncertain negotiations being undertaken in Nairobi between the National Resistance Army and the then-incumbent regime of Tito and Bazileo Okello's military council at the very time the conference was held, two more general factors also inhibited analysis of Uganda's post-colonial nightmare by concerned outsiders at this time. One was partisanship for or against Obote's second presidency. Another was the breakdown in scholarly communication between students of Uganda within the wider academic community dating back to Idi Amin. As our initial 'call for papers' in December 1984 had put it:

> At present, scholarly discussion of Ugandan affairs is deeply fragmented between fierce defenders of the Obote government and fierce opponents, and there is little theoretical tie-in between discussions of human rights and refugees, economic reconstruction, and state collapse as a result of the Amin regime. Our workshop ... should provide an excellent opportunity to 'pool resources' and discuss the interrelationships between these currently quite separate areas of discussion, amongst scholars in the international community who have done some research in Uganda [recently] but not yet had adequate opportunity to compare their findings with fellow researchers.

There was therefore at the outset a recognition of the *multiple character* of Uganda's crises since independence. But there was also recognition that these multiple crises also mirrored a wider dilemma currently shared by many other black African countries. As our earlier 'call for papers' had also pointed out:

> Economically, C.C. Wrigley's words on Uganda 25 years ago still seem relevant: 'It does not, for one thing possess any great mineral wealth, so that the quickest of all roads to fortune has not been open to it. Nor, although it lies across the Equator, is it well suited to the growth of those products of the hot and humid tropics, such as cocoa, cloves or rubber, the peculiar properties of which bring really large returns to their fortunate producers. Nor again has its development been either assisted or complicated by an influx of alien colonists. Large-scale irrigation is neither necessary nor possible. These negations make the recent economic history of Uganda in a sense the more interesting in that it may be taken almost as an abstract type of tropical, non-maritime, newly discovered, political dependent country' (Wrigley, 1959). Politically as well as economically, of course much has changed in 25 years ... Now, especially as a result of the Amin years, the government-taxed economy of Uganda has shrunk considerably and the black market expanded to such an extent that it is arguably the more important for ordinary Ugandans, while the confused character of the immediate post-Amin period appears to have much more deeply politicized the country's small farmers along with the urban workers.

There is one further point that should be extracted from our original 'call for papers'. This was the hope that the conference at

Lyngby Landbrugsskole would prove 'academic' in the best sense of that word:

> The idea therefore is for a workshop of between 25 and 30 experts from Africa as well as Europe and America to convene for three days to present and discuss papers on a variety of aspects of political, economic and social crisis in Uganda that should lead to at least one scholarly publication (most probably in symposium form) on the problems of the country since independence which might well be of interest to planners and aid and refugee personnel as well as to scholars. The workshop will therefore essentially be an academic and research enterprise rather than any propagandist attempt to vilify the present Ugandan government – or uncritically defend it.

As it turned out, our numbers were closer to 40 than 30, with additional aid personnel. But we did attempt a balanced rather than a narrowly focused assault upon Uganda's multiple crises since independence, and do so too in presenting this resultant book to a wider public.

The conference opened with a provocative survey of the problems of the post-colonial state in Africa by Ali Mazrui (Chapter 22). Was there too little government attempted by post-colonial states, or too much? Which produced the greater number of atrocities and refugees in post-independence Uganda, anarchy or tyranny? It was a stimulating and scintillating survey, but in its nature not one to set a conference off on any single path towards consensus. The two dozen or so revised analyses of Uganda's agonies published in this volume cannot therefore be claimed to argue for any single overview. But what this book by more than twenty separate authors therefore lacks as regards internal polemical coherence, we trust it more than makes up for in intellectual debate about the causes and possible cures of Uganda's developmental nightmare.

What, then, are these causes? And what are the principal debates about them? As Christopher Wrigley has argued in two separate contributions, Uganda's developmental problems can be viewed in two separate ways. On the one hand, as Wrigley pointed out as long ago as 1959, Uganda can be considered typical of the generality of poor, dependent countries. On the other hand, as he argues in Chapter 2 of this book, Uganda can be considered the victim of very specific 'historical contingencies' in one especially unfortunate poor country. Clearly, both approaches are possible along a variety of development trajectories, and both are needed for any convincing final overview. However, in his contribution to this volume, Wrigley takes the one-country approach and underlines the 'four steps towards disaster' that he considers were taken before Uganda even acquired final political independence from Britain. In Chapter 19, Dan Mudoola also takes this path and explores the specificities of what he terms Uganda's 'political pathology' within this second paradigm. He analyses the intricacies of Ugandan politics after independence, and focuses especially on the years following the downfall of Idi Amin. In Chapter 18, John Rowe analyses the Amin years themselves, and probes into the political action of Islam in the country also in a most specific and original manner.

The political significance of religion in Uganda has been the subject of a number of scholarly studies. It was a leading theme in David Apter's pioneering study of Baganda nationalism during the struggle for independence from Britain 25 years ago (Apter, 1961), as well as of a number of other important studies researched around this time (Low, 1957; Taylor, 1958; Welbourn, 1965). Connections between Roman Catholicism and the Democratic Party are well known, indeed probably too much taken for granted (cf Twaddle, 1978), as too are connections between Anglican Christianity and both the Kabaka Yekka movement in Buganda and the UPC in areas outside it. But Islam is far less well explored, though Abdul Kasozi's recent survey of its spread throughout the country (Kasozi, 1986) is important in understanding Obote's success in penetrating it politically during the first post-independence years. John Rowe's chapter in this volume is extremely important here, too, in analysing the political action of Islam in Uganda at the height of Amin's tyranny.

In essence, Rowe examines how a minority Islamic government managed to maintain dominance over a non-Muslim majority between 1971 and 1979. For, at least nominally at the moment of Amin's seizure of power, Uganda was predominantly a Christian country; not for nothing had it been the first independent black African country to be visited by the Pope in 1969. Clearly the Nubian factor amongst Amin's supporters was crucial in tying his regime to Islam, as is underlined by Peter Woodward in Chapter 15 (cf also Hansen, 1977). Also important here were new external associations developed by Amin with Islamic states such as Libya and Saudi Arabia. Yet, in Rowe's view, the most important factor of all was the socio-religious structure of Uganda in general and forms of Western education and bureaucratic employment throughout the country for more than two generations. It was therefore not surprising that Ugandan Muslims responded so positively to a leader who promised to act as their spokesman. It is extremely sad that Amin should have then proceeded to serve Ugandan Muslims so badly in this respect; tragic, too, that his period of power was marked by widespread regime-stimulated atrocities at the very time Amin himself was paying such public allegiance to Islam.

In this regard Yusufu Lule, Amin's immediate successor as president of Uganda, deserves to be remembered as a peacemaker. For though his period of office was extremely brief, as a Muslim himself Lule did manage somewhat to cool the strong politico-religious tensions aroused (in Ali Mazrui's opinion) by Amin's political dethronement of the hitherto dominant Christian-educated elite groups in the country. These tensions had a long history in colonial Uganda (Hansen, 1977 and 1984), to be sure, but increased political manipulation of Islam took place after independence both during Obote's first presidency and under the Amin regime. As a result, the political manipulation of religion in Uganda was a political tradition that the incoming Museveni government was most concerned to counter. For, as the sections on 'sectarianism' in the '10-point programme of the NRM' indicate (and as Michael Twaddle stresses in Chapter 21), Museveni's government considers such 'sectarianism' to have been principally manipulation of the masses by opportunistic elites.

In Chapter 11, Nelson Kasfir stresses another respect in which the Amin period was to be of immense importance for subsequent socio-economic developments in the country. This is with respect to peasants and land. As a result of the Agreement of 1900 with the British protectorate government, quasi-freehold tenures were legalized in the Buganda kingdom; and upon the resultant pattern of landownership there developed a very distinctive system of social stratification that is well-known to scholars of Uganda (for the fullest account, see Fallers, 1964). Outside Buganda, however, this pattern of quasi-freehold tenure was only rarely introduced. There, though less studied and reported upon, communal tenures appear to have predominated. That is, until Idi Amin seized power throughout the country. In 1975 a new land law was introduced. Superficially, as Chango Machyo remarks, this law appeared progressive in vesting 'the ownership of all lands in the public under the control of the land commission'. However, 'closer examination exposes [its] oppressive, neo-colonial character'. This is because under the new law individual Ugandans have been able to acquire and register 200 or more hectares of land, 'with the consent of the minister responsible for lands'. 'The act' of 1975, Machyo remarks (1985, p.53), 'has thus facilitated the acquisition of large tracts of land by the bureaucratic bourgeoisie plus their local and foreign allies'. Furthermore, because under the 1975 law intending leaseholders are required to develop land to a standard acceptable to the Ugandan land commission, evictions of poorer peasants unable to comply with the

Introduction

commission's requirements have proceeded apace 'in areas like Masaka and Kabale' (Machyo, 1985, p. 54). Because Uganda has additionally experienced increased pressures upon the land as a consequence of high rates of population increase in recent years, the number of landless peasants has increased still further in areas of the country as widely separated as Rukungiri, Mbale and Nebbi (Machyo, 1985, p. 62). Nelson Kasfir further points out in this volume that the increased number of game parks gazetted during the period of Obote's second presidency in particular adversely affected poorer cattle-keeping groups in Uganda. Indeed, Kasfir's evidence here illumines an important area of grievance specifically stressed in the '10-point programme of the NRM'. This helps us to understand further the origins of the NRM itself, in the very specific grievances of a disinherited Bahima intelligentsia in western Uganda during Obote's second period of political office.

Kasfir also stresses population growth as a factor increasing commercial pressures upon the land of Ankole in recent years. To be sure, this is an extremely contentious issue too in discussions of African developmental issues at the continental level. It is often argued that there is a substantial negative correlation between population growth and economic development in Africa, not least with respect to growth in per capita incomes. Indeed, this view has now entered into the conventional wisdom (see Wolfson, 1985 for a recent survey), and the Governor of the Central Bank of Kenya has recently recommended that all African countries should make immediate efforts to reduce the rates of increase of their populations (Ndegwa, 1985). However Ali Mazrui holds a different view. This he both expressed to the opening plenary session of the conference at Lyngby Landbrugsskole in September 1985 and repeats in Chapter 22. In Mazrui's view, population growth in Africa is more a blessing than a curse. It enables Africans to fight back against seemingly universal processes of decay by reincarnating the next generation. With intellectual supporters like Esther Boserup behind him (cf Boserup, 1965), Mazrui's argument here cannot be dismissed lightly. In the age of AIDS, too, it is not an argument to be simply smothered in conventional wisdom.

Nonetheless, crucial though the population issue is to debate about African developmental problems at the continental level, it is not an issue to which a single-country symposium not specifically devoted to a discussion of it can make a very decisive contribution. All really we can do here is note that two prominent Kenyans differ about it. One argues principally in economic terms, about land shortages, unemployment, underemployment and the like (Ndegwa, 1985). The other emphasizes the importance of there

13

being a specifically *African answer* to Westernized ways of looking at this particular aspect of the developmental process as of others. However, both agree that another, very closely related issue of central importance to the developmental debate in all African countries is education. So, too, in this volume do Oliver Furley; and Hugh Dinwiddy and Michael Twaddle.

In Chapter 12 Furley provides an account of the Ugandan educational system since independence from Britain. A special feature of this period, especially in the very first years of independence, was its over-emphasis upon secondary education. This can now be seen to have further divided the country, and to have led too many Ugandans to think of themselves as the masters, and 'the uneducated' as their servants. It is an issue of no mean significance in causing the 'sectarianism' to which the '10-point programme of the NRM' takes such exception. It is also a theme that Christine Obbo develops further in Chapter 14, where she analyses mass discontent with elite privilege in several crucial areas of Ugandan life. It follows from both Furley's and Obbo's contributions to this volume, and additionally Hugh Dinwiddy's and Michael Twaddle's on Makerere (Chapter 13), that too much in post-independence education in Uganda has been excessively Eurocentric. According to Furley, very few attempts were made to correct this bias in Ugandan education. Nor was there much effort made to stem the consequently still greater drift of educated and semi-educated Ugandans to the urban and peri-urban areas. Nor was any really successful attempt made locally to supply those types of trained manpower in which Uganda was so deficient at the moment of independence. In each of these areas, therefore, lie still further policy challenges confronting the latest rulers of post-independence Uganda.

Here, again, are also aspects of Uganda's developmental history during the last 25 years that fall within both a single country framework of reference – as Christine Obbo stresses amongst other things – and within a continental African context. They also both raise questions of ideological orientation. In his influential analyses of peasants and production in Uganda's southerly neighbour, Tanzania, Goran Hyden also underlines the importance of ideology (Hyden, 1980). Philip Ndegwa, too, attaches great importance to the alternative ideological challenges of capitalism and socialism throughout independent Africa: between the advocates of private producers and market forces on the one hand, and the supporters of state ownership of the means of production and collective action generally on the other (Ndegwa, 1985). In Chapter 10 Apolo Nsibambi introduces these alternative ideological frameworks into a discussion of food policy, but, like Ndegwa, he warns against a monolithic approach: in the real world there is often a mixture of systems and strategies. Indeed, this is the assumption made by most contributors to this symposium. Under its successive political conjunctures since independence from Britain 25 years ago, Uganda cannot be placed clearly within either a wholly 'capitalist' or 'socialist' framework in any meaningful sense, and it is unlikely that this difficulty will disappear to any substantial degree in the immediate future. Nelson Kasfir expressly underlines this point with reference to the peasant farmers of Bushenyi and Mbarara districts. Kasfir sees these smallholders as having been created by capitalism. But by a capitalism that has still not managed to unhinge their earlier, essentially pre-capitalist modes of production. Furthermore, these particular small farmers appear to retain a very high degree of autonomy, and they shift from the informal to the formal sectors of the national economy and back again largely as they please. Aidan Southall (Chapter 4) even asserts that Ugandans *must* pursue capitalism as their principal developmental strategy in the immediate future. There is no other framework within which the Museveni government can work in order that a different kind of social order may emerge. Ali Mazrui takes this argument to the continental level. In his discussion of the twin evils of dependency and decay, he argues that the essential problem in independent Africa generally is not too much, but too little, capitalist penetration.

It is remarkable how much conventional wisdom has changed here in recent years. During the last years of Obote's first presidency, when much scholarly attention was paid to attempts to build socialism peacefully in a number of newly independent African countries (e.g., Friedland and Rosberg, 1964; Resnick, 1968), it would have been academic heresy to suggest that further steps along the capitalist path were first necessary before socialism itself was possible and a dynamic could be established that might transform 'uncaptured peasants' into ones 'captured' by any newly independent African government and its formal economy (cf Jeffries, 1978; Hyden, 1980). Indeed, as David Fieldhouse has recently reminded us, even supposedly capitalist independent African governments at this time exhibited many 'socialist' features. Rapid industrialization seemed more important then than more efficient peasant agriculture, and 'development' was essentially something that needed to be directed by the post-colonial state and its associated experts rather than by any kind of private enterprise, local or foreign (Fieldhouse, 1986, pp. 85-90). Today African economics has a very different conventional wisdom. In Fieldhouse's words,

The left tends to explain it in terms of self-seeking bourgeois or petty bourgèois regimes, representing small elites, who use political power to extract the surplus from the masses and so accumulate private capital, freely collaborating with international capital as their main ally and source of finance ... The alternative 'conservative' assessment, typified by publications of multilateral agencies such as the World Bank, accepts the basic premiss of governmental lack of wisdom, but discounts the radical approach on the grounds that it does not in fact make much difference what political label or style African rulers adopt ... African states must accept the discipline of economic management. Exchange rates must be made realistic in order to help exports, discourage imports and eliminate the huge 'black' sectors of their economies. Protectionism must be modified so that only potentially viable domestic industries survive. State enterprises should be overhauled to eliminate inefficiency, overmanning ... a larger role should be given to private enterprise, both foreign and indigenous. The government itself must be made more efficient; in particular, its size and costs must be reduced ... Above all, however, agriculture must be made more productive ... by paying more realistic prices for export crops and food supplies ... The strategy is based on the peasant (or 'smallholder' in World Bank terminology), who is assumed to be a conventional economic man who can and will respond to market forces if these are favourable (Fieldhouse, 1986, pp. 91-3).

Fieldhouse's capitalism is the thinking man's variety at work, or not sufficiently at work, in post-colonial Africa. Essentially it is a Schumpeterian, liberal view. It is a view defended vigorously by a number of the contributors to this book, Keith Edmonds (Chapter 7) and Deryke Belshaw (Chapter 8) especially. But it is not the only view espoused in this symposium. In particular, Dani Nabudere (Chapter 20) and Aidan Southall (Chapter 4) view capitalism very differently. On their view, capitalism at the global level must be considered synonymous with a much less liberal phenomenom: the imperialist or neocolonial world system.

This profoundly affects socio-economic developments in poor and peripheral countries such as Uganda. On this view, the world capitalist system is essentially exploitative, and in fact initiates a process of class formation whereby local collaborators emerge to sustain the continuance of external exploitation and internal dependency by allying with foreign economic interests. Mahmoud Mamdani has pursued this particular analytical line with vigour in earlier studies of Uganda (Mamdani, 1976, 1983), and in their respective contributions to this volume Southall reproduces it with very few modifications, Nabudere with at least one important change. Nonetheless, there are problems with all these approaches.

Introduction

The closer one moves towards the present time, the more difficult it becomes to apply a global neocolonial analysis of interactions between politico-economic developments and capitalism in Uganda: Idi Amin was *not principally* the product of international capitalism, nor can more recent politics be seen principally as its issue either. Moreover, in his more recent writings (1984 and 1987) Mamdani himself has followed other earlier devotees of the 'development of underdevelopment' theory in switching from stress upon the influences of external forces of all kinds upon tropical Africa to the more complex and difficult study of internal class differences. However, even where these internal socio-economic cleavages can be thoroughly researched in contemporary Uganda, the problem remains of reconciling them with the other continuing and *perceived* cleavages of an ethnic character also stressed in Aidan Southall's contribution and in the other chapters.

This is a continuing dilemma for students of Africa's developmental difficulties, whether or not they are concerned primarily with questions of political economy continent-wide or just in one particular country. Should most explanatory emphasis be placed upon external factors (for the increasing burdens of foreign debt and falling prices for coffee are not difficulties confronting Uganda alone)? Or should answers be sought effectively first in domestic, internal concerns? The dilemma was raised initially by Mazrui in his plenary address to the Roskilde conference. But it runs through all contributions to this volume, though most of the authors focus primarily upon internal rather than external factors and, insofar as they 'rank' these factors, give primacy of importance to what happens in the political arena.

Dani Nabudere stresses the importance of external factors. Indeed, Nabudere lays stress upon the particular importance of foreign powers in sustaining Obote's position. Nonetheless, while most blame is accorded by him to 'imperialist and neocolonial powers', Nabudere also attributes responsibility to Tanzania in both reinstating Obote in power and in subsequently sustaining his dictatorship for several years. While the neocolonial position of Uganda internationally is considered by Nabudere therefore to have been *initiated* by Western imperialism, a neighbouring East African leader is not entirely absolved of responsibility for assisting its continuance in a state of global dependency. And, in Nabudere's opinion, one of the principal instruments inducing continuing dependency for Obote's Uganda was foreign aid. This aid was principally provided by the major Western countries, both bilaterally and through the European Community and the World Bank/International Monetary Fund. Foreign aid was instrumental in sustaining Obote's second presidency directly, through financial support for his government; and indirectly, by giving his regime an image of legitimacy and respectability. Foreign aid is thus seen by Nabudere as a neocolonial tool. Instead of contributing towards the reconstruction of Uganda in the earlier 1980s, it had the opposite effect: it increased the devastation of the country during these years.

Without supplying a similar neocolonial framework for his arguments, George Kanyeihamba (Chapter 5) arrives at a very similar conclusion. The reason he gives for the devastation, however, is different: basic infringements of human rights during Obote's second presidency as well as earlier under Idi Amin. For, as Kanyeihamba himself makes clear, his chapter was originally written on behalf of the Uganda Group for Human Rights during some of the worst excesses of the second Obote regime. It is reproduced here substantially in its original form. This is not only because, as Uganda's current Minister of Commerce, its author is now an extremely busy person, but because his argument bears repetition. Western donor countries closed their eyes during the earlier 1980s to violations of human rights in Obote's Uganda, of which they should have been aware, and which they should not have condoned at the time. Indeed, Kanyeihamba stresses that development aid can never be neutral in this respect. Human rights should not have been ignored by donors when exile groups, information media, and humanitarian organizations all provided substantial evidence of the infringement. Additionally, as Obbo (Chapter 14) also stresses, considerable quantities of foreign aid went into the wrong pockets as a result of widespread corruption in government circles during this period.

The issue of foreign aid was the subject of a special additional session of discussion during the conference at Lyngby Land-brugsskole in September 1985. Officials from the World Bank, European Community, and Danish government agencies and NGOs took part in this as well as the assembled social scientists. It was an unscripted but valuable opportunity for discussion. A number of specific development projects started in Uganda during the early 1980s were reviewed; there are references in more detail to them in succeeding chapters. Ugandan academics who attended the conference from Uganda itself expressed considerable scepticism about IMF/World Bank-assisted structural adjustment programmes inaugurated by the second Obote regime. Foreign aid, these Ugandan academics pointed out, would probably be a necessary evil for Uganda for some time to come. But it needed to be approached with great caution. Walter Elkan summarized much of the ensuing discussion of aid policy in Uganda by stressing the weakness of all aid channelled through governments. Foreign aid inevitably gives enhanced powers to the governments that receive it, Elkan stressed; and it is essential for foreign donors to discover alternative ways of bringing assistance to African peoples without undue intervention by their governments. However, this seems easier to say than to ensure, even when alternative channels for the disbursement of aid through more decentralized means can be found.

Nevertheless, despite the inevitably considerable importance for the Ugandan economy for the immediate future of foreign aid, Deryke Belshaw (Chapter 8) argues that aid cannot of itself be the main engine of growth. Instead it should be concentrated upon the task of removing bottlenecks as well as assisting employment-creating measures, in accordance with whatever wider development strategies are worked out by government authorities in Uganda. In this regard, a representative of one of the principal donor agencies suggested that priority in the country ought now to be given to restoring its productive capacities. This meant priority for an agricultural rehabilitation programme – in other words, better water supplies, posts and telecommunications improvements and much better roads – supplemented by action to rehabilitate social sectors like education and health. But, in order for such rehabilitation to be successful, Belshaw stresses that the macroeconomic and microeconomic levels of analysis and assessment must be combined, not considered separately. It would be misguided only to look at one of these levels by itself. Yet this is done far too frequently in discussions of African developmental problems.

Keith Edmonds (Chapter 7) provides a vigorous defence of adjustment policies implemented during Obote's second presidency from the macroeconomic point of view. Edmonds had first-hand experience here through secondment to the Ministry of Finance during Obote's second presidency. In his opinion, Uganda was confronted in 1980–4 with an economic crisis of both a short-term and long-term character. It was necessary to restructure the economy; and, as a condition for growth and development, there was a need for major investments of money that could only come from foreign funds. Edmonds considers that in a number of respects the second Obote administration's experiment in economic rehabilitation in association with the International Monetary Fund was a success; the substantial reduction in the inflation rate that took place between 1980 and 1984, the achievement on the supply side, the increases in exports of cash crops, and the stemming of the widespread retreat by many small Ugandan farmers into subsistence agriculture: these were some of its principal benefits. Moreover, Edmonds believes that these successes have important lessons for the rest of Africa. He admits there were also problems. There were certain in-built weaknesses in the overall economic policy. This depended for success upon a precarious balance between the second Obote government's domestic policies, donors' commitments of funds, and a restoration of growth in the officially recorded sector of the country's economy at the expense of the parallel economy or black market. When Obote's second regime therefore gave its civil servants a substantial pay rise in the middle of 1984, in order to halt the substantial erosions in the value of their fixed incomes that had continued to take place as a result of inflation persisting even at a reduced rate of increase, the overall policy immediately went awry. This single act itself fuelled further inflation, and thus helped to bring the national economy of Uganda still closer to collapse. Deteriorating security during 1984-5 clearly made an already dire economic situation still worse. In this, the end of Obote's second government came to mirror very closely the immediately post-Amin crisis of 1979–80.

Deryke Belshaw stresses the importance of not leaving the analysis at this level. He argues that it is crucial to marry measures at the macroeconomic level with activity at the microeconomic interface. For Belshaw, the main reason for the failure of the second Obote government's economic strategy was that the necessary micro-economic actions and corrections were not properly integrated into an overall strategic design. The second Obote government paid insufficient attention to the rural contribution to the national economy of Uganda. While coffee performed reasonably well, the contributions from other major export crops such as cotton and tea remained unrealized, while restoration of import-substituting commodities such as sugar and vegetable oil was totally inadequate. Any recovery strategy that the Museveni government finally decides upon should therefore take account of the failures of the 1981–5 period. Two factors especially should be noted. First, the desirability of stimulating export products and thereby increasing the country's earnings in foreign exchange. Secondly, the *magendo* or parallel economy should be reduced in size and growth restored to the formal economy by bringing unrecorded transactions in the rural sector into the formal economy. The informal economy is clearly more flexible than the formal one in Uganda nowadays, and peasant farmers engage in it for good economic reasons. This, Belshaw remarks, any central government in Uganda needs to remember.

Two other contributors (Michael Whyte and Apolo Nsibambi) follow Belshaw in focusing on the microeconomic sides of the Ugandan economy. But they differ in expressing less enthusiasm for an export-based cash cropping strategy. Michael Whyte (Chapter 9) describes recent economic developments in the Bunyole county of eastern Uganda in which he earlier undertook anthropological fieldwork. He describes a local economic situation that can only be described as transformatory. For, to start with, during the last 15 years there has been a substantial diversification of agricultural production in Bunyole, with the expansion of food crops and the introduction of rice cultivation at the expense of previous cash crops. This transformation, and the resultant withdrawal into the informal, *magendo* economy, has come primarily in response to market incentives. A saleable surplus of foodstuffs for 'export' to nearby urban areas is much more lucrative than growing cotton for more distant markets overseas. As regards Bunyole, local people have not been looking at the agricultural economy as something from which to escape, but rather as a source of cash incomes and security. But Whyte insists that this economic transformation has, contrary to Belshaw's recommendation, turned attention away from earlier export crops like coffee or cotton, towards more 'domesticated' agro-economic activity.

In his suggestions regarding food policy (Chapter 10), Apolo Nsibambi strongly advocates this kind of development. Agricultural policy, in his opinion, should be centred on food production instead of the traditional export crops of coffee, cotton and tea. Food crops are also cash crops, and as such fall within the domain of market forces. Nsibambi considers that it should be possible to reduce the dichotomy between the official and *magendo* economies in Uganda, and also provide sufficient 'space' between the two in order to enable peasant farmers to undermine any undue stranglehold on the official economy by the urban elite and any other unfair practices by the state regarding smallholders. At the same time, Nsibambi points out that food crops also have export potential.

The question of whether to give priority to food production or to alternative cash crops is a key issue in the current African developmental debate at the continental level. From the peasant farmers' point of view Nsibambi's strategy has many advantages, but both Belshaw and Edmonds view it differently. From the macroeconomic perspective they consider this kind of agricultural strategy a setback as regards stopping the drift towards the parallel economy that has been such a marked feature of life in the country since Amin seized power in 1971. Their chapters also imply that it would have definite negative implications, particularly as regards raising sufficient revenue for investments important for the country as a whole, if it becomes formally part of central government policy as well as informal practice in areas where the central government writ presently runs weakly, such as Bunyole. Nsibambi himself admits that his proposed strategy presupposes continuance of a particular kind of landownership; others might point out that it also implies continuance of class formation of the kind analysed by Nelson Kasfir in Ankole. Nsibambi counters both criticisms implicitly by advocating the continued individualization of land tenure in Uganda *and* the safeguarding of peasants' rights to hold land under customary tenure. In this respect he recommends an amendment to the Land Reform Decree of 1975.

This throws the developmental ball decisively back into the political arena. Much other data presented in this symposium also suggest that any serious economic strategies for Uganda must depend upon the stability and strength of its central political system. It is generally accepted that there are many backward and forward linkages between politics and economics in African countries. But Uganda represents a case where 'order in the political house' is a precondition for any future improvement in the national economy. The point is repeated again and again in the chapters that follow. It is primarily within the political arena that we must look for an answer to the question: What went wrong in Uganda?

Why is Uganda's position so particularly serious? Most of its problems are not unknown in other parts of Africa. However Uganda does seem extraordinary in the degree to which its difficulties cluster, congeal and seemingly fester at all levels of society. Christine Obbo (Chapter 14) looks especially at the interpersonal level in order to reveal the political culture influencing ordinary people's attitudes and behaviour. She provides gruesome examples of villagers' behaviour that indicate the existence of a very widespread culture of violence in the countryside. This expresses itself in successive scenarios of sorcery, poison and murder, often associated with the summary exercise of popular justice. From Obbo's chapter it certainly does not appear that Ugandan soldiers enjoy a monopoly of violence in the countryside; her research indicates that in the 1970s the sanctity of human life appears to have been violated on a very broad scale. Less spectacular, but equally important for prevailing political culture, is the corruption that has penetrated all corners of Ugandan society, not just the upper echelons constituting the conspicuous *Wabenzi* group. Obbo places prime responsibility for this tragic state of affairs upon successive political leaders of Uganda. In her opinion, too, the only hope for the future is a leader who undertakes seriously to rebuild moral institutions in society. And not least among the problems this leader will have to confront, in her opinion, is the prevailing elitism of educated groups that creates such a grave imbalance in Ugandan society as a whole. This arises at least in part because the country's educational system has unduly favoured access to white-collar jobs by one particular ethnic group, the Baganda. This has further divided Uganda, making the south into the country's richest region and the north its labour reserve.

This cleavage is apparent, in Obbo's view, in many aspects of Ugandan life, not least its cash economy. Anthony O'Connor (Chapter 6) analyses it in terms of spatial differentiation. His basic division is the core–periphery dichotomy, complicated by often overlooked regional variables. During the 1970s and 1980s the result has clearly been a very high degree of national disintegration. Relations with Sudan have further complicated matters. The sociological fluidity of human ties in the areas bordering upon the southern Sudan has deepened the core–periphery problem. Peter Woodward (Chapter 15) indeed argues that cross-border influence from Sudan was instrumental in initially bringing the periphery to power in Uganda in the person of Idi Amin. This was because Amin's power was based so substantially on the Nubian element in his army. The Nubis clearly represent an unusual example of sociological fluidity and cross-border influence resulting from the earlier British colonial era and indeed before. John Rowe shows this in Chapter 18. Woodward suggests that the Nubian group in Amin's army should more properly be classified as mercenaries, but this makes Amin's regime in Uganda into even more of a paradox. Nonetheless, the southern Sudanese connection during the Amin era has had considerable subsequent repercussions in Uganda regarding who are to be considered true citizens of the country and who simply refugees.

As Louise Pirouet points out (Chapter 16), the distinction between citizens and refugees is a difficult one to draw in Uganda because of the comparative smallness of the country and the sociological complexity of many areas bordering on neighbouring countries. Another dimension is added to the problem of national disintegration when doubts may be so frequently and easily raised about individuals' citizenship upon this score. From being a host country for refugees during the 1960s, Pirouet outlines how it was transformed into an exporter of refugees in the 1970s and 1980s. Uganda's refugee problem inevitably reflects the country's successive political conjunctures during these years, but it is remarkable how few refugees were exported from it under the Amin regime by comparison with the much larger numbers expelled during Obote's second period of office. One especially sad case concerned the Banyarwanda of Ankole. Their eviction was made easier partly by their political vulnerability as well as visibility as a marginal group of cattle-keepers locally, partly by the vigorousness of competition at the time for land as described by Nelson Kasfir in Chapter 11. Nonetheless, while it was easy for the second Obote government to get rid of the Banyarwanda physically from Ankole, it was not so easy to deal with them politically after they had become exiles outside Uganda. Here George Kanyeihamba's discussion (Chapter 5) is interesting in underlining how influential political exiles, like these Banyarwanda, could be in mounting international pressure upon an unpopular African government, and indeed how important they were in contributing decisively to its overthrow.

The sociological fluidity of Uganda's northern frontier with the Sudan was also crucially important. This fluidity created the possibility of a regional political consciousness emerging that might undermine the national integration that most of Uganda's politicians had sought during the 1960s. This point is elaborated further by Peter Woodward in Chapter 15. The national goal of Ugandan politicians during the 1960s is stressed by both Anthony O'Connor (Chapter 6) and Martin Doornbos (Chapter 17). Indeed, Doornbos in particular stresses the fragility of the prospects for national integration in Uganda and poses the question whether we are witnessing the beginning of the end of the Ugandan colonial-state formation. Will Museveni's newly installed government be able to restore Uganda as a viable nation-state, or should it face honestly the challenge of political divorce?

Doornbos envisages at least two possibilities here. There is the possibility of further spatial differentiation taking place along the lines of the north–south dichotomy already mentioned, where ethnic cleavage between Bantu and non-Bantu peoples is paralleled to a considerable extent by unequal distribution of indigenous wealth. In the present situation of central government by an essentially southern-based NRM, this may result in an enhanced regional political consciousness in northern Uganda (and possibly in southern Sudan too?) accompanying the effective breaking-up of Uganda into two separate African states. Whether this does or does not happen, there remains the problem of the 'uncaptured peasantry'. Most Ugandan peasants are unconcerned about the niceties of national integration, and indeed the Ugandan state has seemed of little relevance to most of them in recent years. On the contrary, the *magendo* system has shielded them against excessive exactions by an over-demanding as well as under-performing state in its successive political manifestations. Peasants have further suffered from successive avalanches of army violence under the Amin regime, its immediate successors, the second Obote government, and the short-lived Okellos' regime.

Doornbos concludes by expressing some optimism about the other possibility. This is that the Museveni government will be able

24

to break out of the downward spiral of political fragmentation, provided that in its various policy measures it seeks to gain the political trust of northern and well as southern Uganda. One crucial problem area remains army recruitment, not least because of the NRA's earlier predominantly southern recruitment bias. But here, as in other areas of decision-making, the NRM government cannot just start from scratch, much as it would like to do so as a truly revolutionary African government. It has to take account of existing administrative frameworks. It cannot totally ignore alternative political forces in the country. For it was indeed remarkable how those two pioneering political parties from the period of anti-British agitation twenty years before – the DP and the UPC – recovered so quickly after the Amin years and recaptured the political arena in Uganda. It is also remarkable how quickly after the collapse of the second Obote government and the short-lived dictatorship of the Okellos, political agitation revived within the area of the Buganda kingdom demanding its formal reconstitution. Michael Twaddle puts this latter story into context in Chapter 21. Of course, what the future holds for Uganda, God only knows. But we hope that the 21 mere mortals, Ugandans and non-Ugandans alike, who have studied its problems and contributed to this book, may help others who care for the country's future to understand at least some of its problems more fully.

TWO
Four steps towards disaster

Christopher Wrigley[1]

There are two basic ways in which a tragedy such as Uganda's might be discussed. One way would be to take it as an extreme manifestation of the malaise that afflicts the whole of post-colonial Africa and diagnose it by means of the familiar categories of 'tribalism', underdevelopment, neocolonialism and the like. But though theories of general crisis do have their uses, they are of limited value as explanations of particular catastrophes. Chronic poverty is one thing, famine is another; and authoritarian government, whether by soldiers or by party bosses, is not to be equated with rule by thugs and sadists. These terms do not refer to any member of the Okellos' administration or its predecessor, but to the men who have actually had power over their fellow citizens for most of the last fifteen years. Large numbers of Ugandans know the difference only too well, and many others knew it before they died. No African state is a smoothly functioning democracy, but collapse into tyranny, anarchy and civil war is not the norm, and when it occurs it requires specific historical explanation, which is the second line of approach. Within the overarching frame provided by the great dilemmas of Africa, and of the Third World in general, it is still necessary to explore the peculiar malignancies of the Uganda problem.

It is not at first sight obvious that there are any problems, either economic or political, that are peculiar to Uganda. At the time of independence the economic prospects looked good, the country being neither as poor as Tanzania nor as class-ridden as Kenya. Deteriorating terms of trade in the next two decades affected all African countries, other than the oil producers, and some were hit harder than Uganda. The cake still seemed large enough, on any rational view, to be divided without violence, certainly without violence of the extreme kind that has occurred. On closer inspection, however, the very lack of apparent contradictions may provide a partial clue to the trouble. Uganda's prosperity being almost entirely agricultural, without important foreign penetration of the rural sector, the capitalist class was small, and what there was of it, in the commercial and industrial sectors, was almost entirely alien, as was most of the proletariat. Society thus consisted effectively of a mass of peasant cultivators, living in communities that had not wholly lost their tribal character, and a small ruling class composed mostly of state officials. The development of an indigenous commercial bourgeoisie had been inhibited by colonial policy, which first reserved the cotton and coffee industries for established, foreign firms and then began to transfer them to state-sponsored co-operatives, thus confirming the belief that economic advance could most easily be achieved by favour of the government. For individuals, however, the upward path lay more directly through the hierarchy of the state. Social aspirants thus sought above all to control the levers of government power for their own and their communities' benefit, and economic competition was heavily politicised from the start. Even the Ganda landowning aristocracy was not a truly independent social power; for it had acquired its wealth by gift of the state in the first place and perpetuated it by using its capital endowment to purchase education, and thus access to the bureaucratic elite.

This overdevelopment of the state was certainly among the predisposing factors in the breakdown, but was hardly a sufficient cause; for it is by no means peculiar to Uganda, and competition within the governing elite has not usually reached the point of political collapse. So we still have to look for more specific structural defects.

Uganda is of course an arbitrarily delimited, culturally heterogeneous, historically shallow collection of peoples with none of the attributes of a nation state. But again, that goes for most African states, and there is nothing in the ethnic composition of Uganda that sets it apart from the rest. The division between Bantu, Nilotic and Sudanic peoples is no more an intrinsic reason for conflict than the division of Europe into Latins, Teutons and Slavs was the cause of the First World War. Such categories become politically significant only when politicians find use for them. People were not aware that they were 'Bantu' or 'Nilotes' until European linguists told them! The individual, mutually unintelligible languages have much more real significance, but no more so than in other states whose recent history has been relatively placid. And one of the most recent political fissions has no linguistic basis at all, since Langi and Acholi speak virtually the same language. Nor is it especially relevant that some people used to live in kingdoms while others did not. For in the first place the distinction is not clear-cut (the Alur and Acholi chiefdoms were small-scale offshoots of Bunyoro) and in the second place some of the fiercest feuds have been within, not between, the kingdom and non-kingdom groups: Buganda versus Bunyoro, or more recently Langi and Acholi versus Lugbara, Madi and Kakwa.

It could well be argued, indeed, that in most respects the structure of Uganda favoured stability, since its conflicts and rivalries were multiple and variously defined. In particular, religious divisions, more politically potent here than in any other African country except Sudan, cut across the lines drawn by language and political tradition. There was thus ample scope for those recombinations and realignments that, according to widely held political theory, should have kept the system in dynamic equilibrium. There has in fact been a series of recombinations, but they have been violent and disorderly and have not been contained within a rational political framework. To explain the disorder we must turn to historical contingency; and there are perhaps four points at which history may be seen to have taken a wrong turning in Uganda.

The first lies so far back in time and is so well known that it needs little discussion here. It consists of the events that gave the country its revealing name, which reminds us that it was in origin the kingdom of Buganda with such bits and pieces as the British found it convenient to tack on. Althought they soon abandoned what seemed to be their original intention, to keep the expanding Protectorate coterminous with the kingdom, and although they later reined in the enthusiastic sub-imperialism of their collaborators, early decisions left the country with a crucial imbalance. Three provinces of the Protectorate were ethnically and politically fragmented, but the fourth and central province consisted of a single, especially close-knit society that was both a linguistic and a traditional political unit. Its members also believed it had earned a privileged relationship with its British overlords. This province, moreover, contained the headquarters of the colonial government, of the main commercial enterprises and of the Christian churches and educational agencies; and since it was also very well endowed by nature its inhabitants became by some margin the most affluent, the best equipped and the most self-confident of Uganda's peoples. Both recent and earlier history, in addition, had given them an especially strong sense of political identity. In many ways their situation was like that of the Prussians in nineteenth-century Germany, and they would be no more willing than the Prussians had been to merge into a larger entity unless they were able to control it. The difference was, however, that they were not in a position to control Uganda. In one sense Buganda was too big for its context, but in another sense it was not big enough. That is why a political engineer would have been justified in protesting that in order to design a state with a good chance of a stable and peaceful future it would be necessary to dismantle the existing edifice, which was inherently unstable, and start again.

It would be pointless to blame the architects of the Protectorate for this flagrant structural flaw; for they were not designing a country but only a colonial administration, which they thought would endure for the foreseeable future. It was only when decolonisation came on to the political agenda – placed there by the British themselves – that an impasse became apparent, and even then tragedy was not predestined. It was in fact an attempt to avoid the impasse that led to the second wrong turning, the 'Kabaka crisis' of 1953–5.

The British authorities had started trying to cut Buganda down to size in the 1920s, but the first real crunch came when Sir Andrew Cohen abruptly deported Mutesa to London in 1953. This well-meant but ill-judged action (as it appeared to me at the time and still appears) had consequences exactly opposite to the ones intended.[2] Cohen, a civil servant with unusually clear and radical aims, had come to Uganda determined to initiate the process of transition from colonial dependency to nation-state, and he saw the kingdom as an obstacle to be removed from his path. He did not, however, fully understand the forces of resistance he would encounter. He undoubtedly believed that he was breaking the power of a conservative hierarchy in order to open the way to progressive nationalism. But in reality support for the kingship came not from the chiefly hierarchs, who by this time were servants of the Protectorate rather than of the monarchy, but from precisely those aspirant sub-elites, the clerks and teachers and traders and successful farmers, that in other countries supplied the dynamic of the nationalist movement. The removal of the Kabaka was seen by such people not only as an affront but also as a sign of the British Government's determination to hand them over to white-settler domination, against which the autonomy and special status of Buganda had long been perceived as the sole effective defence. And indeed there was confusion of purpose on the British side. While Cohen himself aimed to incorporate the kingdom into an eventually independent, African-ruled Ugandan nation, his political masters had not decided whether the ultimately sovereign state should be Uganda or East Africa (or East-Central) Africa, nor what form its government should take. The Baganda were thus asked to forgo their entrenched rights in return for a quite uncertain future, and this blank cheque they solidly refused to sign.

It is possible that, having started his coup, Cohen would have done better to carry it through; and, if so, the British liberals (myself obscurely included) who helped to persuade him to retreat must take some responsibility for the unhappy long-term outcome. In the event, thanks mainly to Sir Keith Hancock's brilliantly conducted seminars with the Baganda politicians, the impasse was apparently broken and all parties seemed to get what they most wanted. The Baganda got their king back, but they conceded what to Cohen was the essential point: they agreed to elect representatives to the Legislative Council, and thus accepted in principle that there would be a Ugandan state that would have the right to control their destiny, since they had consented to its formation. But there would also still be a kingdom of Buganda, and its exact position in the scheme of things was left deliberately obscure. Hancock rejected a federal solution, that seductive compromise that has so often caused more conflicts than it has resolved; for he knew that federations are the most difficult of all political systems, requiring a fundamental consensus and a political tradition of restraint, a willingness to abide by the rules, such as could not be expected in a newly formed political society. So the Uganda that began to take shape in 1955 was a unitary state, but its unitariness was concealed by the continued functioning of a kingdom too large and too ceremonious to be easily cast in the role of a local-government unit.

To describe the 1955 settlement as a fudge would be in no way a condemnation. Fudges are often essential devices, and above all they are a way of buying time, the usually correct assumption being that problems eventually solve themselves. Sir Harry Johnston's fudge, after all, had worked quite well for half a century, which is quite as long a duration as can be asked for any politicial arrangement. Hancock and Cohen, and Lyttelton did not imagine that they had 50 years to work with, but they could reasonably have expected a minimum of 20 years. Young Englishmen were still being recruited to the colonial service, with the implied premise that they had a career ahead of them. Hancock himself, as a historian of the Commonwealth, was very familiar with the stately sequence of transitions by which colonies had hitherto progressed to independence, and he could not have foreseen that the whole process would be telescoped as drastically as it was and that the settlement would buy so little time. In 1955 there was not anyone in Uganda, European or African, politician or administrator or academic, who believed that there would be a sovereign Republic in Uganda in 1962.

The third great turning-point was in fact the decision taken in London that Uganda should be given almost immediate independence. We do not know – or at any rate I do not know – exactly when that decision was taken or how, for the archives are not yet open and published comments have been very uninformative. It was, however, part of the great review of Britain's place in the world that certainly took place after the Suez fiasco of 1956. In the first post-war decade eastern Africa, together with the Middle East, had a key role in Britain's struggle to remain a world power. But the hinge of that strategy was in Egypt, and it had to be abandoned when the control of Egypt was finally lost. In place of power, it was now decided, there would be a delicate manipulation of influences through the Special Relationship, the European alliances and the Commonwealth connection. In this new perspective colonial dependencies, even in eastern Africa, became costly liabilities to be discarded with all possible speed, hopefully being transformed into 'Commonwealth partners' instead.

In this acceleration, pressures from within Uganda did not play a decisive part. The economic grievances that caused unrest in the late 1940s had been alleviated by the commodity boom and a sharp reduction in the rate of colonial exploitation; and economic aspiration focused antagonism on the Asian business community rather than on the colonial system. Though the Buganda crisis had quickened political consciousness throughout the Protectorate the nationalist movement was in its infancy, and the idea of a Ugandan nation had hardly begun to enter the consciousness of the vast majority. When a number of rural Baganda were asked in 1953 how they saw the future of Buganda in a self-governing Uganda, the question was simply not understood. 'Yuganda' was an English word, and the government at Entebbe was 'the English government'. In the term 'self-government', *kwefuga*, the self was obviously Buganda, which would resume the independence it had temporarily surrendered to the British. If pressed, respondents were willing to suppose that other people might be allowed to join the kingdom if they so desired. Nor was this simply a case of Ganda chauvinism. The Bagisu, it was said a little later, assumed that after independence they would have an ambassador at Entebbe.

Kwefuga, moreover, was a rather artificial term. The word that really expressed the political idea of the Baganda in the mid-1950s was *mirembe*, 'peace', with a strong connotation of being left alone, not being pushed around. It evoked the defensive mood of the African population, the profound insecurity, the fear of impending change, which proved to be better founded than the somewhat facile optimism of the decolonisers. Here I must confess to a hindsight that may still be uncongenial to many. When I identified the speeding up of the transition to independence as a turning-point in Uganda's history, the context of this essay implied that it was a wrong turning. And indeed I have come to believe that nothing in Britain's dealings with Africa did her less credit than the haste and manner of her departure. Another decade at least of colonial rule, devoted to the serious planning of workable political structures, would have given the launch a better chance of success. But the British – not those on the spot but their masters in London – were anxious to be gone, and so they simply took the existing administrative units and turned them into states, handing the African people a governmental framework and telling them to build themselves a nation around it. The chances that this could be done without blood and tears were slender everywhere, but nowhere more slender than in Uganda, where the basic structural defect, the size and solidity of Buganda, had been plastered over but not properly repaired.

The 1955 settlement with Buganda had far-reaching consequences for the shape and character of the new states of Eastern Africa, not just for Uganda. For an essential ingredient was the Secretary of State's declaration that Uganda was a 'primarily African state' and his acceptance of the corollary, an African majority among the non-official members of the Legislative Council. This was the first breach in the principle of multiracial balancing that had been prescribed by the Colonial Office for all the emergent states of the region. At the time it may have seemed a minor change, Uganda having been simply transferred to the West African category of states. But the domino effect was rapidly decisive here. If African majority rule was right for Uganda, could it really be denied to Tanganyika, whose non-African communities were not all that much larger? And if Tanganyika, why not Kenya, or the Rhodesias? So it was soon evident that when power was transferred it would be assigned unreservedly to the African people. That development was both necessary and right: power-sharing between rigidly defined, numerically unequal communities is not a feasible arrangement. But another feature of the settlement was much more debatable. In order to coax the Baganda into Uganda it was necessary to convince them that they were not being inveigled into East Africa as well; and so whatever plans there may have been for wider union were tacitly shelved. They were not actually abandoned but the moment had been lost. To make East Africa acceptable to Ugandans and Tanganyikans it would have been necessary to break the power of the Kenya settlers first. But when this was eventually done it was too late, for by then both Uganda and Tanganyika were well on the way to separate independence. This was a great pity on many grounds. A united East Africa would have had far more economic and political value than the sum of its components. But what is more to our present point, in that larger context it would have been not too difficult to solve the problem of Buganda, which in the narrow confines of Uganda was insoluble – except by force, which as we know, would destroy the state itself.

Independence was launched with a supreme display of fudging talent, almost certainly provided by the departing rulers. The division of functions between a constitutional head of state and an executive head of government is itself a very British proceeding; but to make the hereditary ruler of one part of the country president of the unitary republic was to set up just the kind of anomaly that the British pride themselves on being able to make workable. The British, however, were not going to be there to work it, and the arrangement was obviously going to break down in a very short time. There followed the fourth misdirection, the army mutiny of 1964.

This East African event has not received as much attention from historians and politicial analysts as it deserves, for the varying responses to the mutinies had a profound effect on the future evolution of the three territories. Tanzania, the hardest hit, also took the most drastic corrective action, which developed into one of the most interesting and successful components of the Tanzanian experiment. Once the situation had been restored by British arms, energetic steps were taken to transform the ex-colonial force into a people's army, integrated into the Party and the State. The result was the most efficient army in black Africa and the one least likely to substitute itself for the civilian power. (Anyone who makes statements like that about Africa takes terrible risks with his credibility, but I venture it none the less.) Kenya, by keeping its armed forces small and by careful ethnic balancing, has also managed – just – to retain civilian control. But in Uganda the mutineers were bought off with lavish pay increases and promotions instead of being suppressed. Obote resorted to the personal allegiance of the troops. He knew that once the Democratic Party had been defeated there would be no further reason for the alliance between himself and Mutesa; and that once the Lost Counties problem was out of the way the kingdoms were likely to make common cause with one another and with other elements hostile to himself. So he needed to have in reserve the instrument of armed force. But when he had thus made himself dependent on the soldiers it could hardly be long before they took power into their own hands.

Milton Obote is by no means the only person to have believed that the armies of Africa could be used to secure political objectives. Idealists eager to purge corruption, developers hooked on the concept of modernizing despotism, radicals seeking to hasten the revolution, conservatives seeking to pre-empt the revolution, foreign intriguers promoting their own multifarious interests have all looked avidly into the barrel of the gun, and all have paid the price – or rather the people have paid it. The truth is that soldiers are good at killing. They have no other competence and no useful role in present-day Africa. There will begin to be hope when they have retired, not just to their barracks, but to their villages. And the liquidation of the armies is just one, though the most urgent, aspect of a highly desirable development: the drastic reduction in the power, the cost and the pretension of the state. The one good result of the turmoil in Uganda, by many accounts, is that local communities have relearned self-reliance and self-management. And it is just possible that with the exhaustion of the politicians and the gunmen the people of Uganda may be about to win.

Three points need to be made about this final sentence. (1) When I wrote it I was inclined to include the National Resistance Army among the 'gunmen'. At the Workshop I began to learn, among much else, that this uncomplimentary term was not rightly applied to people who had taken up arms to rid the country of intolerable affliction. All the same, it is to be hoped that they too will soon be able to go home. (2) The people's victory, if that is what it is, has been dearly bought. When I first learnt that guerrilla resistance had been launched in Buganda my blood ran cold, because it was obvious that the consequences for the people would be horrendous. So we must pray that the survivors can now enjoy a lasting peace and freedom. (3) Popular justice is commonly a rough justice, and it is to be hoped that the *gogolimbo*, the cleansing, will be tempered by the knowledge that vengeance belongs to the Lord.

There is also the need for a general clarification. This essay has highlighted the 'Buganda problem' and the emphasis could be misleading. That problem now belongs to ancient history, and for some considerable time the real task will be a much more fundamental one: the restoration of civil order.

Notes

1. Apart from minor editing changes, this paper remains as I wrote it early in September 1985. However, a few clarifications have been added in February 1986. These personal reflections make no claim to academic status and therefore are not dignified by scholarly apparatus.
2. A similar criticism of Cohen has been uttered by those who wish to insinuate that this great public servant may have been a Communist traitor. So I must dissociate myself entirely from that absurd smear.

THREE
The dislocated polity

D.A. Low

Over 15 years, from early 1971 to early 1986, and some would think before that too, Uganda seemed the worst possible case. It was for a time closely paralleled by Equatorial Guinea, but its trauma lasted longer. It was not merely that there were all the grotesque slaughterings of the years of President Amin (1971–9) and of President Obote's second term (1980–5). There were the gross structural defects that lay behind these as well.

We are beginning to understand the crucial importance of structural elements in sustaining a great many new states. Their effectiveness often seems vital for securing some measure of political order. There seem, moreover, at least some regularities in the way these operate, and in probing the reasons for Uganda's agony some of the available comparisons may be brought into focus.

The most important political development in Africa over the last hundred years has not been fragmentation but the huge process of unification. Whereas there were once a thousand or so actual or latent political systems in Africa, by independence these had been reduced to a mere 50 or so. That process has nevertheless entailed profound social and political difficulties, as many new aggregations have found themselves ensconced in an arbitrarily concocted new state.

A *tour d'horizon* suggests that there are several methods by which the process of national aggregation in new states may be assisted, at any rate to secure that sufficiency of political authority necessary to maintain a civil order and thus a modicum of personal security. A major role can be played, as in India and China, by a single dominant party. It can be played as well by a continuing sequence of open parliamentary elections. It is just not the case that 'poor countries cannot afford free elections'. In the ten or so new states in the Southwest Pacific, in the Caribbean, and elsewhere, free and open elections have sucessfully met the strains to which new states are prone (Fry 1983). It is one of the unexplained tragedies of post-independence Africa that they have so often been abandoned there.

The dislocated polity

Where there is neither an established dominant party, nor regular elections, nor an effective dictatorship – a third possibility – the simplest manner in which 'sub-national' socio-cultural aggregations that lie within a state's borders can be accommodated to its requirements has been where at the core of a country one such community is its 'natural' majority. This has been crucial to state formation in Indonesia (where the Javanese outnumber the rest of the population), in Burma (where the Burmese substantially outnumber the hill tribes), and in post-Bangladesh Pakistan (dominated as it is by the Punjabis, as the Sindhis, Pathans, and Baluchis know to their cost). There are three interesting instances of such core natural majorities using their primacy after independence against a formerly pre-eminent minority: the *bumiputras* vis-à-vis the Chinese in Malaysia; the Sinhalese against the Tamils in Sri Lanka; the Shona against the Ndebele in Zimbabwe. Such situations can be very detrimental to the minority (as the Catholics have found in Northern Ireland, and as Ulster would have found in Eire), but they have nevertheless provided the basis for several effective new states.

Where such natural majorities do not exist – and that is more frequently the case – composed majorities can be constructed. There is the interesting case of Fiji, where whilst there is a clear majority of Indians, the Fijian Prime Minister successfully put together a government of Fijians and Indian Muslims and Gujaratis so as to leave its North Indian majority in a political minority (Lal, 1983). In Africa, Senghor successfully composed a Wolof-speaking majority so as to maintain his regime in Senegal. By all accounts Banda's position in Malawi is based upon a southern majority centred in his own people the Chewa; whilst over the years Kaunda has fashioned a succession of such coalitions so as to maintain himself in power in Zambia. In Uganda, as we shall note, there were no less than five attempts in the early 1960s to compose a governing majority, and it is a large part of its tragedy that none of these was sustained.

Where there is no natural majority, and a composed one is difficult to effect, all is not lost. There is, to begin with, the Prussian possibility where (as in late nineteenth-century Germany), in the absence of an effective majority, a cohesive group moves to the centre. For twenty years after independence in 1947 the Punjabis held just such a position in pre-Bangladesh Pakistan. In Africa the Sara clans under President Tombalbaye (1960–75) occupied a like position in Chad (where they only composed a third of the population). In Ivory Coast the landed–commercial–administrative elite under President Houphouet-Boigny hold a similar position; while latterly Sekou Touré in Guinea employed his Mandinké (one-

third of the population) in a similar role there (Dunn, 1978). Much
the most striking example in Africa of the Prussian model was to be
found, however, in Kenya, in the predominance there of the
Kikuyu. More recently this has been transmuted into a composed
majority under the Kikuyu President Kenyatta's successor, the
Kalenjin President Moi; but it is a moot point whether its core is not
still the 'Prussian' Kikuyu.

There are at least three further possibilities as well. The Prophet
Muhammed showed long ago at Medina how feasible it was for one
man to hold the interstitial position between warring groups who
were unable to prevail over each other and establish a position of
dominance over all of them (Watt 1961). In more recent times this
was precisely the procedure followed by the Grand Sanusi in
Cyrenaica (Evans-Pritchard 1949). It seems to have been the one
followed by the Kabakas of Buganda, where the Kabaka was the only
Muganda who was not a member of any clan, and married (as
Muhammed did) into several of them (Southwold 1961).

In post-independence Africa there have been a number of
instances of this procedure being of major importance to a new state.
Gowon in Nigeria was assisted by the fact that he was a Christian –
like most of its southerners – from the generally Muslim north.
Ahidjo, the long-running President of Cameroon, enjoyed similar
advantages:

> His father was a Fulani of middling status, and his mother was
> from a non-Islamic northern group. Because he was not tied to
> the Fulani aristocratic or clerical class, he could be relatively
> acceptable to the south. Because he had northern antecedents,
> even if he lacked high customary status, he could quieten Fulani
> fears of southern domination (Young, 1983).

The principal example in Africa of the use of the interstitial
possibility has been in Tanzania. For whatever Nyerere's personal
gifts, nothing was more fundamental to this position than the fact
that in a situation where there was no natural majority, nor much
sign of anyone composing one, let alone of any aspiring 'Prussians',
his own provenance in a small, numerically insignificant community
enabled him to hold the interstitial position between the larger ones
– the Chagga, the Nyakyusa, the Nyamwezi and so on. It is in these
terms no surprise that his successor, President Mwinyi, should have
come from Zanzibar, a classic interstitial figure once again.

Where all these further expedients prove difficult to effect, it may
still be possible to create a working regime in which the head of
government is no more than *primus inter pares*. This is the situation

that prevails in the Southwest Pacific state of Papua New Guinea. There every cabinet has to have some nexus with each part of a country in which regional governments are very much stronger than is usually the case (Ballard, 1981). The prime minister is little more than just one regional representative and thus little more than the first amongst equals. This scarcely makes for a stable regime. Late in 1985 Michael Somare, for the second time, found himself toppled from its prime ministership. But at least there was never a coup or a military takeover – as indeed there has not so far been in any of the so much better ordered Southwest Pacific new states. The most interesting example of this expedient in Africa has been in Somalia. There, prior to the 1969 coup there were serious clan conflicts. But under General Mohamed Siad Barre, the Supreme Revolutionary Council carefully included members belonging to all the major clan communities, with much more satisfactory results.

Beyond this there seems to be one further possibility for which it is necessary to allow. This is the fifty–fifty arrangement. Belgium is probably the prototype here, with its Flemings and Walloons. It surfaced briefly in India's interim government in the months preceding independence in 1947. It used to be most deliberately employed in Lebanon. Because of the disastrous outcome in both these last two instances, it is hardly to be commended to others.

The tragedy of independent Uganda is that none of these expedients, some at least of which have more than half worked elsewhere, were successfully operated there. The attempts of both Presidents Obote and Amin to pursue instead a populist course proved entirely useless, and that led them to the last resort of the politically bankrupt: terror. That very fortunately destroyed their regimes from within, though not before there had been terrible loss of life. In 1979–80 there was an inept attempt to operate the Prussian possibility. It was left to President Museveni to try once again in 1986 to work one of the more promising structural alternatives outlined above; but with what success only the future can tell.

We may remind ourselves that like most African countries Uganda was an artificial creation, comprising the northern inter-lacustrine Bantu along with the south-central Nilotes; that it encompassed a large assortment of pre-colonial polities (upwards of 70 or so rulerships for a start in the southern areas alone); and that at its core it had the large kingdom of Buganda. It is an old point that from the early 1950s there was scarcely a doubt that it would have independence as a 'primarily African state'. Since the issue thereby became, not whether independence would come, but the distribution of power upon its attainment, the Uganda National Congress, which originally sought to mobilize a unified nationalist campaign, never had very much chance. From the mid-1950s Uganda saw instead political parties that approximated more to its old political cleavages between Protestants and Catholics – the various fragments of the Uganda National Congress (and such, briefly, as the Progressive Party) culminating in the Uganda Peoples' Congress on the one side, and the Democratic Party on the other (Low, 1971).

Unlike Zimbabwe (or as we have seen Indonesia and Burma) Uganda has no natural majority. The Baganda at its core might well have become its Prussians. There have certainly been some Baganda politicians who have always seen its future as lying principally in playing a major role in the larger Uganda – from the early nationalist Ignatius Musazi to his long-running former associate Paulo Muwanga (and certain others besides). At independence Buganda held, moreover, an extraordinary plurality of elite positions in the country as a whole; it enjoyed great prestige; it was relatively well endowed economically; and it straddled the country's heartland. But in contrast to the Kikuyu in Kenya next door, they had early on been used by the British as 'sub-imperialists' in the wider Uganda, and long before independence had come to be greatly resented and feared in the rest of the country (Roberts, 1962). They made their first serious attempt to protect the remnants of their primacy either by a separate independence for their kingdom or by entrenching special privilege for it in a federal constitution. All this was reinforced by the prominent role in pursuing these ends played by their Cambridge educated Kabaka Mutesa II. In 1953 he was deported by the British for pressing his case for the separate independence of his kingdom (as in different circumstances was to be achieved by the comparable royal dynasty in Swaziland). But he was then returned in triumph in 1955, and thereafter as a hereditary ruler with next to no chance of operating politically outside his kingdom as the principal political leader of the whole country, and fearful of the threat to his own position and to that of his kingdom in the larger Uganda from the free play of the ballot box, he encouraged his people to support the neo-traditionalist Kabaka Yekka 'Kabaka only' political movement, and so passed up their principal chance of becoming Uganda's Prussians. These antics compounded the opposition to them in the rest of the country, and that gave Milton Obote, a rising politician from northern Uganda, the chance he seized to compose in his UPC a non-Baganda majority against them (Apter, 1961; Low, 1971).

It is of central importance to an understanding of the Ugandan story to note that in the years 1961–6, before and after Uganda's independence in October 1962, there were no less than five successive attempts to compose a governing majority in Uganda, none of which succeeded for any length of time. In varying sequence three of these were constructed by Obote himself; one by some of his opponents; one, against him, by some of his colleagues. His first attempt, institutionalized in the principally anti-Baganda, largely Protestant UPC, seemed headed at first for political control of the whole country via the first full Ugandan national elections of 1961. Precisely because these looked like delivering Uganda to his anti-Baganda UPC, those elections were widely boycotted by the Baganda under Kabaka Mutesa's increasingly evident leadership. But that had the extraordinary effect of handing the victory at the 1961 elections not to the UPC but to the countrywide Democratic Party, which had largely Roman Catholic support and which took it upon itself to mobilize some of its following in Buganda notwithstanding the more general election boycott there. In the outcome the DP only won a minority of seats outside Buganda, but on an exiguous poll it won almost all of the seats in Buganda itself, and thus secured a majority in the country overall. Under the Muganda Catholic, Benedicto Kiwanuka, it thereupon formed the first African government in Uganda.

This second composed majority was not quite as ephemeral as is sometimes suggested, for in Uganda as a whole there were almost certainly more Catholics than Protestants. But its very success led its opponents to think furiously, and out of that came the second of the attempts Obote made in the early 1960s to compose a governing majority. For against the DP he was persuaded to concoct a quite extraordinary alliance between his own anti-Baganda UPC and their erstwhile foes, Buganda's neo-traditionalist Kabaka Yekka (KY). Together they forced a further general election in 1962 in which they trounced the DP, and thereafter constructed the coalition government that before the end of 1962 took Uganda into independence.

That coalition was then shored up during the following year when Obote supported Kabaka Mutesa for the Presidency of Uganda whilst holding on to the office of Prime Minister himself. The alliance rested, however, less upon a securely composed majority than upon a fifty–fifty split, and very soon suffered from all the ills to which such regimes are prone. There was a special crisis over the Lost Counties, which at the end of the nineteenth century the British had transferred from Bunyoro to Buganda and which Obote was committed in the rest of the country to restoring to Bunyoro from Buganda by referendum. If this was to be effected something other than the fifty–fifty regime with Buganda would be required. The difficulty here was that at the 1962 elections Obote's UPC had not won an overall majority, and was critically dependent on KY support. Obote, however, quietly proceeded to put together his third composed majority by wooing some of the disheartened DP to his side. During 1964 several ex-DP followers were given positions in his Cabinet, and before long, following the referendum on the Lost Counties, which was won for Bunyoro, its KY members left his government.

But no sooner had that happened than Obote's third composed majority began to fall apart as well. It is often argued that the rift that now opened within his government did not follow precisely the north–south lines; but it certainly had that appearance. There are clear indications too that, in the aftermath of the referendum on the Lost Counties, there were moves to oust him from within his own government through a combination of western kingdom leaders and some easterners (including the army leader, Opolot, from Teso) in conjunction with a number of Baganda, or in other words by means of yet one more, again differently composed, majority (Low, 1971).

The crisis came early in 1966 when, in the course of a tangled dispute concerning the provision of financial and other assistance to a rebel group in the Congo (Zaire to be) in which the Uganda army's second-in command, Colonel Amin, was involved, and with which Obote himself came to be tarred, the whole of Obote's Cabinet during his absence from Kampala unanimously decided to institute a committee of inquiry that among other things was palpably directed against him personally. Such were now the uncertainties, with one composed majority tumbling over another – five indeed in so many years – that, feeling cheated of his rightful inheritance as the man who had finally brought Uganda into independence, now at the end of his tether with all this politicking, and wondering where any further majority he might compose could come from, Obote succumbed to the spreading African political disease, arrested five of his ministerial colleagues at a Cabinet meeting, and suspended the constitution fashioned at independence. Mutesa and the greater part of the Baganda naturally erupted. Obote was told to remove himself and his government from off Buganda's soil, and popular disturbances in Buganda quickly ensued. Obote's fateful riposte was then to despatch armed forces, principally of northern Ugandan troops under Colonel Amin, against the Kabaka's palace, from which Mutesa was lucky to escape with his life to London (Mutesa, 1967).

By these means Obote hamstrung the moves to create a newly composed majority without him. But his own third composed majority had now collapsed as well. By contrast, say, with Senghor's composed majority in Senegal, or Kaunda's successive coalitions in Zambia, he had entirely failed to hold any of his together. Accordingly after 1966 he not only had no majority behind him. He found himself operating in a limbo without any of the structural expedients that have been canvassed here to give him support. Worse; having turned to the army to cut his Gordian knot, he was now more at its mercy than he would have cared to admit. For Uganda the bells began to toll.

In these circumstances it is very instructive to see what Obote did next. He first proclaimed himself as Uganda's executive President. Throughout his ensuing first term he then made sustained efforts to undermine and cut across existing ethnic entities so as to create a quite new kind of majority for himself based upon populist appeals. His principal efforts were directed at destroying Uganda's kingdoms, the 'feudalism' they represented, and their institutional quasi-replicas in the rest of the country. Then, whereas at the climax of the 1966 crisis he had dictatorially handed down a new constitution, in 1967 he promulgated a revised constitution, and deliberately encouraged its discussion for three months on end. At the same time he embarked on a speech-making tour in outlying parts of the country. In the following year he went further still. In March 1968 he held a large rally in Kampala to which religious leaders and the diplomatic corps were invited. In June he called a meeting of Secretaries-General of Districts (key local figures he had decided to retain). Immediately afterwards he held the first UPC Conference since 1964, to which President Nyerere and Kaunda were both invited. In September he summoned a further conference, for senior officers of the army, the police and the prison services, and meanwhile embarked on a series of 'meet-the-people' tours in most of the non-Baganda parts of the country, in the course of which he not only denounced Uganda's elite but proclaimed that he and his ministers had come 'to meet their masters'. It was soon fairly clear, however, that he was making very little progress, particularly at the core of the country in Buganda. When at the end of 1968 he announced that he would address a meeting at Bombo in Buganda, the hour for this was suddenly brought forward; troops and police were much in evidence; and no more than 100 people attended (Low, 1971).

Economic and class considerations have been advanced for his next steps, and these are not to be gainsaid (Mamdani, 1976). But taken in the round it is evident that they were principally designed to promote still further his continuing efforts to secure popular support for his regime. To this end he launched in 1969 his 'Move to the Left' with his *Common Man's Charter* (Uganda's surrogate for

Tanzania's Arusha Declaration, which Nyerere had issued two years before). This was designed to foster a 'new political culture' from which all traces of 'feudalism' would be removed. That objective seemed assisted by the death of Mutesa in London at the end of the year, and in May 1970 Obote followed it up with his Nakivubo Pronouncements in which he announced that his government would take majority holdings in the major commercial enterprises in the country. In July 1970 he capped all this with his *Proposal for New Methods of Election of Representatives of the People to Parliament* by which, within the constraints of a one-party state, candidates were to be required to secure votes both in their own 'basic' constituencies, and in three other regions of Uganda as well. This remarkable concoction was explicitly designed to break up the persisting ethnic matrices which he believed so plagued the country, and thereupon secure a new political legitimacy for his regime (Low, 1971).

But by now he was becoming increasingly beleaguered. There had been several attempts on his own life, notably in December 1969 as he was leaving a further UPC conference. That turned out to be a particularly ominous occasion, for not only did elements of the army go on a rampage in Kampala, but Amin, the head of the army, disappeared, and upon his reappearance was accused by his second-in-command, Brigadier Okoya, of deserting his post. Soon afterwards Okoya was found murdered, and there were clear indications that this had been done at Amin's bidding. Violent tendencies were clearly mounting. It was becoming increasingly clear too that Obote did not have the political authority to bring them to a halt. Not only was police morale slipping. As Okoya's murder had shown, there was growing cleavage within the army. This was exacerbated by Obote's increasing alignment with the Sudanese President Numeiri – a move that threatened the Anya Nya guerrillas operating against the Khartoum regime in the southern Sudan, which had Uganda-based support from Israel. For that fed into a growing rift between Obote, who was giving promotion in the army to his own Langi and their Acholi neighbours, and Amin, whom Obote now promoted out of control of the army, but who nevertheless was enlisting Anya Nya and other recruits into it, especially from his own West Nile district (Martin, 1974; Smith, 1980).

The denouement came in January 1971 whilst Obote was away at a Commonwealth Conference in Singapore (Twaddle, 1972a). Before his departure he had left instructions that Amin was to explain his involvement in yet another financial imbroglio. Having survived his dependence on the army for nearly five years, and no doubt believing that having formally promoted Amin out of direct control of the army he had drawn his teeth, Obote disastrously underestimated Amin's likely reaction. There is some evidence that the chief Israeli representative in the country, perturbed at Obote's rapprochement with Numeiri, bolstered Amin's resolution at the critical moment, and that British firms and the British Government, much concerned about the Nakivubo Pronouncements, were party to what was soon afoot. Warned that a coup was planned, Obote's ministers summoned the army's principal officers other than Amin, and attempted to prevent it. But the plotters were too quick for them. The coup erupted on 24 January 1971. The Obote regime was quickly toppled. Amin was installed in his place, and, in an almost literal sense, all hell was then let loose (Martin, 1974).

At the time of the major assassination attempt on Obote in 1969, the army had already shown its fangs. Its ruthless tendencies were now greatly aggravated. Amin's more recent recruits were inherently more hardened and less disciplined than their predecessors. They were not just set loose by a failed assassination attempt, but by a resoundingly victorious military coup. All this entailed sharp conflict between the recently recruited West Nilers and Anya Nya on the one side, and the lately Obote-favoured Acholi and Lango on the other. It also involved bitter cleavage between the victorious Amin and a considerable number of senior army officers who had given their support to Obote's ministers' attempt to forestall the coup. It happened, moreover, that Amin had a long-standing record of inflicting the utmost personal brutality upon those against whom he proceeded. Any military coup is almost bound to be accompanied by violence. On this occasion it entailed not only the extensive slaughter of Lango and Acholi, but the brutal killings of senior officers who had not switched swiftly enough to Amin's side. The homicidal patterns of the Amin years thus became set very early (Martin, 1974).

It is important to recall, however, that initially these did not engross the scene, and that there are many indications that at the outset Amin set himself to face the same fundamental problem that had confronted Obote, the need to create popular support for his regime. For a start he was careful to call it the 'Second Republic' of Uganda, so that he could draw all the legitimacy from such state authority as had attached hitherto to it. He made an early bid, moreover, for the support of the Baganda by arranging that Mutesa's body should be returned to be buried near his forebears. By these means he distanced himself from Obote. But in a fascinating way he then went through a whole series of exercises, remarkably comparable to those pursued by Obote himself. During 1971 he too went on much publicized visits to all parts of the country. He did not of course laud 'the common man', for that had been

Obote's gambit. Rather he acclaimed 'the elders', and before very long held meetings of 'representative elders' in several parts of the country. He then tried the notable innovation of donating 'Shs. 100,000 each to the Muslim, Roman Catholic and Protestant Faiths'. In 1972 he followed that up by launching an appeal for the Anglican Church; granting money and land for a new headquarters for the Supreme Muslim Council; and presenting the Catholic Archbishop with a sizeable cheque with which to build a martyrs' memorial at Namugongo. The climax here was reached when in his official party to an OAU meeting in Rabat he took one of his wives, one of his ministers, the Anglican Archbishop, the Catholic Archbishop, and Uganda's Chief Khadi. Clearly he was looking for support from Uganda's extensive religious networks with their close associations at 'grass-roots' level (Low, 1973).

Yet as Obote had found before him, such contrivances availed very little. So in August 1972 Amin made his most eye-catching move. Having earlier rescinded Obote's decision to take a majority holding in Uganda's principal private enterprises, he now mounted his own 'economic war' – by expelling Uganda's Asians (Twaddle, 1975).

But having gone through his own series of Obote-like efforts to establish his political legitimacy, at roughly twice the pace Obote had done, Amin found himself no better off. For the second time over populist contrivances had totally failed to secure the political authority that, in different ways, Nyerere currently enjoyed in Tanzania and Kenyatta in Kenya. This suggests that a populist policy cannot of itself provide an adequate basis for a state's authority. If he had had more nous Amin might perhaps have played the interstitial role, not just because as army chief he could have stood above the political fray, but because as a Kakwa from one of Uganda's numerically smallest peoples away in the distant north-west, he shared in this one particular Nyerere's vital advantage. But he made no attempt either to create a composed majority, or to take the Prussian road, or the interstitial one. Despite his initial success in securing support in Buganda, he soon squandered this entirely by breaking the kingdom up into separate districts to an even greater extent than Obote had done. At the same time by remorselessly setting loose his own troops against both the Acholi and the Langi, he totally alienated the two most important of the northern peoples (while following the earlier murder of Brigadier Okoya, there was not much support for him in Teso either).

By the latter part of 1972 his situation had indeed become even more parlous than Obote's. The Asian expulsion had given him no more than passing popularity (as, to his chagrin, he very soon realized). It had gravely aggravated the economic crisis he had inherited. *Kondoism* (armed robbery) was by now out of hand. From the outset the army had been out of control too. In June 1971 he had announced that, 'Any soldier caught looting property will be treated as a kondo and will be liable to be shot on the spot.' In March 1972 he summoned a large meeting of 'all of the country's top Army, Air Force, Police and Prison Officers' and administered 'a very severe address' to them to 'see that civilians got the full protection of the law of Uganda'; and in July 1972 he issued a dire warning to 'high ranking officers in the Police Force and civil service who are connected with highway robbery and killing of innocent people by assisting kondos, that he is going to deal with them very mercilessly.' All of this availed little. His operational capacity as President was then destroyed by his decision in April 1972 to retire 22 senior officials, 10 of them permanent heads of government departments. In making his decision to expel Uganda's Asians, he had never consulted his Cabinet. At the end of 1972 he sent all of its members on indefinite leave (Low 1973). Meanwhile he had faced an invasion of armed exiles into southern Uganda, who under Obote's guidance had been training in the Sudan and Tanzania. The invaders as it chanced quite incredibly mismanaged their assault. But it was an ominous development. For while Obote's principal opponent, the Kabaka, had remained a focus of opposition in London, at least he had not set about creating a military force to overturn the Obote regime. From the outset Amin always faced a much greater threat from Obote, and the other exiles across Uganda's borders, and that clearly stoked his already established paranoia. Following the September 1972 invasion, he loosed his troops once again against both the Acholi and the Langi.

Against this background, it is not too difficult to see that under threat from without, with his successive attempts to win popular accord all proving fruitless, with armed robbery now going unchecked, with a governmental regime in collapse, and an evidently restless, often uncontrollable army, Amin by late 1972 was politically at his wits' end. Given his personal and cultural background, it is not at all surprising that he should now have turned to the one expedient that so far had most unerringly put his enemies to flight – terror. We seriously misjudge the Amin years if we fail to recognize that such an outcome represented the final solution of a hamfisted and politically obtuse soldier-dictator now at a loss to know how else to secure his regime in power. That he should so evidently have relished the course to which he now so wholly succumbed made his commitment to it all the more reckless and bestial.

The slaughter that eventuated, of communities at large and of symbolic individuals, such as the Chief Justice of Uganda, Makerere's Vice-Chancellor, and the Anglican Archbishop, made the killing by Kabaka Mutesa I of Baganda seem very limited. When Amin originally came to power he had appointed the most technically expert Cabinet Uganda had seen. In a very short while every one of its members had either fled the country or been killed. More portentously his initially none too broad army support soon steadily shrank as well. From an early date amongst his own West Nilers the Alur were squeezed from influence. At the end of 1972 some Madi began to be killed. By 1974 the Lugbara were being attacked as well, and soon his own position came to rest upon little more than his own numerically tiny Kakwa, upon the Nubian miscellany to which he also belonged, and upon some wandering mercenaries from the southern Sudan and Zaire. In due course even these were assaulted, and by 1978 he was at odds too with his principal Kakwa henchman, his brother-in-law, Vice-President Adrisi, whom he unsuccessfully tried to have murdered. Terror thus steadily devoured his regime from within. In a classical manner he desperately sought at the end of 1978 to rally his remnants by launching a diversionary attack upon Tanzania. Nyerere's army, however, riposted, with numbers of Ugandan exiles now in tow, and shortly afterwards found their advance to Kampala little resisted by Amin's now disintegrating forces. By April 1979 Amin's regime simply collapsed.

The aftermath was pregnant with better possibilities, but the offspring was dreadfully stillborn. There had been various refugee groups of Ugandan exiles; Obote had enjoyed Nyerere's patronage and succour; the Acholi officers, Ojok and Okello, headed a number of military recruits; and various elite figures had scattered into jobs, in Africa and elsewhere. As Amin's regime started to crumble, so, very hesitantly, they came together – but without Obote, who was *persona non grata* to most of them – at the Moshi conference late in March 1979, and from that sprang the Presidency of Makerere's former Vice-Chancellor, Yusufu Lule.

The political ingredients here need to be specified. Amin might have been toppled by another military officer. There were some suggestions that his last chief of staff, the Sandhurst-trained Brigadier Emilio Mondo, might have mounted a coup against him. It was accordingly of great significance that Amin's army simply disintegrated, as that left the way open for a civilian regime. That possibility was reinforced when Colonels Ojok and Okello accepted Lule, not just as President of Uganda but as Minister of Defence. It was initially encouraging too that Nyerere did not push the claims of his confidant, Obote, and that Obote himself accepted the wisdom of remaining offstage. The significant fact about the post-Amin regime was that Lule was not only a Muganda but a non-royal Muganda at that. Since the Baganda stand at the heart of the country it is difficult to see how any Uganda government that aspires to permanence can operate without them. Mutesa II's personal position as a royal figure had hitherto made this peculiarly difficult to effect. But he was now dead, and that allowed a non-royal Muganda to sit in the principal position in Uganda in a way that Benedicto Kiwanuka, Uganda's DP Prime Minister back in 1961–2, had never been able to do. That in turn meant that in 1979 the ingredients were in place once again to enable the Baganda to play in Uganda the role of the Prussians that the Kikuyu had so successfully played in Kenya next door. There were rifts along ideological lines amongst those who attended the Moshi conference, both before and after their grasp of power; but the fact that the leftists soon fell out amongst themselves hardly suggests that they were a major obstacle.

It was clear, however, that a Baganda-topped regime would need to establish a close bond with the Ojok–Okello army, and that in emulating the Kikuyu they would need to do so to the full, namely by embracing a sufficiency of others in their support. In the past Buganda had thrown up adept politicians: Mutesa I, Apolo Kagwa, Martin Luther Nsibirwa. It totally failed to do so now. At first Lule included in his Cabinet a convincing spread of ministers from all significant parts of the country. But he then set out to assert his own primacy as President before either his own or his regime's authority had been effectively established, and then capped this by the crass error of reshuffling his Cabinet so as to introduce four more Baganda and demote three non-Baganda so as to give the Baganda no less than 10 out of 19 positions all told. He soon realized his mistake, made a further reshuffle, and publicly announced, 'That the various regions of the country would be proportionately represented in the Cabinet.' But it was too late. In effect he was no more than *primus inter pares* and had no standing of his own. In an overnight coup he was swiftly replaced by Godfrey Binaisa. Binaisa was a Muganda too; but a great many Baganda soon took to the streets to protest at Lule's replacement, and that boded ill for Buganda's continued support for Uganda's new government. In particular it meant that Binaisa never secured the political legitimacy he needed to establish his government's authority at the heart of the country. Amin had disappeared, but sporadic, especially nightly, violence appallingly persisted, in Kampala more particularly.

Then within a few short months Binaisa threw away even such shreds of authority as he retained. It was clearly crucial that he should maintain his nexus with the Ugandan army. But in November 1979 he sacked Museveni, the Minister of Defence, and in May 1980 the rising Army Chief of Staff, Colonel Oyite-Ojok, as well. Thereupon the army moved into control. Binaisa was replaced by another Muganda, Obote's old associate – and one time secretary of the long-since dead Uganda National Congress – Paulo Muwanga. But he had no personal support either, least of all in Buganda. So for lack of any other credible political figure to whom to turn, and following the now total collapse of the further Prussian possibility, the way stood open for Obote's return.

There followed the Uganda national elections of 1980, the first since the pre-independence elections of 1962. Formally these were fought between the same two political parties that had last competed 23 years before: the UPC and the DP. But despite the continuing undertones of one being Protestant and the other Catholic, the first now principally represented the old Obote alliance (now supported by the new Uganda army led by Obote's fellow Langi, Oyite-Ojok), the second Baganda and all the other southern opposition to it. The results were highly disputed. Muwanga was evidently determined they should yield a victory for the UPC. The DP initially claimed the victory, but in the event this was secured by the UPC. As a consequence Obote was now installed as Uganda's executive President for the second time.

But it was never a rerun. Obote probably possessed even less legitimacy than during his first Presidency. Civil (dis)order was now in a far worse state. The composed majority that Obote's election victory should have implied was essentially spurious. Revealingly he made no attempt to mount anything comparable to the gamut of populist measures he had run in his first term. Such expedients were now completely discredited. Witin four months he was faced, moreover, not with a remonstrating opponent in London, nor just with an exile movement on Uganda's borders, but by a National Resistance Army operating right within Uganda itself under the leftist leader, Yoweri Museveni. It was particularly active in Ankole, from which Museveni himself came, but also in Buganda and Toro. It operated, moreover, on Mao's principle of winning popular support by treating peasants with every consideration. There followed as a consequence civil war in Uganda. That in turn triggered a new reign of terror from Obote's side that was far worse in its slaughter of hapless villagers than even Amin's had been. Yet, just as the terror in Amin's regime had gnawed at its heart, so terror during Obote's second term ate at its vitals as well. As under NRA pressure Obote's Langi–Acholi army found itself under increasing strain, so in the end it broke apart, once its Acholi members sensed that Obote's Langi were leaving the brunt of the conflict to them. Oyite-Ojok had been killed in an aircraft accident. That had left the Acholi leader Tito Okello in command of the army. When he and his fellow Acholi eventually turned on their Lango associates in July 1985, Obote was forced to flee, and Okello took over.

Momentarily the ever resilient Paulo Mwanga daringly tried to seize the interstitial position. But Okello quickly realized how completely *non grata* he was to the Baganda and to all who abhorred the Obote regime. Okello seems to have understood, moreover, that he had now very little choice but to negotiate with Museveni. That became complicated, however, because some of his fellow Acholi, realizing that even with the Langi they had not been able to withstand the NRA, turned to the residue of Amin's following to take their place. Museveni thereupon became all the more determined that he would not settle easily. Skilfully, laboriously, and at great cost in lives he had built up the first military organisation of southern Ugandans the country had ever seen. 'The NRA,' he now declared, 'will never accept a settlement that could perpetuate the same problems of insecurity, misuse of the army, corruption and murder that have been the order of the day for the past 23 years.' Specifying that time-frame was very significant. It looked back over all the years, not just to Obote's (and Amin's) attack upon the Kabaka's palace, but to the original independence concordat of 1962.

For a while, the principal ethnic groupings in northern and southern Uganda now became quite explicitly represented by two armed forces, Okello's essentially northern, Acholi-led army on the one side, and Museveni's essentially southern-supported NRA on the other. They could either now fight, or Okello could provide the southern elements, not only with a major place in a political settlement, but in a new Ugandan army as well. After several months of negotiation President Moi of Kenya eventually pressured the two sides into the Nairobi Agreement of December 1985. But that essentially comprised a fifty–fifty arrangement which had as little chance of working as the UPC–KY concordat of 23 years before. With his accustomed caution, Museveni thereupon inched his way forward. In the new year he finally captured Kampala, and within a bare six weeks of the Nairobi Agreement had himself installed there as Uganda's eighth President. The NRA then pursued the northerners' diminishing forces to the distant borders of the country, whilst he himself set about fashioning a new order for Uganda.

His regime possessed three sets of attributes that gave it more chance of success than any of its predecessors. Above all it comprised as credible a composed majority as Uganda had ever seen. It came very close to being the kind of coalition Obote's Cabinet colleagues had been trying to put together twenty years earlier and that was so abruptly cut short when Obote delivered his fateful blows early in 1966. It included representatives of the country's former political parties and of its non-Amin military factions. But principally – though by no means exclusively – it was built upon an alliance of Uganda's numerically preponderant Bantu southerners. More particularly it included within its ranks the Baganda at the core of the country. But they were not at its head: Museveni from the neighbouring ex-kingdom of Ankole was; and that was probably as satisfactory a structural position for Buganda to hold as its own interests and those of the rest of the country call for. These ingredients were exemplified by the calculation that within Museveni's first 33-man government, there were 13 Baganda, 12 more southern Bantu, and 8 from various other districts in the east and north of the country. Museveni's own position closely accorded, moreover, with that of Kenya's President Moi. Both headed substantial composed majorities. Neither of them came personally, however, from their largest entity. Perhaps that gave each of them something of an interstitial position, with some at least of the advantages that that can provide.

Secondly, Museveni's NRA, for the first time since independence, gave the southerners an army to back them. Hitherto Uganda's armies had all been dominated by northerners of one kind or another. Southerners were unlikely to allow that ever to happen again. Moreover – if only to draw the sharpest contrast between his NRA and the murderous armies of Amin, Obote and Okello alike – Museveni was committed throughout to the Maoist principle of the people's army, under which the most serious offence that any of its soldiers could commit, entailing exemplary execution when the occasion warranted, was the abuse or killing of members of the ordinary populace, whom it was there to defend and with whom it must live. This was a far better populist expedient than either Obote or Amin had ever attempted.

There was a further consideration too. Not only was there a deep-seated desire in so much of the country, the north included (which had suffered so much along with the rest) to see the interminable killings come to an end. Because there was now a southern-based regime holding the levers of power in the capital, which lies in the south, it did not have to be as paranoid as its predecessors, all of whom, coming from the north, invariably felt themselves to be in considerable danger there. The new southern-based regime had, that is, a great deal less need to take to terror to maintain its dominance than any of its predecessors. Correspondingly, in the course of any crisis it had less need to terrorize the north, which could be so much more easily marginalized than the south could ever have been by the northern regimes.

The record nevertheless calls for caution. Too many have misplayed their hand in Uganda to have any clear assurance that its nightmare years are over. Skill, patience, a readiness to make the creative compromise, are all at a premium. But at least in the terms adumbrated here the structures underpinning the state look to be rather more promising than before. The point to watch will be whether these continue intact, or are at any rate modulated into some effective alternative.

FOUR
The recent political economy of Uganda
Aidan Southall

The question posed by the long crisis in Uganda is a version of that posed throughout Africa. What kind of economic policy and what type of regime, in the context of superpower confrontation and the severe constraints imposed by the international economy, can transcend ethnic conflicts and provide production incentives while avoiding the exploitation, corruption and inefficiency asociated with excessive bureaucratic centralization? In Uganda and East Africa as a whole, a significant number of both local and general studies have built up a formidable indictment of Uganda's recent history from the viewpoint of political economy and class analysis.

Meanwhile, Crawford Young's study, *Ideology and Development in Africa* shows that, for whatever reasons, African countries attempting socialist options have been a failure. But at the same time, the capitalist development theory that has informed and dominated the post-war Western impact on Africa is also in disarray. The state of confrontation between the United States and the Soviet Union makes the capitalist and Soviet models the only options available in the international field, although experience to date suggests that both these models are disastrous in Africa.

Crises of development are common to the whole of Africa and beyond. I view the colonial period and its aftermath, with all the suffering it has caused and is still causing, as a part of history. The actions of its perpetrators and participants cannot ultimately be criticized adequately without some conception of alternatives and futures. I regard the present big business of foreign aid by the major donors, consultants and multinational corporations as a fraud, whose real goals are masked by most statements about it. On the other hand, I regard the current form of capitalist development as inevitable during the next few decades, because the African peoples and nations are too weak or too compromised to oppose it. From this point of view, most of the current development debate is a waste of time. Worse, it is part of the smoke screen that conceals what is actually going on. Since major development projects of the kind now in vogue are inevitable for the time being, there is a case for serious criticism of them, in an attempt to inject or salvage something positive. But a much more important task is for Africans and non-Africans of goodwill to think, plan, and experiment with the greatest concern and commitment for future alternatives, neither Soviet nor Western. Correct interpretation of the past is an essential basis for this. I therefore now attempt some account and assessment of the most important critical period of Uganda's recent history.

Cautious historians interpret events in the light of their own background, as the archives open to them. Those who are more impatient must tread dangerous ground. After Mukherjee's lone pioneering effort many years passed before the spate of recent studies such as those of Brett, Van Zwanenberg, Jorgensen and Mamdani. Brett covers the whole of East Africa, Van Zwanenberg compares Uganda and Kenya. Only Jorgensen and Mamdani concentrate specifically on Uganda and bring their analysis up to the recent period. Mamdani's is the only systematic class analysis.

I give a brief sketch of Mamdani's analysis, because it is the most sharply delineated and most clearly raises questions for the future. He starts off from the precolonial situation, in which social formations expressing both a feudal mode of production in the south and a communal mode elsewhere where to be found.[1] The colonial settlement turned the feudal lords of Buganda into landlords, and their serfs into a tenant peasantry, while the communal (or as I would say kinship) mode of production remained predominant elsewhere. An Asian merchant bourgeoisie and commercial petty bourgeoisie became established under British protection and attempts were made by Europeans to establish a settler bourgeoisie. The latter were driven to the brink of bankruptcy by adverse conditions at the end of the First World War. By then they had become irrelevant to the major policy goals of the metropolitan bourgeoisie, so they were allowed to dwindle into an insignificant factor in the political economy of Uganda. For it had been found that the peasants of southern Uganda could grow the very cotton most needed by Lancashire, while the kinship societies of the North could be compelled, by taxation and administrative pressure, to supply most of the unskilled labour needed by the new society, through temporary migration. Both European metropolitan and Indian capital established cotton ginneries, but as the latter were more cost effective they were, in the end, more in the interests of Lancashire and metropolitan capital as a whole, despite the complaints of their European rivals. The African landlords tried to exploit the new wealth of their tenants, but, once again, it was more in the interests of metropolitan capital and Lancashire to protect the cotton growers (who had become restive), so they were given security of tenure and immunity from unregulated landlord exactions.[2]

Southern peasant prosperity produced a nascent class of 'kulaks', forming one arm of the emergent African petty bourgeoisie, along with the growing numbers of mission-educated clerks and civil servants; African traders came rather later. Pre-existing African trade and artisan production had been smashed by the new capitalist import trade and the wholesale–retail network established by the Asians.

Fierce competition reigned in cotton buying and processing, raising the price to growers but lowering local capitalist profits. Colonial government sided with the capitalists (the Europeans being most vociferous) and a system of monopoly processing was established, which lowered growers' receipts and raised those of processors, although it was said to be to protect the former from being cheated. Both African and Asian petty bourgeois middlemen were eliminated.

The Second World War had a profound effect upon the economy, class structure and future of Uganda, and its relation to the metropole. The war destroyed the European image of invincibility. Tight control was exercised over Uganda and little change occurred. Ugandans who went to fight in foreign countries and travelled overseas acquired knowledge, sophistication, skills and savings. They would not return to the same situation they had left, nor could Britain or the colonial government escape a special obligation towards them. They significantly swelled the ranks of the petty bourgeoisie and raised its consciousness level. Britain had changed from a major creditor to the greatest debtor nation and the influence of the United States was correspondingly greater.

Meanwhile, all three branches of the African petty bourgeosie found their aspirations blocked: kulaks by controlled low crop prices, and lack of representation in the Buganda Lukiko, civil servants by racially discriminatory salaries, and traders by both Asian and European monopoly dominance. Urban workers were equally dissatisfied by low wages, poor housing, health and general services. Government reacted to widespread popular unrest in 1945 and 1949 by symbolic changes in the workers' favour, through conferring war service bonuses, fixing minimum wages and appointing labour officers to improve working conditions and encourage segmented unions under strict control while banning *general* unions. Government then soon switched its efforts to creating a 'stable and responsible middle class' by bringing popularly elected members into the Lukiko, encouraging controlled co-operative organization, trying to extend individual landownership (but without success), opening bus routes to African entrepreneurs, promoting African civil servants, and permitting the formation of political parties.

Britain's changed economic position made it worthwhile for the first time to establish manufacturing industries in Uganda, aimed at saving dollar expenditure and earning dollars to assist Britain's foreign exchange, instead of as before merely promoting commerce with and industry in Britain. Since Britain had already lost the East African textile market, it was worth trying to win it back from within by creating a textile industry, which Lancashire had previously opposed. The Owen Falls hydroelectric dam, Nyanza Textiles, and many other manufacturing, mining and financial ventures were expressions of this change, creating an industrial proletariat for the first time and adding a new element to the petty bourgeoisie.

The Uganda National Congress was formed by Baganda traders and professionals, with support from cash-cropping peasants outside Buganda. It picked up Baganda kulak support by organizing the trade boycott to press for the Kabaka's return from exile. But when he did return, they had better representation through the Lukiko and its secessionist tendencies, so they left the UNC, which became an expression of petty bourgeois bureaucrats and traders elsewhere, especially in the other cash-crop producing areas, while the Catholic-oriented Democratic Party was strongest in the non-cash-crop areas where the Roman Catholic Church with its schools and teachers was the main reservoir of petty bourgeois strength. But Baganda secessionism, with its boycott of the first national election, allowed the DP to win the seats in Buganda and hence a majority throughout the country. Subsequent recognition of the necessity of taking part in the destiny of Uganda as a whole forced the Kabaka and Ganda bureaucracy to create the Kabaka Yekka Party and to go into an alliance with the UPC in order to defeat the DP and form the first independent government, winning for the Kabaka the position of President and Head of State in uneasy tandem with Obote as Prime Minister.

Political independence had brought a surge of popular enthusiasm and energy. The co-operatives were set free of controls and enabled to take over many ginneries. Elected local governments were running their own affairs. Party youth wings organized grass-roots activities. Popular education and health services were greatly extended. But African entrepreneurship was still blocked by the Asian presence, and the political scene was darkened by continuing Ganda ambitions. The bright hopes of independence were not and could not be fulfilled. Local government overspending, peasant and worker disaffection and strikes, mutinies in the army and confrontation with the Kabaka over the Lost Counties and divisive secret involvement with the Zaire rebels rocked Obote's regime. Results: the free labour movement was crushed and brought under government control, and the army was paid off with high salaries and lavish equipment, the Kabaka was driven into exile in a bloody battle, further alienating the Baganda and increasing dependence on Amin the army commander. Both the left and the right wings of the UPC were in turn crushed, the kingdoms abolished. Obote and the UPC were without mass support, a pipeline of patronage left more dependent on Amin and the army, lacking a popular base.

The answer was to concentrate control of rural production in the Produce Marketing Board and of trade in the National Trading Corporation in addition to the previously established Lint Marketing Board and Coffee Board. These measures were sabotaged by the Asian commercial and petty bourgeoisie on one side and the African petty bourgeoisie and peasants on the other. Obote and his party were thus pushed further into the 'Move to the Left', which was actually a new alliance through the controlling parastatals in paradoxical co-operation and partnership with the Asian bourgeoisie, oil companies, banks and major multinationals at the expense of the African peasants and petty bourgeoisie, especially in Buganda. The co-operatives were again strictly controlled, and African small traders and processors were crushed in favour of large concerns. The ruling elite thus enriched itself publicly through directorships, patronage and pay-offs instead of privately through entrepreneurship and profits. Response came in the attempted assassination of Obote and the killing of Brigadier Okoya, one of his chief army supporters. Increasing pressure was put on the Asian bourgeoisie through citizenship requirements.

The economy worsened, with unfavourable trade balances, inflation and increasing unemployment despite rising productivity, as it was based on labour-intensive technology. Strikes were outlawed, Kenyan workers expelled and all other parties banned. The number of Acholi and Langi officers in the army was greatly increased, and the military Special Force and the GSU spy organization were aimed at weakening army influence. With the Sudan civil war coming to an end and improved relations with Numeiri, Israel was refused landing rights for assistance to the Anya Nya. Obote had alienated his international support from the mass of the people, who were now ready to jump at any saviour. When Obote charged Amin with defence overspending and tried to arrest him while he himself was out of the country, alienating the capitalist world by his anti-South African campaign at the Commonwealth Conference, Idi Amin was left with little choice but to seize the opportunity thus

practically thrust at him and to take over. With the army as
government, the weakness of the previous regime vis-à-vis the
people was overcome. The major remaining problem was the
continuing economic dominance of the Asians, to which Amin soon
provided his radical solution.

Against the background of the inexorable deterioration of the
Obote regime, the initial popularity of Amin, powerfully boosted by
the expulsion of the Asians, is somewhat comprehensible. The rest
of his career can be quickly summed up. The 'economic war' and the
'double production campaign' stood for economic disaster and
production decline. One ethnic group was murderously set against
another as never before. Brutality and corruption pervaded all
sections and levels of society. A whole generation was brought up
knowing no other way of life. Of the productive equipment that was
still left, in transport, buildings, schools, hospitals, industries,
plantations, finance, much was taken or destroyed by Amin and his
followers in their flight. Objectively, therefore, the material plight of
Uganda was even worse after than before he left (Southall, 1980).

Against this background the dice were loaded heavily against
Amin's successor regimes. Nonetheless, the alacrity with which the
first liberation leaders adopted the corrupt practices of their
predecessors was profoundly shocking. Whatever else may be said
of him, Obote still seemed to stand as the least corrupt of all
Uganda's rulers so far. There must certainly still be the gravest
doubts about the conduct of the 1980 election, but even if Obote and
Muwanga did decide who was to win each seat during the following
night, the resulting balance of power may not have been so
fundamentally different from what a fair election would have
produced. The DP were certainly not the dominant element in the
UNLF and no civilian government could have ruled at that point in
time without the confidence of the army.

A history of political economy, or a diachronic class analysis,
naturally reflects increasing role differentiation, institutional diversification and growing complexity of class composition, factions,
fractions, and interrelations. This impression may be accentuated by
the greater proximity and immediacy of recent events and the more
detailed popular knowledge of them, even though archives are not
available. Thus, it is the accounts by both Jorgensen and Mamdani
of the sequence of events during the first Obote regime that are most
impressive from a Marxist point of view, startling for those more
familiar with the conventional accounts of events in Uganda: of how
Obote and the UPC interacted with the various class forces, both
internal and external, as they unfolded within the political economy
of Uganda; how these changed from what was presented as a

popular, democratic, anti-colonial, left of centre force, with socialist inclinations, into an unholy alliance with the Asian merchant–industrial bourgeoisie and even the major international capitalist firms, against the Baganda in particular and the mass of Uganda's peasants and workers in general.

By contrast with this era, Amin's rule is harder to present through class analysis and even Mamdani tends to get bogged down in the plethora of spectacular detail. Doubtless, as he says, Amin's activity had the effect of intensifying capitalist penetration and increasing Uganda's dependence, despite his renown as 'conqueror of the British Empire'. But at the same time the comprador economy was weakened and the masses went back to subsistence. *Contra* Lofchie and Mazrui, an army is not a class, nor directly involved in the process of production (hence Mazrui's substitution of 'destruction') and instead appropriates surplus through whatever class it serves. (Of course, there may be many different patterns of linkage between classes and different types and categories of persons in an army in different historical situations).

In a sense, Amin's violent onslaught on Uganda society simplified matters at least for the moment. Many of the conflicting issues and factions from which Obote's first civilian regime had suffered were ridden over roughshod and temporarily expelled or obliterated. Complex issues were often reduced to the stark question of life or death. After all the intricacies of the previous analysis, Mamdani (1976) concludes in a correspondingly simple way: the struggle is against imperialism. Mamdani (1983) rams this home with the external evidence.

By taking a different analytical point of departure we may say that the new country of Uganda was created by Britain on the basis of Ganda dominance. Not only were the Baganda accorded enormous privileges denied to all other groups, but they partly paid for them by assisting the British in conquering the other peoples of the area. But if conquerors can hardly be fair to the conquered, they can extract a sense of virtue from imposing a limited (and in political outcome disastrous) fair play *among* the conquered. This precluded the British from turning Uganda into an indirectly ruled, enlarged Buganda empire, as the Ganda might have hoped. Western Uganda, apart from Kigezi, shared much of the general culture and monarchical aspirations of the Baganda and therefore tended to stand with them in a supportive if rival position. Eastern Uganda was fragmented into far more diverse groupings, some culturally similar, some markedly dissimilar and antipathetic to the monarchical regimes. The north was much more consistently and decisively marked off in language, culture and political behaviour, so that in the attempt at democratic settlement that was hurriedly made as a preliminary to political independence in 1962 it was inevitably the north that provided the effective counterweight to Buganda, (Southall, 1975) although all major parties did make serious attempts at a Uganda-wide appeal. After the failure of the northern-based regimes of Obote and Amin to create an effectively united Uganda, it was also almost inevitable that the west should hold the reservoir of a possible alternative power. Buganda and the north were discredited and the east was too fragmented.

This is certainly not to give an unredeemed ethnic interpretation, let alone the 'tribal' interpretation that is the only one the international mass media fancy, without understanding. It is rather to admit that the colonial system crystallized or created ethnic differences, which acquired a regional complexion through its differential policies in economic development and non-development: encouraging cash-crop production in the south and migrant labour in the north, permitting intensive education in the south and relative neglect in the north, leading to army recruitment in the north and training for civilian bureaucracy and the professions in the south. Not that this was a Machiavellian preconceived plan, but rather that it took the line of least resistance and greatest immediate benefit, allowing a polarization that it belatedly tried to counteract. The south did have better rainfall and more fertile soil than the north. The Christian missions did acquire their first converts in the south, and the unhappy coincidence of mission aims and government needs accentuated the polarization. Up until the Second World War the main objective was to make Uganda pay. When the requirements of Uganda as a future 'nation state' began to be envisaged in the 1950s, strenuous efforts were made to develop production, education and general services in the north, but by then it was too late. In this light, it is reasonable to see the dominance of Buganda in the colonial period, the political dominance of the north – for it was only political dominance despite Obote's efforts to redress the balance – from 1964 to 1985; and the rise of leadership from the west in 1986, as a dialectical process of thesis, antithesis and synthesis. It must be emphasized that Obote, and probably even Amin, did not wish to rule as northerners, but under pressure they had to mobilize support wherever they could best enlist it. In a certain sense both Obote and Amin were nationalists, however far their own weaknesses and the forces of history diverted them. Nor is Museveni a westerner in principle or intention. However, he did raise his own army in the west at the expulsion of Amin and he did begin to create his new society in the west as the Obote II and Tito Okello regimes crumbled.

This brings us to a consideration of Museveni himself and his movement as factors in the situation vis-à-vis Obote's second political coming. His credentials as a socialist student at the University of Dar es Salaam, a freedom fighter in Mozambique and an exile in Tanzania are beyond question. The paradox is that, when he took to the bush in protest against Obote's political arrangements after the elections of December 1980 – whether this was as a matter of principle, or in pique at lack of preferment – he became allied with the anti-Obote UNLM led by Yusufu Lule. The Far Left acts against the Left by allying with the Far Right. Lule was regarded by some as a charismatic figure capable of uniting the varied factions and ethnic groups of Uganda, and by others as a conservative Muganda representing the landed gentry, decoyed by history from the quiet pastures of the academy to the jungle of politics. Few regarded him as a charismatic or effective leader except those in his own faction. The rest regarded him as ineffective and corrupt. There is no doubt that a significant part of the Ganda and other southern intelligentsia and propertied classes came to look upon Museveni as their saviour from what they privately regarded as barbaric northern domination. Nonetheless, Buganda must be considered one of the most infertile grounds for socialism, and the alliance of Museveni, as commander of the military wing (NRA) with its civilian umbrella (the UNLM–NRM) under its late chairman Lule, as one of the most politically unnatural and contradictory. It can be rationalized as a strategic class alliance, but against what class?

Museveni has produced a very sophisticated manifesto, that not only outlines the virtuous and essential goals of peace and national reconciliation, army discipline, justice, personal security, social equality and economic development, which any sensible leader must assert, but also displays an intelligent awareness not only of the internal situation of Uganda, but also of its position in an indifferent and exploiting world (See Chapter 21).

Until 1984, with the Ugandan economy showing marked improvement and impressive annual growth (see Chapter 7) – although it never regained its level of 1975 when Amin's economy was already in decline – it still seemed possible that Obote might be able to survive and to succeed; might even gradually gain more disciplined control of the army through Oyite-Ojok, who was greatly respected and had an honourable record in anti-Amin resistance. Ojok's death in a plane accident in December 1983 left a gap that was only filled eight months later, by a controversial appointment of a more junior Langi military commander. This alienated Tito and Basilio Okello and the Acholi, signalling Obote's increasingly exclusive ethnic dependence on his own Langi. This, combined with the downturn of the economy, never again arrested, and the failure to make any headway against the guerrillas, sealed Obote's fate.

There are logical reasons for supposing that only a small force, completely cut off from all antecedents, could succeed in making a new start. Such were Museveni's guerrillas. Those who joined him had to be dedicated men and women. Although by no means true of all guerrilla forces, in the circumstances of Uganda Museveni's NRA could only hope to prevail if it proved to the people of Uganda that it was more disciplined and less brutal than the Uganda army, that even though forced to live off the country it would behave with restraint, decency and humanity, not looting and burning or raping and murdering civilians; that it would not only prove that an uncorrupt army was possible in Uganda, but would also begin to establish new and uncorrupt government in liberated areas as soon as it had the chance. All these tests Museveni and his army passed, and this was what brought back hope to Uganda.

Being hardly supported or opposed by either superpower, because of its bad reputation and its lack of strategic importance, Uganda was essentially un-newsworthy and was left in a blanket of silence by most world news media – other than the BBC, and the London *Times*, *Guardian* and *Observer* newspapers – except on the rare occasions of drama. In this blackout it was very hard to tell what was going on, or which rumours to believe. Yet all news media – outside Uganda – were unanimous in commenting favourably on Museveni's forces by comparison with the Uganda army, whose continuing atrocities kept its evil reputation vividly alive. It was no mean feat on Museveni's part to achieve and maintain this reputation and to survive in the bush without substantial outside aid. For arms and ammunition he had to rely on successful raiding of Uganda army supply points, such as the temporary capture of Masindi barracks. Clearly he had to win the support of local populations, or it would have been impossible to live off them without alienating them. Indeed, by 1985 there were some signs of strain. It seems that the NRA may have been getting frustrated with being cooped up largely in the Luwero triangle, patience and restraint was becoming exhausted and might have broken down, with disastrous consequences, had it not been for the fact that the Obote regime had also reached the end of its tether. Obote himself was ceasing to be able to cope and seemed not entirely reluctant to allow himself to be pushed out by Tito Okello. The machinations of Paulo Muwanga, the great political survivor, with both Tito Okello and Yoweri Museveni, which led up to the coup, make a fascinating story but are no longer very relevant. It is certainly to Muwanga's credit that political principle weighed more with him than ethnic loyalty, although this branded him as an ethnic traitor.

What was more important was that Tito Okello's coup was only a partial change of horses and was, in effect, the replacement of a deteriorating regime with one of even greater ineptitude. This saved Museveni from the possible consequences of increasing stress, by giving him the chance to break out of the Luwero triangle and begin an important new phase of his campaign by taking possession of other parts of the west and demonstrating that he had civilian administrative as well as military skills, in his establishment of reformed local governments in liberated areas. In the less restrictive and more easily supportive context of the west, the NRA seems to have recovered its standards. It had to be accorded the accolade of a purified and potentially purifying force, such as Uganda has never had before. Tito Okello may take credit for having recognized his weakness and having begun negotiations with Museveni almost immediately.

Museveni is the first guerrilla leader to overthrow an African government. Although he actively recruited and trained his own army in western Uganda, as did other regional military leaders of the invasion force during and after the expulsion of Idi Amin, he is reported to have taken to the bush with only 27 followers. In 1983–4 Colin Legum reported that the tide had finally turned in favour of Obote; Museveni had disappeared and was banned from Britain, Kenya and possibly Libya. But this was the very point at which the fortunes of Obote had reached their peak and were going into decline, while those of Museveni were unobtrusively going into the ascendant.

The Luwero triangle, in which Museveni was based and largely confined for the first few years, was not a particularly favourable environment for guerrilla activity. Although it was a marginal area, more sparsely populated that the rest of Buganda and near the traditional border between Buganda and Bunyoro, it was not very remote and although somewhat hilly in parts and swampy in others it was not all that easy to defend. Museveni's survival there must in itself be a testimony to the loyalty, efficiency, and determination of his followers, or else to the inefficiency and pusillanimity of the Uganda army, or both. It was a strategic position in that it gave the possibility of striking at the heartland of Uganda round Kampala, while giving access on the other side to western and northern Uganda. Museveni's move away from the Luwero triangle to the west in 1985, which the government could count as a retreat, marked his confidence that he could actually take full possession of western Uganda and establish an alternative system of government there.

When Tito Okello and Basilio Okello took possession of Kampala in July 1985, ousting Obote and proclaiming a new regime,

Museveni took possession of all the western towns: Hoima, Masindi, Fort Portal, Mbarara, Kabale, and eventually Masaka. The barracks of the Uganda army in some of these towns held out for a while, but Museveni was in effective command of the west. He quickly established a new administration and system of justice, with a high degree of popular participation, and set up political education centres where large and enthusiastic audiences were encouraged to debate and think about the future of Uganda. He did not, as a socialist, attempt any immediate transformation of the system of production. Presumably he had decided that winning political control of the whole of Uganda was the first priority before any disturbing changes were introduced.

Tito Okello had endeavoured to isolate him, with some success, as the other, smaller guerrilla groups agreed to negotiate. Museveni and the NRA were left as such a major stumbling block that negotiations at a much higher level were required. As President Nyerere was the liberator of Uganda from Idi Amin, he had a certain primacy of interest in Ugandan affairs. But as a long-time faithful supporter of Obote, to whom Tito Okello was a kind of successor, Nyerere was at first unsympathetic towards Museveni. So when the possiblity of negotiations began to be seriously entertained in August 1985, the first attempt was made in Dar es Salaam, but Tito Okello and his delegation waited there for Museveni in vain, while the latter demanded that Tito Okello should represent the Uganda army and not the government. The talks were then transferred to Nairobi, on Museveni's insistence, where President Moi staked his reputation on their success. There was some consternation when Museveni, regarded by some as a waning force, demanded the position of Vice-Chairman of the Military Council, with half the seats for his followers. Tito Okello offered him 4 out of 28. The talks dragged on and off for nearly four months, with accusations and counter-accusations of violations of the cease-fire on either side. Neither force could afford to lose momentum, least of all the guerrillas.

Tito Okello was accused of recruiting ex-Amin soldiers 'to destroy Museveni' and it was reported that 10,000 ex-soldiers from the Sudan had been absorbed into the Uganda army, although some of them complained of being used as scapegoats. On the other hand, claiming (with justification) that the Uganda army had violated the cease-fire with their customary looting, raping and murdering of civilians, Museveni's guerrillas appeared within three miles of Kampala to emphasize their increasing strength. The Roman Catholic Archbishop of Kampala fled to Nairobi to exert his influence in securing a resumption of the talks, which had stalled.

On 7 December 1985 an amazing agreement was signed; it granted Museveni almost all he had asked for. He was to be Vice-Chairman of the Supreme Military Council, next to Okello as Chairman and Head of State. His forces were to have seven seats, equal to the seven seats of Okello's Uganda National Liberation Army. But Okello won his point in getting five seats for the minor resistance movements. While it is suicidal for a guerrilla leader to give up his military power before he is absolutely certain of his civilian authority, it is also probable that Okello was unable entirely to curb the atrocities committed by his troops, so that Museveni had the excuse to claim violation of the Nairobi agreement. Almost too good to be true was the provision that all soldiers on both sides should voluntarily lay down their arms and a new army be developed under the supervision of a monitoring/observer force from Kenya, Tanzania, Britain, and Canada; the new army to represent the old Uganda army and Museveni's NRA in almost equal numbers – 3700 and 3580 – together with 1200 from the minor resistance groups.

Unfortunately this never appeared to have any chance of occurring. As the countercharges multiplied, Museveni closed in upon Kampala, creating a very tense situation in which some of Okello's troops began to desert and flee while others took to further looting. Towards the end of January 1986 the position became untenable and Museveni was able to move into Kampala, with some heavy fighting but relatively little bloodshed. The pattern was the same as in the defeat of Idi Amin: Okello and his forces retreated east to Jinja, then north to Mbale, Lira and Soroti. Tito Okello gave up, but Basilio Okello was rumoured to have 30,000 Acholi waiting to make a stand at Gulu. However, Basilio fled and Museveni took Gulu in three hours on 8 March and West Nile by the end of the month, thus completing his possession of the whole of Uganda.

This was a much less destructive conquest of Uganda than the one that had ousted Idi Amin. Museveni appears to have exercised great restraint. On the other hand, Okello's army, reduced to its Acholi redoubt seems still to have the will to fight.

In the short time since Museveni gained control of the whole of Uganda and became Head of State events have proceeded smoothly and the early optimism has been maintained. Two overriding and interlinked questions remain: will Museveni's relatively small, hand-picked, highly trained and bush-hardened army be able to retain its standards and propagate them throughout the country, or will they be dragged down by the *magendo-mafutamingi* economy and way of life of the capital? Secondly, will Museveni's government be able to reconcile the ethnic hatreds that have been continuously exacerbated for the past fifteen years and more? It is too early to tell, but the Cabinet is at present grossly overweighted with southerners, partly, of course, because the north was so recently liberated. This matter needs to be tackled urgently. In the longer term, economic and development policy will be more important in restoring the ravaged areas and above all in giving the deprived, embittered northern peoples a sense of belonging, participating and progressing equally. One good sign is that a Rehabilitation Plan was drawn up with remarkable speed, in great detail and with very restrained budgeting – with a sum for rebuilding a country that after all is no larger than the sums expected by the Nicaraguan contras for destroying a country.

The dramatic events of coups and guerrilla campaigns, with the high level of local violence and harassment of the rural population, distract attention from the underlying facts of political economy, masking class processes. Nonetheless, the principles of Mamdani's analysis still hold. In his earlier book he gave a penetrating class dissection, but in *Imperialism and Fascism in Uganda* (1983) he does not. He castigates those who make false claims of neutrality and 'proclaims his partisanship from the roof-tops: he is anti-fascist and pro-people' (1983, pp. 1–2). But *who are* the people? Museveni's guerrillas, the prosperous southern peasantry, or the economically deprived and neglected peoples of the north? Imperialism is always 'able to take advantage' and 'bend the outcome to suit its own interests' (p. 107). However, this becomes a redundant theory, since imperialism and monopoly capitalism profit whichever way the pendulum swings. They profit from the rise of Amin, they profit from the fall of Amin. All this really says is that capitalism is the dominant system. Uganda has no hope of escaping from it in the short or middle term, even if it wished to - which perhaps even a majority of its population would not – as Museveni has recognized in what amount to essentially middle-of-the-road proposals for a mixed economy.

The Museveni programme is indeed a remarkable document to have been produced from the bush – with some sojourning in Sweden – and although produced in the name of the National Resistance Council and National Resistance Army, it bears the distinctive stamp of a single brain. The general argument is realistic and convincing. I will take issue with only one point. Africa and Uganda must pursue capitalism under duress, because they are powerless to implement any other option. But the flaws of capitalism must be clearly recognized, as Museveni partly does. They cannot be cured by adding some drop of socialism and shaking up the bottle – state control of export–import licensing, of commercial banking, basic industries, physical infrastructure and social services. They are *contradictory* principles that do not mix well. What is socialism? 'African socialism' has become a joke or a fraud. 'Socialism' unqualified must be either the 'muddle-headed revolutionary ideologies of Fabians' ridiculed by Museveni or else the dominant Soviet model, the Chinese having virtually withdrawn from Africa. The Soviet model has not worked in Africa (Young, 1982) for whatever internal or external reasons, and much more fundamentally it is high time that progressive Africans recognized that the Soviet model, however important historically, is a disastrous distortion of Marxism. Socialism has to be rethought and, whatever the outcome of this process, it must be rethought along the lines of complementing *and enabling* political democracy with economic democracy. This means *not* state farms, nor parastatals, nor any other large-scale bureaucratic organizations, which have amply proved their inefficiency, underproductivity, and corruption in Africa. It must mean grass-roots experiments in both agriculture and industry, with small-scale production units ruled and run by the workers themselves, small enough to be capable of preserving individual initiative, incentive, and enterprise, large enough to make profitable use of all appropriate production technology.

Co-operatives have acquired a bad name in Africa, including Uganda. The Museveni manifesto mentions them briefly as a third force – 'use of state and private sector as well as co-operatives' – but surprisingly leaves them out in a later statement. The Yugoslav model of worker self-management may need further modification, but as a serious 40-year-long experiment (Horvat) it deserves far more attention than it has received, especially in Africa. Museveni's Uganda is surely ripe for such an experiment. Such small, democratic, self-management production units are the ultimate answer to the worst ills of the colonial agrarian political economy: its low productivity, excessive inequality, over-centralization, over-bureaucratization, exploitation, and corruption. They do not directly solve the problem of external imperialist exploitation. But they do provide sound building blocks for a fair and productive economy and a strong and democratic state under popular control: a system that offers the best possibility of autonomous prosperity and effective resistance to external exploitation.

Non-Ugandans should offer help, and help when called upon, not otherwise. Development projects proposed by foreign agencies should be rejected unless they are firmly in line with Ugandan development policy and can be implemented without counter productive side effects. Western liberal capitalism, in its contradictory development and despite its inherently exploitative nature, has also thrown up Marxism and socialism and is still capable of

throwing up occasional relatively unselfish intellectuals and professionals, as it has also done in Africa; people who are sufficiently
aware of the suicidal tendencies of our world and from a kind of
enlightened self-interest are motivated to throw in their lot with
oppressed peoples and classes, and find genuine satisfaction and
fulfilment in *participation without dominance*. They can help to work
out solutions together with Africans in complementary equality,
contributing their theory to be confronted and transformed by their
companions' praxis, until the theory of one becomes praxis and the
praxis of the other becomes theory, in a progressive, mutual
confrontation with the hard realities of our catastrophic age.

Notes

1. The designations feudal and communal modes of production are out of date as
   applied to Africa here. All pre-capitalist states came to be described as 'feudal' by
   orthodox Communists during the Stalinist era because the concept of 'Asiatic
   mode of production' was banned. 'Communal' derives from Engels' 'primitive
   communal mode'. In the light of present knowledge it has to be divided into two
   quite distinct modes of production, the foraging mode and the kinship mode
   (Southall, 'Mode of production theory'; the foraging mode of production and the
   kinship mode of production', *Dialectical Anthropology*, forthcoming).
2. The Busulu and Nvujo Law of 1927.

FIVE

Power that rode naked through Uganda under the muzzle of a gun

George W. Kanyeihamba[1]

The title of this chapter is taken from the book *Politics in Africa* by Dennis Austin, published in 1977, a year that was a landmark in the history of Uganda. For 1977 was the centenary of the founding of the Church of Uganda, an institution that witnessed in its early years – together with its sister denomination, the Roman Catholic Church – the first large-scale martyrdom of Christians in modern Africa. The Archbishop of Uganda, Janani Luwum, who was in 1977 presiding over the organizing committee that was preparing the centenary celebrations, became the prominent centenary martyr under the Amin regime. Although news of his death particularly shocked the world, he was one of thousands of Protestants, Roman Catholics, other Christians, Muslims, followers of traditional religion and non-believers who perished under the same regime. His assassination was a culmination of acts of wanton murder, destruction and carnage reminiscent of events in Europe in the Second World War. In Uganda this orgy of barbarism resulted in the loss of thousands of lives, destruction of property and demoralization.

In the wake of the Archbishop's murder, the Ugandan exiles in Britain resolved to found the Uganda Group for Human Rights to publicize the atrocities committed in Uganda and to fight for human rights; this was also in 1977. Hitherto most Ugandans had chosen to keep silent for fear of displeasing the regime, lest it avenge itself against their loved ones who were still living in Uganda. The risk we took in coming into the open against a ruthless regime was not without danger. Nonetheless, we have persistently stood up for our principles and objectives. Because we persevered, many other Ugandan associations with more or less similar aims mushroomed all over the world. It was these organizations and ourselves that campaigned for and succeeded in convincing others to join in a national conference at Moshi whose success was underwritten by the Tanzanian government and that metamorphosed into the Uganda National Liberation Front (UNLF).

The death of Archbishop Janani Luwum was just one incident in the ritual progress of the Amin regime, that eliminated thousands of Ugandans as well as a few foreign nationals. All the same, the world stood by while this carnage went on and on and seemed to paralyse the ability of a caring world to do anything about it. Amin misruled Uganda for nine terrible years. When eventually the Tanzanian People's Forces in collaboration with Ugandan guerrilla fighters forced him to flee the country, the world sighed with relief in the belief that the likes of Amin would never rise again in what they saw as the new Uganda. Nearly every Ugandan welcomed the passing of the Amin regime and hoped for a future in which peace and tranquility prevailed and citizens would no longer witness inexplicable killings or arbitrary arrests and detentions of thousands of innocent people, all seemingly sanctioned by government officials.

Those of us who had participated in the UNLF government made a solemn promise to the effect that never again would our country pass through terrible years of persecution and instability. We were to nurture an administration under a climate designed to enhance freedom and the seeds of democracy. The UNLF would preside over free elections which would have been preceded by the right of everyone to associate, found and join any political party or movement of his of her choice. The armed forces would be national and impartial and subordinate to the will of the people. Indeed, for a while these dreams appeared genuine enough under the UNLF administration. The UNLF was an organization representing all Ugandan political, military and humanitarian groups, whose members mirrored the Ugandan nation in opinions, ethnicity and regionalism. This is the government that took up the reins of power after the fall of Amin and in which I served as Attorney-General and Minister of Justice.

In early 1985, a seminar was held in London under the auspices of the Uganda Group for Human Rights with the object of examining the status of Ugandan refugees in other countries. Eminent experts on Uganda sat in on the discussion. Among those present were foreign journalists and others who had visited Uganda and investigated claims of human rights violations there. There were many Ugandans in attendance too. Most of those present had lived for varying periods of time in Uganda under Idi Amin and under successive Ugandan administrations since Amin's overthrow in 1979. There was unanimous agreement that, unspeakably awful as the Ugandan situation has been under Idi Amin, it was now, under Milton Obote, considerably worse in many respects. The situation was exacerbated by the presence and activities of an uncontrollable army, Obote's party's youth wingers, and the resuscitated intelligence-seeking organizations.

The testimony of those participating in the seminar, backed up by reports in the international and British press media and the evidential report of the State Department personnel in the US, contradicted very sharply the propaganda often put out in support of the Uganda government that things were improving in Uganda or that the government under Obote was the only organization that could put things right. Everyone who spoke at the seminar, whether Ugandan or non-Ugandan, dismissed this propagandist view as not only incorrect but as helping to perpetuate the state of chaos that still prevailed in Uganda. For some time it had become obvious that the country was experiencing a political crisis of such dimensions that Uganda's human rights record was as bad as could possibly be imagined. On the other hand, several governments in Africa and the West, briefed by an inattentive corps of diplomats who had been well fed by an effective propaganda campaign mounted by the then Uganda government, seemed to yield to and accept the avowals that the situation was actually improving in Uganda. It was as if these governments in general, and their spokespersons in particular, did not wish to hear the constant and consistent evidence to the contrary in the areas of security and the state of the economy.

Spokesmen of the British Government were some of the worst examples of a duped officialdom. When in 1984 Elliott Abrams, the American Under Secretary for Human Rights said that between 100,000 and 200,000 people had died in operations by the Ugandan army, the British High Commissioner queried these figures, asserting that things were improving since Amin's overthrow. As late as 1985, the same British High Commissioner congratulated the Uganda Government on its improved human rights record and on the growing harmonious relations between civilians and army. However, a Christian missionary who returned from Uganda at the same time, and who had lived there through the Amin era, lamented: 'In Amin's time I never saw so many dead bodies. I never saw so much looting and raping by the soldiers. Things in the Baganda area at least, have got worse since Amin.' Amnesty International also believed that the situation warranted the gravest concern, and reported widespead detentions without trial, torture, disappearances and death. It estimated that in the Luwero triangle, where the Uganda government suspected the local population to be sympathetic to the guerrillas' activities, half of the population had been eliminated.

Amin may have used spectacular methods to kill his prominent opponents, but the peasants and non-political members of the elite were by and large left alone. Under the second UPC government there were many reports of soldiers, youth wingers of the ruling party and chiefs who supported the government sweeping through the villages, killing and looting as they went. In a long article in *The Times* newspaper of London on 3 May 1985 by Richard Dowden headlined 'Uganda: Britain's blind eye to terror', it was reported that the number of refugees was further evidence that the situation under Obote was much worse than it had been under Amin. He noted that whereas there were about 25,000 refugees from Amin's Uganda, there were then about 280,000 from Obote's Uganda.

LET OTHERS SPEAK FOR UGANDANS

It is often alleged that Ugandans, especially those who live in exile, tend to exaggerate the human rights situation at home. Although the Uganda Group for Human Rights prided itself on its impartiality, objectivity and evidential comment, we were as anxious and passionate as any other Ugandans when our people were killed or deprived of their humanity, and our passion was often mistaken for partisanship. Consequently, we were not always immune to this accusation. It was therefore reassuring that our conclusions about the grave situation were borne out by independent testimony.

From time to time foreign visitors – analysts, journalists, and politicians, as well as organizations – observed and studied the Uganda scene at close quarters and came to devastating conclusions. Not long before the second Obote regime's final overthrow, the Uganda Group for Human Rights received a letter from a well-known supporter of the Obote-UPC government who, having stated that he hoped the UPC party would always be the only party of government, went on to reveal his fears. He wrote:

> I hope the year brings some hope in the hearts of the suffering Ugandans both at home and in exile. The immediate worry for us is the continued slaughter of innocent citizens by the Uganda army. If this can be stopped, it would give some relief to our people. We are however a long way from total freedom because we have degenerated so low that even the right to life is not guaranteed by the government. In fact, the government through the army has concentrated on taking away this right from the people. If human rights are not considered important how can we dream of political rights!

Ministers in the Uganda government were asked to comment on these damning words of one of their supporters and they freely admitted that the army was uncontrollable, and that not even the President of Uganda himself could give them orders. Other evidence tended to disprove what these ministers said. Obote and his close associates were truly in charge of government in Uganda and few could accept their excuse that it was the armed forces who were responsible for the atrocities.

Perhaps the most widely publicized and widely read reports were those of Amnesty International, with which the Uganda Group of Human Rights collaborated on issues of human rights. Reports prepared by Amnesty's missions and reporters since 1980 had not only revealed many examples of serious violations of human rights by the Ugandan authorities, but also ample evidence of illegal arrests, beatings, indiscriminate and arbitrary detentions (sometimes for very long periods of time) of government party opponents, non-political members of the elite and peasants alike. Among its reports, there were cases of torture, beatings with sticks, batons, rifle butts, leather whips, electric wires and chains. Many victims of torture were known or believed to have died or suffered serious injuries. Because of the unlimited number of officials exercising arbitrary powers of arrest and detention, Uganda prisons were severely overcrowded and prisoners lacked the barest necessities of life including food. Many of such people either died or simply 'disappeared' from records.

A number of British newspapers and periodicals reported from time to time that Ugandan armed forces in their search for so-called bandits continued to unleash a reign of terror on the civilian population. Whole communities were decimated by rampaging hordes of soldiers who pillaged, raped, and looted with lust and enthusiasm. In retaliation against the operations of guerrillas, government forces moved against whole communities of civilians where they committed 'many horrendous atrocities'.

One of the organizations most respected by the then Uganda government was the UK-based Church of Uganda Association whose many members generally sympathized with the UPC-led government in Uganda. The overwhelming number of its members were ex-missionaries, teachers, and civil servants who had worked in and loved Uganda both during and after the colonial period. One of their publications contained a report of members sent to Uganda to investigate and report on the situation since Obote's second return to power. It concluded: 'We sense that the greatest problem is one of security. There is shooting every night. The roadblocks where there is frequent looting and even killing are a source of income for the soldiers who man them.'

At the same time, Dr Barbara Harrell-Bond of Oxford University also reported on the horrors she had discovered among Uganda refugees in the Sudan. She had evidence of hundreds of Ugandan refugees 'facing slow death by starvation and disease, having been continually running from raids carried out by Ugandan armed forces in that part of the country.' These refugees were bitter because few people from outside their camps visited them. They felt there was an international conspiracy of silence. They wrote: 'We have no means of expressing ourselves; no means of proving our Ugandan identity, the identity of our miserable orphans, widows and helpless peasant farmers. No one sees the families of small children with no parents to guide them. No one sees the frustration of our youth whose education has been cut off by no fault of their own.' There were other horrors and sufferings confronting Ugandan refugees in places as diverse as Rwanda, Zaire, Kenya, not to mention the relatively luckier ones in Europe and the Americas.

Despite the intransigence shown by the British Government, the British Parliament contained distinguished members of both Houses who cared about human rights, and several of them had specialized in the fate of human rights in African countries and in Uganda in particular. Hansard reported that many MPs of all parties condemned the 'bloodshed, terror and violation of human rights in Uganda', and it further reported that all sides of the House 'urged Her Majesty's Government to use its undoubted influence and special position in this Commonwealth Country (Uganda) to help bring these evils to an end.'

Also during 1985 *La Croix* of France headlined 'Eight Months in Uganda – Daily Terror'. The medical co-ordinator of a humanitarian body, Michel T., a doctor aged 34, had just returned from Kampala. He already knew Thailand, Somalia and Angola and was therefore familiar with conflict and death and was not one to exaggerate unduly. He stated: 'What was new for me, wasn't the poverty or the violence, but the daily and accepted terror. Ugandans live by the day and their own hope is that they survive ... When in 1980 Milton Obote returned to power aided by Tanzanians, it was believed that Uganda would be coming out of the nightmare where Idi Amin had plunged it. Four years later, the opinion finds that the country is sinking deeper into murderous chaos.'

A British medical doctor, Nick Metcalfe of Manchester, who had gone to Uganda at the invitation of the Uganda government wrote to British ministers on his return on 15 May 1985:

I dearly loved the country and the people from its many different tribes. However I grieve very much for the gross abuse of human rights that is going on in Uganda. My main concern here is not the restriction of basic liberties but mass murder. Uganda reflects the problems facing all African countries, the collapse of democratic government ... but it is an exception on the scale of not only killings of political opponents but the mass murder of innocent people. From my experiences in Uganda, the Obote regime is guilty of all the crimes of Amin ... I base this on having worked in one area for a year and subsequently working and travelling around a majority of the country.

A final word on violations of human rights in Uganda may be quoted from *Munnansi*, which was published in Uganda itself. Its issue of 24 April 1985, having stated other violations, concluded: 'Luzira Maximum Security Prison was built by the British to hold no more than 500 prisoners. Now over 2000 inmates are crammed in Luzira Prison in an environment unfit for human or animal habitation. They lack food, medicines, beddings or anything else a British might consider decent for her dog or horse ... none of the inmates have ever appeared in court'.

THE BREAKDOWN OF THE ECONOMY AND THE CONSTITUTION

At independence the Ugandan economy was in excellent shape. It was one of the strongest in black Africa. Comparative world economic data of the period excluded Uganda from the very poorest countries of Africa. By the time the first Obote government came to be overthrown by Amin in 1971, the economy had already been shaken to its foundations. Obote had overthrown the Uganda constitution, declared himself the new President, dismantled the traditional infrastructures of the country, established an authoritarian regime, suppressed the electoral process and negated much of what many Ugandans had aspired for with the coming of independence. He was aided in all this by his chosen army commander, Idi Amin. As if all this was not enough to dampen the morale of the country, his government preached what it called socialism, attempted to impose a theoretical philosophy of the so-called 'Move to the Left' while at the same time his cabinet ministers and UPC elite were greedily grabbing every available asset for themselves. Ownership of land, company shares, firms, and personal chattels such as expensive cars and large houses were mysteriously transferred from legitimate owners to ministers, their families and friends. In some cases even wives and other women were seized. In between these acquisitions, ministers toured the country advocating 'socialism'. People were not fooled. They recognized the campaign for what it was: a cleverly staged smoke-screen behind which members of the government and their close associates could rob the people of their national birthright and inheritance under the principle 'what you have we share, what I have I keep'. What the people had, the ministers would share with them. What *they* had, they would keep. This was the kind of Move to the Left they meant – move to the left while I take everything on the right. In reality few of the cabinet ministers knew what socialism meant or even cared to know.

Whenever general elections were due, the Obote government declared a state of emergency and postponed them; between 1962 and 1971 (the year of Amin's coup) there had been no elections in Uganda, although the independence constitution had guaranteed that they would be regular, free and fair. It is no wonder that on the overthrow of Obote's government there was jubilation throughout the country, even though at that time people did not know who had taken over or what kind of policies would be pursued subsequently.

Consequently, whatever else may be said about Amin when he took office, the Ugandan economy was in the last stages of disintegration. Indeed, in spite of his acrobatics in government, for nine years he managed to hold the economy together, albeit tenously. The economic situation was still bad by African standards, but it became much worse under the second administration of Milton Obote.

A number of Western governments were heavily committed to supporting the Obote government both financially and militarily. The economic sustenance was spearheaded by the IMF and the World Bank. In a bid to win international recognition and the badly needed foreign exchange, the Obote government accepted all the conditions imposed by these bodies in spite of the fact that Mwalimu Nyerere of Tanzania, the mentor of Obote, condemned as corrupt governments that accepted such conditions. A study by the Uganda Human Rights Activists in Scandinavia showed that this money did not benefit the common people: 'The man who bears the full burden of the economy. Indeed one sees more new cars on the unrepaired streets and shops stocked with video sets, colour TV's and the like'. Quoting from *The Tablet*, an international Catholic weekly publication, the activists went on, 'Uganda imported a hundred Mercedes Benz cars for her own top men and women. These cars were ordered during the period when lack of drugs and starvation were rampant in Luwero, Karamoja and West Nile. Not all illicit gains of the powerful come from loans made by the IMF and other aid donors. The ancient art of smuggling, particularly of Uganda's main crop, coffee, is in the hands of individuals who control instruments of government in Uganda today.'

In his budget statement of 1984, Obote as Minister of Finance increased the minimum wages for group employees to 6000 shillings per month, and the ignorant applauded. But this sum could hardly cover a family's weekly shopping. A family of three in Kampala consumed at least 3 bunches of *matoke* a week. At 3000 shillings per bunch, expenditure on food alone was 9000 shillings a week. Daily transport for a single person resident outside the city centre was some 300 shillings a day. Milk for children, sugar and other items of food – if they could be obtained – cost well over 2000 shillings a week. It was little short of a miracle that any Ugandan families living in urban centres could survive at all. On the other hand, ministers, their families and their retainers became extremely affluent. The scale of corruption was such that many Ugandan leaders of the incumbent administration were able to open personal bank accounts in foreign countries and deposit in them large sums in foreign exchange donated or loaned to assist in the rebuilding and rehabilitation of Uganda. Economists and bankers who studied the Uganda phenomenon during 1985 observed that since the fall of Amin, Uganda had earned or received sufficient funds and equipment to rebuild its infrastructure, roads, buildings, and to equip and staff its schools and hospitals as well as to resuscitate its economy. Unfortunately, these funds had been so diverted that even Kampala, the capital, remained a ghost city without regular running water or properly maintained streets or buildings. There was a chronic shortage of water, medicines and personnel in Ugandan hospitals, schools and other institutions. The educational system had become corrupted and standards had fallen.

The Uganda *Democrat* – a publication of the Democratic Party (DP) UK-branch – reported the remarks of Akena Adoko, then a bulwark of the UPC and a confidant and cousin of Milton Obote, published earlier in a Uganda magazine called *Weekly Review*. (In the first Obote government Akena Adoko had been the head of the most feared police, called the General Service, and it was widely believed that not only was this unit back in business but that he might still be associated with it.) Adoko is said to have remarked that not only were the 1980 elections 'won' by UPC corruptly, but also that the resultant UPC government contained corrupt ministers. Here was a member of Obote's ruling oligarchy castigating his own government, yet foreign spokesmen, including representatives of governments of the West, had the temerity to suggest that things in Uganda were improving.

On whose side were they exactly? Did they really believe the words of Shafiq Arain, the Ugandan High Commissioner in London and chief propagandist of the UPC, when he addressed a meeting at the Commonweath Institute and claimed that since his government had come into power the economy of Uganda had made so many tremendous leaps on its way to recovery that recently Uganda was the only country in East and Central Africa whose balance of payments was in the black? Although many knowledgeable people in the audience, including Shafiq's counterpart from Tanzania were incredulous and the latter gave a contradictory speech, Shafiq's claim appeared to have been a rational one. If a government does not pay its armed forces so that soldiers are forced to pay themselves by preying on the civilian population through terrorism, robbery and looting; if that government does not pay its civil servants, policemen and teachers for months; if it neglects to repair the infrastructure of the country, roads, streets, buildings and factories; if there is no equipment for hospitals and schools; if no medicines, books and paper are bought for hospitals, for schools and for courts of law; if threats and insecurity force thousands of the country's professional men and women to become refugees in other countries so that the government does not have to pay their wages and salaries; if a government allows foreign organizations to run the country's economy and become the de facto minister of finance in all his various manifestations and they are allowed to authorize the minutest of official expenditure; and if the only people to be rewarded are ministers and important government and army officials so that they can remain happy and contented making fortunes in foreign banks while their fellow citizens suffer in abject poverty, there would be no economic reason why that government's balance of payments would not be in the black.

Several Uganda ministers who passed through London and other capitals of the world, often staying in very expensive hotels at the expense of the Uganda taxpayer and IMF donors, were asked to comment on this state of affairs over which they were presiding. Some dismissed this grave situation as unimportant. Others claimed that they, including Obote, were prisoners of the Uganda army, which called the tune and was master in the land. If this was the truth, then they had no business remaining in office.

However, the truth lies elsewhere. Grace Ibingira, writing in *African Upheavals since Independence* correctly observed that Uganda had a remarkable tradition of respect for law and order. The police force had a long and reputable tradition of acting fairly and within the law. It was not until the UPC government began to instruct the police to suppress opposition parties and their meetings and to victimize suspected opposition supporters that the public became apprehensive and the police appeared ruthless.

Few Ugandans have forgotten that Milton Obote commissioned Idi Amin on the eve of independence againt the advice of the Governor of Uganda, Sir Walter Coutts. The Kenyan colonial administration submitted evidence to Obote that Amin was wanted for murder: it wanted to try him for the murder of a number of Turkana tribesmen whose mutilated bodies had been discovered in an area previously patrolled by Amin's platoon. Not only did Obote refuse to hand him over but later he placed him in charge of the Uganda army and promoted him in preference to better-trained and more capable officers. Be that as it may, Obote was soon to be rewarded. Amin assisted him in the overthrow of the Uganda constitution and in the dismantling of Uganda's kingdoms and traditional infrastructures. It was widely believed in Uganda that the subsequent overthrow of the Obote government by Amin was sparked off by an internal quarrel. Indeed, in the initial stages Amin was anxious to describe what had happened as a mutiny rather than a full-blooded *coup d'état*. It was for these reasons that most Ugandans believed that authoritarian rule had become conventional since the mid-1960s, albeit briefly interrupted in 1979 by the UNLF administration. What occurred in between was nothing more than a game of musical chairs in which members of the same ruling oligarchy changed seats.

Regardless of what the legal constitution of Uganda provided in relation to elections and to succession to office, UPC leaders had no intention of relinquishing the office of government through constitutional means. To this end they often engaged in systematic campaigns and activities designed to destroy anyone said, or imagined to be, a possible successor, and this occasionally included their own members. Meanwhile the general public was subjected to indiscriminate harassment, arbitrary arrests, and detention by a regime that had lost the support of the general population. The more this loss of popularity was manifestly evident and widespread, the harsher was the treatment meted out to citizens. At various stages of this repression in Uganda, the more capable, qualified and experienced citizens fled from the country and found homes and employment in other countries. The departure of these refugees effectively deprived the government of the necessary personnel for its bureaucracy and development. As a result public service became inefficient and the development of the country was retarded. The regime was then forced to rely on foreign aid and support. In a publication, *Contemporary Crisis no. 8* of 1984, a member of the Uganda Group for Human Rights wrote,

> Thousands of Ugandans continue to flee the murderous brutality of the Uganda government army and the size and number of these camps (refugee camps) continue to grow, with apparently no end in sight. In recent weeks many international observers and human rights organizations have recorded the atrocities and outrage perpetrated by the Obote regime. There are arbitrary arrests, mass killings and wanton destruction of property. Hundreds of people are dying from torture, disease and starvation in

squalid government prisons ... The question is now no longer whether President Obote is the right man to solve Uganda's problems but why he is the wrong one.

CONCLUSION

Uganda's problems in the second Obote era were political and not, as some spokespersons in the West are fond of saying, economic. Nor was it true that Obote was the only person capable of governing Uganda. In fact Ugandans have always found this assertion by Obote's apologists to be a grave insult to Uganda.

The Uganda Group for Human Rights and others including international pressure groups appealed to all sides in Uganda to agree to a conference at which the various political interests in and outside the country could discuss peaceful options to the crisis during Obote's second presidency. The Obote government showed neither the will nor real ability to translate its propaganda rhetoric of national reconciliation into the reality of government policy. This inability led Obote's opponents to argue that he could not find the solution to Uganda's problems for much the same reason that a thief cannot find a policemen to investigate his crime. Obote and the UPC often claimed that they were gen-uinely attempting to serve the national interest. It will have become clear from the evidence I have presented that what Dennis Austin wrote was true: 'Attempts to serve the national interest [by a party] may easily end by [that party] being the chief interest itself.'

The killings, anarchy, suspicions and hatred in Uganda were such that the UPC government and its military force together with foreign aid and military hardware were incapable of providing solutions. This is a political truism that all genuine Ugandans and those who call themselves friends of Uganda had to accept. The truth of the matter was that Uganda was in the middle of a civil war and for every Ugandan who claimed that those fighting the Obote government were bandits there was another who claimed that it was the members of the government who were the bandits. One Ugandan scientist whom I would call a model of moderation in our divided land, described the guerrillas who were waging war against the Obote government in the following terms:

What is happening today in Uganda is a culmination of what has been brewing all these troubled years of that country's history; it is a logical conclusion of all truisms and prophecies about the trends of justice. When one hears or reads about the guerrilla warfare which is now raging, it is at first difficult to understand or distinguish it from a civil war but, on looking more closely or more nationalistically, one identifies a new Uganda in the making. What started as the disaffections of a group of people has

81

now grown into a national sentiment involving the support of many Ugandans from all parts of the country. For many there is renewed hope that at least those people who perished at the hands of the dictators will not have lost their lives in vain ... The military training team and all the outsiders who are trying to keep Obote in power, for whatever reasons, are playing a losing game for no one can ever win against the instruments of change, especially when the change is backed by a true and justifiable cause.

A need has arisen in Uganda for her leaders to reconstruct a national ethos. A great deal of compromise and co-operation between the opposing factions must be encouraged before the suspicions and hatreds are replaced by mutual trust and common interest. Only then can the processes of true democracy begin. Above all in cases of societal conflict as in the case of Uganda, it is absolutely essential that predetermined rules of constitutionalism and legitimacy must be adhered to. An important aspect of the new art of compromise must be the realization by any leadership that neither it nor anyone else has a monopoly to the right policies or solutions. Ugandan leaders need to be educated in appreciating and accepting political defeat and loss of power as attributes of democracy, freedom and constitutionalism. Ugandan leaders have to appreciate that equitable distribution of the national wealth is as important as the maintenance of law and order; legalism is as important as the political reality of the situation; and the claims of democracy must be tempered with the right of the population to be governed well and efficiently. Only when that appreciation is noted by the general populace, will the system of public law guarantee the lives of previous and ousted leaders in a way that will discourage them from clinging to power by whatever means available as the only sure way of keeping alive.

Notes

1. This chapter was originally given as an address in the middle of 1985 when the author was still chairman of the UK-based Uganda Group for Human Rights, a post that he had held since the start in 1977. In 1979 the author was briefly Attorney-General in the first post-Amin government presided over by Yusufu Lule.

PART TWO

ECONOMIC PERSPECTIVES & AGRICULTURAL CHALLENGES

SIX
Uganda: the spatial dimension

Anthony O'Connor

The vast majority of recent writings on Uganda both on the traumas experienced by its people over the past 15 years and on priorities in reconstruction, have related to the country as a whole. Little attention has been given to variations from place to place within the country, except in discussions focused explicitly on ethnicity and political relationships among people of different ethnic groups. Such an emphasis on the aggregate national situation was also a characteristic of most discussion of 'development' in Uganda in the 1960s, including official Development Plans, and it is again evident in volumes such as the World Bank (1982) survey. While this has often been necessary, an inevitable result has been a great deal of overgeneralization, with critically important regional variations overlooked.

The differences between, say, Acholi areas in the north and Bugisu in the east are not merely those of ethnic identity: they include also density of population, physical environment and structure of the local economy. Some contrasts pre-date colonial rule, others result from its differential impact, and others again reflect variations in the nature and extent of post-1970 institutional breakdown. All are relevant to policies for the future – concerning food crops versus cash crops, road-building versus school-building, or whatever. To some extent such policies can be formulated at the national level, but often they must be area-specific if they are to be appropriate and effective.

An emphasis on the aggregate national scene was perhaps very understandable in the first decade following independence, when everyone was encouraged to think in terms of 'nation-building', even though it was essentially the extent of regional diversity that made that task so difficult. In various respects a process of national spatial integration was taking place during the 1960s, both gradually through such agencies as the education system, and more abruptly in such cases as the imposition of centralized authority on the former kingdoms. However, the 1970s and 1980s have witnessed a reversal of this process, and a substantial degree of national disintegration, so that for many people 'Uganda' has become a less and less meaningful entity. In this situation there is more need than ever to give explicit attention to the residents of particular areas, and to their distinctive problems.

Of course, this will raise politically sensitive issues. This is inevitable wherever there are tensions among ethnic groups each of which is associated with a particular tract of territory. A Development Plan may make little reference to *where* change is to take place, either because this is thought unimportant, especially by economists; or alternatively because it is thought too important, or at least too sensitive, by those engaged in politics. A geographer might suggest that issues of *where* must be confronted, and that neither short-term rehabilitation nor long-term development can be tackled effectively behind a smoke-screen of national aggregates.

FEATURES OF UGANDA'S GEOGRAPHY

In one short Chapter it is impossible to discuss all the aspects of the geography of Uganda that are relevant to the theme of this book. Readers are referred to the national *Atlas of Uganda* (Uganda, 1967). All that I can do is highlight a few such aspects, and then selectively illustrate regional variations in conditions during the early 1980s. In comparison with much of Africa the country is often considered as having a highly favourable physical environment: but while this is true of much of the south, it is far less true of the north, where soils are in general less fertile and where rainfall is much more seasonal. Climatic conditions are especially harsh in the former Karamoja District of the north-east, where the rains are highly unreliable. Within the southern half of the country regional variations may be exemplified by two highland areas, Bugisu in the east with its particularly fertile volcanic soils, and Kigezi in the far south-west where the non-volcanic soils are far less fertile. Both of these highland areas are very densely populated, with over 1000 people per sq km, and any plans for them must take into account extreme land scarcity. Much of the south and south-east also has more than 300 people per sq km, but elsewhere there are extensive tracts with less than one-tenth of that density, not always reflecting a poorer resource base. Wildlife is of course one resource particularly associated with sparsely settled areas.

The well-distributed rainfall of much of the south permitted a traditional food-crop economy based on the perennial banana, whereas to the north this gave way to cultivation of millet and sorghum during the short wet season, complemented by a greater reliance on livestock. In Karamoja, the harsh environment has enforced a predominantly pastoral economy, and this has remained the area least integrated into Uganda as a whole. Elsewhere, colonial rule brought the spread of cash crops on small farms. But whereas in much of the south, especially the former Buganda, both the climate and the high-yielding banana allowed extensive planting of coffee, in the north farmers could only plant cotton, which brought in much less income and also clashed more severely with food production.

With respect to the spread of a cash economy, the south and south-east had further advantages over the north and to some extent the west. Notable among these was more direct access to the sea by way of Kenya, an advantage reinforced by the whole orientation of the national economy towards Kenya and Tanzania rather than Sudan and Zaire both before and after independence. Equally important considerations were sharply contrasting pre-colonial political structures, discussed by other contributors to this volume, and imbalance in the spatial distribution of 'Western' education throughout this century. All this meant that Uganda attained independence in 1962 with a space-economy that offered a classic example of a core and periphery structure. Within it, a whole series of circular processes operated: for example, the point at which the Nile flows out of Lake Victoria was much the best site for the country's first hydroelectric power station, and this gave further advantage to the south and south-east as the location for manufacturing industry. Not only the chief city, Kampala, but also the next largest urban centres, Jinja and Mbale, developed in this part of the country, while the district headquarter towns of the west and north remained extremely small.

While a core–periphery dichotomy may be drawn far more readily than in the case of countries such as Tanzania or Nigeria, it is dangerously crude. For most practical purposes further disaggregation is essential. Within the 'periphery', the environmental, economic and political circumstances of the far north and the far west are quite different – the political circumstances even more different in the mid-1980s than ever before. Now that people from the north are no longer in control in Kampala the north may in a sense have become more peripheral, while the west has moved closer to the core. Where once the relative isolation of the south–west perhaps softened the north–south economic division, this may now be sharpened, with serious implications for national integration. As for the 'core', there are many differences between the former Buganda kingdom and the areas lying to the east of the Nile. Advantages enjoyed by the latter depend to a far greater extent on the orientation of economic change resulting from colonial rule. This extension of the 'core' in economic terms towards the Kenya border

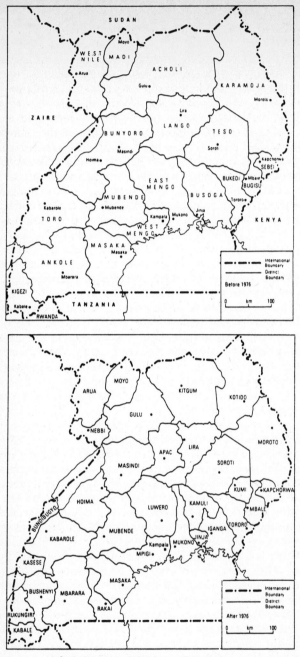

Administrative Divisions of Uganda

may be highly significant in reducing the probability of the Baganda occupying as dominant a position in a new Uganda as the Kikuyu in Kenya. (Why they did not seize the opportunity to dominate in the past is a question outside the scope of this chapter.)

A proper understanding of most aspects of Uganda requires not merely differentiation between north and south or core and periphery, but disaggregation at least to district level. Unfortunately, this is complicated by the changes in the administrative divisions of the country that have occurred in recent years. It is perhaps a reflection of the gravity of other political issues in Uganda that nothing has been written on the implications of the replacement of most of the ex-colonial districts by smaller units in 1976. Indeed, many maps of the country published quite recently continue to show the pre-1976 boundaries, while almost all discussions of contemporary Uganda continue to refer to Ankole, Toro, Acholi, West Nile and so on, despite their disappearance as administrative units. One might assume that it indicates the irrelevance of the state for most aspects of life throughout the country, but it even applies to government publications such as the Ministry of Information's *Uganda 1983 Yearbook*. (See maps on page 86.)

In any case, it would be impossible here to deal with every district, even on the basis of the larger pre-1976 units, so attention will be concentrated on certain areas that have either always been, or have more recently become, particularly distinctive, just to illustrate the theme of spatial differentiation at this level.

SELECTED AREAS

One of the most distinctive areas is the north-east, which formed Karamoja District until this was subdivided in 1976 into Moroto and Kotido. The land here provides a livelihood for only a sparse population, most families traditionally depending on cattle herded on a semi-nomadic basis by the men, and sorghum grown in the very short rainy season by the women around the home base. Culturally, the Karamojong and related groups have far more in common with the pastoral peoples of northern Kenya, such as the Turkana, than with groups in the rest of Uganda. Education levels lag far behind those in other regions, and by the 1960s commercialization had made scarcely any impact. To a large extent other Ugandans then still 'disowned' the people of Karamoja.

In some ways, therefore, Karamoja was the area least affected by the partial collapse of the cash economy during the 1970s. It was less affected also by some aspects of the breakdown of law and order, since this had never been effectively imposed. For most people there, life in 1978 was little different from life in 1968, though even by 1978 military misrule had led to a very disturbing diffusion of guns to replace the traditional spears. This latter process intensified greatly following the overthrow of Amin, especially as a result of the looting of the large armoury at Moroto. Warfare between rival groups quickly escalated, and vastly expanded the scale of cattle-raiding, so that before long cattle were far more unequally distributed than before. The Dodoth people of the far north, for instance, with fewer guns than others, are reported to have lost most of their cattle between 1979 and 1981. The dire problems particular to the former Karamoja District were compounded by severe drought in 1980. The drought was of the sort that most people would have survived in earlier years, though not without great hardship, but by now the usual survival mechanisms were for many people not available. Communities that had a little cash could not use it to buy grain, since the insecurity had discouraged traders from bringing any in. In any case some of the cash became worthless when the post-Amin government changed the currency notes, for most people had no access to any bank. The result was a famine to which Kampala was unable to provide any remotely adequate response, and by early 1981 numerous international relief agencies were operating in this region, generally gaining access to it through Kenya. The grim conditions are fully described in several papers in Dodge and Wiebe (1985).

Fortunately, the rains were good in 1982 and 1983, in sharp contrast to the situation in Ethiopia to the north. At the same time the security situation seems to have improved during that period. Both situations could change again for the worse, however, and any assessment of the condition of Uganda at any time must give specific attention to what is happening in the semi-arid, semi-pastoral north-east.

In other parts of northern Uganda subsistence production continued to dominate the economy in the 1960s far more than in the south, but people here are essentially settled cultivators. Many families by then supplemented their subsistence food crops with either cotton or tobacco grown as a cash crop, using the proceeds to pay taxes, pay school fees and buy a few consumer goods. The fact that cotton and tobacco sales from Uganda fell away far more sharply in the 1970s than coffee sales has been noted by many observers (World Bank, 1982, etc): less often has it been noted that this meant the near-disappearance of cash from districts such as Acholi. There is no question of cotton being merely unrecorded as with much smuggled coffee: it would not be worthwhile for anyone to smuggle such a bulky crop as cotton anywhere, least of all across the Sudan border.

If the economic circumstances of the former Acholi and former West Nile districts were fairly similar in the late 1970s, their political circumstances differed sharply, since Amin was himself of West Nile origin. By 1980 the contrasts were even greater, for Amin's supporters had retreated to that area, and violent clashes between them and the Uganda National Liberation Army were taking place. One result was a massive exodus of the local population across the borders into Zaire and Sudan. The number of people involved is estimated at 250,000 to 300,000, sufficient to leave vast tracts of the former West Nile District almost empty. Very little has been published on this situation, but some indications are provided in Barbara Harrell-Bond's (1986) volume on Ugandan refugees in Sudan.

A third area to which specific attention must be given is totally different in its geographical location from 'peripheral' Karamoja and West Nile. This is an area in the heart of the country, north and north-west of Kampala, which became known as the 'Luwero triangle'. This was in no way distinctive during the Amin period, but it experienced devastation in the early 1980s, and especially in 1983, as government forces waged a long campaign against armed dissident groups, one of which later became the National Resistance Movement. The devastation was intensified by the indiscipline of the government troops, and by the extent to which their attacks were on the ordinary local population who were said to be sheltering and supporting the 'guerrillas'. Many thousands of civilians were killed, and well over 100,000 were displaced from their homes.

Presumably the takeover of national administration by the NRM has particular significance for this area. Its people have suffered terribly, and might reasonably expect that special concern will be shown for them as reconstruction programmes are put into effect. On the other hand, their proximity to the capital and location within the generally more prosperous part of the country means that there is a better prospect of spontaneous rehabilitation here than, say, in the far north-west.

Meanwhile, what has been happening in various other parts of the country over the past 15 years? Have both the tyranny of the Amin period and the anarchy of later years been less devastating for Kigezi, later Kabale and Rukungiri districts, in the extreme south-west, than for most other areas? The main news of this corner of Uganda to reach the rest of the world has concerned the long-standing problem of people originating from neighbouring Rwanda who have settled on the Uganda side of the border.

Certainly both political and economic life seem to have been rather less disturbed in the extreme south-east, close to the Kenya border, than in some other areas. Whyte reports rather favourably on the Bunyole area of Tororo District in one of the few contributions to this volume that is focused on a specific area. On the slopes of Mount Elgon in Mbale (formerly Bugisu) District the cash economy has long been based on the cultivation of high quality arabica coffee. Its high value-to-weight ratio and the fact that this is the type of coffee most widely grown in Kenya, as well as physical proximity to the border, must have made smuggling an even more attractive proposition than in the main robusta coffee zone of Uganda. So it is likely that most farmers in this area continued to receive a substantial cash income, and to have some access to imported goods on which to spend it, as well as feeding themselves through banana and maize cultivation much as before.

Neighbouring Teso (now Kumi and Soroti districts) must have suffered greater economic deprivation, since this was one of the areas depending most heavily on cotton. (The national decline in cotton production is documented by Edmonds and Belshaw in Chapters 7 and 8.) It also suffered greatly at one stage from the large-scale rustling of cattle by military forces. However, it appears that this is one of the areas that has been least involved in specifically political conflict. Very few Iteso individuals have been in positions of great influence in any of the various administrations, apart from Peter Otai, Obote's deputy minister for the army in the early 1980s. Amongst other things, this reflected the prominence of Iteso soldiers, as well as Acholi and Langi ones, in the second Obote regime's army.

SELECTED ISSUES

An alternative approach to the geography of Uganda's critical problems is to consider these one by one with special reference to spatial variation across the country. The only problem for which this is well documented is the physical destruction resulting from military campaigns. Reports of these (e.g. Avirgan and Honey, 1982) include much reference to specific places. With regard to most other problems the situation is very different.

One of the best known characteristics of Uganda in the late 1970s and early 1980s was the replacement of much of the officially organized cash economy by a 'parallel economy', generally known within the country as *magendo*. Naturally, this has not been the subject of much academic study, although one extremely valuable, and brave, investigation of it has been undertaken by Green (1981). Green provides much valuable insight into the working of the *magendo* economy, but he has very little to say about where within the country it is of greater or lesser importance. Kasfir (1984) also discusses *magendo* essentially at the national level.

In absolute terms, the growth of this parallel cash economy must have been essentially a phenomenon of the south, and most particularly of the former Buganda kingdom. The relative prosperity that the people of that region have long enjoyed has rested primarily upon coffee cultivation, and most of the perennial coffee bushes continue to yield despite some degree of neglect. In the late 1970s the official figures for coffee exports fell sharply, but it is generally accepted that a shift to smuggling accounts for most of this fall. Cash continued to circulate, and many new forms of trade emerged as ingenious ways were found to satisfy the wants of those in a position to pay. While there was some reversion to subsistence activity, in other ways the level of commercial activity in and around Kampala probably increased.

In some other areas, where export crop production virtually ceased, the *magendo* economy cannot have developed to the same extent in absolute terms. However, it is possible that its share of such cash transactions as did take place, at least at certain periods, was even higher in these areas. It should at least not be assumed that the process of displacing this new parallel economy by officially approved transactions will be the same in every part of the country.

Two further topics merit attention with regard to what has happened where within Uganda in recent years. One concerns the ecological devastation that has been widely publicized. As people have been obliged to fend for themselves small-scale poaching of wild animals has increased to maintain food supplies, while at the same time large-scale slaughter of animals such as elephant has made fortunes for a few. It really forms another element in the *magendo* economy, and smuggling is often involved. Woodcutting for fuel has similarly increased, often in forest reserves where it would have been prevented in the past (Hamilton, 1984). There have been cases of charcoal being exported quite openly by rail to Kenya without any sign of the necessary approval from the Forests Department. It is well known that these things have been happening, and it is known that they are widespread, from urban fringes to remote corners of the country: but remedial action will require knowledge of just what kind and degree of ecological damage has been taking place in every locality.

Equally well known is the deterioration in the availability of social services such as health care and education. In 1965 there was one doctor for every 11,000 people, but by 1980 the ratio was only one for every 27,000. There is no published information on the regional incidence of this decline, but in this case the data must exist and in broad terms the spatial dimension of the problem must be known. However, a major policy dilemma remains. Should every effort be made to restore the pattern of service provision that once existed, or should the opportunity be taken to try to establish a more equitable distribution, even if this would involve somewhat higher costs and somewhat greater delays?

A further dimension of spatial variation that should be mentioned is that between town and countryside. It has been argued for poor countries in general (Lipton, 1977) that this is the most significant of all divisions, and the matter is now the subject of much debate (e.g. Harriss and Moore, 1984). In countries such as Uganda, where the vast majority of people are rural dwellers, does the channelling of government resources to the towns constitute 'urban bias'? Or does future prosperity depend on a substantial degree of urbanization taking place, including urban job-creation? With regard to most expenditure of effort and funds, both on rehabilitation and on development, allocations must be made between urban and rural areas, and also between the capital city and smaller urban centres. Of course, the urban–rural dichotomy must not be overdrawn, especially as there are few parts of the world where urban dwellers maintain such close links with their rural areas of origin. But a sharp distinction can be made between urban and rural *places*, even if not between urban and rural *people*.

Have most urban places been affected more or less than most rural places by the events of the past 15 years? If they have been more affected, would this alone justify special attention being given to them? At certain times some degree of exodus from Kampala seems to have taken place, even long-standing urban residents returning to their rural home areas for security. This has not prevented an overall growth in the city's population, but the rate of growth since 1970 seems to have been only about half that of Dar es Salaam or Nairobi. This might be seen as a blessing in disguise, or as an artificial situation that will require planning for extra-rapid urban growth in the near future. With regard to most smaller towns absolutely no information is available, although there are extreme cases such as the West Nile District headquarters, Arua, which apparently lost almost all its population in the early 1980s, at least for a few months.

One might expect the 1976 subdivision of the country into an increased number of districts to have had some impact on the very small towns such as Bushenyi, Kamuli and Kitgum which have become district headquarters for the first time; and especially on places such as Apac and Rakai, which were no more than minor trading centres before the reorganization. However, the breakdown of government may in some cases have been far more significant than its nominal restructuring, and the crucial decisions for these small towns may still remain to be made.

I suspect that a considerable degree of concentration on the towns is inevitable in Uganda in the years ahead, if only because of the role that they must play in the organization of space and of the national economy. However, there is a strong case for efforts to avoid over-concentration on the capital city, and to ensure that some urban functions are effectively performed in every district. This may be especially important in a period when people from the south hold a larger share of power at the national level than in the past.

Meanwhile, the extent to which families tend to have a base in a rural area even when some members are in the city has proved to be of great value in Uganda; indeed it has often provided a lifeline. If it can be maintained, it may be both to the advantage of those families and also of advantage to the nation in countering the emergence of a privileged urban elite whose members neither know nor care about the countryside. Such urban–rural links, and many others such as the supply of food and fuel to the towns, can of course be maintained far more easily from a scatter of small urban centres than from a single metropolis.

All of this requires thought and decisions not just about Uganda as a whole, nor even about urban versus rural sectors, but about each part of Uganda. For many people in the former West Nile District, for example, the critical question with respect to urbanization is what will now happen to Arua. The future of Uganda depends to a considerable extent on the attention paid by central government to such concerns.

CONCLUSIONS

This chapter has been concerned both with space as a critical dimension of Ugandan affairs and with the country's regional diversity. Both issues are important in any country at any time, but the present circumstances of Uganda greatly enhance that importance, with profound implications for public policy.

Every national government must make decisions about the location of investment in schools, medical facilities, water supplies, roads and so on. Every government has some influence, direct or indirect, on the spatial pattern of new agricultural or industrial activity. These decisions and this influence are especially significant in countries where diverse ethnic groups are strongly attached to specific areas, and in Uganda today they impinge on almost every aspect of reconstruction as well as longer-term development.

For many years there have been substantial spatial disparities in Uganda with respect to all forms of economic infrastructure and the level of commercial activity, but in many respects these must have been greatly intensified by the events of the past fifteen years. To some extent this can be viewed in simple 'centre' and 'periphery' terms, with many pressures now for yet further increase of disparity between the two. In the short term the financial returns from public investment in Kampala, Jinja and surrounding areas will often be greater than from investment in Kigezi, West Nile or Karamoja, but the dangers involved in acting on this must be recognized, especially as private enterprise may then become even more spatially concentrated. There are severe limits to the degree of dispersal that can be achieved. But at least every effort should be made to avoid positively favouring concentration, for instance by hidden subsidies, and to ensure that the poor peripheral areas have some source of cash income, and to assist local small-scale enterprise. There are instances where such enterprise arose through the need for local self-sufficiency during the crisis years, and it would be most unfortunate if it were obliterated by the restoration of interaction with the more prosperous centre.

Regional diversity is of course not just a matter of disparities between a prosperous centre and poor peripheral areas. Many other differences between places are not a matter of equity at all, but they still cannot be ignored when policies are being formulated and plans are being prepared.

The Museveni government, like others before it, would no doubt like to regard Uganda as a single unified entity as far as possible, and it will be encouraged in this by most external agencies. However, it no doubt knows far better than these agencies that Uganda is actually a collection of very disparate parts, especially since it had to establish its control over various areas one by one, and since this must have been much more difficult in some areas than in others. The prospects for a future Uganda enjoying some measure of national unity will not be improved by ignoring regional differences. These must be acknowledged, and appropriate policies must be formulated for each part of the country in the light of its natural resources, its demographic and cultural characteristics, its development experience up to 1970, and its particular experience of collapse and destruction since then. The appropriate future path for Kigezi will perhaps have little in common with that for Karamoja or that for Kampala and its surroundings. Of course, national policies and plans are needed. But they must be complemented by policies for, and formulated in consultation with, specific groups of people in specific places.

SEVEN
Crisis management: the lessons for Africa from Obote's second term

Keith Edmonds

INTRODUCTION

The world's attention in the past years has been focused by the media on the food crisis in Africa, which a widespread drought turned to famine. However, most of the countries of Africa face economic crisis even when better weather prevents famine, and they have been doing so for the past decade. Though less dramatic, the pervasive nature of this crisis warrants careful analysis of its causes and the policies adopted to manage them.

Of particular interest is the longer-term nature of the crisis, which generally stems from the need to restructure the economy so as to reduce its dependence on one or two tradables. Such restructuring is necessary as a basis for sustainable growth and development but requires major investments to be undertaken. Clearly, the cost of these investments is greatly in excess of the current savings capacities of any least developed country, so foreign funds have to be mobilized for it. Mobilization of such monies (and their efficient use) is the key to the solution of this longer-term aspect of the crisis.

When addressing more short-term aspects of the crisis, this longer-term objective is often forgotten, but conflicts can arise that, if ignored, can undermine both more long-term development effort *and* the short-term stabilisation measures themselves.

This chapter concentrates on Uganda, whose history since independence has hardly been a shining example. However, the extremities touched by its policies had produced by 1980 a dramatic picture not too dissimilar to other African countries today. Thus, any lessons learnt from Obote's subsequent effort to stabilize and restructure the economy may be usefully applied elsewhere.

UGANDA BEFORE 1980

Since independence in 1962, Uganda's economy has undergone many changes, both in the level of economic activity and its structure. Development has not been a continous process. Indeed, the military regime's mismanagement of the economy in the 1970s

95

led to a dramatic reversal of the process, increasing Uganda's underdevelopment and dependence. Broadly speaking, four distinct periods emerge when a variety of economic indicators are analysed.

1963–71

Between 1963 and 1971, the economy performed impressively, developing steadily and reducing the problems associated with underdevelopment: poverty, ignorance and disease. Looking at Table 7.1 one can see that there was a steady growth in output and income per capita until 1971. Over the period, gross domestic product (at 1966 prices) grew at an average annual rate of 4.5 per cent, from UShs5272 million in 1963 to UShs7497 million in 1971. Since this rate was greater than the estimated population growth rate, real income per capita increased, from UShs694 in 1963 to UShs752 in 1969.

Moreover the structure of the economy was changing, with economic activity becoming broader based, shifting away from agriculture (both monetary and non-monetary) and towards industrial and service-related activities. Looking at Table 7.2, one can see that between 1963 and 1971 the share of agriculture declined by four percentage points, from 53.3 per cent to 49.2 per cent, whilst the share of industry rose from 7.8 per cent to 8.5 per cent and that of services (including those provided by government such as health care and education) increased from 27.0 per cent to 30.1 per cent.

During this period, export volumes generally increased, with the basis for new peak levels being laid for cotton (78,100 tonnes in 1970), coffee (214,200 tonnes in 1972) and tea (20,700 tonnes in 1972). Other non-traditional exports were also flourishing, as diversification started to take place. Almost 17,000 tonnes of copper were exported in 1971 and some manufactured goods were starting to find markets in neighbouring countries.

Finally, the 1969 census revealed a crude death rate of 19 per 1000 and an infant mortality rate of 120 per 1000, both of which represented a steady decline in mortality rates. Unfortunately, no other social indicators are available.

Therefore, one can conclude that between 1963 and 1971, Uganda was growing, restructuring and developing its social services. Significant progress towards its long-term developmental objectives was being made.

1971–77

However, such positive developments were increasingly affected by poor economic management, following Amin's takeover in 1971

Table 7.1: Gross Domestic Product, Population and Gross Domestic Product Per Capita, 1963–84

Year	Gross Domestic Product at 1966 prices		Population (estimates)		Per Capita Gross Domestic Product at 1966 prices	
	Ush. m	% change	Thousands	% change	Ush.	% change
1963	5,272	–	7,602.1	–	693.5	–
1964	5,516	4.6	7,894.7	3.8	698.7	0.7
1965	5,787	4.9	8,198.5	3.8	705.9	1.0
1966	6,119	5.7	8,513.9	3.8	718.7	1.8
1967	6,296	2.9	8,841.5	3.8	712.1	-0.9
1968	6,459	2.6	9,181.7	3.8	703.5	-1.2
1969	7,171	11.0	9,535.1	3.8	752.1	6.9
1970	7,282	1.5	9,793.2	2.7	743.6	-1.1
1971	7,497	3.0	10,058.4	2.7	745.3	0.2
1972	7,542	0.6	10,330.8	2.7	730.0	-2.1
1973	7,496	-0.6	10,610.5	2.7	706.5	-3.2
1974	7,509	0.2	10,897.8	2.7	689.0	-2.5
1975	7,357	-2.0	11,192.9	2.7	657.3	-4.6
1976	7,411	0.7	11,496.0	2.7	644.7	-1.9
1977	7,527	1.6	11,807.2	2.7	637.5	-1.1
1978	7,181	-4.6	12,126.9	2.7	592.2	-7.1
1979	6,330	-11.9	12,455.3	2.7	508.2	-14.2
1980	6,115	-3.4	12,792.6	2.7	478.0	-5.9
1981	6,351	3.9	13,143.8	2.8	483.2	1.1
1982	6,873	8.2	13,513.1	2.8	508.6	5.3
1983	7,207	4.9	13,893.6	2.8	518.7	2.0
1984	7,582	5.2	14,280.2	2.8	530.9	2.4

Sources: IBRD Country Economic Memorandum (1982), Table 2.2 pp.129/130 Background to the Budget 1985/86 Table 1, p. 44; Table 35, p. 79.

Table 7.2: The Changing Structure of the Economy, 1963–84 (selected years)

Industry	1963		1971		1977		1980		1984	
	USh.m	%	USh.m	%	USh.m	%	USh.m	%	USh.m	%
Monetary Sector										
Agriculture (1)	1,334	25.5	1,727	23.1	1,675	22.3	1,334	21.8	1,711	22.6
Mining and Quarrying	103	2.0	112	1.5	21	0.3	6	0.1	10	0.1
Industry (2)	412	7.8	638	8.5	480	6.4	26	4.3	306	4.0
Electricity	47	0.9	100	1.3	92	1.2	70	1.3	91	1.2
Construction	97	1.8	95	1.3	45	0.6	25	0.4	35	0.5
Transport and Communications	175	3.3	323	4.3	266	3.5	168	2.7	214	2.8
Services (3)	1,421	27.0	2,257	30.1	2,178	28.9	1,950	31.9	2,231	29.4
Sub-Total	3,599	68.3	5,252	70.1	4,757	63.2	3,822	62.5	4,598	60.6
Non-monetary Sector										
Agriculture (1)	1,469	27.8	1,960	26.1	2,422	32.2	1,943	31.8	2,609	34.4
Others (4)	204	3.9	285	3.8	348	4.6	350	5.7	375	5.0
Sub-Total	1,673	31.7	2,245	29.9	2,770	36.8	2,293	37.5	2,984	39.4
Gross Domestic Product (5)	5,272	100.0	7,497	100.0	7,527	100.0	6,115	100.0	7,582	100.0

Notes: 1) Includes Forestry, Fishing and Hunting
2) Includes Cotton Ginning, Coffee Curing, Sugar Manufacture, Manufacture of Food Products and Miscellaneous Manufacturing
3) Includes Commerce, Government, Miscellaneous Services and Rents
4) Includes Construction and Owner-occupied Dwellings
5) At factor cost and in 1966 prices.

Sources: IBRD Country Economic Memorandum (1982) Table 2.2, pp. 129/130
Background to the Budget 1985/86 Table 1, p. 44

and his subsequent declaration of 'economic war'. This 'war' led to the departure of many skilled persons, notably important Asian families who dominated industrial and commercial activities and, increasingly, qualified Ugandans and aid-financed technical assistance personnel.

Consequently, the performance of the economy became erratic and growth marginal. Between 1971 and 1977, economic activity increased by only 0.4 per cent as GDP increased from UShs7497 million to UShs7527 million. This 1977 level was below the peak achieved in 1972. Although according to the 1980 census the population growth rate also slowed, the extent of the slowdown in economic activity was such that per capita income fell to UShs638 by 1977, at an average annual rate of 1.8 per cent from its peak level.

Previous structural changes also started to be reversed. Subsistence agriculture grew sharply in relative importance to account for 32.2 per cent of economic activity in 1977, whilst as one might expect the importance of industry, services and monetary agriculture declined. As the monetary economy faltered under the burden of poor economic management placed on it by the military regime, there was a retreat into subsistence activities.

Export earnings started to depend more and more heavily upon coffee and its officially exported volume fell to 132,400 tonnes in 1977, 62 per cent of its peak level. Cotton exports declined precipitously from a peak of 78,100 tonnes in 1971 to only 9,900 tonnes in 1977. Also tea exports dropped to 8,800 tonnes as bushes were left to grow unpruned. Imports were thus increasingly dependent on one export and its price, and the decline in import volumes adversely affected economic activity, notably in the industrial and transport sectors given their dependence on imported inputs.

1977–80

After 1977, the economy collapsed. The economic chaos engendered by eight years of military mismanagement of the economy was followed by a war to free the country and eighteen months of political instability. Looking at Table 7.1, one can see that between 1977 and 1980 GDP declined by 18.8 per cent to a nadir of UShs6115 million, or at an average annual rate of 5.9 per cent over those three years. Even more disastrous was the accelerating decline in living standards: per capita income fell from UShs638 in 1977 to UShs478 in 1980, or by 25.0 per cent to a level only 68.9 per cent of its 1963 level!

Perverse structural changes continued. In particular, the decline in monetary activities, whose share fell to 62.5 per cent in 1980, and the increase in subsistence ones. Monetary agriculture, industry and transport and communications once again fell in importance whilst monetary construction joined mining and quarrying as a marginal activity. Comparison with 1971 reveals a halving in the importance of industry (to 4.3 per cent) since this sector was particularly vulnerable to the dislocation that occurred, given its dependence on imported inputs, skilled management and organized marketing channels. In general, compared with 1971, there was a narrowing in the range of significant economic activities.

The export picture was also bleak. By 1980, Uganda depended on one crop, coffee, for 98 per cent of its export earnings as cotton (at 2300 tonnes), tea (at 500 tonnes) and tobacco (at a mere 300 tonnes) exports became negligible and copper exports ceased. Even the volume of (official) coffee exports had declined to only 110,100 tonnes, a level barely half the 1972 peak.

By 1980, not only had economic activity declined precipitously: the foundations of past and future development had also been seriously eroded. The co-operatives and marketing boards had ceased to function effectively. Roads started to crack up through lack of maintenance to such an extent that their reconstruction was required. The rail network also deteriorated. Industries that had been painstakingly established ceased to function, as machines wore out or became technologically obsolete; as spare parts were no longer imported; and skilled manpower was no longer available. Vital social infrastructure such as schools, hospitals, clinics, boreholes and urban water and sewerage systems deteriorated, instead of being improved to meet the greater needs of a growing population. Morale declined in the public services as numbers employed increased but real wages and facilities did not. Army and police discipline fell to unacceptable levels. In the Liberation War, three towns were so badly damaged as to require major reconstruction programmes.

The need to rebuild these foundations was the longer-term aspect of the crisis Uganda faced in 1980. In addition, the economy had to adjust to the two increases in oil prices that occurred in the 1970s, such adjustment having been postponed through controlled domestic prices. Also, the break-up of the East African Community and its shared services, especially East African Railways, precipitated the need to urgently invest in wholly Ugandan entities. Such investment was far from complete by 1980.

In the short term, stabilization measures were required to correct the disequilibrium between aggregate demand and supply, caused by financial indiscipline as well as the collapse in real supply outlined above. Past attempts to increase supply through importation had left very large short-term and medium-term commercial debts and external arrears, both of which had either to be repaid or rescheduled.

Moreover, attempts to control the prices of traditional exports and most consumer goods together with interest rate and credit controls had led to significant black market activity, (e.g., coffee smuggling, petroleum products re-exportation) that further undermined the government's solvency, resulting in an economic crisis of unprecedented proportions.

UGANDA: 1980 AND AFTER

Following the election of December 1980, a UPC government was formed, headed by Dr Apolo Milton Obote, who was also Minister of Finance. Quite radical measures followed, to reverse the catastrophic decline in economic activity, to increase the efficiency of resource allocation and to reverse the erosion of the accumulated infrastructure of the economy. Moreover, the government recognized the longer-term need to restructure the economy away from further dependence on agricultural activities, and in particular quota-constrained coffee (as the sole export and principal source of taxation).

Six complementary policies were adopted as a package aiming to achieve financial stability, greater efficiency and recovery insofar as this was possible in the short term.

I. A flexible exchange rate

In December 1980, the *official* exchange rate was about UShs7 1/2 to the US dollar. However, since the country's reserves were minimal, its main exports were smuggled or stored when produced (with official exports only half their peak level) and smuggled re-exports of petroleum products were significant, the official market was of small relevance to the majority of traders. The unofficial, or 'kibanda' rate was by that time over ten times the official rate. Customs duties and export duties were undermined, as the majority of international transactions passed through the unofficial market. Efficiency was impaired and the opportunities for corruption in allocation were rife.

In recognition of this, and as a precondition for IMF standby credits subsequently agreed, a flexible exchange rate was introduced in the June 1981 budget. The rate immediately floated to UShs78 to the US dollar and subsequently depreciated steadily to UShs98 to the US dollar in August 1982. Nevertheless, the 'kibanda' rate was still four to five times this official rate. In order to undermine this unofficial market further, and to provide foreign

Table 7.3: Merchandise Exports, 1966–84
(thousands of tonnes)

Year	Coffee	Cotton	Tea	Tobacco	Maize	Copper
1966	167.1	69.8	9.0	2.5	–	15.8
1967	159.5	72.0	9.6	2.9	–	15.0
1968	151.6	61.7	11.4	2.1	–	15.6
1969	180.6	52.9	15.9	2.4	–	16.6
1970	191.2	78.1	15.1	2.0	–	16.4
1971	174.6	68.7	15.3	2.2	–	16.8
1972	214.2	66.1	20.7	2.5	–	14.1
1973	192.4	64.7	19.2	1.5	–	9.7
1974	187.2	36.2	16.7	1.1	–	9.0
1975	176.6	25.6	17.1	1.3	–	7.8
1976	153.1	19.2	11.7	1.1	–	5.4
1977	132.4	9.9	8.8	1.8	–	2.5
1978	113.7	11.7	8.7	1.2	–	7.1
1979	143.1	3.6	1.4	0.4	–	4.4
1980	110.1	2.3	0.5	0.3	–	–
1981	128.3	1.2	0.5	–	–	–
1982	174.7	1.8	1.2	–	1.6	–
1983	144.3	7.0	1.3	0.7	30.3	–
1984	133.2	6.7	2.5	n.a.	29.7	–

Sources: IBRD Country Economic Memorandum (1982) Table 3.2, pp. 135/136
Background to the Budget 1985/86 Table 3, p. 46.

exchange in a timely manner to importers with cash, a dual exchange system was introduced in August 1982.

The lower rate (called Window I) was used to import oil, to repay debts, and for government and other priority imports. It was slowly depreciated by a committee, whilst the higher rate (called Window II) was determined by a weekly auction. All export proceeds (except those from coffee and cotton) were convertable at the Window II rate, providing a significant incentive for the exportation of other products through official channels. The two rates were merged in June 1984 at the rate of UShs300 to the US dollar, though the auction system was retained almost unmodified until November. By then, the rate was UShs550 to the US dollar, following a very sharp depreciation in the second half of 1984.

The adoption of this flexible exchange rate policy was heavily criticized by the opposition parties in Uganda, as it is when proposed to many African countries with inflexible exchange rate regimes, e.g. Tanzania. However, in view of the extensive and very damaging black market activity that it was beyond the ability of the government to control, flexibility seems a necessary condition for a recovery in traditional exports (though not a sufficient one). It was (see Table 7.3) notably successful in the case of coffee, and it seems in general to have been a necessary condition to reduce 'kibanda' activities. Its role in increasing government revenues, both directly and indirectly, was very significant, and greatly eased the need to resort to deficit financing.

In particular, the dual system had many advantages, allowing petroleum prices to increase slowly without explicit subsidization and reducing the shilling magnitude of debt servicing, as well as having the political advantage of allowing allocation of some foreign exchange at a preferable rate whilst simultaneously allowing a 'float' or 'free-market' rate to be determined. Finally, and not least, it allowed agreement to be reached with the IMF and so access to significant donor funds.

However, two valid criticisms of the policy measure can be made. First, even though many retail prices were set with regard to the 'kibanda' rate, in line with the scarcity of the goods, retail prices did increase following the float, eroding the income of those on fixed incomes. Especially adversely affected were civil servants and industrial workers, including those in the large parastatal sector. Black market earnings were also squeezed, as transactions and the margins fell. Second, the industrial sector, with minimal stocks to revalue, low production levels and a reluctance to revalue assets, saw its working capital eroded. Since access to credit was also tight, attempts to rehabilitate this sector in pursuit of longer-term aims were often frustrated by its inability to purchase foreign exchange, even when this had been allocated from donor credits. Ignoring these criticisms had repercussions on the flexible exchange rate policy after the merger of the two rates.

II. Regular increases in minimum producer prices of traditional exports

Producer prices for a number of traditional exports were increased. For example, the price paid for robusta coffee rose from UShs7 per kg in April 1981 to UShs210 per kg in October 1984. The producer prices were based on regular surveys of farm costs, allowing a 20 per cent margin for 'profit'. The aims, to encourage the production and rehabilitation of cash crops and to curtail their smuggling, were largely achieved. The marketed production of coffee rose from 97,500 tonnes in 1981 to 138,700 tonnes in 1984; that of cotton from 4100 tonnes in 1981 to 12,200 tonnes in 1984 and that of tea from 1700 tonnes in 1981 to 5,200 tonnes in 1984. Smuggling of coffee was very much reduced. These regular reviews were necessary to provide incentives to farmers to produce and market their cash crops through official channels, and the response of farmers was positive and significant. By 1982, official purchases of coffee were limited more by the ICO quota than a lack of marketed output at the government's minimum producer prices.

III. Price controls for most other commodities were removed

Since price controls were in the main ineffectual, their removal made little difference to the general price level. However, those who had previously had access to controlled price commodities did suffer income losses. The equity effect in countries where such controls are effective would of course be greater.

IV. The taxation structure was rationalized

Various rationalizations were made to the tax structure. In particular, specific import duties were replaced by ad valorem rates, sales tax rates on imports and domestic production were equalized, and increases in the effective rates of sales tax and excise duties on a number of major revenue producing items were implemented. In an inflationary situation, the move to ad valorem rates allows, to some extent, government to index its revenue, whilst maintaining constant real taxation levels. This rationalization led to customs duty, excise duty and sales tax collection increasing from UShs1.7 billion in 1980/81 to UShs30.5 billion in 1983/84.

V. The introduction of more remunerative and flexible interest rates

Restructuring of interest rates was not pursued as vigorously as the other policies: throughout the period real interest rates remained significantly negative. Thus to the debate on financial repression, the experience of Uganda can add very little.

VI. Credit ceilings

Finally, starting in May 1981, ceilings were imposed on the budget deficit, government borrowing and domestic credit expansion in the context of three consecutive standby agreements with the IMF. By the end of June 1984, when the last agreement ended, net purchases totalling US$305 million had been made, allowing the balance of payments deficit (which totalled US$224 million) to be financed and reserves to be accumulated. Moreover, the ceilings were the most important part of the government's stabilization effort and it was within their framework that the fight to re-assert control over government expenditure and inflation was fought. Although simple regression analysis fails to find a significant relationship between measures of the money supply and inflation, time series graphs strongly suggest one exists. Inflation declined from an annual rate of over 100 per cent in April 1982 to 16 per cent in June 1984, when monetary growth, in particular net borrowing by the government (and so, in turn its expenditure), was limited by the ceilings agreed with the IMF. In the following fiscal year (1984/85) when no such ceilings were agreed (principally because of the acceptance of the criticisms listed below), monetary growth and government expenditure (notably recurrent) accelerated in an uncontrolled manner, in association with a resurgence of inflation (to an annual rate of 141 per cent by May 1985).

Like the flexible exchange rate policy, the imposition of ceilings was criticized. Ignoring the debate over the role of monetary aggregates in explaining inflation, which cannot be resolved by examining the Ugandan case (suggestive though the evidence is), three criticisms should be noted. First, though they effectively limited expenditure, they did not discriminate between different types of expenditure: in particular, development and recurrent expenditures were treated alike. Many examples occurred of development projects being delayed or halted through lack of the necessary counterpart funding from government. Often external disbursements of aid funds failed to occur because of this or because of the government's inability to guarantee timely disbursements in the face of these ceilings. In this way the ceilings frustrated the efforts to correct the longer-term aspects of the crisis and in some cases urgent remedial work required to increase production was significantly delayed. Secondly, the need of marketing boards for timely access to credit to procure export crops sometimes led to conflict with the ceilings, given the seasonality of such demands. Speedy payment of the farmers was essential if the producer price incentives were to have the required result, but delays were in evidence due to the quarterly ceiling on domestic credit expansion. Finally, as mentioned above, the industrial sector required access to credit to compensate for the effects of the float on its working capital, but satisfaction of this need proved difficult in the context of a ceiling on domestic credit. Again, the longer-term aim of rehabilitation was frustrated.

As well as these six policies aiming at dealing with the short-term aspects of the crisis, three other notable policies were implemented to attempt to deal with the longer-term aspects of the crisis.

First, the Expropriated Properties Act was passed in 1983 in an attempt to resolve ownership disputes over properties 'abandoned' or 'expropriated' under Amin. Uncertain ownership was a limiting factor on credit access, especially for some major industrial enterprises.

Secondly, technical assistance was sought from abroad for government ministries and important parastatals, in recognition of the skilled manpower gap. In addition, training programmes for Ugandans, both at home and abroad, were initiated, in particular for those personnel working in the three central control ministries: Finance, Planning and Economic Development, and the Bank of Uganda.

Finally, and most importantly, strenuous efforts were made by the government to mobilize resources for priority projects to rehabilitate the productive structure of the economy. In April 1982, the government presented to donors in Paris a Recovery Programme, which was subsequently revised in October 1983. This development plan was for three years initially and listed close to one hundred projects, with planned expenditure totalling US$828 million (if one excludes expenditure incurred before mid-1982 and that to take place after the three-year period). Donors welcomed this project-based approach and responded positively. Looking at Table 7.4, one can see that by the end of June 1985, donors had committed about US$1.1 billion to these selected projects. However, disbursements in each year were less than planned, partly because of the problems involved in mobilizing counterpart funding outlined above and partly because of slower than anticipated government and donor procedures. Nevertheless, over the three years the implementation ratio averaged 57 per cent, with close to US$600 million having been spent in total, a significant investment yielding dividends by 1984/85.

Table 7.4: Mobilisation and Utilisation of Resources for Development

Resources allocated to:	Funds Secured US$m	Disbursements US$m Pre-June 1982	1982/83	1983/84	1984/85 (Estimates)	Total to 30.6.85	Undisbursed 30.6.85	Planned Expenditure US$m 1982/83 (RP)	1983/84 (RRP)	1984/85 (RRP)	Total (RRP)	Implementation Ratio% 1982/83	1983/84	1984/85	1982-85
a) all coded projects in:															
i) Agriculture	306.6	30.7	50.4	36.9	39.7	157.7	148.9	78.9	64.78	94.60	238.28	63.8	56.9	42.0	53.3
ii) Industry and Tourism	293.1	30.2	30.5	28.6	45.3	134.6	158.5	62.2	73.25	92.70	228.15	49.0	39.0	48.9	45.8
iii) Mining and Energy	17.6	0.6	1.0	2.3	4.4	8.3	9.3	15.8	12.27	13.53	41.60	6.2	19.0	32.1	18.4
iv) Transport and Communications	242.7	36.8	17.6	50.9	55.2	160.5	82.2	41.7	38.10	68.40	148.20	42.3	133.6	80.7	83.5
v) Social Infrastructure	234.8	31.9	27.7	30.1	37.4	127.1	107.7	42.5	32.18	76.78	171.46	65.0	57.7	48.8	55.5
vi) Public Administration	13.7	0.4	2.4	3.8	3.1	9.7	4.0	–	–	–	–	–	–	–	–
Sub-total (a)	1,108.5	130.6	129.6	152.6	185.1	597.9	510.6	241.1	240.58	346.01	827.69	53.7	63.4	53.5	56.5
of which															
External	989.1	108.1	97.2	127.6	152.4	485.3	503.8	–	–	–	–	–	–	–	–
(Loans)	(715.5)	(76.6)	(61.7)	(79.1)	(97.0)	(314.4)	(401.1)	–	–	–	–	–	–	–	–
(Grants)	(273.6)	(31.5)	(35.5)	(48.5)	(55.4)	(170.9)	(102.7)	–	–	–	–	–	–	–	–
Domestic	119.4	22.5	32.4	25.0	32.7	112.6	6.9	–	–	–	–	–	–	–	–
(Budget Releases)	(85.5)	(22.2)	(31.4)	(20.3)	(11.7)	(85.6)	(–)	–	–	–	–	–	–	–	–
(Project account drawdowns) (2)	(33.9)	(0.3)	(1.0)	(4.7)	(21.0)	(27.0)	(6.9)	–	–	–	–	–	–	–	–
b) Development Budget Projects (1)	173.1	n.a.	70.2	33.9	69.0	173.1	–	n.a.	n.a.	n.a.	n.a.	n.a.	n.a.	n.a.	n.a.
c) Commodity Aid (1)	180.6	110.5	29.0	21.3	6.5	167.3	13.3	–	–	–	–	–	–	–	–
d) Project Aid (1)	73.6	10.1	19.7	2.5	3.9	36.2	37.4	–	–	–	–	–	–	–	–
e) Technical Assistance (1)	24.0	4.7	1.0	1.0	7.1	13.8	10.2	–	–	–	–	–	–	–	–
f) Balance of Payments Support (1)	446.3	222.7	141.3	59.7	-34.5	389.2	57.1	–	30.00	30.00	60.00	–	–	–	–
Total Resources	2,006.1	478.6	390.8	271.0	237.1	1,377.5	628.6	–	–	–	–	–	–	–	–
of which															
External	1,713.3	456.0	288.1	212.1	135.3	1,091.5	621.7	–	–	–	–	–	–	–	–
(Loans)	(1,181.4)	(246.5)	(217.5)	(133.8)	(70.9)	(668.7)	(512.7)	–	–	–	–	–	–	–	–
(Grants)	(531.9)	(209.5)	(70.6)	(78.3)	(64.4)	(422.8)	(109.1)	–	–	–	–	–	–	–	–
Domestic	292.8	22.6	102.7	58.9	101.8	286.0	6.9	–	–	–	–	–	–	–	–
(Budget Releases)	(258.9)	(22.3)	(101.7)	(54.2)	(80.0)	(259.0)	(–)	–	–	–	–	–	–	–	–
(Project account drawdowns) (2)	(33.9)	(0.3)	(1.0)	(4.7)	(21.0)	(27.0)	(6.9)	–	–	–	–	–	–	–	–

Notes: 1) Excluding that associated with coded projects and so included in sub-total (a).
2) i.e. from the shilling equivalents generated by the purchase of aid inputs.

Source: Ministry of Planning and Economic Development

The net result of these measures was mixed. By June 1984 inflation had fallen to around 20 per cent and the current account was in surplus for the first time since Liberation. External arrears were steadily being repaid and debts had been rescheduled to reduce debt servicing to manageable proportions. Thus the short-term goal of financial stability had been more or less achieved by June 1984.

On the supply side, economic activity had grown continuously since its 1980 low-point. By 1984, Uganda's gross domestic product had attained a new peak level of UShs7582 million. Given the deteriorating international situation over much of the period and the precipitous decline in the country's infrastructure in the Amin period, this was a remarkable achievement. Average annual GDP growth over the period 1980–4 was 5.5 per cent, leading to positive annual per capital income growth averaging 2.7 per cent, the first growth in living standards since 1971. Furthermore, the significant investments undertaken in Recovery Programme projects and the undisbursed balances secured from donors suggest that the foundations of future growth and development were being laid.

At the sector level, the recovery had been uneven, leading to further changes in the structure of the economy. Subsistence agriculture continued to scale new peaks as can be seen from Table 7.2. In 1984, it accounted for 34.4 per cent total GDP and the non-monetary sector taken as a whole for 39.4 per cent. Monetary agriculture, with the recovery in cash crop production, had since 1980 started to increase in relative importance, in contrast to its previous trend. However, industry continued to decline, so that by 1984 it accounted for only 4.0 per cent of GDP.

Finally, the composition of exports had started once again to become more diversified as their shilling returns increased as the exchange rate depreciated. In addition to the recovery in traditional exports, 30,000 tonnes of maize was exported in 1984 and beans, simsim (sesame), and hides and skins were becoming significant exports.

Unfortunately, frustration stemming from the impact of the measures on longer-term objectives led to policy changes in the 1984/85 fiscal year. The government's stance shifted radically to an expansionary one, ostensibly in order to restore public servants' living standards (wages and salaries were increased on average three and a half times, and allowances were similarly increased) and to allow for a significant increase in development expenditure (but much of this was not connected with the priority projects included in the Revised Recovery Programme). Such an expansion in expenditure occurred at a time when no agreement had been reached with the IMF for further funds for the first time since May 1981 – indeed significant repurchases had to be made in 1984/85, reducing the amount of foreign exchange available to meet the increase in demand; no increase in the coffee quota allocated to Uganda was anticipated, so further dramatic increases in revenue from this source were unlikely; the non-bank sector (notably the marketing boards and government suppliers) held an unprecedently large amount of Treasury Bills that they were likely to want redeemed in 1984/85; and increases in the efficiency of the collection of other taxes were only occurring slowly.

Consequently, net borrowing by government from the banking sector (and all other monetary aggregates) rose sharply, by 128.5 per cent from UShs41.8 billion in June 1984 to UShs95.6 billion in March 1985 (whereas it had *fallen* in 1983/84 from UShs45.0 billion) and this was associated with the re-emergence of growing financial instability as inflation accelerated (to an annual rate of 141 per cent by May 1985) and the exchange rate sharply depreciated following the merger of the two windows, reaching a rate of UShs600 to the US dollar in November 1984 (after which its 'flexibility' resulting from the weekly auctions was significantly reduced so that it remained around UShs600 to the US dollar until the July 1985 coup).

The return of such instability resulted from the failure to refine the policies pursued (especially the exchange rate and credit ceiling policies) to meet the criticisms levied. For example, by applying selective expenditure and credit controls, by offering selected, skilled employees wage increases and by continuing with the dual system. Frustration at the resulting conflicts led to the government's over-reaction in 1984/85.

Conclusion

The lesson to be drawn from Uganda's experience under Obote is that the stabilization measures outlined above when complemented by strenuous efforts to mobilize funds to rehabilitate, expand and diversify productive potential can yield substantial benefits if adopted when facing crises like the one Uganda faced in 1980. However, careful consideration is required where conflicts arise between policies aimed at dealing with different aspects of the crisis. For the frustration of longer-term objectives, in particular by some aspects of the flexible exchange rate policy (notably the merger of the two rates in June 1984) and that of strict and indiscriminate credit ceilings, undermined stabilization efforts in the final year of Obote's second term, leading once again to financial instability and crisis. By July 1985, in terms of inflation and to a lesser extent the balance of payments, the situation was once again similar to that of

December 1980. Avoidance of such a reversal is probably the most important lesson to be learnt from Obote's second term.

EIGHT

Agriculture-led recovery in post-Amin Uganda:
The causes of failure and the bases for success

Deryke Belshaw[1]

INTRODUCTION

This chapter focuses on the question of the design of the short-term strategy for economic stabilization and recovery after a period of severe disequilibrium, with a parallel economy arising to challenge the hegemony of the officially controlled sector. After the ravages of the Amin government from 1971 to 1979, Uganda was faced with just such a situation (see Commonwealth Secretariat, 1979; Green, 1981). The period 1981–5 saw an attempt to apply one such stabilization strategy. After early indications of success, particularly against the parallel or *magendo* economy, it lost momentum and internal support. By 1985 it was clear that the attempt had failed to meet its objectives. The new government that came into power in early 1986 under President Yoweri Museveni was now faced with an economic situation at least as difficult as that left behind by Amin. The careful analysis of the 1981–5 experiment, therefore, is of vital importance to the design of a successful new strategy. Explicit analysis is particularly necessary since the widespread revulsion at the unlawful activities of the security forces under the two governments in power between 1981 and 1986 may quite understandably lead to a rejection of all economic policy components of the failed strategy. The lessons that analysis may draw from Uganda's failed 'experiment' are likely to have a wider relevance, especially to other African countries facing similar reconstruction problems, whether more or less severe than Uganda's. This group of countries currently includes Angola, Ghana, Madagascar, Mozambique, Somalia, Tanzania and Zambia.

Whatever the long-term development options, the Ugandan economy in the post-Amin situation desperately needs to increase imports in order to restore the real consumption levels of all its citizens to previously experienced levels. Imports are required of direct consumables, raw materials and intermediate products for the run-down domestic industrial sector, and capital goods and fuel for transport and other infrastructure. The most important way of

Table 8.1: Selected Economic Development Indicators: Uganda, 1979–85

	1979	1980	1981	1982	1983	1984	1985
Rate of annual growth of GDP (%)	–12.6	0.3	5.5	8.2	4.9	5.2	0.6
General price index (1966=100)	1702	3527	6800	9581	13097	–	–
Kampala Middle-Income Consumer Price Index (Apr. 1981 = 100) year average	–	–	156	200	248	343	800
Annual change in CPIs (%)							
(a) 1966 = 100	86	107	93	45	33	–	–
(b) 1981 = 100	–	–	56	28	24	38	133[1]
Exchange rate UShs: US$							
annual average	n.a.	7.4	502	94.5	250.0	300.0	677.5
beginning of period	–	–	7.6	86.0[2] 99.2[3] 300.0[1]	107.0[2] 235.0[6]	241.4[2] 299.1[8] 307.2[2]	540[10] 1500(e)[11]
end of period	86.6	98.7	104.8	240.0	233.8	302.5	292.3 326.4 551.6 1400 3500(e)

Sources: Government of Uganda, *Background to the Budget* (various years)

World Bank (1985) *Uganda: Progress Towards Recovery and Prospects for Development.* Washington D.C.

Notes:
1/ The equivalent change for the Kampala low income CPI was 147.1
2/ Unified rates, Jan-July 1982
3/ Window 1 rates, Aug-Dec 1982
4/ Window 2 rates, Aug-Dec 1982
5/ Window 1 rates, Jan-Dec 1983
6/ Window 2 rates, Jan-Dec 1983
7/ Window 1 rates, Jan-May 1984
8/ Window 2 rates, Jan-May 1984
9/ Unified rates, June-Dec 1984
10/ Unified rates, Jan-Dec 1985
11/ Unofficial rates, Jan-Dec 1985
(e) author's estimates

financing imports, particularly when aid and international finance are in short supply, is through merchandise exports. In Uganda the only short-term source of export earnings is the primary sector drawing on the country's relatively abundant, fertile and reliable natural resource endowment. Inevitably, in the short term, particular attention falls upon the major export-earning cash crops of the period to 1970, where there are underemployed production assets, skills and processing capacity that can be utilized to achieve rapid increases in foreign exchange earnings. These crops are coffee, cotton and tea. An equally important role for agriculture exists in increasing the production of import-substituting commodities, where significant foreign exchange savings can be diverted to meet other priority import requirements. Because of their relatively large and price-insensitive domestic demand, sugar and, to a lesser extent, vegetable oils are the major items in this category.

The intention here is to connect analysis of the macroeconomic framework, at the level well-treated within a broader historical framework by Keith Edmonds in Chapter 7, with the microeconomic, technical and institutional factors in the agricultural sector where, it is argued, the crux for the ultimate success of the 1981–5 stabilization strategy lay. The implications for a second economic stabilization strategy for Uganda, and the more general implications for countries in broadly similar situations, are discussed in the final section.

PERFORMANCE UNDER THE SECOND OBOTE GOVERNMENT

In Table 8.1 a few key indicators give a clear picture of the trajectory followed by the recorded economy in the seven-year period 1979–85. The GDP growth data and price indices indicate the economic stagnation combined with hyperinflation experienced in 1979–80 and the second collapse in 1985, which has continued to today. Both periods, however, are associated with the rise of the parallel or *magendo* economy. As this is poorly reflected in the official statistics, the decline in total economic activity indicated in Table 8.1 is exaggerated. A further flaw in the statistical record is that the estimates for the so-called subsistence economy relate not only to autoconsumption at the household level but also a significant quantity of unrecorded monetary transactions within the rural economy.

Nevertheless, these indicators adequately monitor the degree of success achieved by the government, i.e. the restoration of growth in the official, recorded sector at the expense of the parallel economy and the conquest of hyperinflation. The changes in both consumer prices and exchange rates suggest that by the first half of 1984 the

Table 8.2: Selected Balance of Payments Variables: Uganda, 1979—85 (US $m.)

	1979	1980	1981	1982	1983	1984	1985
Merchandise exports	397	319	246	347	368	408	379
Merchandise imports	-322	-504	-415	-422	-428	-342	-264
Grants, loans and net IMF credits	n.a.	n.a.	215	179	249	105	4
Overall balance of payments	n.a.	n.a.	-118	-33	-36	159	67[1]
Financial reserves (end of year)	17	4	25	60	87	65(e)	30(e)
Accumulated arrears (end of year)	116	257	217	240	248	281(e)	309(e)

Sources: Government of Uganda, *Background to the Budget* (various years)

Notes: (e): Author's estimate

1/ The improvement in the overall balance of payments was more than offset by the repayment of the short-term IMF credits received in the period 1980–83; there was no IMF agreement between March 1984 and April 1987.

Table 8.3: Officially Marketed Output of Principal Cash Crops: Uganda, 1978/79–1984/85
('000 metric tons)

	1978/79	1979/80	1980/81	1981/82	1982/83	1983/84	1984/85	Increase 1978/79–1984/85 (%)
Coffee (all types)	103.0	135.2	97.5	166.6	157.4	138.7	155.0	50.5
Coffee (robusta)	98.3	130.4	93.0	152.3	142.8	128.6	144.4	46.9
Coffee (arabica)	4.7	4.8	4.5	14.3	14.6	10.1	10.6	127.7
Cotton (lint)	7.6	6.1	4.1	5.1	9.8	12.2	14.4	89.5
Tea (made)	1.8	1.5	1.7	2.6	3.1	5.2	5.6	211.1
Tobacco (cured)	0.8	0.4	0.1	0.6	1.6	1.9	1.3	62.5
Sugar (raw)	5.2	4.3	3.7	4.6	3.1	2.9	0.8	–84.6

Sources: Government of Uganda, *Background to the Budget* (various years). World Bank (1985) *Uganda: Progress towards Recovery and Prospects for Development*. Washington D.C.

Note: Figures for coffee and cotton are on a crop year basis (October–September) and for tobacco, tea and sugar are on a fiscal year basis (July–June)

Table 8.4: Composition of Merchandise Exports: Uganda, 1979–85

	1979	1980	1981	1982	1983	1984	1985
Volume ('000 metric tons)							
Coffee	143.1	110.1	128.3	174.7	144.3	133.2	151.5
Cotton	3.6	2.3	1.2	1.8	7.0	6.7	9.6
Tea	1.4	0.5	0.5	1.2	1.3	2.5	1.2
Tobacco	0.4	0.3	–	–	0.7	0.7	0.3
Maize	–	–	–	1.6	30.3	29.7	9.8
Value (US $ m.)							
Coffee	425.9	338.7	241.6	341.0	339.7	359.0	344.0
Cotton	6.4	4.3	2.2	3.3	11.6	12.4	15.4
Tea	1.4	0.3	0.3	0.8	1.2	3.2	1.0
Tobacco	0.9	0.3	–	–	0.9	1.5	0.5
Maize	–	–	–	0.6	11.3	10.1	3.1
Other exports	5.1	2.2	2.5	0.7	2.1	6.6	4.3
Total (adjusted)	439.7	345.8	246.6	346.4	366.8	392.8	379.3
Coffee as % of total value	96.9	97.9	98.0	98.4	92.6	91.4	90.7

Source: Government of Uganda, *Background to the Budget* (various years).

battle against inflation had been won; for a few months the annual equivalent rate of inflation was probably in single figures. Economic growth, assisted by an improvement in international coffee prices in 1982, had been restored to at least a reasonable pace.

The second collapse was reflected most quickly in the exchange rate for the second half of 1984. This corroborates the view that the three and a half-fold increase in the public sector wage bill of July 1984 was immensely inflationary: rising defence expenditure and financial indiscipline by ministers with the commencement of the election run-up are widely viewed as contributory factors. Also, the increases in the coffee producer price in 1983 and 1984 were greater than required on the basis of economic considerations alone.

On the other hand, the tight control up to this time of increases in public sector wages had been a consequence of controls on money supply enforced under the IMF standby credit arrangements. While this contributed significantly to the decline in inflation rates, it did so at the marked expense of the living standards of fixed-income workers. The inevitable pressure for redress overrode economic analyses, which suggested that a more gradual adjustment was needed. If the sudden increase in wages in 1984 was a major policy error, so also were the failures to ameliorate gradually the fall in real wages and to reduce the size of the civil service in 1982 and 1983. It is argued here that if the performance of the output side of the economy in 1981–3 had been closer to what was attainable, there could have been some improvement in real wages at an earlier date, through a combination of increased budget expenditure and improved consumer supplies. These would have obviated the self-destructive wage increases of 1984.[2] Why was the supply-side performance of the economy not considerably better than it was?

Table 8.2 presents data for selected variables from the balance of payments accounts for the period 1979–85. These suggest that the economic strategy had already run out of steam by 1983, when export earnings had still failed to reach even the 1979 current dollar level of earnings. It is true that enhanced coffee producer prices, financed through depreciation of the Uganda shilling, had enabled the official market to recapture a large part of smuggled exports by 1982 (see Tables 8.3 and 8.4). But this still left the economy dangerously dependent for foreign exchange earnings on the output and official sales of this one commodity. Coffee did not contribute less than 90 per cent of the value of total merchandise exports throughout the period. The output level had begun to suffer from the destructiveness of security operations in the Luwero area in the coffee–banana zone by 1983/84; 20,000 to 25,000 tonnes output is estimated to have been lost each year since then. The economy was also very dependent on the probity of the marketing board officials, who were selling the crop through a system of direct sales treaties rather than putting them through an open auction system such as that operating in Kenya (Kakooza-Semanda and Schluter, 1986). By 1984 the repayment of the IMF's short-term credits, and the decision not to seek new ones, had begun to reduce the total value of external capital transfers (Table 8.2). This, combined with the continued sluggishness of exports, was reflected in a 20 per cent fall in the dollar value of imports and by deterioration in the financial reserves and accumulated arrears positions.

Compared with the rehabilitation strategies envisaged by the Commonwealth Secretariat team in 1979, and the World Bank in 1982, the primary deviations and probable main causes of failure were the low output and exports of cotton and tea and the low output and poor import-substituting performance of sugar (Tables 8.3 and 8.4). These shortfalls were far from being compensated for by increases in other exports, such as the well-publicized sales of maize in 1983 and 1984. Commodities other than coffee, cotton, and tea never reached 5.0 per cent of total export value throughout the period; in 1985 they amounted to only 2.1 per cent of the total.

The highest output recorded for cotton in the period 1980/81 to 1983/84 was only 14.1 per cent of the 1970 production peak. The corresponding proportions for tea and sugar were 22.5 per cent (of the 1973 peak) and 3.2 per cent (of the 1970 peak). If in 1984 only 50 per cent of peak output had been achieved, it is estimated that an additional US$86 million of foreign exchange would have been generated. This would have permitted, for example, a 25 per cent increase in merchandise imports in 1984. The full explanation for the failure of Obote's economic strategy has to proceed, therefore, to the specific institutional and policy arrangements for these three commodities; here one discovers a failure to incorporate the necessary microeconomic actions and corrections into the overall strategic design.

The largest unrealized contribution to economic recovery was from cotton. Initially cotton-ginning capacity was seen as a major constraint, but this has been tackled under a large World Bank-funded project. International prices have been attractive in the 1981–5 period. The constraints in practice have arisen in the production and marketing areas. These include:

(1) Inadequate supplies of reliable cotton seed due to a breakdown in the Ministry of Agriculture's two sequential breeding and bulking-up programmes;

(2) Non-availability of and/or inflated prices for farm inputs,

especially insecticides, ox-ploughs and fertilizers;
(3) The non-restoration of production credit arrangements;
(4) Lack of road transport, including vehicle and bicycle spares, and poor road and bridge maintenance;
(5) High ginning and marketing costs, associated in large measure with poor capacity utilization arising from low output levels and from the protected purchasing monopolies enjoyed by co-operative unions;
(6) Unreliable power supplies to ginneries, leading to processing backlogs and cash-flow problems.
(7) Inadequate crop purchase finance, or its diversion to trading and direct production activities, within the co-operative marketing system, leading to late and non-payment of cotton growers;
(8) Inadequate and inappropriate donor support for smallholder cotton production.

Despite the establishment of a cotton task force in 1984, an effective package of measures has yet to be devised. The World Bank's 1984 agricultural sector mission had proposed a cotton expansion project, but its focus was on experimenting with new high-input production methods rather than with tackling the constraints on the tried and known extensive systems of production. This appears to reflect an obsession with yield levels that is inappropriate to the land surplus/labour scarce farming systems of the cotton-growing northern districts of Uganda. The mission's target of 350,000 bales (64,000 tonnes) by 1989 was scaled down by the subsequent general survey mission (World Bank, 1985) to only 200,000 bales (36,000 tonnes) in the early 1990s. This report also reached the conclusion that 'sub-optimal agro-ecological conditions' made it unlikely that the output levels of the 1960s could be reached again. In the absence of evidence of long-run climatic change or environmental deterioration this view is surprising. Given the Obote government's political base of support in the northern cotton growing districts and the undisputed contributions to both growth and equity objectives that a revived cotton crop would have made, the explanation for this policy failure seems to lie less in the realm of political economy than in a set of inappropriate and ineffective institutional, technical and microeconomic measures taken by both national and donor agencies.

In the case of both tea and sugar, on the other hand, delays in rehabilitating the capital-intensive processing plants have been the most serious factors. In part, this has reflected uncertainty about ownership of assets abandoned by Ugandan Asians, both between new and former owners and within the families of previous owners. Also, to the extent that almost all sugar and 55 per cent of the tea

Table 8.5: Agricultural Development Budget Expenditure: Uganda, 1982/83–1984/85 (US $m.)

Sub-sectors	1982/83	1983/84	1984/85	3-year Total
1. *Crops*				
Planned	59.6	39.8	55.0	154.4
Actual	27.3	25.6	18.5	71.4
Impl. (%)	45.9	64.2	33.7	46.2
2. *Livestock*				
Planned	9.8	14.4	23.4	47.6
Actual	17.3	8.5	7.7	33.6
Impl. (%)	176.9	59.2	33.1	70.6
3. *Co-operatives*				
Planned	8.8	8.6	12.1	29.5
Actual	8.6	3.9	1.8	14.2
Impl. (%)	97.5	44.8	14.7	48.1
4. *Fisheries*				
Planned	0.5	1.8	2.5	4.8
Actual	0.2	0.9	6.8	7.9
Impl. (%)	39.8	48.3	271.6	164.6
5. *Forestry*				
Planned	–	0.2	0.6	0.8
Actual	–	0.1	0.9	1.0
Impl. (%)	–	67.3	147.7	131.6
Total				
Planned	78.7	64.8	93.6	237.1
Actual	53.4	39.0	35.7	128.1
Impl. (%)	67.9	60.2	38.1	54.0

Source: Bank of Uganda

area is organized on a plantation basis, uncertainties have arisen over profitability in the short term due to alternative employment opportunitites in food production and in *magendo* trading, which had driven up real wages in the rural areas. Nevertheless, the lower cost modes of smallholder settlement and outgrower production have long been successfully demonstrated for these crops in Uganda, as well as elsewhere in East Africa. Given the leasehold arrangements whereby plantation companies hold land and the important effects that continuing delays in investment have had on the national and local economies, the absence of effective government pressure for speedy implementation of investment by private companies is puzzling. The lack of an adequate sense of urgency and priority in the relevant ministries of government – agriculture and industry – appears to be the most probable explanation. Delays on the part of donors in putting investment projects into effect must also share some of the responsibility in the case of tea.

Disappointments have occurred elsewhere in the agricultural sector; the decline in veterinary disease control for traditional cattle herds, the resurgence of animal (and human) trypanosomiasis, and the failure to revive the vegetable-oil industry (groundnut, sunflower, sesame and cottonseed oils for both domestic cooking oil and soap manufacture and for export) are the most striking. In most cases, the needed investment projects had been correctly identified and donor funds secured in principle. The overall balance between activities within the agricultural sector (Table 8.5) appears generally satisfactory, with the exception of an undue emphasis (from the perspectives of economic efficiency and income distribution) on intensive livestock production and the neglect of agro-forestry. The rate of implementation, however, was far from satisfactory, as Table 8.5 indicates. The poor levels of achievement in the crop production and the marketing and co-operative sub-sectors had particularly serious effects. The marked falling off in activity levels in 1984/85 clearly reflects the rapidly deteriorating security situation in the country.

AGRICULTURAL ISSUES IN THE SECOND RECOVERY STRATEGY
Only careful analysis of the successes and failures of the 1981–5 period can provide a reliable guide to the design of a new strategy that has a reasonable chance of achieving its objectives. After the period of food shortages in 1979/80 smallholders had demonstrated their ability to generate food surpluses both for urban consumers and, when the opportunity sporadically presented itself, for export. For once in Africa the supply of staple foods does not present itself as a major cause of concern, in the short term at least. The capture by

Table 8.6: Price Relationships for Food Crops, Coffee and Non-Food Consumer Goods Inferred from Urban Consumer Price Indices: Uganda 1981–6

Year	Quarter	(i) Kampala Low-income Consumer Price Index (LICPI)	(ii) Kampala LICPI – food items	(iii) Kampala LICPI-non-food items	(iv) Robusta Kiboko (UShs/kg)	(v) Coffee price index	(vi) Food: non-food (ii-iii)	(vii) Coffee: food (v/ii)	(viii) Coffee: non-food (v/iii)
1981	3	101.0[1]	102.4[1]	97.7[1]	20.0	100.0	1.05	0.98	1.02
	4	88.1	88.5	87.2	35.0	175.0	1.02	1.98	2.01
1982	1	102.1	100.6	105.6	35.0	175.0	0.95	1.74	1.66
	2	111.3	116.2	99.9	35.0	175.0	1.16	1.51	1.75
	3	122.4	134.5	94.2	50.0	250.0	1.43	1.86	2.65
	4	136.8	152.6	99.9	50.0	250.0	1.53	1.64	2.50
1983	1	129.8	138.6	109.3	50.0	250.0	1.27	1.80	2.29
	2	145.6	160.0	112.0	60.0	300.0	1.43	1.88	2.68
	3	167.1	187.7	119.0	80.0	400.0	1.58	2.13	3.36
	4	170.2	189.9	124.2	80.0	400.0	1.53	2.11	3.22
1984	1	173.6	189.5	136.5	100.0	500.0	1.39	2.64	3.66
	2	181.5	197.9	143.2	130.0	650.0	1.38	3.28	4.54
	3	225.1	250.8	165.1	210.0	1050.0	1.52	4.19	6.36
	4	339.7	393.1	215.1	210.0	1050.0	1.83	2.67	4.88
1985	1	418.8	462.3	317.3	210.0	1050.0	1.46	2.27	3.31
	2	511.0	579.2	351.9	210.0	1050.0	1.65	1.81	2.98
	3	600.3	669.1	439.8	270.0	1350.0	1.52	2.02	3.07
	4	932.5	1013.8	742.8	470.0	2350.0	1.36	2.32	3.16
1986	1	974.1	1024.4	856.7	470.0	2350.0	1.20	2.29	2.74
	2	1235.1	1362.4	938.0	850.0	4250.0	1.45	3.12	4.53

Source: Calculated from data in Government of Uganda, *Background to the Budget* (various years).

Note: August 1981 = 100

1981/82 of the major part of the coffee sold in the parallel economy represented a major achievement for official policy. But, as we have seen, the rapid restoration of production in the three next most important agricultural commodities eluded the grasp of government. Which features of agricultural policy does analysis suggest should be retained and which abandoned, and what new approaches should be introduced, if the economic record of the new government is to improve significantly upon the old?

An issue of some controversy concerns the weight to be given to price policy, on the one hand, and to non-price measures, on the other, in once more routing as much of the potential coffee sales as possible through the official marketing channels. Certainly the new government will have good will on its side for a time, as well as the chance to replace or bypass officials and others believed responsible for organizing illegal trading in the past. Non-price methods of combating the parallel economy – exhortation, tightened policing, exemplary court sentences, etc. – are likely to have some effect in reducing leakage from the official channels. But coffee producers have been fully educated by two periods of hyperinflation as to the difference between real and nominal producer prices. Their decisions about not only to whom to sell, but also when to sell (or store) and also how many variable inputs to apply to existing coffee and whether to replace ageing coffee bushes or to switch resources to other income-generating activities, are likely to be fully informed by current and expected levels in their terms of trade and in relative rewards to effort and investment. Table 8.6 provides estimates of shifts in the domestic terms of trade (taken as the coffee: non-food price ratio) and relative price (coffee: food price ratio) that faced coffee producers between 1981 and 1986. Taken together with the changes in officially marketed coffee output shown in Table 8.3 and bearing in mind the loss of an estimated 20,000 to 25,000 tonnes of coffee from Luwero District from 1983 onwards, the data strongly suggest the importance of improving both terms of trade and relative prices. Given the absolute export dominance of coffee in the short term, any strategy that fails to restore the competitiveness of official coffee prices, or to maintain it thereafter, appears to run a tangible risk of the loss of a significant fraction of coffee, and therefore of total exports. This requires the careful use of exchange rate policy. An unwillingness to devalue would protect the predominantly urban interests that benefit from an overvalued currency – traders in and consumers of imported goods – but at the cost of a possibly disastrous spiral of declining exports and tax revenue, falling imports and the further acceleration of the domestic rate of inflation.

The restoration of cotton and tea exports and of domestic sugar production have the next highest priority in the short term, followed by vegetable-oil production for both the home and export markets. Clearly, the availability of adequate international investment funds and short-term technical expertise is an important, though not sufficient, condition for success. The problems that have arisen in the supply of cotton and oil-seeds inputs through the extension service, and their marketing and processing by some of the co-operative unions have had the effect of closing off large farming areas from producing these commodities altogether. Problems of input supply, finance and management in these traditional institutions are intractable in the short term. An alternative institutional model that has proved succesful is provided by the tobacco crop. Its production is vertically integrated with the national cigarette corporation, which provides inputs, production credit, advice, crop marketing finance and processing capacity (for a recent general review of similar institutional arrangements see Goldsmith, 1985).

There would appear to be a compelling case for setting up a government task force to establish the role of the domestic textile and oil-mill companies in the parastatal and private sectors in facilitating the rapid recovery of cotton and oil-seed production in areas where existing institutions have failed to perform adequately. In the case of cotton, such a reform would represent the reproduction in a domestic context of the type of linkage that led to the crop's introduction into Uganda in the first instance. The balance between state, parastatal, co-operative and private institutions could be left to emerge on the basis of several measures of performance (rural equity and consumer prices as well as exports and profitability) rather than being predetermined on the basis of ideology or vested interest.

Finally, there are the tasks of restoring tea (least expensive given the fact that bushes are standing on 23,300 hectares) and sugar production (requiring crop planting and factory construction) to previously attained production levels. More stringent timetabling for investment by the original owners or claimants seems in order, with the outgrower and settlement scheme modes of production being actively explored as alternatives to plantations. The repossession and releasing of land, with compensation for fixed assets payable from future earnings, should be a step of very last resort and one which is necessary, one would hope, in only the most intractable cases of delays in making incumbent contributions to the recovery of national output.

If the focus is turned to medium-term and longer-term issues in the agricultural sector, a long agenda awaits attention. The restoration of research, training and extension capacities in a wide range of disciplines and skills is only one of several areas requiring major investment where the case for new institutional arrangements seems to deserve consideration. Wider issues of the effective role of the state in securing growth and rural equity objections need to be re-thought in the light of Uganda's experience over the last 15 years (for an extended discussion, see Belshaw and Livingstone, 1981). The rural contribution to further diversification of the national economy is an important policy area, with scope for a wider range of primary activities, for enhancing value added through further processing and raising the quality and timeliness of products (through irrigation, for example). Nor do these exhaust the list: related issues in rural energy supply, food and nutrition policy and rural transport, for example, strongly deserve attention. The primary foundation for progress in these areas, however, requires the successful implementation of the stabilization or structural strategy. On the next time around in Uganda, it is crucial that the economic measures are integrated with the specified set of activities, with timetables and performance targets, at the microeconomic level. In other countries facing similar economic difficulties, many of the specific issues and measures at the grass-roots level will be different, of course. But the need to fully specify the required changes, to monitor their implementation and to adjust both macroeconomic and microeconomic policies in the light of performance is likely to be a common requirement.

Notes

1. The author was a member of the Commonwealth Secretariat's economic rehabilitation mission to Uganda in 1979 (the Seers Mission) and the Canadian Government's (IDRC) economic stabilization mission in July 1986. The responsibility for the views expressed here rests solely with the author.
2. Other factors, especially internal security from 1983 onwards, would still have caused government expenditure to rise faster than purely economic considerations would support. But the collapse of the economic strategy and of the official sector of the economy could probably have been avoided.

NINE
Nyole economic transformation in eastern Uganda

Michael A. Whyte

My wife and I left Uganda in April 1971. We had spent over two years living with and carrying out anthropological research among the Nyole of Bunyole County in Tororo District (then Bukedi District). Much has happened in Uganda since 1971; all too often Uganda has made headlines, and all too often with reports of still another horror, killing or step down the road to political and economic collapse. This short note, however, is not about disaster. Instead I want to draw attention to a small agricultural and economic revolution in progress in a corner of Uganda that I once knew well.

The 'revolution' involves two major changes. Cotton, the universal cash crop in 1971, is being abandoned by many Nyole, thus radically transforming the farming system (based on cotton and millet) that had existed in Bunyole for over 60 years. Wet-rice cultivation in reclaimed swamps, introduced by a Chinese development team, is spreading rapidly, the first major technical innovation in Nyole agriculture. Both developments are exciting, but they are also tantalizing. Both have occurred since I left the field, thus I have very little data to draw on. My wife and I returned very briefly to Bunyole in 1979 on what was properly speaking simply a visit to old friends, though of course we were both intent on discovering as much as we could of the events of the preceding eight years. In the spring of 1985 we received in turn a visit from a Nyole man who had been our field assistant in 1969–71, again an opportunity to be brought up to date but hardly a research situation. Thus in describing events after 1971 I have recourse neither to surveys nor to figures nor – except for one week in 1979 and a few weeks in 1987 – to direct observation.

The development of wet-rice cultivation in Bunyole since 1973 is certainly the most dramatic of the events I wish to recount. Wet rice had never been cultivated in Bunyole so its technology was completely foreign. Nor was there any tradition of, or experience with, large-scale co-operative ventures in agriculture. Thus the

Chinese development agents who began work in 1973 started from scratch, teaching both water engineering and cultivation techniques. By the mid-1970s they had completed an extensive demonstration project, which we visited in 1979. Although a few of the paddies had clearly been abandoned, most were being actively cultivated by scheme participants. I was told that the Chinese had set severe limitations on plot size; rice cultivation was meant to be a family affair, based on family labour alone. Sharecropping and the hiring of outside labour were forbidden. But my Nyole friends hastened to point to those plots that were in fact being farmed as a unit by a local businessman, using hired porters. Control was not strict.

Rice cultivation caught on to a remarkable degree, and in the late 1970s and throughout the 1980s new swamps continued to be drained. Indeed I was told in 1985 that Nyole farmers had begun to quarrel with one another over rights to swamp areas considered useless and ownerless a few years earlier.

Rice was of course known to Nyole long before 1973, when the Chinese began their work. It was considered a luxury food consumed by members of the elite and wage earners. Local cultivation occurred on a small scale, without transplanting. Today more rice is eaten in Bunyole but it has not by any means replaced millet as the staple food. Instead rice is cultivated for sale in Jinja and especially in Kampala. A new railway station has been opened near Busolwe, the county's major trading centre. Traders and middlemen abound, both Nyole and 'foreigners' who compete with each other in bidding for a rice crop not even harvested. Indeed, the picture our visitor painted in 1985 was that of a classic boom. Nyole, he insisted, have never had it so good. 'We are leading now in Bukedi and soon we will be as rich as Bagisus', he proclaimed.

The other major change in Nyole agriculture over the past 14 years has to do with the progressive abandonment of cotton as a cash crop. This has occurred simultaneously with the 'rice boom' described above, but it is not, so far as I can tell, a consequence of the introduction of wet rice. To understand this aspect of the Nyole agricultural revolution, we must go back to the pre-Amin period and look briefly at the characteristics of the Nyole agricultural economy when I studied it in 1969-71.

At that time, Nyole practised a variant of what Hall and Belshaw (1972) call the cotton–cereals farming system. This system was established at the time of the First World War and continued unchanged through the 1970s. In Bunyole cotton and subsistence food crops were grown as part of a complex rotation, integrated at the level of field management. A given plot was opened with cotton in the short rains season, to be followed by millet during the long rains. The plot was cultivated for five to seven seasons before returning to fallow (and cassava) for another seven seasons. At least two croppings of cotton were taken from the plot, which was otherwise devoted to subsistence cultivation (millet, beans and peas, groundnuts and sesame). Only trivial amounts of these foods were ever sold.

I have argued elsewhere (Whyte, 1977–8) that this system functioned so as to block any further development of commercial farming. From the point of view of a Nyole farmer, cotton, the universal cash crop, paid taxes, provided new clothes and perhaps school fees. It failed to generate enough income to allow for capital investment; indeed cotton income did not even meet the average family's yearly cash needs. Intensification of cotton was not possible without cutting into subsistence production, yet the return from cotton, even when well cultivated, was not sufficient to purchase the food necessary to reproduce the family itself. Nyole responded to this situation by giving subsistence cultivation their highest priority and by seeking to increase their cash income through a wide variety of subsidiary – often only indirectly agricultural – economic activities. These included trading in commodities and livestock, sale of livestock and poultry, craft production, service activities and wage labour. Of all cash-generating activities, only cotton was universal, yet few families failed to supplement their cotton income in one way or another. Often the supplementary income was larger than the cash return from cotton.

What appears to have happened during the Amin period was that the state and private structures that supported cotton cultivation began to fail. By this I mean not merely the system of local growers' societies and marketing boards, but also the transportation system generally, as well as the maintenance of sufficient public order. Under these new conditions it appears that in 1979 Nyole had reacted by drastically reducing their cotton acreage. Some had reverted to nearly 'pure' subsistence agriculture; others had begun to explore alternative cash crops. Nyole told me that a thriving 'grey market' in food exports, groundnuts, maize, even millet and bananas, had grown up, centred around exports to urban areas, including Kampala. Often it was a question of barter for commodities in short supply in the countryside rather than simple sale. As the food supply situation in the towns deteriorated, this trade became more and more lucrative. For probably the first time in their history, Nyole – some Nyole – experienced the rewards of a sellers' market.

The cotton–cereals farming system had begun to break down. Individual Nyole farmers discovered different mixes of crops that could satisfy their specific needs for both food and commodities. The sellers' market in food that had developed in many parts of Uganda was a crucial impetus here, but the progressive abandonment of cotton cultivation was equally a necessary condition. It had the effect of 'freeing' significant amounts of land and quantities of labour that could, in turn, be put to a variety of lucrative uses.

It was this situation that my wife and I observed during the course of a brief visit to Bunyole in 1979. We had been working in western Kenya (some few hours drive from Bunyole) and had just completed a village survey that had revealed that over half of the Kenyan households we interviewed had not been able to produce sufficient food to cover consumption. From March or April until the new crops were harvested in June these people had been dependent on remittances from migrant family members. Our visit to Bunyole took place in June, after the long-rains crops had been harvested, yet many Bunyole told us of shortages of all kinds and pointed to children born during our absence who had for example never tasted sugar. Yet no one, they insisted, was hungry and certainly gifts of sesame butter, groundnuts and vegetables with which we were showered bore witness to their dietary well-being. This relative abundance of food was a point of pride for the Nyole with whom we talked and it was clearly the result of conscious strategy. Our friends explained that while most Nyole were still growing some cotton, many had cut back on both acreage and labour input. It was both smarter and safer to grow food instead.

To summarize: the Nyole agricultural revolution can be simply stated. In the years between 1971 and 1985, cotton has lost its position as the universal cash crop. Food crops (including such innovations as maize) are being grown instead and many farmers are experimenting with new rotations. Food crops are being grown for sale, new markets for these crops – grown under 'traditional' conditions – are being developed in towns and the wealthier coffee-producing areas in Bugisu. In addition wet rice, an entirely new crop, produced with a new technology on drained swamplands never before used, is gaining in popularity. Furthermore wet-rice cultivation is being spread largely by local initiative. I was told that a few Chinese technical advisers were still resident in the country headquarters but that their active involvement in spreading the new technology was no longer necessary. Finally, I was told that rice exports – especially during the last five years – have been expanded enormously and that this export is largely controlled by the Nyole themselves.

What all this means for Bunyole, let alone for Uganda, is far from clear. Many regions of Uganda have been thrown back on their own resources have made the shift from cash cropping to a greater dependence on subsistence crops. Stephen Bunker gives a case in point from Bugisu to the east of Bunyole. There coffee has long been the mainstay of the rural economy, and a significant foreign exchange earner for Uganda. From observations made in 1983 he notes: 'Increasingly ... coffee is being relegated to the status of a single component within diversified income and subsistence strategies.' The Bagisu, in common with other African peasantries, 'Appear to be withdrawing from cash markets, *especially those controlled by the state*' (1984, p. 588, emphasis added). Nyole evidence suggests that withdrawal – in their case from the cotton–millet farming system and the clutches of the Lint Marketing Board – need not mean withdrawal from the marketplace. Indeed, I have argued that withdrawal, for Nyole at least, is a precondition for such developments as have taken place. Neither food sales nor rice cultivation would have been possible to the extent described were cotton still king.

Bunyole has become a more diversified agricultural economy and it seems unlikely that the cotton–millet system will be able to re-establish its pre-Amin dominance. Indeed, it is possible to envisage a number of possibilities for growth and development in the newly 'released' Nyole economy. A saleable surplus production of foodstuffs is surely significant these days in Africa. It is doubly significant when – as here – it is based on local initiative and a significant degree of local control of both production and marketing.

On this reading, events in Bunyole could be significant for the future of agricultural planning in Uganda. Certainly they appear to support the argument that agricultural productivity – and innovation – will respond to market incentives. In essence the events of the Amin years – and the second set of Obote years that followed – served to expand the demand for a variety of agricultural products while at the same time opening marketing networks in a direction that favoured producers and, more generally, rural people in the peripheries. Anyone with something to sell could get his price. Indeed, the small producer was perhaps for the first time at an advantage: he had a lower political profile and a smaller accumulated capital to tempt official or unofficial expropriation.

On the other hand the politics of the last 14 years make something other than an ideal laboratory for economic theory-building. Nyole food exports are more or less directly a response to extreme political repression and military destruction in once wealthier and certainly more centrally located regions such as Buganda. Put bluntly, does it take a civil war to give a periphery a chance?

BUNYOLE 1987

In January 1987 a grant from the Danish Council for Development Research enabled me to pay a brief visit to Uganda, including a few weeks in Bunyole. On the whole I was able to confirm the transformations described in this chapter.

The Doho rice scheme, run by a Ugandan staff with advice from a resident team of Chinese experts, is flourishing. Another Chinese team is completing construction of a headquarters unit and there are plans for a significant expansion of the area under irrigation. At present some 870 acres are under cultivation by 830 farmers, most of whom have an acre of irrigated land. Average yields are 1200kg paddy per acre per season. Rice cultivation has also spread to the many seasonal swamps of Bunyole and Bugwere. There it is a long-rains crop, for the most part broadcast rather than transplanted. I was unable to discover how many farmers grow swamp rice but local people agreed that the practice was spreading very rapidly; acreages were estimated to have doubled within the last two years. It was unclear whether more rice was produced from the swamps than from the scheme, with its two seasons. As marketing is not centralized and some significant portion of the crop is consumed locally, a reliable figure for total rice 'exports' was not available. Yet one indication of the extent of this trade is that Bunyole County is well known for its rice in Kampala.

Other food crops are also cultivated for sale on a wide scale these days. Millet (which is still the main staple) is now sold, but not so readily as sorghum and especially maize (grown from hybrid maize seed from Kenya). Beans are the most popular of cash foods, followed by cassava (which can also be eaten and distilled locally). Groundnuts have recently suffered from blight and are being deserted in favour of soya. Other cash foods include cashew nuts, cocoyams, vegetables (cabbage, onions, tomatoes) and – on swamp fringes – plantain bananas.

Cotton is still being grown, though in greatly reduced amounts. The plots I saw had not been well picked. A number of Nyole told me that they continued to grow cotton intercropped with beans or peas as an opening crop for millet, but prices were still so low that few would waste time with thorough picking. Nonetheless the local agricultural staff showed me figures indicating that, after a low point in 1979, more cotton *is* being sold to Nyole local growers' societies. A World Bank programme to encourage cotton cultivation is being prepared for the next season.

In general, it is clear that the agricultural economy in Bunyole has been transformed. Rice has played a role in this transformation – especially the Doho scheme – but the single dominating factor has

Table 9.1: Inflation, 1971–87
(Prices in Uganda shillings. Data from Busaba Market, Bunyole)

Item	1971	1987	increase
millet – kg	0.80	1000.00	
groundnuts – kg	1.10	5000.00	
beans – kg	2.00	1500.00	
cow peas – kg	0.65	1000.00	
rice – kg	4.00	3500.00	
cooking bananas			
(small bunch)	5.00	6000.00	
			x 1328
woman's gown (egomasi)			
Nytil quality	28.00	45,000.00	
man's cotton trousers	25.00	35,000.00	
			x 1509
sugar – kg	0.65	10,000.00	
			x 15,384
primary school teacher			
salary p.m. (apx)	600.00	19,000.00	
			x 320

been the market. Nyole farmers grow whatever can be sold for prices that make their labour worthwhile. By so doing they have not become rich, but they have fared significantly better than others. Between 1971 and 1987 the prices of basic foodstuffs – grown in Bunyole – have increased 1300 times. The prices of basic clothing (ladies' gomesi dresses, mens' long trousers) have increased 1500 times. The wages of a grade II teacher have increased 320 times (see table 9.1).

Ugandan inflation and the problems it has brought to those attempting to survive on wages are commented upon elsewhere in this volume. In Bunyole at least, civil servants are now farmers first, of necessity. The agricultural economy is no longer seen primarily as something from which to escape; today it represents both security and a new kind of future. A teacher continues to teach, despite earning the cash equivalent of two kilogrammes of sugar a month, because a small rice plot provides both food and cash: 400kg of rice, kept for some months to avoid the low prices at harvest, can bring in

1.2 million 1987 Uganda shillings. Rice is only one of a series of food crops that play this role; beans, cassava and maize, for example, are also common cash sources. Yet none provide enough cash to equal the purchasing power of the salaries paid out in 1971. In this sense both the civil servant turned farmer and the farmer himself are worse off today.

The cultivation of food for consumption and sale has made possible a tolerable living standard for many Nyole, but it has also brought problems. Labour shortages/bottlenecks abound and it has become common to hire workers, who are paid daily for piecework. Rice cultivators – both irrigated and swamp rice – are major employers. The present quite extensive use of hired labour is probably a transitional phenomenon. As farmers become more familiar with the labour demands of the new mixes of crops with which they are dealing, many will discover field strategies that minimize labour bottlenecks and the need to depend on porters. Should tractors become available once again this too will be of great help. Yet in so far as the future does in fact lie with food crops – and in particular with rice – then it would seem that for Bunyole as a whole, an agricultural labour market is here to stay.

And what of the future? In my brief visit I observed a formal economy very nearly in ruins, and a local, agricultural economy that appeared to be dynamic and inventive. New crops and new agricultural techniques were spreading from farmer to farmer. Equally important, people who once would have ignored farming were now actively engaged in innovative cash cropping. There was a clearly expressed pride in local achievement, in particular the growth of local trading centres. Busolwe, which had one mill in 1971, boasted of six mills processing maize and rice and a community centre where video films were shown and a weekly disco was held. Permanent buildings were being put up despite severe shortages of cement, roofing materials, even nails.

These developments were based on a transformed agriculture, which in turn had its roots in the free market of the last decade. Of this Nyole were only too aware, for I was told again and again that if they were forced to sell crops at the 'government' prices, life would be impossible. Yet at the same time, Nyole had demands to make: farm inputs, better roads, water supplies, electrification, more and cheaper consumer goods, medicines, building supplies, a stable currency, salaries that were an inducement to work. They worried about erosion control, deforestation, sleeping sickness, bilharzia and the leeches that attacked them in their rice paddies. They were glad for the improved security situation, credit for which was given to the Museveni government, and for the Resistance Councils that were being elected. They were, nonetheless, deeply suspicious of 'Kampala'. In short many Nyole seemed to want the return of effective centralized government, but they also wanted to retain free markets for crops and indeed the *de facto* decentralization to which they had become accustomed.

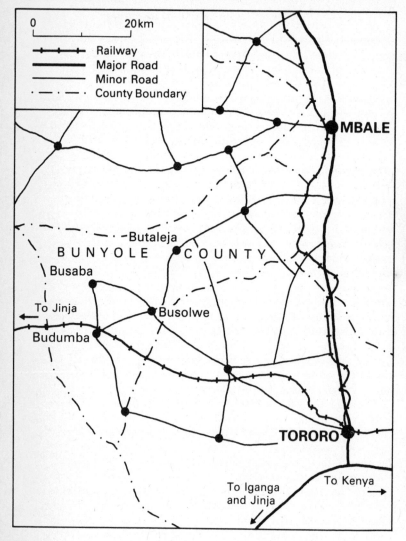

Bunyole County

TEN
Solving Uganda's food problem

Apolo Nsibambi

This chapter seeks to show that despite the frequently officially stated policy of realizing food self-sufficiency and a balanced diet, Uganda's post-independence governments have adopted strategies that have effectively undermined the realization of the stated policy.[1] Three reasons may be given for this. First, since 1966, governments have been so preoccupied with political survival that they have not had enough time and energy to re-examine the policies inherited from Britain, the former colonizing power. The second argument concerns political economy. Peripheral countries like Uganda, it is suggested, cannot have an independent food policy and finance capital must ultimately dictate the policies they must adopt. This particular argument is largely rejected in this chapter. Thirdly, and rather more persuasively, the failure is seen to have been caused by the fact that agricultural policy has been centred on nursing the traditional cash crops such as coffee and cotton to the detriment of food crops. This has been so because the governments have been getting easy and dependable money from the cash crops.

It will be further argued that post-independence Ugandan governments, which used institutions such as the Produce Marketing Board, essentially followed the same approach as British colonial agricultural policies. These governments only made minor changes. To a large extent food policy represented the interests of urban elites.

WHAT IS THE LINK BETWEEN POLITICS AND THE FOOD POLICY?
David Easton suggests (1957) that people may be said to be participating in political life when their activity relates in some way to the making of policy for a society. Making a food policy is a political activity *inter alia* because the exercise entails striking a balance between the various conflicting domestic and external groups. The domestic forces have been well documented by Robert H. Bates. They include the 'revenue hungry' governments, urban industrialists, workers, and progressive farmers who betray their

fellow farmers who are less successful. To use Bates's own words:

> To secure revenues, to promote industry, the elites seek taxes from agriculture. To safeguard their urban-industrial base, they seek low-cost food. They get allies from progressive farmers who have become dependent on state-sponsored programmes of subsidized inputs. Allies include tenants and managers on state production schemes. The bureaucracy is a key element in the emergent social order. It spans markets which governments manipulate (Bates, 1981, p. 120).

Most of the elites, who stay in the urban areas and whose interests are normally different from those of farmers, tend to concur when it comes to exploiting the peasant farmers, who are isolated, localized and lacking in organizational power. The remedy of the peasants lies in exercising autonomy by withdrawing labour from economic activities that are not financially rewarding. Goran Hyden's thesis on the 'autonomy' of the peasant will be discussed in more detail at a later stage.

The external interests include industrialized countries possessing the farm technology that enables them to produce surplus food. These surpluses require markets outside their national political systems. Such countries will not provide us with markets for most of our surplus food. They are also more likely to assist us by importing such items as coffee, tea, and cotton. Yash Tandon (1978, p. 21) observes that, after satisfying the local market, US grain monopolies have available for export nearly 60 per cent of wheat and rice, 50 per cent of soya beans, 25 per cent of sorghum and 20 per cent of maize. The United States export food to the Soviet Union despite the ideological differences that have tended in the past to stand in the way of exchanging other goods on a large scale. It appears that the availability of so much surplus food in the United States dictates either that part of it is destroyed or that it is exported to non-traditional markets.

Preoccupation with political survival

In 1966 Dr Obote, who was then Prime Minister of Uganda, suspended the Ugandan independence constitution and later abrogated it. In 1967 he replaced it with a highly centralized constitution under which he became the President. Monarchy and federalism were abolished. In this struggle for power, the army was the most decisive instrument enabling him to retain power. However, Uganda's politics, which had been characterized by vigorous constitutionalism, were transformed. They became militarized. Furthermore, political survival became a major preoccupation of the government after acquiring office. In 1971, there was a military coup and Amin took over power. Amin's preoccupation with survival was aggravated because his opponents were openly assisted to overthrow him by Tanzania, a neighbouring state. Eventually he was overthrown with the assistance of Tanzanian troops in 1979, and replaced by three short-lived governments between 1979 and 1980. Obote regained the leadership of the country as a result of the very controversial elections of 1980. However, effective dissident groups and a devastated economy weakened his government, which was overthrown in 1985 in a military coup.

This is a sketchy summary of complex developments (see Willets, 1975; Glentworth and Hancock, 1973; Nsibambi, 1980; Gertzel, 1980). The major point to grasp here is that absence of primary consensus, and the use of the army as an instrument of domestic politics for political survival, preoccupied Ugandan leaders. Under these circumstances, it was difficult to formulate a comprehensive food policy and to adopt effective strategies to realize the policy. In the event, the leaders settled for an incremental food policy.

THE 'INCAPACITY' OF PERIPHERAL COUNTRIES TO PLAN THEIR ECONOMIES

Another important link between politics and the absence of viable food policies in Africa is currently offered by many political economists. They argue that peripheral countries cannot plan their economies independently of international finance capital. For example, Tandon, who examined the food question in Tanzania, tried to explain why Tanzania, which has been independent for 15 years, could not anticipate and overcome serious food shortages. He argued that:

> What is missed out in this argument is that Tanzania is in no way able to plan 'its' economy independently of finance capital ... the Tanzanian economy is merely a link within the chain of world economy dominated by finance capital, and as long as it remains a link in this chain, it cannot stray too far away from its moorings. Governments with bigger and economically stronger economies than Tanzania, such as that of India and Brazil, have sometimes had 'independent' ideas of their own and tried to stray away, but were always whipped back to their senses by the representatives of finance capital, the World Bank and the IMF (Tandon, 1978, p. 10).

The major problem with Tandon's argument is that it underestimates the local capacities and initiative of peripheral countries to
harness their domestic resources to the advantage of their countries.
Indeed, Tandon downplays the mistakes by the leaders of the
peripheral countries by referring to them as contributory factors to
famine as opposed to fundamental causes of the food shortages.
The available evidence suggests that food production in Tanzania
declined in the mid-1970s in part because of drought, and in part
because of the government's Ujamaa policy, whereby farmers were
forced to abandon established farms and move into villages.
Furthermore, whereas food prices rose, the prices offered by the
marketing agencies did not (Bates, 1981, p. 84). C.K. Eicher informs
us that Tanzania paid farmers throughout the country a uniform-
ly low price for maize, encouraging the sale of maize in black
markets. The distribution of food in Tanzania has also been poor
because of poor communication systems. There are also administrative measures that interfere with the flow of food within Tanzania.
Lastly, government-operated grain boards have been 'plagued with
overstaffing, corruption, mismanagement and high marketing
costs' (Eicher, 1982, pp. 160–2).

What we have discussed thus far suggests that peripheral countries such as Uganda and Tanzania can have a viable food policy, but
that they have to contend with external interests that do not always
coincide with their interests. We have also rejected Tandon's view,
which tends to belittle excessively the domestic mistakes that
peripheral countries make and which themselves cause serious food
shortages. Since we have basically followed colonial food policies, it
is essential also to discuss the colonial legacy here briefly.

THE COLONIAL FOOD POLICY IN A DISARTICULATED ECONOMY

When the British controlled Uganda from 1894 to 1962, they
centred their agricultural policy on growing cash export crops,
mainly coffee and cotton (Van Zwanenberg, 1975, p. 60). They had
a narrow food policy under which food was not treated as a cash
crop. They emphasized the need to keep famine reserves and
famine crops such as cassava. The need to provide food to the
African population was emphasized because 'if the natives were well
fed, their masters could work them as hard as they liked' (Stigand,
1914, p. 35). However, this narrow food policy was operating in a
disarticulated economy whose parts lacked complementarity and
reciprocity. Production focused on use-value – the feeding of
'natives' – and not exchange value.

Solving Uganda's food problem

POST-INDEPENDENCE GOVERNMENTS PURSUE DISJOINTED INCREMENTAL POLICIES ON FOOD AND EXPORT CASH CROPS

The post-independence governments in Uganda abolished the colonial practice of maintaining compulsory famine crops and food reserves because the practice was associated with interfering with the freedom of the peasants to decide what to grow. However, President Amin attempted to revive the colonial policy, but he lacked the institutional and administrative capacity to implement it. He tended to announce several policies, some of which conflicted with each other, and many were frozen at the very stage at which they were advocated. The post-independence governments pursued food policies that M. Lofchie described as almost anarchic laissez-faire ones (1972, p. 560). Why do African governments pursue almost anarchic laissez-faire food policies that eventually force them to use scarce foreign exchange to import food? The answer is linked to the pressing need to get 'easy' revenue.

THE LINK BETWEEN THE REVENUE IMPERATIVE AND THE DESIRE TO NURSE THE TRADITIONAL EXPORT CASH CROPS

The imperative to collect local revenue through indirect taxation and to procure foreign exchange through centralized marketing agencies lures African governments to focus their agricultural policies on the export of traditional cash crops such as cotton, coffee, and tea and to ignore food, which the peasant is in any case obliged to grow for his domestic consumption. Additionally, the industrialized countries have a keen interest in buying coffee, cotton, and tea whereas they are not interested in buying food from the periphery countries since they themselves produce excess food. In Uganda coffee exports account for nearly 95 per cent of Uganda's export earnings. The revenue for 1985/86 (i.e. from 1 November 1985 to 31 October 1986) has been estimated at UShs114.8 billion. The foreign exchange earning has been estimated at US$397.5 million. Some of this money has been procured. The peasant farmer, however, still only gets 31.45 per cent of the export price. The export duty is 48 per cent. The temptation to concentrate the policy on the export crops is thus obvious.

INSTITUTIONAL ARRANGEMENTS TO MARKET COFFEE AND COTTON

Whereas detailed institutional arrangements exist to market coffee and cotton, arrangements to market food are inadequate. The Coffee and Lint Marketing Boards which were set up during the colonial period, have persisted. These boards, which enjoy a monopsonistic status to market coffee and cotton, accumulated funds that were used for capital development from the 1950s onwards. These included the construction of the hydroelectric power project at Jinja, a project that incidentally mostly benefited the elites who are the main users of electricity(Walker and Ehrlich, 1959). The recently constituted Agricultural Policy Committee (APC) and its secretariat monitors price changes and advises the government concerning prices that should be paid to the farmers for their cash crops.[2] Crop finance exists for the main export crops.

<h3>INSTITUTIONAL ARRANGEMENTS TO ASSIST FOOD PRODUCERS</h3>

Institutional arrangements for improving the production, storage, and distribution of food were either missing or weak in the years immediately following independence. For example, there were no viable institutional means for the peasant to procure food crop finance.[3]

The Produce Marketing Board (PMB) was a parastatal body set up under the Ministry of Co-operatives and Marketing in 1968, and was assigned the following functions:
(1) To purchase all controlled produce from the growers, buyers, or licensed processing factories and sell any controlled produce;
(2) To provide and maintain storage, handling, grading, transport, and processing facilities for controlled produce;
(3) To ensure provision of efficient marketing facilities for controlled produce at reasonable prices;
(4) To provide market intelligence and market research to farmers and government;
(5) To take steps to stabilize prices of controlled produce;
(6) To import or export any controlled produce. In this regard, it would facilitate government to government food purchases.

It should be obvious that the PMB was given a task that was not commensurate with its capacity. The peasants demonstrated their capacity to evade government controls by selling the food outside the controlled prices. Table 10.1 clearly shows that the market prices were much higher than the government controlled prices (Byarugaba, n.d.).

The major disparities between the government-controlled prices and the market prices encouraged malpractices. For example, officials who managed to get food at official prices were tempted to sell it at the high open market prices. Furthermore, the PMB found it more difficult to procure the food until the government was forced to reduce the number of controlled food items. In 1981, the government decontrolled the prices.

Table 10.1: Government Prices Versus Market Prices, 1970

Item	Statutory price (cents per kg)	Market price (cents per kg)
1. Groundnuts (shelled)	40	70
2. Simsim	25	80
3. Mixed beans	15	30
4. One-colour beans	20	40
5. Maize	7	15
6. Finger millet	15	35
7. Paddy rice	40	50
8. Cow peas	25	40
9. Small chillies	75	100

THE POWER AND AUTONOMY OF THE PEASANT

The refusal of the peasant to surrender his food produce at low prices endorses Hyden's thesis (1980, 1983) that although the peasant might appear 'small', he is powerful and that he enjoys some degree of autonomy that enables him to evade repressive government measures. In 1976, the Provisional Military Administrative Council (PMAC) of Ethiopia set up a new agency, the Agricultural Marketing Corporation (AMC), to ensure adequate supplies of grain for public distribution systems. The peasant resisted successfully the attempt of the AMC to lower prices. Lirenso observes:

> The peasant reaction to lower AMC producer prices than market prices was strong. They showed reluctance to sell over-quota grain to the AMC in local markets, and even tended to withhold their grain from markets, but instead, sold it to private traders at home and this encouraged black markets, grain shortage, and price inflation (Lirenso, 1983, p. 79).

This quotation needs no clarification. When the peasant in Uganda realized that he was getting a small fraction of the proceeds from selling cotton and coffee, he concentrated on selling food crops (Nsibambi, 1984). In 1985, the government of Uganda was forced to raise the proportion of the coffee export price paid to peasants to 31.45 per cent.

When we talk about the autonomy of the peasant, we do not suggest that he abandons the cash economy. Nelson Kasfir (1984) has rightly observed that the peasant is habituated to purchasing many of the factors of production as well as an increasing number of consumer goods. This argument does not, however, nullify the suggestion that the peasant enjoys some degree of autonomy from state control. The debate should be about the extent of autonomy and not about whether or not the peasant enjoys some autonomy.[4] Several studies have already shown the ability of the African populations to use the labour market to exit from areas where economic conditions have declined and to enter areas where the economic conditions are more favourable by comparison (Bates, 1981; Barnhum and Sabot, 1977).

There are also studies dealing with cross-elasticities that measure the percentage change in production of one crop associated with the percentage change in the price of another. For example, in Zambia, changes in the price of tobacco and groundnuts compared with maize led to a widespread decline in the production of these cash crops as farmers shifted to maize production (Bates 1981; Adesimi, 1970).

What is the link between the autonomy of the peasant and food policy? When the elites use institutions such as the PMB to extract surplus from the peasants, the peasants cannot use political or physical force to challenge a lopsided relationship. Instead, they use market forces to evade the unfair practices of the state. We must, however, state that some of the alternatives that the peasant resorts to are extremely costly to him in the long run. For example, when the peasant refuses to sell his food to PMB he must sell his food to a private businessman who realizes that the peasant does not have lasting and viable storage facilities. In the long run, the businessman will also pay the peasant a price that is less than he really deserves. The state must ultimately intervene in marketing in order to provide better food stocks and it must provide security and ensure that a viable and integrated transport system exists. We must therefore assess the existing capacity of the PMB, beginning with its storage capacity. (See Table 10.2.)

THE CURRENT STORAGE CAPACITY OF THE PRODUCE MARKETING BOARD[5]

Each of the warehouses in Kampala, Kasese, Gulu, and Tororo has a weighbridge, a laboratory, and drying and cleaning equipment. However, they require rehabilitation. The quality of the remaining warehouses is very low. While the PMB has tried its best to fumigate regularly, it lacks sufficient fumigation inputs.

Table 10.2: The Current Storage Capacity of the Produce Marketing Board

Town	Tons
1. Tororo	13,500
2. Mbale	2,000
3. Gulu	4,500
4. Kasese	4,500
5. Jinja	5,000
6. (a) Kampala	13,500
(b) Kampala	6,000
7. Masaka	600
Total	49,600

The PMB is mostly involved in buying maize, beans, and rice. It buys small amounts of millet, groundnuts, simsim (sesame), and soya beans. It has several major problems. First, it lacks vehicles to go to the countryside in order to collect food. The absence of security and the presence of many useless road-blocks at which soldiers and policemen demand large portions of the food being carried, have greatly increased the hazards of transporting food. The poor state of roads damages the vehicles. Individual farmers are required to transport their food to the warehouse of the PMB. Secondly, a lot of Uganda's food is being smuggled to Rwanda, Kenya, Sudan, and Tanzania. Consequently, the PMB is increasingly finding it difficult to get adequate supplies of groundnuts, simsim, rice, and maize. Thirdly, it only buys dry food because it has no cold storage facilities to preserve perishable food such as plantains (matoke). Its warehouses for dry food are neither adequate to cater for the entire country, nor are they sufficiently modernized to cope with the difficult task of storing food for long periods. Fourthly, administrative methods to prevent theft of food have not been very successful because some 'guardians' must be guarded. Fifthly, the Minister of Co-operatives and Marketing is given too much power of intervening in the affairs of the PMB. For example, apart from the fact that the Minister appoints the most senior members of staff who include the chairman of the PMB, he is empowered to give directives to the PMB members.[6] Sometimes, the directives given to the PMB have only promoted narrow political interests. Lastly, the PMB lacks sufficient qualified people to carry out market research.

Because of these various problems, the PMB has concentrated overmuch on procuring food to feed the army. It has also been involved excessively in government to government food purchases. For example, in 1982/83 and 1983/84, it exported 20,000 tonnes and 30,000 tonnes of maize respectively to Tanzania.

It should be clear that the PMB is an institution that has been manned by members of the elite since 1962, and that it has mostly catered for the interests of the elite, including army personnel. Worse still, it has been protected by the state through such mechanisms as 'lending' it money and granting it monopolistic powers of exporting food amidst a stated policy of open trade. The extensive powers given to the Minister of Co-operatives and Marketing to intervene in the affairs of the PMB have also enabled the government to treat the PMB as a source of political patronage. The consequence of all these actions is that state capitalism has acted largely to prevent the rise of indigenous Ugandan entrepreneurs outside the parastatal structure (cf Turok, 1979, pp. 50–2).

OTHER ASPECTS OF MARKETING FOOD

Marketing entails the collection, storage, distribution and selling of food. When we discussed the activities of PMB, we dealt with all these aspects at an institutional level. However, it should be noted that the PMB covers only roughly 10–15 per cent of the food market. Food marketing is thus primarily organized by small private traders who face several security and business risks. Only a few co-operative societies are involved in food marketing. Otherwise, the co-operative movement has traditionally focused its attention on exporting cash crops. Shortage of storage facilities at the village and district levels is a major obstacle to the realization of price and market stability. For the traders must dispose of their food stocks as soon as possible in order to avoid losses that might arise through theft or through the deterioration of food. Food marketing is also handicapped by the absence of viable and modernized wholesale systems. These problems are aggravated by the absense of a nationwide information system on the food situation. Many producers and traders are not continuously in touch with each other. Consequently, one area of Uganda may be starving while another may be having surplus food. The traders thus take advantage of food producers in the remote areas of Uganda, who are not aware of the changing market forces, though the extent to which they do this consciously or unconsciously is of course debatable.

Railway transport, which should normally be cheaper than lorry transport for food collection and distribution, is either not available to many parts of Uganda or is unreliable. Consequently, lorries are used to transport food.

Lorry transport has become very expensive because of, first, security. Following the rigged 1980 elections, which were 'won' by the Uganda People's Congress (UPC) led by Dr Obote, different sections formed guerrilla movements to topple Obote's government.[7] These were the National Resistance Movement (NRM), led by Mr Yoweri Museveni; the Federal Democratic Movement of Uganda (FEDEMU), led by Dr David Lwanga; the Uganda Freedom Movement (UFM), led by Dr Andrew Kayira; the Uganda National Rescue Front (UNRF), led by Major Amin Onzi; and the Former Uganda National Army (FUNA), led by Major General Lumago. On 27 July 1985, Obote's government was overthrown. As the resistance movements collided with Obote's ill-disciplined soldiers for over four years, sometimes villagers were wiped out after the guerrilla movements had tactically retreated. The villagers were treated brutally because they were suspected of collaborating with guerrilla movements. Obote's soldiers tended to torture civilians, hoping to intimidate them and extract information that would lead to the capture of guerrilla camps. In contrast to the inhuman behaviour of these soldiers the guerrilla armies were courageous and kind to the civilians. Consequently, they won the respect and co-operation of the civilians. The areas that experienced cruel treatment on a large scale included West Nile, from where the former President, Idi Amin came, the Luwero triangle (in Bulemezi, Mpigi, and Mubende). The three latter places are in Buganda. Many road blocks, some of which were illegal, were mounted in the countryside. A transporter passing through the countryside could face any of these threats. Pay money at the road blocks; give away a portion of his goods; lose the lorry; or lose his life if he refused to pay the necessary 'dash'.

The second problem concerned the main and feeder roads which have been in a terrible state of disrepair for more than a decade. These roads frequently damaged the vehicles, at a time when motor spare parts were either unobtainable or were extremely expensive.

Lately, since insecurity became widespread in the country from 1966 onwards, many peasants have been displaced or killed. People who have been on the 'run' cannot produce food. This has created food shortages. The cost of collecting food in small quantities from scattered dangerous areas is correspondingly high. All these factors have made transport costs soar. Scattered populations in the countryside have also tended either to starve or to suffer from malnutrition.

DISJOINTED POST-COLONIAL POLICY ON AGRICULTURAL INPUTS

Although the post-colonial Ugandan governments have been importing a few tractors and fertilizers for elites on an ad hoc basis, they have basically followed an incremental policy on agricultural inputs. This means that, like the former colonial power, they have basically left the peasant to devise his own means of grappling with soil fertility, weeds, and insects. Worse still, the peasant now lacks the hoes that he needs in order to produce enough food, cotton, and coffee.

The agricultural inputs are fertilizers, agricultural chemicals, new varieties of crops, and capital equipment. The traditional methods that have been used, either to retain or to restore soil fertility have included use of cow dung, shifting agriculture, mulching an area with elephant grass or other types of grass, crop rotation, and covering an area with coffee husks. It should, however, be noted that in areas like Kigezi, where there is serious land shortage, these methods are losing efficacy. Coffee husks are also becoming expensive. The large-scale use of inorganic fertilizers cannot therefore be avoided. Indeed, they have been instrumental in causing in Europe and Asia a green revolution. However, using inorganic fertilizers entails adopting a scientific package. For example, the quantities to be used and how often they must be used should be scientifically determined. Furthermore, there is evidence to show that fertilizer nitrate leached from corn fields in Illinois in the United States has caused a health problem (Clapham, 1981, p. 157; Wallace, 1981, pp. 258–9). Agricultural chemicals such as insecticides, fungicides, and herbicides, however, have not been used in recent years in Uganda on a wide scale despite research findings indicating the possibility of high returns, because of the deteriorating economic and security situations (Lawrence and Livingstone, 1983, p. 73).

During the 1960s there was a quality seed production scheme based at Masindi in Bunyoro, but this virtually came to an end in the 1970s. Consequently, there is a general shortage of seeds of improved varieties of staple and horticultural crops. However, in 1983, the EEC gave the Uganda government a grant of 9 million European currency units (ECU) to revive plant breeding and the production of breeders' seeds at three agricultural stations.[8] These were Kawanda for maize, beans and soya beans; Serere for groundnuts, simsim, sorghum, and finger millet; and Kasindi Seed Multiplication Centre for other seeds.

The Department of Agriculture buys seeds from the out-growers and sells them to farmers, co-operative unions, and private traders. The co-operative unions sell them to primary societies, which sell them to farmers, often doubling the Department of Agriculture's prices.

This is a welcome scheme which is, however, totally dependent on modern technology. For example, the seeds that are to be sold to the farmers will require inorganic fertilizers at specified intervals. The scheme is using tractors, combine harvesters and maize shellers. The EEC grant has only a little input for the hoes that the ordinary farmer uses. Yet there is a serious shortage of hoes.

Before launching such schemes there are important policy questions that require the calling of a national seminar in which the peasant farmers must participate. They include the following: What is the scientific package of the scheme? For example, the new maize variety requires a sophisticated technology involving the use of expensive perennial inorganic fertilizers, which must be imported. What will be the cost of the package to the farmer? Will the cost enable him to forgo his traditional methods of growing maize using the local seeds, which are resistant to a number of local diseases (Feistrizer, 1975)? Where shall we export the surplus food? Is the scheme labour-intensive or capital-intensive? As I write this paper, these questions remain unanswered. Eicher (1982, p. 163) warns that 'For example, hybrid sorghum varieties from India have not been successful in Upper Volta, Nigeria, and Mali because of unforeseen problems such as disease, variability of rainfall, and poor soils.' His warning is pertinent to Ugandans as we plunge into new agricultural ventures.

CAPITAL EQUIPMENT

In 1963, the government of Uganda decided to provide the peasant farmers with access to mechanization. The Department of Agriculture set up tractor stations all over the country and then hired them out with drivers to the farmers who wished to use these facilities. By 1966–7, there were 870 tractors in service. The advantage of such a system was that an individual farmer could make use of a tractor without incurring the full expense of purchase, when, on a small farm, he would not want to use it continuously. Experience showed that the tractors were only used at the beginning of the planting season and left idle at other times. Van Zwanenberg observes that 'Even in the scheme's most successful year (1963) the tractor service was operating at a loss of 13 shillings per hour or 500,000 per year' (1975, p. 73). The failure of this scheme suggests that using tractors tends to be uneconomic. For apart from the question of obtaining foreign exchange to import these tractors and their spare parts, they have low rates of utilization, especially in relation to small plots of land. However, Zwanenberg fails to point out that one major reason why the tractor scheme failed was because it was misused by politicians and top civil servants. Additionally, tractors that were unsuitable for Ugandan soils were bought.

THE LAND QUESTION AND THE IDEOLOGY OF DEVELOPMENT
Two major ideological models have been juxtaposed to each other regarding the land question. These are the Marxist and the capitalist models. Important advocates of the Marxist model, which entails the nationalization of land in Uganda, include Chango Machyo (1984), Mahmood Mamdani (1984), and Obol-Ochola (1971). Machyo says that the introduction of the private ownership of landholding in Uganda was not a mark of development but rather of under-development. For what it did was to benefit one small minority and deprive the masses of peasants economically and socially. He advocates nationalization of the land (Machyo, 1984, p. 33). And Mamdani adds that the wretched condition of the peasantry 'is not an outcome of either their 'traditional' or 'backward' way of life, as some would have us believe. It is the bitter fruit of very modern forces of exploitation, both landlord and comprador' (Mamdani, 1984, p. 24). Our reply here is that there has been failure and exploitation in both capitalist and socialist models of development. For example, in Tanzania where land was nationalized, corruption, mismanagement, and even the failure of the state to feed its people have been documented (Eicher, 1982; Hyden, 1980; Tandon, 1978). These problems have also been documented in Ethiopia where land was nationalized. Similar problems have been documented in Kenya and Uganda, where capitalism has been allowed to flourish. However, the socialist model has faced greater problems of settling the question of promoting incentives in a communal arrangement and the peasant's desire for the security associated with having his own piece of land. As J.R. Raeburn (1959) has aptly observed, '... even within African polygamous families, it seems so necessary to get direct responsibilities and incentives for labour that usually each wife has her separate plot.' The issue of private ownership has been institutionalized in Uganda. So much so that when President Obote participated in socialistic documentary radicalism in 1969, the system of private ownership of land was not even nibbled at. He was so realistic in his second term of office that

he embraced the capitalist model fully. The system of individualization of land must continue to flourish because it provides important
incentives for economic development. However, some bad aspects
of the Land Reform Decree of 1975 should be amended. For
example, better provisions must be made to compensate evicted
tenants (see Nsibambi, 1981).

LABOUR POLICY

The colonial practice of dividing the country into labour-providing
and commodity-producing areas, served the colonialists' narrow
purpose of ensuring that there was enough labour flowing from the
south-western and northern parts of Uganda into the south, where
cotton and coffee were largely grown for export to Britain. Around
the 1920s, the policy was slightly adjusted when Uganda began to
receive substantial amounts of cheap labour from the neighbouring
states of Rwanda and Burundi (Richards, 1954). From then on it
thus became possible to allow cotton production to take place in the
north. However, the general pattern under which the people from
the north predominated in the army, and provided labour for the
commodity-producing areas, became institutionalized. This pattern
led to the post-colonial economic conflict between the labour-
providing areas and the commodity-producing areas. J.J. Jorgensen
deals with this problem extensively (1981, Chapter 2). It has serious
implications for the national integration of Uganda.

While the post-colonial governments allowed all areas to grow
cash crops, they did not significantly pursue policies that seriously
undermined the earlier colonial approach to labour supply.
However, the economic disintegration of Uganda since 1970 has to a
significant extent deprived the country of labour from the neighbouring countries. This has been so because as the Uganda shilling
lost value it became increasingly meaningless for labourers from the
neighbouring states to seek jobs in Uganda. Following the expulsion
of Asians from Uganda in 1972, indigenous Ugandans increasingly
left the countryside and became urbanized. These developments
have created serious labour shortages in the countryside, especially
serious during the rainy seasons, when peasants utilize family labour
to grow family food. Another major issue that has contributed
towards increased labour shortages in the countryside is that some
peasants have realized that if they take charcoal, vegetables, local
beer, and firewood to the urban areas, they get paid promptly *and*
recieve more money than they would simply through digging in the
rural areas. They use bicycles to transport these items to town. The
shortage of labour has also been compounded by the shortage of
agricultural implements such as hoes and wheelbarrows. This has in

turn made the food that is grown in the countryside more expensive.

EXTENSION WORKERS

Extension workers have so far concentrated their energy on ensuring that the production of cotton and coffee does not decline. We now need extension workers who will focus their attention on food production.

Three problems have reduced the efficacy of extension workers. First, they have tended to preach down to the peasants. It is essential for the extension workers to realize that the peasant has a lot of practical knowledge which sustains him to overcome several environmental problems. Second, they have lacked transport to enable them to visit the farmers frequently. It is recommended that in addition to providing them with transport, which should include bicycles and motor-cycles, extension workers should be encouraged to stay with peasants for a prolonged period of time. Third, the advice of the extension worker has had limited results because it has not been accompanied by inputs, credit, marketing facilities, and knowledge of climatic changes. Legal arrangements must be made to enable a peasant to present his land held under customary tenure as a collateral against which a reasonable loan can be procured from a bank. It may, for example, be necessary to register land held under customary tenure so that the owner of the land may receive a certificate of ownership for a specified period of time.

Uganda has also been undergoing serious climatic changes that have been partly attributed to serious deforestation. It is essential to rehabilitate the Uganda Meteorological Department in order to get reliable climatic data. The extension worker should be given reliable climatic information so that he may give the farmer early warning information on crop forecasts.

Fourth, the ratio between extension workers and peasants has been very high. Professor Bibangambah estimates it to be at 1:2500.

Lastly, extension workers have not demonstrated any great interest in research in recent years. And yet it is they who must provide a fundamental link between researchers and farmers.

NUTRITION

The Mwana Mugimu Clinic at Mulago Hospital has been rehabilitated through the assistance of the Rotary Club and other institutions, and is grappling with the problem of chronic undernutrition that is widespread in Uganda. About 30 per cent of pre-school children show reduced growth. The principal problem affecting infants and young children is protein energy malnutrition (PEM). The causes for this condition include improper weaning and lack of basic knowledge regarding the protein-containing foods, which are sometimes available but are often ignored. Food and meat have also become very expensive items, especially in the city. Bates estimated that in Africa as much as 60 per cent of the average urban dweller's budget is spent on food purchases (Bates, 1981, p. 75). In Uganda, where the salary of an ordinary wage-earner lasts for two weeks, food alone wipes out the entire salary. The wage-earner must therefore do other things in order to survive. This person is vulnerable to undernutrition. The dominance of *matoke* (plantain) as a staple food in Buganda has been recognized as a significant contribution to the high incidence of protein-calorie malnutrition among children there (Opio-Odongo and Bibangambah, 1984). And yet this diet is still becoming increasingly widespread in Uganda outside Buganda too nowadays.

RESEARCH

The need to revive the research stations at Kawanda, Serere and Namulonge and at Makerere University must be emphasized. Research must also be done in the art of co-ordinating the research activities of government and parastatal institutions and individuals. The National Research Council, which was assigned the task of screening and co-ordinating research activities, has not been given statutory recognition and political support. It should organize several seminars on the food question in Uganda and Africa with special emphasis on research.

CATTLE-KEEPING

Our discussion has so far not dealt with pastoral areas, and yet Karamoja, a pastoral area in the north-east of Uganda, faces perennial problems of raiding, hunger, and malnutrition. The Karimojong live in a semi-arid area and their interests revolve around cattle, which provide milk, blood ghee, meat, skins, bride-wealth, status, and influence (see further Nsibambi and Byarugaba, 1982).

CONSEQUENCES OF HAVING AN ALMOST ANARCHIC LAISSEZ-FAIRE FOOD POLICY

What we have so far discussed shows that post-colonial governments have followed a disjointed incremental food policy. This means that they have not departed much from the colonial food policy, which almost followed a system of anarchic *laissez-faire*. Because of this approach, Uganda still imports food despite its excellent climate. For example, in 1982, Uganda imported food worth UShs3,013,768,370.[9] Rice accounted for UShs118,241,938. FAO

Table 10.3: Daily Average Calory and Protein Unit Availability Per Person and Requirement 1970–2

	Average 1970–2	Average 1981	Requirements
Energy K-cal	2439	1795	2056
Protein g	54,7	43	48
Fat g	30,9	–	–

food balance sheet data estimate that the average food availability per person in 1981 expressed in calory and protein equivalent per capita per day was well below minimum requirements and much lower than the average 1970–2 consumption levels. (See Table 10.3.) In areas like Karamoja, West Nile and Luwero, which had famine and security problems, the situation was considerable worsened. The most nutritionally vulnerable groups were infants and young children, pregnant and lactating women and several old and young people who were displaced from the war zones.

FOOD AID

In addition to importing food, we had to depend on food aid from abroad as the figures in Table 10.4 show. It must be pointed out that food aid can have the deleterious effect of reducing the pressure on governments that they require in order to force them to adopt systematic policies aimed at food self-sufficiency. Food aid is also unreliable. For example, when America disagreed with what was happening in Mozambique in 1981, it cut off aid to Mozambique for six months.

RECOMMENDATIONS

The first proposal must be political because without solving the political problems we cannot implement the food policy. We appear to be reaching a political threshold under which no single military group can impose a lasting formula on Uganda for a prolonged period. Political bargaining must therefore take priority over military solutions. The external powers, whose nationals have been supplying arms to the various fighting groups, must take an active part in showing the relevant groups the necessity of reaching a political agreement.

Eventually all civilians who are over 18 years old must be given military credentials (and not necessarily guns) so that they may defend themselves against the tyranny of a few elite members who currently monopolize the control of lethal weapons.

Power must be decentralized to districts and parishes from which vital recommendations for recruitment in the army, for economic and educational development must emanate. Either a federal or a unitary government with decentralized powers should be adopted.

Our agricultural policy should be centred on the production of food instead of coffee, cotton, and tea. Whereas the quantity of coffee to be exported is limited by quota agreements to 136,000 tonnes per year, our capacity to export food is not yet limited by international agreements. Because of health risks, consumption of coffee in developing countries is declining. Coffee is also facing competition from tea and soft drink abroad. Our cotton is facing the competition of external synthetics producers. There are also large-scale producers of cotton in Ameria and other countries. Tobacco poses health risks which include cancer. Because of birth control and the widespread disinclination to have large families in the countries to which we export our cash crops, there is a low rate of population growth. Because of these considerations, long-term prospects for our traditional export crops are not very bright. Hence our recommendation that we centre our policy on food production and export. The advantages of a well-fed nation must be obvious. It will be energetic and we are likely to reduce crime, which is specifically attributed to absence of adequate food supplies. The gestation period for growing most of our food is much shorter than that for producing coffee, tea, and cotton. Hence, within a year, we can have two yields with some crops. Our capacity to make the necessary adjustments in response to price changes is greater with food crops than with coffee, tea, and cotton.

In view of our historical prejudices, we must be reminded that food crops are cash crops too (cf Bibangambah, 1983). If we export it to our food-deficit neighbours, we can earn foreign exchange. In case there are problems of being paid in foreign exchange when we sell food to our neighbours, there are prospects of procuring it through the Preferential Trade Area (PTA). For exports to neighbouring countries, the best prospects are in rice, maize, sorghum, beans, groundnuts, and cassava. For the European export markets, the best prospects are in soya beans, simsim, and sunflower seeds. As already noted in our previous discussion, we have been selling maize to Tanzania. Some of our maize has been smuggled to Kenya, which is currently importing maize from the United States: Kenya will find it cheaper to import maize from Uganda than from the United States. We can export mangoes to the Middle East and pineapples to the EEC. *Matoke* and *bogoya* are already being exported to Kenya.

FOOD POLICY

In order to work towards integrating our economy, we must get involved in food processing. This strategy will create more jobs for our citizens and will facilitate the preservation of our perishable food. For example, it is possible to make a tasty cake from mixing pounded groundnuts and simsim. Pre-processing activities such as sun-drying, threshing and shelling, which are done manually, should be mechanized. Already the manual methods of grinding finger-millet, sorghum, and dry cassava, between stones, is being replaced by small hammer mills. Local producers of hammer mills must be given official encouragement. For example, they could be given tax holidays. The possibility of developing a large-scale oil-processing industry, for combining the production of vegetable oil with cake animal feed, must also be scientifically studied. We must examine the preservation of fruits and vegetables in the form of jams and fruit juices. The small-scale activity of processing meat, pork, fish and meat, must be enlarged. Food processing is thus likely to create forward and backward economic linkages.

A food and nutrition council should be set up to examine the food policy in Uganda. It should consist of representatives from the Ministries of Defence, Agriculture and Forestry, Marketing and Co-operatives, Health, Animal Industry and Fisheries, and Makerere University. Research institutes dealing with food crops should be represented on the council. Major issues to be examined include crop improvement, seed production and economics of farm mechanization.

The Produce Marketing Board should be leased to a private businessman for a period of five years so that it may be run on a commercial basis. Since the PMB has useful warehouses, which are scarce in the country, the government should negotiate with the manager of the PMB to store buffer food stocks that can be distributed at subsidized prices to famine-stricken areas. However, the PMB should as much as possible compete at par with other organizations (such as Gomil Ltd) that are involved in marketing food.

We must not be condemned to permanent 'peasantization' by being totally dependent on the hoe. Special tractors that are suitable for our soils and cultural conditions should be constructed. In order to alleviate the existing shortage of hoes, we must rehabilitate the company that makes hoes. Current estimates show that we ned 3.7 million hoes per year. In 1984, we received 1.93 million hoes from donors, who included the EEC and IFAD. However, the low level of production of hoes locally and smuggling to neighbouring states have meant that the peasant in the countryside is short of this vital input. Increased production of hoes plus effective policing of the borders should, however, minimize future serious shortages.

154

It is recommended that we should use a mixture of the traditional organic fertilizers and modern inorganic fertilizers. The extent of mixing or not mixing the two systems should be determined by costs and environmental factors. Reformed farmers' co-operatives, managed by trained people who are accountable to the farmers, co-operative banks, and extension workers should provide farmers with fertilizers and credit facilities. Malawi's example of supplying farmers with credit facilities in the form of inputs should be tried in Uganda (see Bisika, 1985).

Labour problems can be reduced by three strategies. There must be greater use of intermediate technology instead of relying too heavily on manual labour. Herbicides must be used on a greater scale for weed control. The labourers in the countryside must be given more realistic wages.

With regard to the improvement of the efficacy of extension workers, the ratio of extension workers to farmers should be raised from 1:2500 to 1:200. The suggested ratio would enhance the impact of extension workers. They must also be provided with transport, which may range from a bicycle, or a motorcycle to a car. It is worth noting that land-locked Malawi, which produces more food than she requires, has a ratio of 1:100. The extension worker should encourage farmers to plant multi-functional trees in order to correct deforestation. Makerere University Forestry Association (MUFA) is already encouraging farmers to plant forest and weedlots in the villages. MUFA's efforts should be supported by the government. Radio and television programmes on new methods of farming and seed production should be started. They should involve extension workers, farmers, school teachers, and university lecturers.

Undernutrition is partly caused by ignorance. Intensive educational programmes should indicate the food that must be eaten in order to have a balanced diet. As for pastoral areas, the recommendations that we made in 1982 (Nsibambi and Byarugaba) are still pertinent. These included focusing attention on ranching schemes, providing water to the area and growing grass that is resistant to drought. Food can also be grown in Karamoja. Another critical objective is encouraging economic interdependence between Karamoja and food producing areas. Improvement of transport, linguistic communication, and security would all enhance this interdependence.

In this chapter, we have recommended that Uganda should depart from pursuing a disjointed-incremental agricultural policy that is basically centred on exporting cash crops of which coffee, cotton, and tea are the key export items. We have recommended a policy that focuses attention on food production for domestic consumption and for export to food-deficient neighbours. Adopting this policy does not

Table 10.4: Food Aid, 1983

Country or institution	Type of food	Amount in metric tons
1. EEC	DSM	4821
2. EEC	Butter oil	400
3. Sweden	Vegetable oil	583
4. Saudi Arabia	Vegetable oil	50
5. Denmark	Butter oil	250
6. Canada	DSM	900
7. Netherlands	DSM	24
8. Austria	DSM	25
9. Finland	DSM	157
10. USA	Maize	120
USA	DSM	528
USA	Vegetable oil	225
11. Save the Children Fund based in U.K.	DSM	50
12. Netherlands	Maize	180
13. E.E.R.	Maize	1000
14. Norway	Maize	800
15. Austria	Maize	1447

mean that we ignore the traditional export crops. It simply means that food must have the first priority and that the traditional export crops, which will also be encouraged, will take a second priority. Adopting the recommended policy entails confronting domestic and international vested interests. Herein lies one of the major links between politics and food policies. The domestic vested interests include the government itself, which has been habituated to getting reliable and easy revenue and foreign exchange from taxing indirectly the farmers who produce the traditional export cash crops. The external forces enter this equation because they have surplus food and it is natural that, despite what they openly declare, they will not go out of their way to provide us with the necessary infrastructure in order to reverse the existing agricultural policy, which benefits them. If we were in their position, we would take the same position. After all, in international politics nations seek to pursue their interests.

The elites in Uganda should take to heart Bates's observation. He says that

... in response to the erosion of advantages engendered by shortfalls in production, the dominant interests may be persuaded to forsake the pursuit of unilateral short-run advantages and instead to employ strategies that evoke co-operation by sharing joint gains. In the face of mounting evidence of the failure of present policies, people may come to believe that short-run price increases for farmers may in the longer run lead to more abundant supplies and less costly food; or that decreases in tax rates may lead to greater revenues as a result of increased production (Bates, 1981, p. 132).

Our paper is a serious attempt to appeal to fellow Ugandans to pursue policies that will in the long run benefit the peasant farmers and the urban elites simultaneously. The policy advocated entails strategies that include re-examining the role of marketing institutions such as the PMB. We must thus reverse earlier disjointed-incremental policies and adopt more comprehensive policies. In order to do this, it will also be essential to agree on institutions and procedures for resolving political conflict in the country.

The chapter with its recommendations was composed before January 1986, but its arguments still appear persuasive to the author.

Notes

1. Our knowledge of food policy in Uganda is based on several interviews that were carried out in the Ministry of Agriculture at Entebbe and the Agricultural Secretariat in Kampala. We also interviewed officials of parastatal bodies. They requested to remain anonymous. Tribute must be paid to them for their co-operation.
2. For example, the new prices were announced in June 1985. See *Uganda's Budget Speech, June 20, 1985*, Government Printer, Entebbe, 1985, p. 1.
3. If the peasant gathered courage to borrow money from the commercial banks, he was required to produce collateral such as privately owned and registered land. Many peasants who held land under customary tenure lacked the required collateral.
4. Mamdani underestimates the options which a peasant possesses, options, which minimize the capacity of the state to capture him. See Mamdani, M., 'A great leap backward: A review of G. Hyden's *No Shortcuts to Progress: African Development in Perspective ...*' *Social Science Research Review*, 1, 1, January 1985, especially pp. 81–8.
5. Source: Interview of officials of the PMB.
6. For example see sections 3 and 5 of the *Produce Marketing Act, 1970*.
7. Some evidence of rigging the elections can be obtained from Avirgan and Honey, 1982, pp. 226–8. For example, commenting on the UPC's picking the 17 uncontested seats out of 126 parliamentary seats, they say that in the case of the six West Nile seats and three in Kasese, the UPC bent the rules to the point of breaking them.
8. Interview with officials of the EEC at Kampala. 9 million ECU was roughly equivalent to 7 million US dollars.
9. Source: Statistics Department, Ministry of Planning and Economic Development.

ELEVEN

Land and peasants in western Uganda:
Bushenyi and Mbarara districts

Nelson Kasfir[1]

Contrary to the widely shared belief that land remains freely available in Africa for any peasant who needs to grow crops or keep livestock, it is, in fact, becoming increasingly scarce. It is no longer useful, if ever it was, to think of African peasants subsisting on their own, independent of both capitalism and the state, because they have continuing and open access to as much land as they can farm. Once land becomes commercially desirable, social relations within the peasantry and between peasants and commercial farmers become more unequal and more antagonistic. At that point fostering the assumption of open land helps to serve the purpose of obscuring this process. The intention of this paper is to investigate the consequences for rich and poor peasants of increasing land scarcity in Bushenyi and Mbarara districts (which at independence made up the kingdom of Ankole) in western Uganda.

Open land tends to be characteristic of systems of customary tenure in which rights in plots are maintained through continuous use rather than legal title to the land itself. If cultivation ceases, the land reverts to the community. For this reason, so long as cattle-owners do not possess dominant social power, grazing provides a weaker customary claim to land than agriculture. But where land is plentiful, rights of way for cattle are more likely to be respected and those who are capable of farming larger plots than they possess – for example, sons who would otherwise divide their father's plot – can cultivate new farms from unused bush.

Open land, in theory, also insulates farmers from dependence on market demands. If it is not necessary to purchase land, farmers have less reason to need to generate cash income. All over Africa, insists one writer, 'With land being no sales commodity, peasant incorporation into the capitalist economy cannot but be marginal' (Hyden, 1980, p. 10).

But there is good reason to doubt whether open land and its hypothetical consequences actually describe contemporary rural Africa. In the first place customary rules vary greatly from one group to another. Some groups practise more individualization of land use, sale and inheritance than do others (Brock, 1968, p. 3 and *passim*). Secondly, and far more significantly, the advent of a monetary economy has placed both open land and customary tenure under considerable pressure. The notion that unused land reverts to the community has become attenuated. The contradiction in the Russian peasantry that Marx called 'common ownership, divided cultivation' (quoted in Post, 1972, p. 228) fits precisely the changes in attitudes toward land that accompanied the introduction of cash crops everywhere in Africa: '... witness after witness has attested all over Western Africa to the tendency to use land as if it belonged to the individual farming it, to the point where communal ownership has even been superseded' (ibid.). In addition a lively land market has spread over much of West Africa. Rural land sales in southern Ghana, for example, have been a familiar practice for well over a century and may have begun before the rise of commercial cocoa farming (Hill, 1963, p. 138–41).

The same changes have also turned open land into a fiction in many parts of East Africa. Increasing land shortages in Bukoba district in Tanzania have strengthened rights in land so that 'there exists today [1965] an assured and permanent individual entitlement to the use of land hardly distinguishable from rights of property ... The large amount of trade in land is remarkable ...' (Friedrich, 1968, p. 180). By 1961 coffee plantations in Mbozi could be sold, even though the formal right to use the land had to be secured from the village headman as representative of the community (Brock, 1968, p. 6). On the densely populated island of Ukara in Lake Victoria, one-third of the fields have been acquired through purchase or trade, often at high prices (Ludwig, 1968, p. 129).

Among the Bagisu there developed an unusually great concentration of rights over land held by the individual farmer, though less extensive than freehold, even before arabica coffee became the local cash crop (Brock, 1968, pp. 6–7). In the 1963 agricultural census of Uganda over 97 per cent of the peasants claimed that they owned their holdings, even though freehold tenure accounted for a very small percentage of farm lands (Uganda Government, 1965, Vol.1, pp. 37–38). Though there once was a lively debate over the communal basis of customary tenure: 'It is now beyond doubt that in many African communities individual title and security of use is recognised by custom' (Ssempebwa, 1977, p. 23).

The notion of a land frontier is used here to refer to the situation where there is an availability of undeveloped land that is so extensive that it has little or no market value. This frontier disappears when land becomes a valued commodity, whether or not it is actually being developed. Furthermore, it is not necessary that legislation recognize individual holdings. Where individuals are prepared to buy and sell permanent improvements on the land – such as perennial crops – it is only a fiction to presume that the underlying land is not also being sold.

Strictly speaking, a land frontier refers to space for expansion. Thus, in addition to open land it might also refer to land that was commercially valuable, but only suddenly accessible to a specific group of inhabitants. For example, the removal of the Kenyan colonial prohibition on African ownership of land in the 'White Highlands' temporarily opened a new land frontier, but through the market. That frontier has closed again. In any case, where there is no opportunity for expansion, competition for land forces farmers to adjust to new and frequently harsh economic necessities.

PASSING THROUGH THE LAND FRONTIER IN BUSHENYI AND MBARARA DISTRICTS

Though long part of the periphery to Buganda's core, Bushenyi and Mbarara districts are probably now expanding faster economically than any others in Uganda. Agriculture – cattle and crops – has continued to be the basis of production, though it is now far more integrated into a capitalist economy than it was in either the pre-colonial period, when this area consisted of several small kingdoms, or when the latter were amalgamated into the kingdom of Ankole within the British Protectorate.[2]

Early class stratification in the area gave social and political dominance to a tiny minority consisting of cattle herders who were ethnically identified as Bahima and who ruled cultivators known as Bairu. However, the introduction of the demands of a cash economy undermined these arrangements. By the Second World War Bairu owned as many cattle as Bahima and by the 1970s owned two-thirds of the cattle in Bushenyi (Muwonge, 1978, p. 170). At independence Bairu leaders had effectively taken political power from the royal Bahima family and its followers, though the new notables were themselves fragmented by religious and other factional divisions (Doornbos, 1970, pp. 1096–1109). The turbulence of post-independence Ugandan politics has resulted in the eclipse of one group of political notables after another, but has not interrupted the steady growth in conversion of land from customary ownership to private freehold or leasehold.

In Bushenyi and Mbarara, public land – what used to be called Crown land or *Karandaranda* – defines the land frontier. Public land in these districts was given legal status during the Protectorate period in order to protect customary tenure. It must be distinguished from the concept of public land created by the Land Reform Decree of 1975, which stripped away the rights securing claims based on customary tenure. Strictly speaking, what public land means today in Uganda is simply ownership of the land by the state. No individual can possess more than a leasehold interest in any plot.

Since independence Bushenyi and Mbarara have also almost completely passed through the land frontier. The once seemingly limitless public land available to cultivators and herders on the basis of customary law has almost entirely disappeared. No longer can the sons of a farmer who want to cultivate more than the share they inherited from their father simply request a chief to allocate unused land. It is not that public land is fully farmed, but that most of it has been leased under Ugandan statutes and much of it has been fenced.

The disappearance of open land has begun to force some peasants out of their customary holdings, while increasing the differentiation among those peasants who have managed to hold on to their land. As a result, migration and resettlement have grown in less densely settled eastern and northern counties in Mbarara district and northern counties in Bushenyi. In addition out-migration to other districts in Uganda has increased. The problems for nomadic herders are even worse, since they depend so greatly on open land both to move their cattle and for fresh grazing areas and available water supplies during the dry seasons. Many herders have moved to Nyabushozi county in eastern Mbarara district, where population density is still low, though growing faster than in any other county.

In addition to these social consequences, changes in the land situation have played a hidden role in intensifying several political issues that emerged during the second Obote regime of the early 1980s. Political manipulation led to the removal by force of peasants from their land. It resulted in the seizure of temporary land by powerful political notables, in the upgrading of Lake Mburo game reserve into a national park, and in the expulsion of the so-called Banyarwanda refugees. Each of these acts indicates how critical a point had been reached. In each instance, force was used to remove peasants from their land.

The most important reason for passing through the land frontier is population growth. Almost everywhere in Africa the population is doubling with each succeeding generation. This, without stopping to consider variations in land holdings, doubles the person–land ratio, causing open land to disappear at an accelerating rate. The situation in Bushenyi and Mbarara districts is no exception, though their initial advantages in soil fertility and rainfall help to explain the larger populations sustained in the richer counties of Sheema and Igara.

On the other hand, migration patterns that were created by the increase in land values have since then led to population shifts to the drier and poorer counties at the edges of the two districts. Peasants unable to maintain themselves on a fraction of their fathers' family plots (held on customary tenure and locally called *bibanja*), and incapable of buying more, move to counties in which land is cheaper. If present average land values were compared by counties, there would probably be a strong *inverse* correlation with percentage population increases. Thus, as Table 11.1 opposite indicates, the different rates at which the counties of the two districts have grown suggest important changes in social conditions, particularly the displacement of poorer peasants.

Overall the population of the two districts more than doubled between the 1959 and 1980 censuses. However, the population of Mbarara district, which is generally less fertile and less densely populated, has almost trebled: while Bushenyi's has grown by a factor of 1.7. This difference in rate of district population growth suggests the continuation of the trend noticed a decade ago (Muwonge, 1978, p. 181) of eastward migration from the more densely populated counties in Bushenyi to sparsely settled areas in Mbarara district, where land remains cheaper. Another earlier trend, which appears also to be continuing, has been the movement of migrants from Shema and Igara counties to Kashari (see Doornbos, 1970, p. 1106).[3] In addition, both districts received pastoral migrants in the 1950s as a result of the revolution in Rwanda, as well as agricultural migrants from Rukungiri and Kabale districts as a consequence of the even earlier closure of the land frontier in those areas. Since 1969, Bushenyi and Mbarara have probably experienced continuing in-migration of cultivators from Rukungiri and Kabale, while the number of immigrants from Rwanda has probably diminished (see Table 11.1; maps p.86).

A second and perhaps even more important contribution to the demise of the land frontier has been the change in the system of land tenure applied to these two districts since independence. Before 1975 a relatively small portion of the land in each district could be bought and sold as freehold. Two kinds of freehold titles existed: native (or *mailo*) and adjudicated freehold. The former consisted of about 270 square miles of land that was given to the *Omugabe* and his chiefs as part of the Ankole Agreement of 1901, and later extended to reward various chiefs during the 1920s (Doornbos, 1975, pp. 62–65). The latter was an unsuccessful attempt by the government in the 1950s to create a class of smallholders who could hold title in

Table 11.1: Population Growth 1959–80

County	Pop. 1948	Pop. 1959#	Pop. 1969	Pop. 1980	% increase 1959–80
Sheema		79,680	115,301	151,009*	90
Igara		107,859	139,924	146,799§	36
Buhweju		20,114	25,401	34,929	74
Bunyaruguru		14,305	26,946	52,161	265
Kajara	}	81,331	103,111	139,771	72
Ruhinda*§	}				
BUSHENYI		303,289	410,683	524,669	73
Ibanda**		38,944	80,769	127,782	228
Kashari§§		41,744	85,869	118,017	183
Rwampara	}	107,859	147,826	188,165	74
Ruhaama	}				
Isingiro		34,985	98,774	176,351	404
Nyabushozi		12,665	37,224	77,838	515
MBARARA		236,197	450,462	688,152	191
ANKOLE	400,924	539,486	861,145	1,212,822	125

1959 county populations were calculated from density per sq. mile figures and aggregate to 529,712 rather than to the census figure.

* For purposes of comparison Kabira division has been added to the 1980 total for Sheema and subtracted from Ruhinda where it is now located.

§ For purposes of comparison Mitooma division has been added to the 1980 total for Igara and deducted from Ruhinda were it is now located.

** Ibanda was called Mitooma county in the earlier censuses.

§§ For purposes of comparison Mbarara municipality has been added to the 1980 total for Kashari. The population of Mbarara was 16,078 in 1969 and
23,255 in 1980.

their property. Further small grants of land were given to missions for religious and educational purposes.

Though the amount of land alienated in these schemes was relatively small, it reinforced important political and social conflicts between fractions of the rapidly forming dominant class. Each fraction was doing what its members could to gain control of the offices of state of what was then the kingdom of Ankole. In particular, conflicts over the schemes deepened the sense of identification and cleavage between Bahima chiefs, who had been the recipients of the *mailo* estates, and their main opponents, Protestant Bairu political notables and emerging entrepreneurs.

The Bahima chiefs defended the *mailo* estates, not as commodities for sale, nor as the means of creating wealth, but to protect a pre-capitalist ethos in which cattle ownership was the basis of their social prestige (Doornbos, 1975, p. 67). Several decades later, Protestant Bairu notables supported adjudicated freehold as a legal tool to gain privileges previously monopolized by Bahima chiefs and to protect investments on their farms (Doornbos, 1975, pp. 71-2). Bahima opposed adjudicated freehold because it impeded the free movement of their cattle, and because by that time Bahima notables could no longer control the allocation of plots under the scheme.

Aside from statutory leases to urban authorities and land occupied by central government institutions, the remainder of the land was public land available for customary tenants. Without title they could not legally buy or sell their land, or use it as collateral for bank loans. To promote economic development, the 1969 Lands Act permitted these customary tenants to apply for leaseholds if they wished. Nevertheless, the vast majority who could not afford the survey fees or just did not bother, engaged in a lively market in the sale of the 'improvements' on the land, their coffee trees and banana plants. For most purposes they should be considered freehold owners with no title to their land (Uganda Department of Lands and Surveys, 1980, p. 10). In addition, however, by the end of the 1960s perhaps 20,000 peasants (predominantly Bairu) held *bibanja* on freehold estates (Doornbos, 1975, p. 66). As tenants of the free-holder they were in a weaker position than those who held *bibanja* on public land. They also appear to have had far less protection from high rents and eviction than peasants in Buganda enjoyed.

The Land Reform Decree of 1975 introduced far-reaching changes into land tenure. No one, however, should mistake the name of the decree for an intention to promote a more egalitarian land policy. The problem it addresses is fragmentation of holdings, which – in the view of its authors – blocked effective exploitation of the land. 'The Decree is intended to facilitate and control economic and social development' (Uganda Government, 1977, p. 20). It did so by providing the opportunity for developers to amalgamate plots of land in order to realize their economic potential, but also forfeiture of their leases to the state if they fail to develop their holdings within eight years.

The Decree's consequences for landlords and tenants are far from what they seem at first sight. It does away with all forms of freehold by giving the state title to all land. While thus appearing to weaken the position of landlords, it actually provides them with the opportunity to acquire long-term leases (99 years) on the land they formerly owned, so long as they economically develop their holding. The effect of such long leases is to provide almost as much social power as did the former absolute title.

At the same time, however, the Decree seriously impairs the rights of customary tenants' holdings on either public or *mailo* land. Here the theory behind the Decree is that previously the freeholder was unable to develop his land because he could not intrude upon smallholders cultivating plots on it. By law he could neither charge them an economic rent nor remove them in order to undertake more productive ventures. In the former region of Buganda, where over 3,000 square miles of the land are held in *mailo* tenure, much of it by commercially alert entrepreneurs, that is a significant change that will have serious consequences for thousands of tenants.

Under the 1975 Decree their status is reduced to tenants at sufference liable to be forced off the land with short notice at the discretion of the leaseholder. They are left with only an uncertain claim to demand resettlement, though the Decree protects their right to adequate compensation (Sempebwa, 1977, p. 21). Since lease arrangements are expensive, require knowledge of complex regulations, and depend on persuading District Land Boards that the applicant will invest in his property, few peasants holding public or *mailo* land on customary tenure are likely to protect themselves under the Land Reform Decree.

Thus peasants are always vulnerable to ambitious entrepreneurs who have the capital to apply for leases in order to seize the new economic opportunities created by the Decree. In order that evicted peasants be resettled, there must continue to be public land on which the District Land Board can place them. If there is, it is unlikely to be the most fertile and well-watered land in the area. Even assuming they actually were 'resettled', there would be no guarantee that someone else would not lease *that* public land and later evict them once again (Nabudere, 1980, p. 205).

Outside Buganda, where *mailo* and adjudicated freehold are relatively insignificant, the more profound impact of the Decree is occurring on public land where customary tenants – no matter how long they have been there – are liable to be ousted upon six months' notice after someone lays claim to the area by establishing a leasehold. Where previously the leaseholder on public land had to entice a customary tenant to leave by making an attractive offer, now he need merely make an offer a court would judge adequate and convince the Uganda Land Commission that he has a plan to develop the land. In the difficult conditions of enforcing land law in Uganda these days, he frequently can get away with doing much less than that. As a government official drily observed: 'Such a situation has not proved satisfactory as hundreds of customary tenants have had their *bibanjas* leased to influential persons without reasonable excuse' (Uganda Department of Lands and Surveys, 1980, p. 19). He added that many who were displaced during the Amin regime never received any compensation (ibid., p. 18).

The process of leasing public land was well under way *before* the Land Reform Decree. In his prescient study carried out in 1973, Muwonge pointed to the rush to lease and then fence farms – which he aptly termed an enclosure movement – ranging from 75 to 3750 acres as compared with an average customary holding of 5 acres (Muwonge, 1978, pp. 175,170). He argued that the reason for the sharp rise in leases was the insecurity over land caused principally by the rise in both human and livestock populations, and to a lesser extent by the requirements of keeping foreign cattle. He identified 1257 enclosed farms in both districts, comprising about 600,000 acres, exclusive of the Ankole Ranching Scheme, or about a sixth of the total land area. This ranching scheme, which contemplated the establishment of more than 100 ranches in eastern Ankole (now Mbarara district), greatly exacerbated these trends. Ranches containing up to five square miles were allocated primarily to Bahima political notables, who became absentee owners and treated the ranches as a capitalist investment (Doornbos and Lofchie, 1971, pp. 168, 178–87). In areas like these, fencing of pasture by Bahima and Banyarwandan herders led to clashes with Bairu cultivators, who could not expand their holdings as their numbers increased, while in other places fencing by Bairu cultivators forced herders to move or give up their way of life (Clay, 1984, p. 27).

The more land rose in value in Bushenyi and Mbarara, the more people acquired leases. Though this has been the situation since independence, knowledgeable local people insist that an acre of land is now worth a hundred times what it sold for in the 1960s. It is difficult to translate that into increases in real value. The Uganda shilling now purchases only a minute fraction of what it commanded twenty years ago, but civil service salaries were at the time of research only about double what they had been then.[4] Not only had land been a sensible hedge against inflation, it is one of the few safe investments in the political turmoil that disrupted all economic ventures during the Amin period and afterwards.

In any event public land clearly became a spectacular investment, because the only cost to the lessee was the expense of surveying the land and registering his title. In the act of putting the land into private hands, the state accepted the basic belief behind customary tenure: that the land itself was a free good! But, for all poor and most middle peasants, these fees made it impossible to think of applying for leases, even though many of them have become aware of what a lease held by someone else meant for them. It is the rich peasant or businessman who can take advantage of this windfall.

The intense pressures to acquire land have been reflected for many years in official reports of illegal fencing and fraudulent boundary changes. Two recent examples will illustrate this. In 1974 the district commissioner warned county chiefs against permitting fences on land when no lease had been obtained from the Land Commission (Bushenyi District Files, C.Lan. 8: 30 October 1974). Chiefs, he added, had generated unnecessary disputes by excluding people from 'public land that should be used by everybody'. The chief magistrate for the two districts noted that 'land encroachments are on the increase' and urged both district commissioners to ensure that chiefs were present when surveyors were demarcating land 'to keep peace in the areas' (Bushenyi District Files, C.Lan. 8: 5 May 1976).

Land law itself was also misused at much higher levels for patronage or self-enrichment by well-placed officials, a problem that existed in the 1960s but became endemic during the Amin regime and appears to have been continued by succeeding governments. By Decree No. 17 of 1973 which has subsequently been repealed the minister responsible for land policy was also appointed to carry out the duties of the Uganda Land Commission, thus removing one level of accountability provided in the land law. As a result 'big chunks of land were leased to individuals by successive Ministers holding the portfolio of Land without due regard to possible repercussions that can emanate from thousands of citizens being rendered landless ...' (Uganda Department of Lands and Surveys, 1980, p. 17). All over Bushenyi there are leaseholders who received their leases during Amin's time, but without the 'benefit' of any survey. Nothing seems to have been done about it, since the Chairman of the Bushenyi District Land Commission warned the Uganda Land Commission that discontent was continuing over lease titles obtained between 1971 and 1978 (Bushenyi District Files, LAN.1, 19 October 1983).

The extent to which political power may be used to take advantage of the law – or even to render it superfluous – is suggested by a 1984 case in which peasants were reported to have been evicted from an area of over 30 square miles of public land in the eastern part of Bushenyi district, which was then fenced and turned into a ranch. An article in *Munnansi* claimed that the displaced peasants not only had nowhere to go nor means to earn a livelihood, but could not complain to either district officials or to their MP, since their MP and their district administrative secretary were part of the group that had taken the land.

By the early 1980s the consensus of officials in several counties was that only tiny bits of public land remained. It is not clear whether the Land Reform Decree accelerated the land rush or not, but it certainly puts at far greater risk those peasants whose *bibanja* were formerly on public land, and who are now the tenants of lessees. In addition it has made the position of nomadic herders, including many Rwandan refugees, utterly impossible. Among the reasons for the expulsion of 80,000 Rwandan refugees (whose numbers actually included many local Bahima herders) in October 1982 were the tensions growing out of many years of rivalry between Bairu and Bahima notables, now complicated by the enclosure of most of the remaining public land (Clay, 1984, pp. 27, 37). Furthermore, the firm party control that the UPC imposed over chiefs after 1980 ensured that patronage for notables would play an important role in determining who acquired control over the land. These chiefs were drawn from the small faction of the Protestant Bairu who threw their lot in with Obote on his return to power.

OFFICIAL EFFORTS TO PROTECT PEASANTS

At both national and district levels officials have put forward suggestions to provide better protection for peasants, though none of these have or seem likely to be put into effect. Part of the problem is the chaotic situation of land records. The Lands and Surveys Department estimated in 1980 that if the Uganda Land Commission suddenly stopped alienating public land, it would still take present manpower ten years to complete the 3000 pending surveys on lease offers (Lands and Surveys Department, 1980, p. 16). At the district level records are in an impossible situation due in part to the shelling of government buildings and looting during the liberation war, several registers are missing and few of the leasehold applications are available in the files.

Official proposals for helping peasants focus on restoring customary tenants' control over their *bibanja*. The Lands and Surveys Department recommended that Provision 24(2) of the Public Lands

Act be reinstated so that customary tenants on public land are required to give consent before land they occupy is granted in leasehold (Lands and Surveys Department, 1980, p. 19). That would restore the most important of the peasants' legal protections, though the help it would actually provide would be limited. That would, of course, defeat the point of the Land Reform Decree by preventing wealthy speculators from acquiring large tracts of public land.

Soon after Amin was overthrown, the Bushenyi district council took a more radical position by urging in an unanimous resolution that holders of *bibanja* be given freehold tenure in their plots (1981: Min. 22/81). Entrenching the rights of smallholders means they would have to be paid the economic value of their holdings by speculators. Since the speculators and high government officials come from the same class, and both see smallholders as the obstacle to economic growth, neither measure seems likely to be adopted.

The local district commissioners took some steps to ameliorate specific problems. They attempted to act as mediators in order to work out patterns of land use where compromise was possible. In particular they tried to protect peasants' use of swamps for growing food crops. If any land had been considered peculiarly appropriate for communal agriculture in Bushenyi and Mbarara, it was swamp land. *Bibanja* stopped at the edge of the neighbouring swamps in order to permit anyone who wanted to grow sweet potatoes, to cut grass for thatching the roofs of their houses, or to remove sand or clay. In addition there is widespread disquiet in the area that draining the swamps would have a serious effect on evaporation, reducing rainfall, and making drought more likely, as well as lowering the water table.

Even though the law did not distinguish between types of public land, an informal administrative practice against leasing swamps to individuals existed during the 1960s, but broke down during the Amin regime. So, as land became scarce, individuals acquired leases over swamps and then drained them for grazing cattle or planting crops. Recently the prohibition has been reinstituted, though in general it is now too late.

Despite the absence of any legal ground to deny such leases, the Bushenyi district commissioner and the district land committee sent a circular to all county chiefs in 1982 informing them that draining swamps was 'an illegal practice' which they should prevent (Bushenyi district files, LAN.1: 7 May 1982). It was an 'administrative lie to protect the people', one of the assistant district commissioners explained. Though the disappointed lease applicant could sue the district land committee, he was not likely to do so because, if he won his case, his fences might be cut, his animals killed and he would be in personal danger. On the other hand, if he had links to political notables, he could probably treat the peasants with impunity.

PEASANT RESPONSES TO THE CLOSURE OF THE LAND FRONTIER
Under the circumstances peasants do not have many options. They can attempt to expand their own customary holdings by purchase – if they are rich enough – or by encroachment. Occasionally they organize and sucessfully resist a lease applicant in court. They may take matters into their own hands and respond violently. Frequently they are forced to live on plots too small to sustain their families and must hire themselves out as day labourers or look for work in a town, leaving the care of food crops to their wives. And in many cases they are forced off their land. If they are fortunate and sell their *bibanjas*, they can try to find cheaper land elsewhere. Alternatively, they are evicted and have no resources to start over again. Though most Ugandans – including the Bushenyi villagers with whom I spoke – continue to deny that many peasants have become landless, this social trend is likely to accelerate over the next few years.

In his monthly security reports the Bushenyi district commissioner reported that violence over land issues was a recurrent problem. In November 1983, for example, he noted that 'land disputes – occasionally erupting into violence – have continued unabated. However, visits by the [Land] Committee and myself have helped to diffuse [sic] most disputes' (Bushenyi District files, Monthly Reports: 4). Still, he felt that land disputes were always close to open violence; there were even cases of sons physically attacking their fathers over land. Many cases, he believed, were never reported. Nevertheless, he felt that most peasants were unaware of how much weaker their legal position had become since the Land Reform Decree had been issued. 'If they knew,' he insisted, 'there would be an insurrection!' (Interview: 7 March 1983).

In one case a rich peasant from a nearby *gombolola* bought a *kibanja* adjoining a swamp, filed a lease application for both and started to drain the swamp. A local Protestant minister whose *kibanja* also bordered the swamp organized twenty of his neighbours to take the rich peasant to court. Eventually, they won their case. But, the local *gombolola* chief added: 'If he had taken the swamp, the people promised to kill him – even in front of the magistrate' (Interview: 14 March 1984).

Frequently, a lease applicant wears down his neighbours in order to force them to sell out. If he intends to change the land use radically – generally from food crops or coffee to fenced cattle grazing – he may offer to trade the peasant another piece of land. In one recent case the *gombolola* chief restored the *kibanja* owner when the leaseholder reneged on an offer of a land exchange *after* clearing the peasant's land of his coffee, avocado trees and his house (Interview: 8 March 1984). In other cases lease applicants, having established a leasehold and hoping to enlarge it, allow their animals to enter the vegetable or coffee plots of their smallholding neighbours to induce them to sell (Interview: 8 March 1984).

When a *kibanja* becomes too small for a man to follow custom by splitting it among his sons, there is pressure to encroach on the *bibanja* of neighbours by uprooting and secretly replanting the *omugorora* plants traditionally used as boundary markers. But when they are unable to expand, peasants are also likely to sell and move to a county in which land is cheaper. Frequently, a peasant will sell strips of land in an attempt to meet his most overwhelming short-term expenses, graduated tax or brideprice. Cases arise where brothers who have left their father's *kibanja* dispute the right of the remaining brother on the land to sell part of it. At the moment many of these sales are not to rich peasants or to lease applicants, but rather to neighbouring middle peasants, who are expanding their customary holding. However, sales to middle peasants who generally are not in a position to pay the fees needed to apply for a lease may merely point to a temporary trend before they too are forced out.

Land-starved peasants often become labourers on the holdings of rich peasants or borrow land to grow enough food to feed their families. One *gombolola* chief estimated that half the peasants under his jurisdiction are hired at some point during the year and are usually paid in cash. A poor peasant could earn his graduated tax in 1984 (UShs1000 – 1500) with about a month's employment in the fields of a rich peasant, working six half days a week. The rent for borrowed land is paid in produce from the harvest and seems surprisingly low compared with well-established sharecropping arrangements elsewhere. Peasants claim they pay (or receive) – and chiefs report similar figures – between a twelfth and a twentieth of the harvest, though it is not clear how much effort the 'borrower' must also put into removing the bush before planting.[5] Chiefs claimed that the practice of renting land began about the time of independence.

The most likely response of poor peasants, especially in areas in which land values are highest, is to leave when their land can no longer support their families. In one *gombolola* 35 families moved out in the first five years of the 1980s. In another containing a little over 3000 taxpayers, there were 27 fewer taxpayers in 1984 compared with 1983. I spoke to more peasants in poorer areas who had moved there within the previous ten years than I met in richer parishes. Nonetheless, while there are many cases of peasants with land inadequate to maintain subsistence, I found only a few cases of landlessness; mostly victims of family squabbles, or labourers who came from other areas and could not earn enough to catch up with continually rising land prices.

CONCLUSIONS: PEASANTIZATION AND THE LAND FRONTIER

Contemporary African peasantries were created by the introduction of capitalist economies, primarily by imperialist penetration from Europe. But they are not fully integrated into capitalism for they continue to depend on their own land and labour for their subsistence (Saul and Woods, 1981, p. 113). It is the complex interplay of factors – varying from one locality to another – constituting the balance between autonomy provided by subsistence and dependence created by the demands of the monetary economy and the state that determines peasant responses (Kasfir, 1986). How, then, does the closing of the land frontier affect the changing dynamics of peasantization?

First, we need to consider how widespread is the disappearance of public land and then what its consequences might be. Growth in population, changes in land tenure legislation, and the machinations of political notables have not only put Bushenyi and Mbarara districts at the edge of the land frontier, but are hastening that day in other parts of Uganda as well. Ugandan population density is uneven: large parts of the north and other parts of the west have far lower ratios of people to land than do Bushenyi and Mbarara. Nevertheless, in each coming generation the country will have to support the same number of people on half the land their immediate predecessors occupied.

The market in land everywhere in Uganda has been sharply expanded by post-independence legislation, particularly the Land Reform Decree of 1975. These changes in land tenure are already having an immediate and widespread impact on control over land. Investment in large tracts promises more profitable returns now that the Land Reform Decree has removed the obstacle of removing peasants from customary tenure. Nabudere argues that within two years after it was decreed, *mafutamingi* – who made money through the allocation of properties taken from expelled Indians – were offering peasants compensation to induce them to leave estates they had leased (Nabudere, 1980, pp. 205–96). He cites a case in Kigezi in which one entrepreneur bought out more than 1,000 peasants whose land totalled 14 square miles, though in that case he apparently then induced them to stay and work for him. There are also reports from the north, particularly Lango, that entrepreneurs are acquiring large leaseholds on what was formerly public land.

What consequences for peasants are likely to follow from the closing land frontier and the new insecurity of farmers and pastoralists whose production continues to depend on customary tenure? The two main considerations are likely to be further capitalist incorporation and further dependence on the state. Further integration into the capitalist economy will be unavoidable for peasants who lose their land, as well as those who acquire large farms that depend on wage labour (Kasfir, 1986, pp. 344–50). That means further differentiation of the peasantry as poor farmers increasingly support their families by working for rich peasants.

Lenin, however, may not have had the last word on Ugandan peasants (1956, pp. 172–89). Capitalism is not advancing so inexorably in Uganda that peasants are close to the crossroads where they must become either petty bourgeois or proletarians. To judge from Bushenyi and Mbarara, for example, the acquisition of land presently seems more a way for entrepreneurs to protect assets from continuing political and economic uncertainties than to introduce large-scale commercial agriculture as the basis of production. Rather, what seems more likely for peasants is a shift in the balance from autonomy toward greater dependence.

Peasant dependence on the state and the incipient social class that controls the state apparatus is already striking (Kasfir, 1986, pp. 350–54). As this chapter has demonstrated, that state of affairs has been important in Bushenyi and Mbarara since the establishment of colonialism. The competitive use of ethnic charters to gain advantage in control over land led to dominance by Bahima notables in the Protectorate period, which then gave way to control by one and then another predominantly Bairu-defined fraction after independence. The ability of political notables to flout laws and regulations that developed during Idi Amin's regime permitted them to acquire land illegally in Bushenyi and Mbarara and undoubtedly elsewhere in Uganda. The expulsion of the 'Rwandan' refugees – orchestrated by the local district council with the connivance of national officials – opened many homesteads to other takers (Clay, 1984, pp. 33–6).

Because the state determines and implements policies of land tenure, peasant security on their land depends significantly on the desire for economic investment in land by those who control the state apparatus. As the frontier closes, land appreciates in value. As struggles for control of the state apparatus become more internecine, safe investment becomes a preoccupation of those in control. If President Museveni can ensure greater political stability, peasants will have a better chance to remain on their land. Finally, what he does about the Land Reform Decree will be a critical indicator of his government's is development strategy.

Notes

1. This chapter is a preliminary inquiry based on field research funded by a Fulbright Senior Research Award and carried out in early 1984. I am grateful to the National Research Council of Uganda and the Department of Political Science and Public Administration at Makerere University, Kampala for facilitating my work. Hakim Kasozi and Jamil Ziyimba, my research associates, made large and indispensable contributions to this project. I also wish to thank Martin Doornbos for his close reading of an earlier draft and his many helpful suggestions. I am solely responsible for all conclusions reached here and any errors of fact that remain.
2. The kingdom was abolished in 1967 and then split into the present two districts in 1974.
3. *Kumanyana*, a movement promoting Bairu interests, promoted the earlier stages of this resettlement.
4. Later in 1984 official salaries were raised by a multiple of three to eight times. However, inflation promptly wiped out much of the increase in purchasing power.
5. In Buganda rent for land seems higher as well as being more expensive, the poorer the peasant (Mamdani, 1984, pp. 56–7).

PART THREE
EDUCATIONAL DISTORTIONS

TWELVE
Education in post-independence Uganda:
change amidst strife

Oliver Furley

'LOPSIDED EXPANSION', 1962–72

Yash Tandon, writing in 1972,[1] gave the education policy of the first Obote regime some degree of praise, but said that educational growth had been lopsided. At independence, there was an urgent need to provide quickly for the trained manpower requirements of the administration and the modern sector in general. Thus there was great emphasis on expanding secondary and tertiary education. Makerere University College, or Makerere University as it became, grew from 1500 students in 1966/67 to 3427 in 1972/73. This was a remarkable rate of expansion, but far too many of the students were in the arts or social science faculties, and this meant that by 1972 many graduates were looking for jobs, the economy being unable to absorb them. Similarly, following the recommendations of the Castle Report (1963), secondary education had been greatly expanded, again without a clear direction as to the proportion of arts or science, technical or vocational graduates required, with the result that those leaving the system with a general academic, arts-based education often found employment hard to obtain.

Secondary and tertiary expansion was inevitably at the expense of primary expansion, and in the early 1960s this lagged behind. The government's second five-year plan, *Work for Progress*, sought to rectify the low numbers in primary school, and aimed at providing places for at least 65 per cent of the primary age-group by 1971, and claimed that the great goal of universal primary education (UPE), which politicians continually referred to, could be achieved by 1981. This had still by no means been achieved, and by 1971 only 29 per cent of the age-group were in primary school. In any case, according to Tandon, on obtaining the primary leaving certificate, 10,000 went on to secondary school, 12,000 to 15,000 to technical training or employment, while the remaining 45,000 to 48,000 looked for jobs to match their qualifications, and drifted to the towns. Yet, as Tandon pointed out, the primary curriculum is still almost entirely oriented to cater for the demands of the one child in seven who ultimately gets admission into a secondary school. It is not surprising therefore, that those who are unable to get into secondary schools should find themselves unfit to go to the rural environment from which they are alienated, but for which their education does not prepare them.

He considered there was need for a drastic change, and the same was true regarding technical education. Here, it was a lack of conviction of the need for growth. There were twelve rural trade schools, five technical schools, one technical college and one commercial college: 'Their total output and rate of expansion have been miserably low.' It is the purpose of this chapter to see whether such criticisms are justified and to detect if there are any recent signs of changes of character as well as scale in the education system.

First one should note that the colonial legacy in education was very firmly entrenched, not least because government ministers, politicians, administrators and teachers were all themselves products of it. Its main features are easily discernible: first of all the missionary tradition, with its emphasis on broad general education coupled with a strong religious element, culminating in an elite system of boarding schools for secondary education; then came government subvention of this system with grants-in-aid for the mission schools and the establishment of government schools very much on the same lines, along with only a limited provision for technical, vocational or agricultural training. The system had been geared to provide clerks and cadres of lower civil servants for the colonial administration, and following the uneven spread of missionary schools in the different regions, no great effort had been made to equalize educational opportunities in more recent times. Above all, the type of education provided was specifically Western and indeed firmly British. How far there was a perceived need to break the mould, and if so how it could be carried out, are questions we shall have to ask in this chapter.

At the time of independence there was no doubt in the government's mind about the need for the expansion of secondary places. Expatriates were still very numerous in the higher ranks of the modern sector and if independence was to mean anything, Africanization of these posts would need to take place speedily. The aim was therefore to double the numbers in secondary schools in five years. The World Bank in its report on economic development, published shortly before independence (1962), urged this, and so did the Castle Report commissioned by the independent government. It echoed the strong missionary tradition in Uganda, being in favour of 'character-building', general education and training for citizenship, and urged a substantial rise in secondary numbers. It assumed that this increase would be based on the existing very expensive boarding school system, and although the report spoke of the need for Africanization of the curriculum – or more specifically of orienting it towards Uganda's needs – it did not consider the linked problem that some 90 per cent of the teaching staff in the secondary schools were expatriates. Nor did it suggest that pupils should be steered towards subjects where manpower was most needed, perhaps for the good reason that there were no up-to-date manpower surveys available at that time. The tradition was still strong that whatever types of education were available in the country, to have more of it was the main solution. The government followed the report's recommendations and placed the main emphasis on the expansion of secondary education: in 1960 there were 21 secondary schools, and by 1965 there were 66. In the process, some of the traditional mission domination of these schools disappeared. The 1964 Education Act aimed to reorganize the ownership and management of schools so that in the boards of governors there would be a predominance of government representatives. Schools were in future to be non-denominational, so that even a famous mission school like Budo should no longer be a 'Protestant' school, or Kisubi a 'Catholic' school. A leader in the *Uganda Argus* (18 December 1963) declared that this would be one of the greatest revolutions ever attempted in Ugandan education. The Act caused great public debate and many protests, but it marked the determination of the government to take over full control of the education system. In practice, the effect was gradual: the big schools remained largely of one denomination for some time, and the character of the governing bodies took time to change (Furley and Watson, 1978, pp. 398–9; Nsibambi, 1976). But it was certainly a big step in the process of breaking the mould: the old mission domination of education went and nationalization took its place. The 1970 Education Act completed the process.

In the later 1960s the main emphasis was still on secondary education. In Uganda's *Development Plan for Education, 1964/65 up to 1970*, there was to be a slight increase in the percentage of children in primary school, but numbers in secondary school were to be tripled: 25 new secondary schools were to be opened in 1965, and 10 more in 1967: 24 new streams were to be added to existing schools, and in 1968 23 converted primary teacher training colleges were to become secondary schools. The aim was to obtain four times as many higher school certificate holders in 1970 as in 1963. The second five-year plan, *Work for Progress*, declared, 'The Government therefore attaches the highest importance to the expansion of secondary education, and much more will be spent on this than on any other branch of education during the Second Plan.' Out of a total of 8 million, 1.5 million was to be spent on the senior sixth forms, which were the higher school certificate classes. In these classes, at last there was to be a government-controlled ratio of science to arts students. The existing ratio of roughly 50:50 was to be changed to a 60:40 ratio in favour of science. School certificate holders were to be 'steered' by a clearing house into the types of training that had the highest priority in the economy, though Uganda was a long way behind Tanzania in this respect, and in Obote's time it never indulged in the forceful 'direction' of students as a policy. By 1969 the expansion in secondary schooling was up to schedule and beyond, so that by 1971 the targets would be exceeded (Uganda Government, 1969).

This expansion was not without its snags. Shortages of qualified teachers, accommodation, school materials and equipment often led to a decline in school morale, which manifested itself in a period of strikes and school riots of surprising frequency, intensity and violence, in the late 1960s. These outbreaks occurred all over the country, in both old and new schools. Buildings, libraries and the laboratories were damaged, while unpopular teachers and head-masters had stones thrown at them, or their houses and cars were burnt. There seemed too many causes. Sometimes it was overcrowd-ing, poor accommodation, especially in the dormitories: at other times it was harsh discipline, or else the efforts of headmasters to impose what they thought was reasonable discipline. These efforts, sometimes involving suspending boys or closing the school for a period, were occasionally undermined by the government, when the decisions of the headmaster were overruled. Other causes were worry over poor examination results and declining job prospects. There were deeper causes too: confused aims among the boys to appear Westernized and yet not 'de-Africanized' at the same time; the still-large proportion of expatriate teachers, who sometimes contributed to this confusion; and sometimes the indifference of African teachers, some of whom were intent on outside businesses. Fundamentally there was a sense of disappointment and impatience that the fruits of independence seemed as yet far away to these students. The advent of Amin's regime put an end to these outbreaks.[2]

Primary education received different treatment in this period. The numbers were not expanded greatly, but much effort was put into reducing the very high wastage rates, and reducing the regional inequalities of opportunity. The Castle Report persuaded the government to reduce the eight-year course to seven years, in the interests of economy and to obtain a higher completion rate. The education given was to be a general preparation for life, yet the Report expressly excluded agriculture from the syllabus. 'Rather than remind them so early of the drudgery of the hoe. Their home *shamba* will do that soon enough.' As for the educationally undeveloped areas, poverty, lack of an economic infrastructure and communications, difficult terrain, absence of missionary activity in earlier days, and often a cultural antipathy towards girls' education, had all contributed to a low percentage of enrolment. The solution to this was to be special 'catch-up-grants' for such areas, making their primary schools truly co-educational, with full provision for girls; inducements could be offered, such as awards of attendance bursaries to girls, free lunches, free tuition, and free uniforms to girls of poor families, and special allowances to women teachers. In Karamoja, the poorest district of all, primary education should be free. This last recommendation was eventually carried out. The seven-year course was brought in, and in 1965 the primary syllabus underwent a major revision, to make it more African in approach, with the necessary re-training and in-service courses provided for teachers. Curiously, the changes involved less use of vernacular languages and more use of English. The National Institute of Education, established at Makerere in 1964, produced the new English syllabus with English as the language of instruction even from Primary I. The Minister of Education, Dr Luyimbaze-Sake, claimed that the teaching of English would prepare children to educate themselves further when they grew up, as African languages did not have the wealth of information that English carried; it would also help to build the nation with one unifying language.[3] It is interesting to note that such a view is totally opposed by the more recently appointed Director of the National Curriculum Development Centre, Mr A.M. Bagunywa, who has long campaigned for a cultural revolution in African education to make African culture feature more prominently in the curriculum, including music, dance and drama, languages, literature, folklore, oral traditions and religions, as well as more African history, and the study of African political, social, and cultural institutions. The 1965 revisions brought in more mathematics, agriculture or domestic science, and the above subjects were weighted in favour of the academically minded child (Bagunywa, 1980, p. 28).

Meanwhile, the goal of Universal Primary Education (UPE), which figured prominently on the political platform of the ruling party, the Uganda People's Congress, was treated with much caution. *Uganda's Development Plan for Education, 1964/65 to 1970*, called for only a slight increase in the percentage of children in primary school, and urged that primary expansion must be related to economic growth and educational opportunity. To establish UPE too soon would not only strain financial resources, but also flood the market with school leavers, with further training only available for a few. It would be difficult enough to keep pace with the rising population, then reckoned at 2.5 per cent to 2.75 per cent per annum. Instead, the plan aimed to make existing primary schools more efficient, cutting down the high wastage rate. In 1966 when the Second Five-Year Plan, *Work for Progress*, was published, there was certainly a change of emphasis, and a substantial expansion of primary education was proposed, with the assertion that it imparted vital economic, personal and cultural advantages. Primary places were to increase by 40 per cent in the plan period, so that by 1971 53 per cent of the age group would be in grant-aided schools, which, with non-aided schools, would mean a total of 75 per cent. An interesting feature was the co-operation of government with parental effort, for in many places it was the parents who collected the money and materials to start building a primary school in their district, in an ever-spreading self-help movement. Government supported this, and in the plan expected to spend £1,650,000, with local authorities contributing £400,000, and parents, it was estimated, approximately £2,000,000, in the value of their efforts.

Teacher training was boosted to match expansion in both primary and secondary education, though the government policy of trying to 'rationalize' the 26 primary teacher training colleges, reducing them to a smaller and more efficient number, proved a slow process, while progress in Africanizing secondary school staff seemed very slow. In 1969, 94 per cent of graduate teachers in secondary schools were expatriates, and even when African graduates were engaged as teachers, they often disappeared quickly into more attractive or lucrative employment. In that same year King's College, Budo, often regarded as Uganda's leading school after 60 years of its history, did not have a single African teacher, although it had had quite a number and had lost them. In a teaching staff of 24, Budo had seen 40 changes in the last five years (McGregor, 1967, p. 157). In 1968, it was still seen as a disquieting problem: Mr E. Nyanzi, Under-Secretary for Education, admitted that of some 1500 teachers barely 200 were Ugandans, and of the Ugandans very few were graduates.[4] In 1965 the government introduced a Grade V teacher scheme, whereby non-graduates with a good school certificate took a three-year course at Kyambogo National Teacher's College, which qualified them to teach in the lower secondary forms, and even up to school certificate in their specialist subject. A two-year course for higher school certificate holders was added.

Makerere University taught a postgraduate Diploma in Education course, and a Bachelor of Education degree was instituted in 1963/64, but numbers were fairly modest, and in 1970/71 an effort was made to speed up production by offering the BA and BSc degrees concurrently with Education. At least some progress was made in Ugandanizing headmasterships, and by 1970 23 out of the 77 secondary school headmasters were Ugandans.

There was still much concern that the type of education given was too Eurocentric, tending to 'turn out a mass of dissatisfied youth looking for white collar jobs only.'[5] It imparted ideas of elitism, it was feared. William Kalema, Parliamentary Secretary to the Ministry of Education, said 'It may be a relic of colonialism, that the school and college products tend to think about themselves as a privileged class who are not always sympathetic to the aspirations of the masses of the people who are, in fact, paying for their education.' Schools must be decolonialized, so as not to produce 'little black whites.' Dr Obote himself echoed these sentiments in addressing Teso College in 1969: the boys were not to regard themselves as a privileged class, with a contempt for manual work. Higher education did not mean behaving like Europeans, but being effective Africans, to serve country and people, identifying with national aspirations.[6] There was also a forthright statement in the leading document of his government's 'Move to the Left', namely *The Common Man's Charter*, 1969:

> We cannot afford to build two nations within the territorial boundaries of Uganda: one rich, educated, African in appearance but mentally foreign, and the other, which constitutes the majority of the population, poor and illiterate ... We are convinced that from the standpoint of our history, not only our education system, inherited from pre-independence days, but also the attitudes to modern commerce and industry and the position of a person in authority, in or outside the government, are creating a gap between the well-to-do on the one hand and the mass of the people on the other ... Our education system aims at producing citizens whose attitude to the uneducated and to their way of life leads them to think of themselves as the masters and the uneducated as their servants.

There were many calls for more technical, agricultural and vocational training at all levels, both to correct this bias and to supply the types of manpower needed. Thus technical subjects were introduced into all secondary schools, with one or more of them to be available in each school, such as agriculture, woodwork, metalwork, technical drawing, industrial art, or commercial subjects. The five technical schools expanded, as did the Uganda Technical College, though the farm schools, which the Second Five-Year Plan had sought to expand greatly, never achieved much growth or popularity, the chief difficulty being the institution of effective settlement schemes for the farm school leavers.

The Move to the Left incorporated other educational schemes of course, including proposals for national service for the whole of the young population. The scheme never materialized because in January 1971 the military coup by Idi Amin intervened.

THE FABRIC SURVIVES IN THE AMIN YEARS, 1971–9

During the eight years of military rule under Idi Amin, it was inevitable, given the nature of that regime, that the education system would suffer. Amin made many declarations supporting the development of education, but in general the army was suspicious of the loyalty of educated people. There were several confrontations between the military and the students on the campus of Makerere University,[7] and others in some of the secondary schools such as Mwiri, where beatings of boys took place in front of the assembled school. In areas of Acholi and Lango, where West Nile troops took revenge on the peoples who had supported Obote, there were massacres and widespread destruction, which meant of course that education was completely disrupted. As is typical in African military regimes, there was much suspicion and dislike of the intelligentsia of the country. Many of the African staff of Makerere University fled into neighbouring countries, often tipped off about their imminent arrest just in time. The same was true among graduates in the teaching profession and the civil service; many of them spent most of these years in exile, though the exact figure is not known. Others were not so lucky and met their deaths at the hands of the army: the most prominent case being that of Mr Frank Kalimuzo, Vice-Chancellor of Makerere University. The effect on the intellectual, educated element of Ugandan society has been a lasting one, and many of those in exile chose not to return to the country after the defeat of Amin, but stayed in new posts elsewhere.

The military regime had disastrous effects on the economy, and enormous proportions of the dwindling budget were spent on keeping the army over-supplied with new weapons, supplies, and cash. Amin's declaration of an 'economic war', in which the Asians were accused of sabotaging the economy, and given until November 1972 to quit Uganda, had a disastrous effect on the whole economic infrastructure, and for the schools it meant that books, paper, supplies, building materials and repair work, etc. – in some cases even food and water – gradually became impossible to obtain, with effects detailed below. The very harsh treatment meted out to the Asians, and the wholesale pillage of their property and goods, had its effect on the European expatriate community, and convinced most of them that it was time to go. This meant that by the end of 1972 the substantial number of European expatriate teachers in secondary schools had disappeared, leaving enormous gaps in the staff. Above all, the effect of these calamitous years on the pupils themselves must have been extremely grave. Bereavement among their families, periods of terror, devastation, deprivation and the prevalence everywhere of *magendo*, the black market and corruption characteristic of the time, must have caused many to wonder whether climbing the educational ladder to collect qualifications was either feasible or worthwhile.

Yet very many did just this, and it is a remarkable fact that the educational process, and the education system as a whole, continued in this period, not unscathed, but by and large intact. 'The collapse, characteristic of the Ugandan economy and many functions of government did not occur in education,' asserts Stephen Heyneman (1983). He cites, among other achievements, the continued managerial prowess shown in the conduct of the primary leaving examinations (PLE) over these years. The examination tests:

> must be delivered at exactly 7.30 am on a given day in December at 4000 different school locations around the country. Accompanying them must be exactly the same number of answer sheets and thick lead pencils, invigilators from neighbouring schools, and (a rival) school's managing committee. In 1978 the exam required a special airfreight flight from London to Kampala; 40 lorries; a military escort – of battalion strength and approximately 3 per cent of the Ministry of Education's current outlays. After three days of testing, the envelopes containing only each individual student's identification number are collected, sealed, and transported back to either Nairobi or London for grading by computer. Results are sent to district education offices and then to each of the 4,000 primary schools within two months. despite extraordinary limitations on foreign exchange, despite (since independence) five changes of government, and despite unprecedented levels of internal strife, each year the PLE has been adminstered on schedule and without scandal.

These valiant effort were also accompanied by very considerable growth, much of it at the primary level, and due largely to parental initiatives and capital. Between 1969 and 1979 an average of 230 new primary schools opened each year, and total primary enrolment grew from 632,000 to 1.2 million (see Heyneman, 1983). The government declared its aims in 1972 were to expand primary education until UPE was achieved, but there was concern that the rate of population increase threatened (even in those disturbed times) to outpace the acknowledged increase in primary places. The *Third Five-Year Development Plan, 1972-76*, stated, 'If no measures to reduce the rate of population growth are taken, and the rate continues its present acceleration, Universal Primary Education will not become a reality until decades after the end of the present century; unless a disproportionately large amount of the country's resources is devoted to the expansion of primary education.' The annual population growth rate in 1972 was reckoned at 3.4 per cent. In the 1950s and 1960s it had been as high as 4.6 per cent, partly due to the inflow of refugees from neighbouring countries. In the absence of firm statistics it was difficult to reckon, but in the 1970s the annual rate had decreased to approximately 2.8 per cent, still very high (Odaet, 1985).

Other worries were the high drop-out rate and the number of repeaters, and the large proportion of primary leavers, some 70–80 per cent, who would get no further education or training. In 1972 less than 65 per cent of the primary age group were in school. The third Five-Year Development Plan set a target of 920,000 in school by 1976, with an annual increase of 100,000, which it was estimated would mean 41 per cent of the age group would be in government aided schools, or 54 per cent if private and unaided schools were included (UNESCO, 1983). By 1974 it was clear that this target would be exceeded, as 901,674 were already enrolled. But there were huge regional differences, with 70 per cent of the age group enrolled in West Mengo, and only 17.5 per cent in Karamoja. In such deprived areas, education had been free for the past five years, with free mid-day meals provided, thus following the recommendations of the Castle Report of many years ago, but it had evidently not done much to improve the situation (UNESCO, 1975).

It is another source of some surprise that in those troubled times great effort were made to reform and Africanize the curriculum. In the early 1970s the primary curriculum was still the one issued in 1965. It contained vernacular and English languages, mathematics, health education, general science, geography, history/civics, religious knowledge, PE, music, crafts and handiwork. The aim was to serve best those who would receive no further education. It was reported to UNESCO that 'The present syllabus achieves some degree of Ugandanization, but leaves much of the general organization of the curriculum, and orientation of syllabuses, as they were in the past – overcrowded and unsufficiently related to the ordinary child's actual experience and interest' (UNESCO, 1973). In 1975 similar comments were made: 'The colonial era did not suddenly cease with political independence, for its roots were also economic, social and psychological...' Education has often led to 'the alienation of the schooled from the unschooled, the desire to imitate imported tastes and cultural norms rather than a dedication to continually develop the African cultural heritage' (UNESCO, 1975). An important new step was the establishment in August 1973 of the National Curriculum Development Centre, with Arthur Bagunywa as its Director, the initial emphasis being placed on revision of the primary syllabus, to produce functional literacy, skills in crop farming, animal husbandry, rural trade skills and crafts – all of these to be part of general science, language and culture. Such aims were of course not a sudden development, and indeed a prime task of the Centre was to co-ordinate the several schemes, some of them supported by international bodies, which already existed. Bagunywa listed these:

(1) The African Primary Science Programme, later the Science Education Programme for Africa, by the Education Development Centre, USA, and the Centre for Curriculum Renewal and Education Development Overseas (CREDO). (2) The Buloba Language Unit, sponsored by the Ford Foundation, for English language training. (3) The Schools Science Report, sponsored by the Nuffield Foundation, relating to O-level but not A-level courses. (4) The Schools Mathematics Project sponsored by the Schools Council for UK, again for O-level but not for A-level courses. (5) The African Social Studies Programme, by the Education Development Centre and CREDO. (6) The Namutamba Integrated Education for Rural Development Project, sponsored by the UNESCO (Bagunywa, 1980, p. 94–5).

This last scheme began as the Namutamba Pilot Project in 1968, in which both teacher training and trial syllabuses in the surrounding fifteen primary schools were tried out. These schools were to be developed into community schools for the non-formal education of youths and adults as well, in order to prevent the alienation of educated children from parents. Much was made of 'the outdoor approach', which included learning about the local environment, rural skills and farming. The Ministry of Education adopted the scheme, hoping that primary schools would become centres for economic development, social improvement and cultural appreciation. The burden of this planned transformation fell on the Curriculum Development Centre, and it produced a five-year plan to redress the curriculum balance in favour of a more practical, environment-based approach. The systematic revision of syllabuses followed, with the introduction of more subjects for rural development. The aim was to prepare primary leavers for a profitable life in their own communities, and to stem the drift to the towns. In 1975 it was asserted that, 'Our textbooks and syllabi reflect this new emphasis' (UNESCO, 1975, p. 11).

Yet there were appalling difficulties, and by the later years of Amin's rule the economy had run down so badly that schools suffered severely from shortages of every kind. The quality of primary provision decreased sharply. Heyneman sketched in a picture of the schools' plight in just one area of Buganda, but it must have been much the same in most areas. In four schools in Buganda with a duplicating machine in 1971 only one had a functioning machine in 1981. In six schools which had an average of 1 chair per 1.2 pupils, by 1981 the average had plummeted to 1 per 8.8 pupils. Few pupils at these schools had pencils or notebooks by 1981, and in some schools not a single textbook was available (Heyneman, 1983). The bland reports to UNESCO do not mention these conditions, nor the chronic security situation in some areas, which must have almost totally disrupted schooling. In addition, the 1978/79 invasion of the country by Tanzanian forces cut a swathe of destruction from the south-west through to Kampala, and caused wholesale looting in many other areas.

In secondary education, the Amin years saw a sharp reversal of previous policy. It was considered by the Ministry that in the 1960s the numbers of secondary leavers needed in the economy had been over-estimated, and the great pressure to expand secondary schools had been uncontrolled. The result was that by 1972 it was reckoned that some 30 per cent of leavers from government-aided secondary schools were neither in employment nor in training. By 1975, of some 8000 Standard 4 (school certificate) leavers, less than 50 per cent found employment 'commensurate with their qualifications and aspirations'. So the third five-year plan called for the strict control of entrants, and in contrast to the Obote period the numbers were held at a fairly constant level, as Table 12.1 shows (Source: UNESCO, 1975).In addition there were 166 private secondary schools, of which 52 were registered with the East African Examinations Council, indicating a recognized level of quality. It should be noted that of the 73 government-aided secondary schools, no less than 62 of them were boarding schools, a balance which was to change soon.

As in primary education, there was a determination to revise and transform the syllabuses, with the emphasis more on technical,

Table 12.1:
Enrolment in Government Secondary Schools,
1964–74

Year	No. of Schools	Enrolment
1964	41	12,044
1966	68	20,582
1968	72	30,309
1970	73	38,805
1972	73	40,300
1974	73	41,293

commercial and agricultural studies. In 1975 the Ministry introduced a new curriculum for all secondary schools, each school having to offer subjects in three areas: the sciences, technical and vocational subjects, and the arts. They could specialize in some of these, but there was a compulsory core of English, history, geography, science and mathematics, and by 1975 two of the curriculum projects mentioned above, the Schools Science Project (chemistry, biology, physics) and the Modern Mathematics course, had spread to all government schools. The new approach was to move away from factual courses, and stress the processes of discovery of principles and concepts, along with experimentation and project work. The 60:40 ratio for science and arts students was maintained, at both higher school certificate and university levels. Africanization of syllabus contents had made big strides by this time. The establishment of the East African Examinations Council in 1968 encouraged the gradual emergence of much more African material at the secondary level: British literature courses became literature in English, with African authors included: mathematics and science courses were oriented to East African problems; language courses included Swahili and Luganda literature. Instead of the history of the British empire, East African history was offered, and the author, who was chief examiner in A-level history for the East African Examinations Council up to December 1972, can testify that by that time there were already a good number of textbooks available to make such courses viable and worthwhile.

The wholesale exodus of expatriates in 1971/72 meant that there was a severe shortage of secondary teachers for a time: in 1973 there were less than 1100 qualified teachers in post, but an additional 1700 were needed. In science and mathematics, UNESCO was told, this 'makes effort to diversify the curriculum almost impossible.' That year, the output of trained secondary teachers at Kyambogo National Teachers' College was 160 per annum, and from Makerere University 182 per annum (UNESCO, 1973). By 1975 this situation had eased, as output at Kyambogo and Makerere had increased dramatically, 'so that today's secondary schools are fully staffed with qualified teachers in the arts subjects. There is still a shortage of teachers in mathematics and physics, and in technical and commercial subjects, but these shortages should be overcome in the next few years, given that the secondary schools will be expanding at a well-controlled pace' (UNESCO, 1975). This official report did not mention another factor that contributed to this improvement in staffing: so many people in top positions of responsibility in the civil service, banks and elsewhere found that their security position was exposed, many of them losing their posts for no apparent reason, or worse, being arrested, detained and even murdered. The survivors therefore often opted for a quieter life out of the limelight and, as many of them had been teachers (such as the late James Aryada, Chief Inspector of Schools), they returned to the safer obscurity of a secondary school teacher's post.

Technical and commercial education was treated in much the same way as secondary: the rate of expansion was slowed. The number of rural trade schools was rationalized down to seven, with five technical schools, and five post-secondary technical institutes. At the top, there were the Uganda Technical College, aided by UNESCO, the Uganda College of Commerce, and the Faculty of Technology at Makerere, the latter also assisted by UNESCO. By 1975 it had produced 45 graduates in the field from two annual intakes, and the government estimated that an annual output of 100 graduates would be sufficient for Uganda's needs. With the technological assets of Uganda in shambles, such estimates must have been guesswork indeed, but the opportunities for trained technologists to rectify matters were obviously very limited. For immediate needs, Amin's government tended to rely on foreign technicians from new allies. In 1972 Egypt sent 14 doctors, two sugar technicians, and two cement engineers, and there were rumours that more would come, though this did not happen. Ghana sent 45 teachers in 1973, and then somewhat surprisingly India,

Pakistan and Bangladesh became suppliers of temporary expatriate personnel, the previous expulsion of Asians having been apparently forgotten. A Ugandan delegation went to Pakistan in 1974, and secured some help; another went in 1977, resulting in the arrival of 400 doctors, engineers, accountants and professors in January 1978 (Mamdani, 1983, p. 94).

MEETING THE DEMANDS OF EIGHT YEARS' FRUSTRATION IN EDUCATIONAL ASPIRATIONS, 1979–83

The war against Amin by Tanzanian troops and Ugandan exiled forces lasted six months and caused much destruction. It was followed by a very uncertain time in which the next President, Yusufu Lule, lasted only 68 days before he was ousted. Godfrey Binaisa's rule lasted somewhat longer until he, too, was ousted by a military clique in June 1980. Milton Obote returned to Uganda to fight for a return victory in the elections, but this period, in late 1980, saw severe famine in the north of the country. His election victory was a hollow one in that very many thought it was rigged, and within three months Yoweri Museveni was leading a guerrilla war against Obote's regime, which lasted for the whole of Obote's second period of office, until the coup of July 1985. This meant that parts of the country were often in rebel control, and other parts, especially the 'Luwero triangle', were devastated by the Ugandan army in a scorched earth campaign. Quite often schools were attacked, looted, and teachers and pupils were either killed or fled. Leading schools with a national reputation did not escape: Gayaza Girls' High School, near Kampala, was attacked in 1983 and nine girls were killed. Whether it was by guerrillas or by the Ugandan army in an anti-guerrilla sweep seemed a minor question.[8] In such conditions, how could the education system possibly develop or even recover?

There were in fact some significant changes, brought about by the Ministry of Education, which was acknowledged to be one of the better and more efficient ministries in this period. Dr Philemon Mateke, Minister of State for Education, outlined the task of Education for 1981–3 as reconstruction and rehabilitation, after eight years of military dictatorship. The need was to expand the educational provision, improve its quality and cost-effectiveness, and revise the curriculum.[9] Somehow, national consciousness and pride had to be restored, with a rebuilding of ethical and spiritual values, social and civic responsibilities, and skills for self-development. Not much could be done in the face of a shattered economy, which showed little sign of recovery until the economic reforms and fiscal measures of June 1981. These enabled exports to grow, and there was a gradual development budget that meant that education was not allocated much.

In primary education there were still only 56 per cent of the primary age group in school by 1980, and government expenditure on these schools was low compared to the average in Africa. This was because the government relied heavily on parents and local communities for the building and equipping of primary schools: government paid only the salaries of teachers and did not pay capitation or block grants to the schools, though some reports say government paid 50 per cent of costs per pupil. The result was that in the government budget the proportion spent on secondary and tertiary education now figured much more prominently. Efforts to improve the primary provision continued however. In Karamoja and other underdeveloped districts, it was free. Eighteen additional primary teacher training colleges were opened, raising the total from 31 to 49. After the Liberation War there was a great influx of children into primary school, but it was recognized that this rate of increase would not continue. By 1983/84 the annual rate of increase of enrolment was 10 per cent,[10] and predictions presented to UNESCO in 1983 forecast that enrolments would fall into line with the annual population growth rate, estimated at 2.8 per cent. In this case the gross enrolment in primary education would reach 100 per cent in the early 1990s, so that the country was within striking distance of UPE (UNESCO, 1983).

In the unsettled state of the country it was hardly surprising that estimates and forecasts differed widely. There was a great need to improve the quality of primary education provided. 30 per cent of primary teachers were untrained, and the desperate shortage of books and materials already described continued. In 1980, Uganda set up its own National Examinations Board in place of the East African Examinations Council (one of the last 'federal' bodies to be disbanded) and the new board tried to take steps to improve teaching for the Primary Leaving Examinations, especially regarding the high failure rates in English and mathematics. The primary syllabus of 1977 was now progressively revised by different subject panels, and the whole curriculum was being restructured in the new format of Basic Education Integrated into Rural Development (BEIRD), which was in line with the philosophy of the previous projects referred to, emerging out of the Namutamba Project.

There was still a high drop-out rate, up to 50 per cent per annum, and the number of repeaters could be 10–15 per cent of each class. Improvement of quality, especially in primary teacher training, was a main concern of collaboration efforts between the National Institute of Education, and the Centre for Continuing Education, at Makerere. The long-term scheme was to upgrade post-primary Grade II training colleges into post-secondary (O-level) Grade III

Table 12.2:
Enrolment in Government Secondary Schools, 1981–3

Year	Enrolment
1981	83,000
1982	101,752
1983	117,087

colleges. But both these institutes were short of staff and equipment (UNESCO, 1983). Improved support to the schools was to be provided by the decentralization of administration, with twelve regional education offices, to be in closer touch with local needs.

Only about 25 per cent of primary school leavers went on to secondary school or further training, and in the 'surge of interest' in education which was reported after the Liberation War, this percentage was considered too low. A third IDA loan, which the Ministry of Education secured from the World Bank, and assistance from the Canadian Agency for International Development, enabled a large increase in secondary provision to be made. A significant change in policy was to drop the traditional emphasis on boarding schools, which necessarily involved high costs, and instead to build up a day secondary school system, rectifying regional imbalances in the process, and again encouraging voluntary efforts by parents and the community through partial grant-aiding. In many cases, good primary schools were now upgraded to secondary schools. The rate of increase in secondary enrolments was phenomenal, as Table 12.2 indicates.

By 1984 there were 410 grant-aided secondary schools, 127 of them offering A-level as well as O-level courses. Such an increase has only been possible because of the government's decision to break with tradition and concentrate on a community-based day school system with the government only undertaking to pay the teachers' salaries and partial grants for recurrent costs. Between 1981 and 1982 the government opened no less than 145 new secondary schools, more than in the whole of Uganda's previous history of education. Because most of these were day schools, this marks the beginning of a breakthrough to a predominantly day school system.

Comparing current building costs and normal standards of accommodation, this means savings in capital costs of a day school place compared with a boarding school place are approximately 35–40 per cent, while corresponding savings in recurrent costs are 50 per cent or more (UNESCO, 1983). Nevertheless it could be argued that, in the face of crippling shortages of teachers, books, materials and equipment of all kinds, it would have been better to shelve this huge expansion programme until a more prosperous time.

It was recognized that these day secondary schools were unlikely to be able to offer the same quality of education as the well-established boarding schools for some time to come. The task would be to achieve a balance of quality, and this could be aided by ensuring that not all the most able primary leavers went to boarding schools. An influx of able pupils into the day schools would raise the standard and as the overall trend towards day attendance became the national norm, the problem would decrease. At the same time, the 1972 secondary curriculum was replaced with a new one in 1982. This broke further away from the traditional emphasis on theoretical and academic subjects. Although English and mathematics were given much weight, and political education was compulsory, the new curriculum moved away from the idea of core subjects, in favour of a wider choice of marketable skills. Agriculture was compulsory in S1 and S2. In S3 and S4, that is up to O-level, English and mathematics were the only compulsory subjects, the other seven or eight subjects being chosen from options, with at least one vocational or technical subject required. The chief concern was to place the practical subjects on the same footing as theoretical subjects, though with severe shortages of tools, machinery and materials, it was often very difficult to introduce new practical courses. Indeed, from a wide range of technical subjects projected, most schools could only offer two in 1980, namely agriculture and principles of accounts.[11] It may well be that this second example of a switch in policy to 'break the mould' will take far longer to implement, except in schools like Mengo Senior Secondary School, which has a pilot project in general technical education.[12]

Technical education also expanded rapidly. Between 1981 and 83, the number of post-primary technical schools was increased from 10 to 23, and the two-year post secondary technical institutes increased from five to 19. In addition there were of course the Uganda Technical College and the Uganda College of Commerce, the Makerere University Faculty of Technology, four vocational training centres operated by the Ministry of Labour, and many apprenticeship training and industrial upgrading courses provided by other ministries, besides the Nakawa Vocational Institute,

Kampala, courses run by the YMCA, the trade unions, etc. Technical teacher training at the Uganda Technical College and the National Teachers' College has been assisted by UNESCO. There were worries about the high failure rate at the Uganda College of Commerce and the Uganda Technical College, however, and in many of the other technical training schemes there was some duplication, overlapping, and under-utilization. This arose partly because there was no single body responsible for co-ordinating manpower training services. The last manpower survey had taken place in 1977, and by 1983 there was urgent need for a detailed survey to identify where the worst shortages of skilled manpower were. UNESCO advised that there should be a central manpower training council in Uganda.

In agricultural education the story was the same. The network of institutions was there, but in very poor shape. At the top, there were the faculties of agriculture and veterinary medicine at Makerere University. Agricultural certificate and diploma courses were run at Arapai College and Bukalasa College, and the College of Agricultural Mechanization, Busitema. Training in forestry, veterinary services, fisheries and co-operatives was given in colleges supervised by the related ministries. In addition, there were eighteen district farm institutes. The Amin years and then the Liberation War had caused immense damage and disruption to these training services at all levels. The Makerere University farm at Kabanyolo had suffered severely, and needed much reconstruction and restoration of even such essential services as water supplies, transport for students, telephones and equipment. The result was that the courses in 1983 were still very theoretical because there was no way that practical work could be taught. At the three agricultural colleges, equipment was either missing or in very bad condition. Arapai College had been badly looted: the Agricultural Mechanization College had no working tractor-renting scheme. Most of the district farm institutes did not have farmers in training because of their losses due to war damage and looting, and because of insufficient funds (UNESCO, 1983).

The conclusion is threefold. First, clearly Ugandan education since independence has seen some wide swings in policy, from rapid expansion in secondary education at the expense of primary education, then a swing to primary expansion, and latterly a huge swing back to secondary expansion with technical and agricultural education rather taking a back seat throughout this period. Second, the military regime imposed colossal strains on the education system with the sudden departure of expatriates, the hostility and violence shown by the military towards the intelligentsia, the university and the secondary schools, and the terrible shortages of equipment, materials, and even food and water for some schools. Buildings and plant deteriorated drastically and this was made worse by the destruction and looting in the Liberation War. The education system and structure survived, but it was almost a skeleton: fleshing it out in subsequent years has proved painfully slow. Third, throughout the period there have been many efforts to transform the colonial legacy and Africanize or Ugandanize the type of education provided. There has been some success: staffing has been in Africanized; syllabuses have been progressively and extensively revised: parental support and enthusiasm has been harnessed, and the predominance of the expensive secondary boarding schools has given way to an emphasis on a day school system.

Notes

1. Supplement on Uganda, *The Times* (London), 25 January 1972.
2. Interview with Paul Beacham, August 1985 (formerly master at Nabumali High School and Mengo Senior Secondary School. See also Kasozi, 1979, Chapter 6.
3. *Uganda Argus*, 16 October 1968.
4. E. Nyanzi, *Uganda Argus*, 16 October 1969.
5. Letter from Alex Banda, *Uganda Argus*, 11 August 1969.
6. *Uganda Argus*, 8 January 1964; 27 May 1968.
7. See Langlands, 1977; 'Makerere Murder – 1976. Progress of the Commission of Enquiry into the Makerere University Affairs, March–August 1976', cyclostyled, 1977.
8. *The Times* (London), 10 June 1983.
9. *The Development of Education in Uganda, 1981-83*. Report to the 39th Session of the Internation Conference on Education, Geneva, 16 – 25 October 1984. Compiled by A. Nakkazi, Assistant Secretary General, Uganda National Commission for UNESCO. Uganda National Commission for UNESCO, Kampala, July 1983.
10. *Ibid.*
11. Uganda National Examinations Board, *First Annual Report, July 1980/June 1981*.
12. Vergise George, *The General Technical Education Project*, cyclostyled, Mengo Senior School, Kampala 1982.

THIRTEEN
The crisis at Makerere

Hugh Dinwiddy and Michael Twaddle

The crisis at Makerere nowadays is not solely a matter of decayed infrastructure requiring urgent material repair. It is also a question of what educational space – if any – the liberal university established towards the close of the British colonial period in Uganda, may reasonably expect to occupy after 25 years or more of political independence from British rule. This question requires reflection. Indeed, without at least some such reflection upon the role of Makerere in the wider context of the country's future, it seems most unlikely that the material damage caused to the university's infrastructure, personnel and morale by successive post-colonial governments will have much likelihood of being remedied at all satisfactorily.

Makerere started institutional life as a secondary school in the 1920s (Macpherson, 1964). 'Makerere is now a school,' remarked the British protectorate governor at speech day in 1934; 'but it is a school which may have a great future ... as the centre of higher education for the East African group of territories ... a place where there shall be provision alike for the sons of the greatest in the land and the poorest' (Mitchell, quoted in Macpherson, 1964, p.23). Sir Philip Mitchell's prophecy was soon realized. In 1950 Makerere formally became the University College of East Africa, to which students from Kenya, Tanganyika and Zanzibar as well as from Uganda and still further afield came to take degrees validated by 'special relationship' with London University. In 1961 it became one of three colleges making up a new federal University of East Africa; a somewhat frustrating relationship for Makerere, because it had to mark time while the two newer colleges forged ahead in Kenya and Tanganyika (Tanzania from 1964, upon the union of Tanganyika with Zanzibar). But in 1970 the federal institution subdivided into three, and Makerere at last became a full university in its own right.

Or so it was initially hoped. However, full university status for Makerere at this time inevitably raised starkly the question of its role in a newly independent country; and this in turn raised further crucial questions about Makerere's future governance and control. All these questions were considered by a commission of inquiry set up by the first Obote government just before the break-up of the federal University of East Africa in 1970. To start with, it was the developmental contributions of Makerere to the newly independent republic of Uganda which most concerned Obote's commission of inquiry. But, as it went round the various departments of the university, governance and control came to concern the commission still more. The headship of Makerere also became an issue of greater importance and, within a short period, Yusufu Lule was replaced as vice-chancellor by Obote's cabinet secretary, Frank Kalimuzo.

Any further major changes Obote might have had in mind for Makerere were overtaken by the Amin coup of January 1971. Makerere now began an era of sustained material decay, inter-spersed with the periods of marked hostility exhibited towards it by the new rulers of Uganda. Before the Amin coup, Makerere's graduates had acted as a political freemasonry throughout the newly independent states of East Africa. Ministers representing the three ex-British dependencies had as often as not been students together earlier at Makerere. After an extremely brief period following the Amin coup – during which civil servants and other graduates became ministers immediately after Obote's overthrow – this was no longer the case. Most of Amin's ministers were now soldiers, and extremely few of Amin's soldiers had been even at school with politicians from Obote's first government. As a consequence, Makerere's regional renown inevitably suffered further decline during Amin's years of power. The simultaneous break-up of the East African Community's regional services still further underlined Makerere's continuing slide from earlier significance. Visiting examiners from Makerere were still to be encountered at Dar es Salaam or Nairobi universities during the 1970s, but the picture they now painted of Makerere was a very different one from the previous decade. It was a picture of things turned upside down in more than one way. For example, during the 1970s, as in the 1960s, a Makerere university teacher's status could be measured roughly by the altitude of his or her residence on Makerere hill. But, whereas under Obote's first government one went up the hill as one's career and family expanded, under the Amin regime the most desirable residences became the ones at the very bottom of the hill and movement, such as there was, was therefore to where water still reached the taps, and where gardens were large and fertile enough for staff to grow more of their own food, as the value of salaries declined with inflation.

This is still essentially the situation. By comparison with their colleagues of the 1960s, Makerere staff now receive minute salaries.

This requires them to supplement their academic incomes by second or third occupations if at all possible. Physically, conditions have also deteriorated markedly, so that almost all sectors of the university require rehabilitation for future use. Inevitably the question arises: is such rehabilitation worthwhile? Is money spent on the rehabilitation of Makerere University money well spent? As indicated earlier, an adequate answer to this question requires attention not only to an extremely long list of material works requiring rehabilitation, but reflection upon Makerere's role in Uganda too.

The stress on Makerere's contribution to manpower planning was not the concern of Obote's commission of inquiry at the close of the 1960s alone, but had been present from the very beginning. Indeed, during the 1920s there had been considerable concern in British colonial circles that not too many schoolboys should pass through its courses, lest there should be insufficient employment for them in Uganda after graduation. Basically it was the sheer expense of continuing to employ European civil servants in top jobs, and Asians in the middle management positions during the financially tight 1930s that led to more ambitious plans emerging for Makerere in the 1940s, because Africans would necessarily be cheaper for colonial administrations to employ than either Europeans or Asians. Nonetheless, despite the utilitarian tinge to British protectorate planning, the idea of a liberal higher education being provided by Makerere was also present from the beginning. To start with, this had been mingled with the moralism inherent in the sort of British boarding school education that provided so many of Makerere's teachers in its earliest days. Further strengthening of liberal education at Makerere through a special link with Oxford University was contemplated just before the Second World War, but this came to nothing; as too did plans during the war itself for educating the new Kabaka of Buganda at Oxford through 'a modified Greats course ... combined with practical training in the growth of cotton' (Symonds, 1986 p.233–5). Nonetheless, the desirability of liberal education was emphatically endorsed by the Asquith Commission, which reported in 1945 and successfully recommended Makerere's upgrading to university status in association with London University.

'An institution with the status of a university which does not command the respect of other universities brings no credit to the community it serves', reported Asquith (quoted in Maxwell, 1980 p.13). Manpower needs in the wider community necessitated diplomas as well as degrees being awarded by the newly upgraded college. However, it was not considered appropriate that those requiring training to become medical orderlies or agricultural assistants should train alongside those about to become medical doctors and those studying more intensively for an agricultural degree. Those seeking more practical courses should be guided into more practical institutions than Makerere. The Asquith Commission laid emphasis, for Makerere, upon a balanced education, 'neither rigidly directed to the training of recruits for professions, nor [so] disdainful of practical needs that its products are unequipped for useful service to the community'. One of the principal aims of educational upgrading, in the Asquith view, was 'the preparation of colonial peoples for self-government'; and this aim could scarcely be seriously upheld, it was also implied by Asquith, without 'balance' between usefulness and uselessness. 'In our view there is no fundamental antithesis between liberal and vocational education. We hold that this distinction can be transcended'. And transcended it was, until the strains of decolonization brought Makerere – along with other educational institutions established during the British protectorate period in Uganda – under severe stress.

This stress was partly a side-effect of decolonization already under way elsewhere in tropical Africa during the 1950s. Partly, too, it was a direct consequence of the type of education by now consciously inculcated at Makerere. One of the pleasures of running a hall of residence at Makerere was entertaining important visitors. In 1961 one such visitor was the British Colonial Secretary, Alan Lennox-Boyd. Unfortunately, Lennox-Boyd's visit to Northcote Hall was not a resounding success, at least in the normal sense of the word 'success'. A number of students were invited to meet the distinguished visitor in the Makerere Arts Building, but when in a jolly way Lennox-Boyd remarked that he wanted to see 'the Kenya boys' about a certain matter on his mind, he was most disconcerted when these particular students retaliated by walking away from him, muttering angrily that Lennox-Boyd considered them schoolboys, that he had a 'settler mentality', and that it was quite unrealistic to expect any sensible constitution to be discussed with such a man. Fortunately or unfortunately, Lennox-Boyd did not appear to hear what these students were muttering about his use of the word 'boys'. But it is perhaps interesting to note that one of the Kenyan students present on that occasion was the novelist and critic, Ngugi wa Thiong'o. Ngugi has also since then written vigorously about the necessity of 'decolonizing the African mind'.

For Ngugi, decolonization of the African mind involves abandoning the English literature taught during his time at Makerere, and substituting for it novels and poetry written by Africans. Ngugi's teachers were of course very conscious of what one of them (Alan

Warner, Professor of English) called 'the problems of the missing background' in the study of English literature. Indeed, in 1958 Warner wrote on this very theme in a piece which opened with the question put to him by one Makerere student: 'Please Sir, who is Father Christmas? The speaker was a member of my final year General Degree course in English' (Warner, 1958). Warner further explains that none of the students in question had either seen anybody dressed as Father Christmas at any time or any picture of him, and one student assumed that he was an early Father of the Christian Church. Without labouring the point any further, it is surely reasonable to point out that Makerere, simply by being there and teaching a course of this kind, was able to solve many such problems of 'missing background', as well as stimulating creative writing by new African writers such as Ngugi himself. From 1958 the English Department at Makerere produced an annual magazine called *Penpoint* that ran to about 25 pages and contained students' short stories, poetry and plays; many of which were subsequently collected and published in the anthology entitled *Origin East Africa* under the editorship of a later head of the English Department, David Cook. Of course, whether it was right to put so much stress upon nineteenth-century British novels and poetry is open to debate. Warner's view, and it was a view very widely shared in his time at Makerere, was that the Britain of Charles Dickens had produced such a rich vein of creative writing in the wake of urbanization, industrialization, and massive social dislocation, that prolonged study of it by students at Makerere would inevitably reap rich rewards for them in terms of liberal education.

But it was liberal education for an elite. Whether it was English history or some other subject in the humanities or social sciences, it was liberal education for a comparatively small number of people. And these people inevitably aroused suspicions amongst both British colonial administrators and European missionaries in their home areas, because of this very elitism. This same elitism also stoked up further political trouble for Makerere students and others because of the students' clear concern to build closer associations with their ethnic kinsmen at Makerere, and because of the corporate antipathy of all Makerere students of the time towards soldiers. All these things created serious problems for Makerere.

As educators of their own people, a considerable number of Makerere students formed ethnic associations before independence from Britain: Kalenjin societies, Luyia societies, the Abana ba Buganda society, Iteso societies, and so on *ad infinitum*. As members of such associations, Makerere students would make a special effort during university vacations to get in touch with people in their home areas, in particular advising them on how they should approach independence. Needless to say, these students were reported to be 'agitators' by local British district commissioners. In a similar fashion, Roman Catholic students from Makerere reported that the very act of taking a newspaper back to their home areas was regarded with suspicion by certain Roman Catholic missionaries. On occasion they were even denounced from the pulpit for 'stirring up the people unnecessarily' and even for 'spreading communism'. This is no exaggeration. Indeed, after early morning Mass at Mbarara shortly before independence, Hugh Dinwiddy was specifically asked by the bishop's secretary there to tell His Lordship 'about all the communists at Makerere'. Visiting Kigezi a few days later, Dinwiddy went to the Roman Catholic mission just outside Kabale and was told while breakfasting with the White Fathers there 'of all the communist spies infiltrating across the border from Rwanda'. In retrospect, these reports seem fantastic. But at the time these European missionaries were sure they knew best, because they were on the spot, and their conspiratorial hunch about what was actually happening in their immediate bailiwick – for hunch was all that it could possibly have been – fitted in with 'communism' constituting the principal enemy of Roman Catholicism in Kigezi every bit as much as in Czechoslovakia. Amongst Verona Fathers in northern Uganda these views were, if anything, even more deeply entrenched. John White, a resident tutor in one of the Makerere halls of residence as well as local corresponent for *The Times* newspaper, went round as many northern Roman Catholic parishes as he could immediately before the Uganda general elections of 1962, and concluded that these missionaries were preaching 'sheer anti-communism' to their parishioners (personal communication to HD at the time). And in such an intellectual climate, Makerere students were inevitably suspected by many missionaries as well as district commissioners to be carriers of unduly subversive doctrines at the time of independence. But it was probably as 'imaginers' of ethnic associations at district level that Makerere students had their greatest political impact upon Ugandan politics, both before and after independence from Britain.

This is an aspect of Ugandan politics about which it is all too easy for the foreign observer to be excessively simplistic. For around the time of independence in Uganda, Makerere students were *both* tribalistic *and* nationalistic in their public utterances. On the one hand, there were many references in Makerere magazines at this time to 'the African personality'. There were also many references to it in the new and most appropriately named monthly journal, *Transition*, founded by Rajat Neogy and published for the first time

in Kampala in November 1961. Indeed, in his first number Neogy
wrote that one of the principal questions to which the new journal
would address itself would be: 'What is our East African culture?'
Stimulation to write about the African personality came partly from
anglophone Africans' need to find something to say in reply to the
earlier, eloquent stress upon 'negritude' by francophone Africans.
But it was hardly surprising that many of the contributions to
Transition on this subject should have been supplied by writers from
Makerere, students as well as staff. Nor, in retrospect, does it seem
especially surprising that many of these contributions should have
proved primarily ethnic in emphasis. For while calls for 'Freedom
now' were increasingly heard at the East African level, most
Makerere students worked to influence events most energetically
through university societies linked to their home areas. And if the
thrust of such associations as the Abana ba Buganda, Makerere
Students' Kalenjin Society, or Makerere Students' Chagga Association, was initially cultural and developmental, during the era of
decolonization they became in practice political. One group of
Kenyan students did request, just before Kenyan independence,
that tribal origins should be omitted from the Makerere nominal
roll, so that national origins could be stressed. But it proved difficult
to go beyond symbolic action, and it was the ethnic association that
received greatest stress at Makerere because, of course, as far as
many students were concerned, these ethnic associations had been
formed before they themselves arrived there.

The principal Baganda group was the Abana ba Buganda. They
waxed and waned in importance at Makerere, depending upon
what the Kabaka of Buganda himself was doing. One afternoon at
Lugogo stadium, Hugh Dinwiddy invited the Kabaka to attend high
table one evening at Northcote Hall since, as Hugh put it, 'your
students would love to see you'. But Mutesa II refused, saying that
he 'lived in a sort of cocoon', and could not expose himself to the
general mass of Makerere students in this way. Nonetheless, the
Abana ba Buganda had its importance when the Kabaka was
suffering in other ways. In 1966 for example they rose up, launched
their own paper, organized their own meetings, and paid special
visits to the Kabakas' graves when Obote attacked the Buganda
kingdom; and the whole idea of the Kabakaship became extremely
important to Baganda students at Makerere at this time. But by no
means to all Baganda students at Makerere, only certain of them.
Indeed, at this time some Baganda went out of their way to show that
they were not as narrow in their attitudes as were the Abana ba
Buganda. Senteza Kajubi was one of these; he was one of the first
leading Protestants to join the Democratic Party, and indeed might

well be leader of the DP today had he been more of a politician and less of an academic.

But far more serious was the massive disdain of Makerere students of all tribes for Ugandan soldiers. Like most students in other countries, Makerere students were primarily concerned with their own careers. While their 'political' activities at the time of independence were of considerable importance, they themselves doubtless regarded them as of secondary importance compared with their own personal advancement through a university education. Decolonization was here a time of extraordinarily high expectations. When white men departed at this time, black men not only took over their jobs, but also their houses. Furthermore, because decolonization in Uganda was so comparatively swift during the early 1960s, and the army was not included in arrangements for it, there were army mutinies in 1964. When African NCOs and officers saw other Ugandans taking over departing Europeans' jobs and houses, when they themselves still had British officers over them, they rebelled. They demanded that British officers should also go within six months. The jealousy of Ugandan soldiers for Makerere students on this score was also considerable for another reason. Students refused to play any games with the soldiers. When Hugh Dinwiddy was president of the students' games union at Makerere, the students resolutely refused to play any game against any army team, not so much because they might lose, but because Makerere students regarded soldiers as rough and uncouth chaps, utterly beneath contempt. It was an appalling attitude. It was also an attitude that reaped a bitter harvest in the soldiers' harassment of students after the Amin coup of 1971. For example, when the Amin soldiers invaded the Makerere campus in 1976, they made all the students lined up in front of the main building lie down, dance, do this, do that, take your shoes off, walk on your knees, do a whole range of things designed to teach 'these upstarts' a lesson. And teach them a very nasty lesson, the soldiers certainly did on this and other occasions (Langlands, 1977).

The earlier arrogance of Makerere students towards the Ugandan army had certainly been strengthened by their elitism. This elitism in turn had to a very considerable extent been strengthened by their education at Makerere. But more fundamental forces had been at work here too. Within the socio-economic structure of colonial Uganda, soldiers had enjoyed wages and status roughly equivalent in value to those of migrant labourers working on sugar cane estates in the southern part of the protectorate. Education essentially accentuated differences between such soldiers and labourers on the one hand, and other Ugandans on the other;

differences that were essentially rooted within the socio-economic structure of the British protectorate. However objectionable 'Makerere elitism' might therefore appear to Ugandan soldiers, it was itself more an expression of these more fundamental differences, and only secondarily objectionable in its own right. Needless to say, Ugandan soldiers did not treat Makerere students any more gently as a result during the 1970s.

Resentment was also widespread in the towns against Makerere's 'elitism', and for much the same reason. And, to a considerable extent, this resentment still persists and makes Makerere's rehabilitation in the devastated conditions of Museveni's Uganda still more problematic. The NRA newspaper, *New Vision*, has printed letters revealing continuing popular resentment against Makerere, as well as defensive replies by the current Makerere administration and still more angry letters by Makerere students and staff. The Makerere administration has appealed to the World Bank, EEC and other foreign donors for 100 million US dollars, 'to repair buildings and laboratories, and buy scholastic materials' (*New Vision*, 5 September 1986). It has replied to criticism that this appeal seems to be dictated by a desire for 'eating' – corruption – on the part of administrators and contractors by stating that

> The university as it is now cannot be saved by Manna from heaven, but rather by friends. A donors' conference is not an 'eating' venture. If such donors give Makerere a new hall or library, then it is the students who will have eaten and not the officials (*New Vision*, 3 February 1987).

However, younger staff clearly chafed at appeals for rehabilitation of a material kind which bypassed their concerns:

> accommodation and the 'I don't care attitude' of some officials. Apart from the laughable meagre salary Makerere offers no single incentive to its employees ... I am really worried about the donors' conference. Some people are going to suggest projects from which they will be able to 'eat' to the detriment of the university (*New Vision*, 2 January 1987).

Clearly, these are concerns not restricted to Makerere, but ones common to a number of public institutions in Uganda nowadays.

Indeed, that was precisely the burden of Professor Kabwegyere's complaint about Ugandans' excessive concern with 'eating' in *New Vision* newspaper:

> The boost to the growth of conspicuous consumption was the

allocation of businesses to any one that pleased the allocation committee after the 1972 expulsion of Asians. This time not the elite but, in many cases, the less-than-ordinary citizens. Wealth was no longer an accompaniment of office alone but ... simply an attribute of an allocated business.

Very little of this money, because it was not really wealth, was ever invested in production to any significant extent. The businesses were literally looted. When looting came later, some people wondered why. A whole decade had been devoted to looting. Every one else became a convert.

Two examples of this problem are obvious: weddings and graduation ceremonies. Several meetings are held to raise money for consumption. This has introduced a culture of beggary.

One would have thought that the few who have made it to Makerere are better. Many of the people who have just graduated have not had any job since they left the campus. Yet sumptuous parties were held to celebrate the graduation which led to no job ... It is high time Ugandans earned the money they want to spend. The opposite of consumption is production. Produce before you consume and Uganda will have started on the journey to recovery (*New Vision*, 30 January 1987).

In his paper to the Roskilde conference, Hugh Dinwiddy quoted the words of a Makerere student leader at the time of Uganda's independence celebrations in 1962:

The benevolent Protectorate Government is no more, and unless we work hard for the good of our nation, this political independence may well mean poverty and misery to the majority of us at least. Let us then forget our differences and join hands with our Prime Minister and his Government in their determination to combat Ignorance, Illiteracy, Poverty and Disease in order to make Uganda a happy and progressive nation (Makerere Students' Independence Celebrations Committee brochure, 1962).

The 1970s and 1980s have proved very bumpy years for Makerere. Elsewhere, too, the idea of a liberal university and the concept that learning is of itself something to be cherished regardless of its immediate usefulness, have come under attack. However, letters to the press like that of Professor Kabwegyere are surely reassuring. His letter may be right. Or it might be wrong. But one thing about it seems indubitably clear. It surely indicates that, amidst enormous material difficulties, the idea of the liberal university is still very much alive at Makerere – and working in one of the university's supposedly least 'useful' departments, Sociology.

PART FOUR
PROBLEMS OF IDENTITY
& NATIONAL INTEGRATION

FOURTEEN
What went wrong in Uganda?

Christine Obbo

INTRODUCTION

This chapter departs from the tendency in Africa to analyse problems and crises in terms of personalities. This is not to deny the importance of attributing policies that result in human suffering, rampant corruption and political instability to political leaders. The position in this chapter is that in order to understand exactly what went wrong in Uganda, i.e. the causes of the present political, social and economic malaise, it is important to examine the internal dynamics of Ugandan society that have produced it. The entity called Uganda is a result of a colonial policy that sought to transform a 'multiple aggregation' of different groups of people into a viable political state. Colonial policies also sowed the seeds of the weeds that have now overrun Uganda. However, Ugandans must take blame for nurturing rather than uprooting and destroying the weeds.

In public discussions Ugandans express passion for human rights and democratic principles, but in interpersonal relationships infringements upon the personal and civil rights of others seem to be taken for granted. When all is said and done, it will be found that the Ugandan tragedy, which led to the total collapse of the economy and unnecessary losses of human lives, was basically a struggle for human dignity (denied through ethnic chauvinism) and a struggle for a decent share in educational and employment opportunities. There is need to analyse the colonial legacy that had demarcated the southern regions for bureaucratic duties and the North as a source of agricultural labour and military manpower. But, for the purposes of this chapter, it is argued that it is the seemingly mundane daily acts of people that provide the essential material for analysing the Ugandan situation.

ELITISM: BUREAUCRATIC POWER

The system has been unfair if scholarships and chieftainships could only go to bona fide Baganda whereas many counties have more non-Baganda tax-payers than Baganda.[1]

Kyagwe and Kyaddondo counties have been my special interest and areas of research. Since 1971 I have collected data in Kampala and in three villages in what is now Mukono district. I start answering the query of what went wrong in Uganda by looking at education, which produces elites with access to employment and other opportunities.

Despite the fact that some villages in the Kyagwe county of Buganda had nearly a quarter to one half immigrants, who had settled in them, who were taxpayers and who supported the school system, none of the immigrant children were recipients of county scholarships. A former teacher at a prominent secondary school explained it this way:

> In all my classes the non-Baganda children were hardworking and often achieved top grades even in Luganda classes! Every time I recommended any of these children whom the fellowships are meant to reward, none of them ever received any. The headmaster always managed to reward the academically poor pupils just because they happened to be his children or those of his friends and relatives.[2]

The headmaster was using his position to give his children a head start. Despite the financial and other manipulation, only one out of his six children went to Makerere University, and graduated with not such a brilliant record.

In the late 1950s and early 1960s, the headmaster was actively engaged in the nationalist politics that sought Uganda's independence. He was part of the new elite termed responsible nationalists by Governor Sir Andrew Cohen. At the eleventh hour the colonial authorities actively groomed a middle class (petty bourgeoisie) of collaborators to eventually assume leadership. The party that the headmaster and his relatives started did not do well in the independence election. He did, however, get a modern leadership job in the capital.

The relevance of this case will be clearer if we take a brief glimpse into history. The Pax Britannica created an elite class that was used to spread and maintain indirect rule. It is therefore important to address the question of elitism in the present Uganda crises. Is the looting and destruction of property that has been the political weapon of the masses since the 1940s a reaction to ethnic competition or to class privileges.

If in 1900 the chiefs, 'friends of the Queen', were demanding the right to an income and the right to bear arms, in 1946 Sir J. Hathorn

Hall was lamenting that:

> As education spreads, so the number of persons prepared to
> undertake any work with their own hands diminishes in inverse
> ratio. Once a boy has passed through the primary school he
> considers that he has automatically joined the ranks of those who
> order others to work, and that physical labour by himself was
> derogatory. Whether responsibility for this failure rests with the
> educational system or with those entrusted with its administration
> ... it is a very disturbing fact and particularly serious in a basically
> poor country like Uganda ... which can only be developed by hard
> and sustained work ... We have thus two serious limiting factors
> [to the development of the country's potential wealth] a predomi-
> nantly peasant agriculture; and an inefficient labour force.[3]

Hall concluded by proposing that the Public Relations and Social
Welfare Departments should take over where the Education
Department stopped: '... on its success or failure must largely
depend the social and political future of Uganda ... If we fail, then
the progress of Uganda will inevitably be retarded and her future,
social and political and economic, will be black (no pun intended)'.

The basic issues that Hall raised are still with us: anyone who has
learned the alphabet wants to have clean nails (i.e. shuffle papers) or
be a superior (i.e. give orders). Until 1945, the educated people with
only primary school education did land jobs as clerks, could be sent
to England (by the British Council) on 'Refresher' courses and by the
time Independence came in the 1960s, many of them were elite
members heading or about to head schools, government departments and were active in political parties. The spread of secondary
school education produced a hierarchical elite that was itself as
elevated by virtue of its members' professional jobs and international connections. However, the semi-educated regarded themselves as equally deserving of high prestige, but they too regarded
the peasants as backward. The real legacy of colonialism as far as the
Uganda situation is concerned was not only the rise of elites and a
semi-educated minority that would not work on the land but also the
implications of this in a country with two distinct areas determined
by colonial policy. The south was the 'productive' region and the
north was the region that supplied labour. The latter provided men
to work in the productive (cash crop) areas; it also provided soldiers
for the army to ensure law and order and to put down peasant
revolts. The south, by virtue of being the site of the administrative
capital, had a head start in schools, hospitals and commerce. The
regional differences in wealth and occupations that originated in
colonial policies are often articulated as natural and in need of

defending. One often hears people from Buganda province tell foreigners that they have the right to rule because they have more people who have been to school.[4] The 'southern' bureaucracy and the 'northern' army syndrome were perpetuated by nepotism, local[5] and regional interests. In 1980 the district of Karamoja was devastated by famine due to no fault of the population; indeed the fleeing Amin soldiers exacerbated the situation by stealing or killing their cattle at an accelerated rate. The attitudes expressed in statements often heard by UNICEF workers in Kampala were even once quoted by a *Newsweek* magazine reporter, as follows: 'The Karomajong have been primitive for a long time. Let them starve. Leave the food, clothing and medicines here.'[6] These eliticist attitudes are deep-rooted among bureaucrats. They manifest themselves in two ways: in what seems to have been a deliberate attempt to block the advance through entering bureaucratic jobs of people who came from the labour areas and, secondly, a general discrimination against peasants seeking to improve their lot by seeking jobs in the public service. Regarding the former, an easterner tells how in 1971, while being interviewed for a civil service job, he was compelled to answer questions posed in the interviewer's language, although the official language of Uganda happened to be English. He was told: 'You are bright. I have never met a northerner like you. You are unusual.' In fact, a poorly qualified southerner was hired for the job. The easterner to this day says, 'Even if I had been a northerner, what mattered is that I had a good Makerere degree and I resented being patronized.' Sometimes, even in public discussions, the issue of regional educational differentials surfaces. In a 1981 newsletter of the National Resistance Movement, its leader, Yoweri Museveni argued that one of the reasons Uganda finds itself in the present political mess is because at independence, men of 'low level of modern education' including 'school drop-outs like Obote found themselves at the helm of state affairs' although Uganda had 'the best trained [elite] in Sub-Sahara Africa.'[7] Yet an examination of Uganda politics throughout the 1960s indicates that members of the elite – professionals, trade unionist, teachers and businessmen – were very active on the political scene.

In the following section, discrimination in the award of vital scholarships among the elites and gruesome elimination of competition at the village level are illustrated with examples. The point at issue is the lack of fair play and the possibility of revenge being taken in the future. Between 1971 and 1979, many Ugandan refugees fled via Nairobi. Many refugees survived because they had good friends. Technically, it was possible to receive financial aid from the United Nations High Commission for Refugees or the National Council of

Churches. The most common complaint was that scholarships to study went to people from the southern part of Uganda where, coincidentally, some of the influential employees of the two regional offices originated. Between 1973 and 1975 many northerners were being persecuted and interrupted their education by fleeing to Kenya. Yet many of the recipients of the fellowships were southerners who in most cases were already abroad on other scholarships. There were cases where money was used to transfer students from European to American institutions. It was also alleged that the relatives of those connected with the scholarships had priority. After 1975 Ugandans from all walks of life and from every region were fleeing Amin's reign of terror. Many did attempt to seek fellowships through foreign friends of Uganda. One clergyman who had previously been in charge of the scholarships in Nairobi and had somehow managed to move to the United States and live lavishly was involved in a hit and run incident and despite encouragement from the Washington DC police, he declined to press charges. Rumour among Ugandan exiles was that he knew that his Nairobi misdeeds were catching up with him.

In 1979 at Makerere University, heads of departments were instructed to write letters to all scholars abroad asking them to return and help rehabilitate education. One department head, who technically had no professional qualifications to be in that department, wrote letters only to people from his own ethnic group. In most cases those contacted were just at the beginning of their university careers and did not return. Even then the head of department saw no need to contact qualified and practising scholars who came from other parts of Uganda.

In 1985, while the head of department was on an official visit outside the country, the acting chairman rushed through a promotion recommendation for a colleague from his part of the country. On paper everything in this department looks regular, but underneath things are rotten. At one point the head of the department attempted to hand over a popular course with the highest enrolments in the department to a lecturer from his home area. He forgot that one important ingredient of courses are the teachers who design and implement them.

The pettiness of these two examples can be laughed off but they should raise concern over current problems and possibilites for the future. During the 1970s such problems were solved by the injured person bringing soldiers to kidnap and eventually kill the culprits and sometimes the favoured pawns in such games. Still, some injured people would personally execute justice. Many people disappeared and lost their lives over such petty affairs. The simple point being made is that the same elites who were helping the international organizations document cases of human rights violations were themselves contributing to such violations, whether by denying deserving refugees fellowships or by overlooking and underplaying the achievements of others. The point at issue is that people who infringe upon the dignity and rights of others cannot right them by shouting political rhetoric about democracy and human rights. It can be argued that engendering trust among Ugandans should take priority over impressing foreigners.

Meanwhile back in Kyagwe county, villages had an interesting tradition of dealing with competition. In 1945 and 1948 there were economic boycotts aimed at protesting against the monopoly accorded to Asians to run business by the colonial government. I was told by informants that poor people or competitors could start a whispering campaign against anyone whose gardens and house indicated economic success. One 68-year-old woman put the whole matter in perspective. She called the persecution of the rich during the 1940s a modernized kind of witchcraft accusation in which one was never confronted with one's accusers but with innuendos and finally a faceless mob in the dark of night. She put it this way:

> When I was young, a prosperous farmer was always accused of using sorcery which sucked the fertility from the neighbours' gardens into his. Most of the accusers were lazy, drunks, or had no means of producing more. In the 1950s, witchcraft accusations were supplemented by arson. Competitors or jealous neighbours simply torched the grass houses at midday when they were likely to burn quickly. This set a trend so that even people who could not afford it made the effort to roof their houses with corrugated iron. Soon after that, strong wooden doors with padlocks replaced moveable reed doors. Robbery by force (Kondoism, i.e. stealing by breaking the padlock, *kakondo*) became common. Thieves would chop down the door with a panga (or big knife) or hurl a heavy stone to open doors. People who were still envious but were not inclined to robbery resorted to poisoning or using home-made guns on others. People died of poisoning from beer they purchased or from gifts of cooked food. The guns never killed anyone but they maimed people – so that they could not work as hard as before. In one case, a rich womanizer had lost a leg from a gunshot, some villagers visited assiduously, hoping he was dying. But as soon as they learned that he was to return home, they went to the hospital and poisoned him to death. Several people were tried and imprisoned for making and using home-made guns.[8]

For some time now (1960–79), factory-made guns have been common. Soldiers have them and others have ways of getting access to them. People in this village say, 'It is the poor who waste time on sorcery, just hire someone with a gun and the score will be settled.' The most feared words in Uganda are 'You will see.' Children learn to avoid kids who invoke such words: and adults get worried in view of this sorcery / poison / gun scenario.

This interview was cross-checked with five other informants who agreed with it entirely. In fact, events in the villages during the 1970s, but particularly recorded by the writer in 1979, revealed a lot about the fate of successful competitors, especially if they had different ethnic background from that of the host community.

One night in June 1979, a Munyankole taxi driver was doused with paraffin and set alight in a nearby forest and his father was threatened with a similar fate if he dared even accord his son's bones a burial. The reason given for this merciless killing, at which most Baganda in the village were present, was that the victim was a bandit. Three months later the real bandit was caught with most of the things in his house and hounded out of the village. He was a 27-year-old son of a Muluka (village) chief, whom no one would have suspected but for providence. During an escape after breaking into a house in a nearby village, he had lost a leg to a passing train. A week later, his best friend killed his father, mother and sister with a shotgun when they confronted him with the facts about the innocence of the murdered Munyankole taxi driver. While most people were revolted by this family execution, they pointed out that threat of death often stopped people from publicly condemning these murders of victims of popular justice. This case emphasizes the point that the victims of popular justice may be innocent people whose most vocal accusers are the real culprits. The Banyankole had moved into the area in the 1930s and 1940s. They were often single men who herded cattle for some Baganda farmers. They lived in huts near the kraal and devoted a lot of time to their work. They were paid poorly and some supplemented their incomes through sales of milk. Cattle owners were always complaining that their cows should be producing more milk and of course customers complained of adulterated milk. As the Banyankole prospered, married, and educated their children, and stopped herding cattle, their achievements were always met with sneers and references to negative stereotypes such as those reducing them to 'trouserless squatters'.

Two weeks after the torching of the Munyankole taxi driver, in a nearby village, a hard-working Munyarwanda who had lived in the village for over thirty years and who sold firewood and pineapples, was awakened late one night and tied up by the villagers. They set his wood in a huge bonfire and threw him on top of it. The crowd sat quietly until he burnt. One villager bragged, 'That tiny man was tough, even after two hours he had not charred. We had to get more wood in the village and even then it took all night. We did not want to leave any evidence for the police.' One might ask what crime necessitated cremating a live person. Apparently, one of his neighbours had died and he had only learned of it three hours later, after he had already been working in his garden. This was felt to be unneighbourly behaviour, and he was condemned to death.

When some villagers were asked why he was not simply ostracized, as was the normal practice, one man said, 'Ostracizing him by calling him a witch would not have worked, he was not a Muganda.' Others privately said that the man had been a good neighbour all these years and he did not deserve to die. 'He had sat for nights on end with us and contributed firewood for mourners to keep warm.' So why did a minor infringement of the etiquette, caused by ignorance about a death, result in such a severe punishment? One of his compatriots felt that the death was due to the general climate against foreigners, particularly those who had (occupier) rights in land and operated independently.[9] 'You see people here want a foreigner to be poor and to work for them.' The Banyarwanda had moved into this particular area during the 1920s and 1930s. Many returned home after working as agricultural labourers but others stayed and bought occupier rights in land.[10] They always tried to demonstrate their adherence to important local customs. Again the word Munyarwanda often had unstated meanings other than a group name. It meant poverty and non-personhood (the latter is a common way used by rich people all over the world to identify poor people).

The death of a popular teacher who had taught many people in the country gave people the excuse to form a vigilante group. He had been gunned down as he slept by bandits who took his watch, eyeglasses, radio and clothes. As an old man of 82 put it, 'For better or for worse, this village has always been vigilant.' In the 1950s, on two occasions, suspected thieves were made to dig their own graves at crossroads and then buried alive! You heard what happened two weeks ago?'

Apparently a woman had deserted her Muganda husband in the village and gone to stay with a Musoga boyfriend plus two visiting friends, a Japadhola and a Musamia. They dragged them back to their village, tied them up and threw them on a firewood bonfire. This episode convinced many foreigners to leave the village. The relatives of the dead men, through courage, managed to take the skulls of the charred men home for burial.

These gruesome village episodes illustrate the violation of the sanctity of human life when people perceive success in terms of a zero sum game in which those who succeed can only do so at the expense of others. A successful taxi owner, farmer and womanizer are condemned to death. Some villagers clearly disagreed with killing people for one reason and accusing them for another to justify their murder. I want to make an analytical connection between these events and the success of the General Services Unit in the 1960s and the Special Force Unit in the 1970s and early 1980s. It was no secret that anyone reported to these bodies would be harassed, tortured or even lose life, yet people continued to sneak in names of their neighbours, friends and acquaintances.[11] In the 1970s people disappeared for being professionally or commercially, successful. University lecturers found threatening notes under their doors and successful traders, particularly women, had their businesses looted and burnt down by soldiers. Still some people disappeared without trace but would be rumoured to have met terrible ends.

A Danish businessman based in Uganda noted: 'Ugandans will not say no to you, but they will waste your time and make you return at least three times, by which time you will know that the answer is a refusal or rejection. Maybe this is why people do not openly rebel against the corrupt leaders.'

These are apt observations for the purposes of this paper. Among groups that were politically uncentralized at the time of colonial contact, there was a great emphasis on debating issues before reaching a consensus, the ideology being that this reduced tension and promoted well-being in face-to-face communities. Occasionally rude people were pressured to apologize.

Most Ugandans who come from societies which had precolonial chiefs often assume that the stateless or segmentary lineage societies had no mechanisms for social control, law and order, or political participation. The arguments is usually put in a way that suggests that the long discussions between opposing parties or between husbands and wives were an anarchical derangement. It is no accident that people from precolonial stateless societies are stereotyped as *loud*.

In contrast, people in state societies regarded the hierarchical chain of common authority as ideal for law and order as well as a politically advanced arrangement. Before colonial rule, people would 'vote with their feet' and either follow a popular chief transferred by the king or abandon the territory of a harsh chief. The colonial laws regarding people's relationship to land and power weakened the authority of chiefs over the people. However, folktales and proverbs suggest that the state was rather coercive. Obedience, and not answering back, and kowtowing to those in authority were virtues. This has not changed much. In Kyagwe county, people would say, 'Yes, Sir' to a chief, or in Kampala, servants would say, 'Yes, Madam' to their employer yet wear murderous expressions as soon as their faces were turned. Women who were about to desert their husbands took care to show extreme deference. During the 1970s, some employers and bosses could hardly believe that they had been betrayed by subordinates who ordinarily kowtowed. A British physician tells of an apparently popular leader who was an alcoholic. The main function of the permanent secretary appeared to be ensuring that the leader was not poisoned. He locked up and served the drinks personally. Precautions against poisoning preoccupied the ordinary people as well. For example, the rule of thumb in the Kyagwe villages studied was that a guest should not be left in the room where food or tea had been served. Parents severely scolded or even punished children whenever they did not observe the rule. At Christmas, gifts of meat or processed food from neighbours were frequently thrown away. These precautions were public knowledge. People continued, however, the traditional acts of gift exchanges and hospitality.

ELITISM AND OPPORTUNITIES

He struck me then as being an unsophisticated man whom people evidently felt they could influence if not exactly manipulate (Elizabeth of Toro, 1983, p. 123).

The view simply stated by Elizabeth Bagaya when describing her first meeting with Amin in 1971 at a state luncheon was shared by many elite members, ministers and foreigners. The elite members who supported Amin underestimated his political shrewdness because of all those old assumptions about northerners. A northern soldier who was apparently all body and no brains could, they believed, be used by those with brains that had been formally schooled. Apparently, having served as Roving Ambassador and Foreign Minister and being publicly humiliated, Bagaya realized that Amin was a 'hectoring bully'.

In the following section it will be argued that elitist attitudes are partly to blame for the present Uganda situation. The problem basically rests on two assumptions, first that the colonial 'labour' areas are natural, i.e. produce people who have no intellectual capacity, and no right to have leadership or a white-collar job; and, secondly, the tendency to entrench the privileged positions of the elites at the expense of the peasants, people from the periphery of the capital Kampala, and the surrounding areas.

It was often said after the coup in 1971 that Amin was a man of the people. He spoke half a dozen languages, a factor due to his ethnic background as well as his career in the army. The Nubi can be said to be the true urbanites in East Africa whose main careers were soldiering and shopkeeping. Although the Nubi were descendants of southern Sudanese groups, they had been alienated from their cultures as they served in Emin Pasha's colonial army in Sudan. Eventually they escaped with him to Uganda at the turn of the century and became a fixture in rural centres and small towns. Although they had their own language (Lunubi) and dress style, and were followers of Islam: they often intermarried with the local populations, spoke the local languages and occasionally converted people to their culture. Amin was a product of this background: a Nubi born in Buganda but claiming to be Kakwa. Amin was therefore the ultimate opportunist indulging in ambiguities.

Soon after his coup Amin invited everyone who mattered in Uganda to meet with him. The elders, the Asians, the monarchists, the women, the farmers, the elites were some of the groups that met with the President. Amin listened to everyone, noting particularly their vulnerable points as they poured their hearts out with demands and highlighted issues of antagonism against each other. Then Amin struck each and everyone of them.

Amin's initial popularity with the common people was due to their perception of him as being anti-intellectual. When he talked of the elite's corruption, nepotism and perpetuation and entrenchment of its privileged position, people understood what he meant. For example, the peasants in their dealings with extension officers were aware that their views or experiences never counted, but they were expected to adopt foreign ideas learned from books at schools and universities. Some of the schemes advocated for rural development, for example the tractor schemes, were way beyond the economic means and skills of the ordinary peasant. When the peasants managed to join co-operative movements, again those with reading and writing skills benefited at the expense of the peasants. Already facing shortage of labour and poorly paid for their crops, the peasants had to cope with the embezzlement of their co-operative societies' funds by some officials.

Some peasants already underemployed because of land shortage and under-productivity migrated to the urban areas. They often found themselves self-employed because the elite members who run cities essentially defined their skills as irrelevant to modern wage labour. Even when they used their traditional skills to create employment for themselves as brewers or food hawkers, they found that those employed specifically to administer certain services such as granting licences, often demanded bribes or else no service. In some cases, women had to kneel down while talking to the bureaucrats. In cases of women bureaucrats, the poor people complained of lack of attention and being dismissed simply with, 'I don't understand what you are saying.'

However, the same elite members would fill jobs with clients, relatives or co-ethnics. This was not a secret. The common saying in Uganda was that 'Whose child are you?' was a much more important criterion for a job than qualifications. A bribe sometimes helped. The elite in Uganda are regarded by the general population as a bogus lot who 'had been privileged enough to receive education and obtain jobs but who behaved as if they had unique abilities that differed from everybody else.'[12] The empirical reality shows that descendants of chiefs and priests, and teachers had a head start in education as compared to the peasants. Furthermore, every elite Ugandan is either first or second generation educated and has many relatives who are poor and illiterate because they lacked access to educational opportunities.

It is not surprising then that when Amin started whimsically sacking and recalling the civil servants, the peasants cheered. In April 1972, Amin sacked 22 senior civil servants and from then on even ministers lived with uncertainty. The peasants laughed at the elite members who were being brought down to size. Some scholars have argued that Uganda is not a class society and therefore a class (Marxist) analysis is only used by those who want to perpetuate hatred.[13] Some elite landlords employed in academic careers still claim that their tenants love them like fathers and would have to be incited by someone else to rebel against the status quo. However, historical evidence overwhelmingly shows that the peasants have looted or destroyed the properties and even threatened the lives of elite members whenever there has been upheaval. The 1945 and 1949 trade boycotts organized by trade unionists to protest against the Asian predominance in commerce in fact resulted in many losses in Kyagwe county as the crops, shops, and houses belonging to local 'progressive' farmers and shopkeepers were vandalized. In 1960 during the Bukedi riots, the 'rich' people in the area had to flee for their lives. In 1979 the ordinary people and particularly the lumpen-proletariat *(bayaye)* felt justified in looting the rich because they were *Mafutamingi* – Amin's class of successful businessmen who hoarded and overcharged on essential goods. These class-based actions must be distinguished from the lootings and destruction of lives and property in 1971, which were acts of revenge directed at particular politicians. Then, ordinary people joined soldiers in hacking to death those suspected of sympathizing with the deposed leader, Obote. In 1955, again in Kyagwe county, a county chief was almost mobbed to death because he had bet with a friend that if the Kabaka ever returned from his British-imposed exile, he would give up a leg. The Prime Minister of Buganda at the time of exile, Paul Kavuma, and members of his family in Uganda and England were treated as pariahs. He was blamed for not having been tough with the British. This was interpreted as a sell-out by his political opponents who acted as sources of information for the masses.

The point at issue is that classes do exist, as can be illustrated by a few expressions such as *Wabenzi* (owners of Mercedes Benz cars), *mafutamingi* (businessmen), *bawajjese* (the disposed), and *banjalananda* (cultivators). It is recognized that one achieves the former two statuses by seizing opportunities. The Ugandans have always been opportunistic. Uganda became a British colony (Protectorate) because there were men willing to grab the opportunity to collaborate. Such men embraced Christianity, the ideological and cultural arm of colonialism which promised and delivered Western education, wealth, power and privilege. The concern over the protection of these privileges is evident in the 3 January 1900 letter which the three regents of Buganda wrote to the commissioner, Sir Harry Johnson. The letter is worth quoting at length.

Sir, we chiefs of the land request you to give us one rupee out of every three rupees collected from each hut, and friends of Her Majesty the Queen as you said. *It is not good for us to be poor and people to laugh at us saying, 'Look at those who call themselves friends of the Queen being short of money.'*

Again, Sir, in connection with the gun licence of four rupees – that is all right, but we beg you to give us a period of three years in which to settle our country down. This is because our guns together with those possessed by the Askari in the service of the Queen *are needed in defending our country* ... Again, some of the big chiefs have got guns, one may have 100, another 50, another 20, another 10, and another 5. All these guns help the Askari of the Queen ... *Kakunguru ... is trying to make Bukedi obey the Queen* ... it is the rules of the Queen which we seek to put into force ... Because of ... inexperience we shall proceed slowly *until we are able to proceed on our own* ... This is indeed my reason for my begging you to leave us to rule so that we may under your tutelage rule wisely ...

We who are called friends of the Queen are afraid of *losing respect for this will make some people laugh at us* ... (Quoted in Low, 1971a, p. 32–3, emphasis mine).

Between 1960 and 1985 the same arguments regarding respectability were used to justify the conspicuous consumption of public officials. Specifically, the Mercedes Benz was justified on the

217

grounds that the peasants needed to look up to their leaders with pride. Writers like the late Okot p'Bitek ridiculed and questioned this and branded the Benz owners or *Wabenzi* as 'a minority clan of urban dwelling, well-fed and overprivileged elites.' Moreover, the *Wabenzi* only went to the countryside at election time to overwhelm the peasants with dust and beer. During my fieldwork in 1971 and 1974, I concluded that the older villagers may have resigned themselves to this situation but the rural dwelling school leaders were determined to do something about it by hook or by crook.

In 1979 and 1985 one of the biggest shocks of watching happenings in Uganda was to see the inevitable Benz in the midst of decaying urban buildings and tatteredly-clothed audiences! It was a shock because the Benz was misplaced and had no business in a scene of such squalor. There were Land Rovers that had been given as gifts by Britain, and which were more appropriate under the circumstances. In 1985, just a month before the coup, a fleet of Benzes had arrived for ministers, permanent secretaries and other heads of department. (These were duly looted by the soldiers who drove them around after 27 July 1985.)

I have shown that opportunism was from the beginning a legitimate political factor at the core of the entity called Uganda. The point being made is that opportunism in itself is not intrinsically negative but that it has landed Uganda in a mess. It seems that many Ugandans are willing to go with the man of the moment as long as it benefits them without compromising them. At the time of the 1971 military coup, many of the people who had been campaigning for elections on a UPC platform suddenly became supporters of the military regime, whether genuinely fed up with the previous regime or not. It was an opportunity to 'fall into things', a euphemism for acquiring power and wealth through the landing of an important job. A lot has been said about how, during the 1970s, peasants converted to Islam in order to get business allocations and to enable their children to get fellowships to study abroad; and about the soldiers who entrenched their economic positions by intimidating opponents and often accusing them of hoarding (a crime then punishable by death). However, little has been said about the elite members who not only enjoyed their ministerial and civil service salaries but used their positions of influence to join the soldiers in reaping economic rewards from business (*mafutamingi*) and black marketeering (*magendo*) activities. Denouncements of Amin by elite members who had accumulated and exported enough money to live overseas, and their protestations about their innocence are not only boring but self-serving, to say the least.

What went wrong in Uganda?

CONCLUDING REMARKS: WHICH WAY UGANDA?

What is new? Lule and Binaisa cleared the treasury during their short rules. Binaisa offered no excuse. Obote is making up for the last time he was kicked out penniless. Everyone is out to make something. My boss buys expensive rather than cheap stationery because he gets good kickback percentages on them.

The above remarks were made by a bank employee on learning that Obote had left with foreign reserves enough to run the country for three years. This cynical view tells a lot about the six years 1981–5. On 27 July 1985, it was clear that the Kampala business district had had no paint for the last fifteen years or so but the shops were stocked with all kinds of material goods, a triumph for periphery capitalism. But perhaps the most outstanding symbol was the Mercedes Benz assembly plant at Kyambogo, a suburb of Kampala. I would argue that the Mercedes Benz mystique is inimical to Ugandan development. Apart from the obvious disadvantage of draining foreign exchange, the example below illustrates its interference with the delivery of foreign aid to the people who really need it and for whom it was intended in the first place.

The World Bank grant to rehabilitate education in Uganda focused on supplying schools with books and writing materials. This grant was administered through the Ministry of Education by a handful of expatriates (each of whom had a Ugandan counterpart) responsible to the permanent secretary. The excitement of the expatriates began to dampen when they began to feel that their immediate boss wanted some financial rewards from the overseas companies that had won the contracts to supply the books. The permanent secretary openly instructed that the discounts given by the companies should go to him because he was 'saving' money to buy or build his double-storey dream house. However, on their bookshopping trips, the expatriates were required to buy him goodies. The other Ugandans in the department who were supposed to deliver the books to the schools not only vied to be the ones to go overseas and buy the books but some demanded that they be given Mercedes Benzes. In fact, they put on so much pressure that about four Mercedes Benzes were procured for them. The Mukono district commissioner blamed the porters for having removed the labels off boxes so that some schools did not get their allotted books. The matter had come into the open when the area's MPs went to complain to the project directors. The minister insisted that the books should be delivered directly to the schools rather than through the DCs. This was impossible given the limited manpower available. But even in cases where the school supplies reached schools safely, the headmasters were accused of either diverting them to the local shops (for a profit) or selling them to the students. This happened despite clearly stamped indications that the books were free and were not for sale. Parents regularly received notes reminding them to pay for school supplies. Parents often paid up because they wanted their children to remain in school and shrugged their shoulders at the futility of protest. On inspection tours, the project expatriates were often confronted with situations where a headmaster would claim to have run out of supplies but would be found to be hoarding books and other supplies which became visible through the accidental opening of a cupboard. Apart from the lying, it was clear that some children had not received the books and were presumably out of school.

This case study is particularly heartbreaking because the argument that had won that particular World Bank grant in Uganda's favour was on the strength of those dedicated teachers and eager pupils who continued school as usual, often substituting the bare ground for books and blackboards. Furthermore, this case illustrates one of the major contentions of this chapter: corruption in Uganda is not limited to the top but that everyone uses whatever situation they are in to rake in a profit at the expense of those who are entitled to it, the public.

Discussions of democracy, civil liberties and human rights, which are foremost in every Ugandan's mind, cannot be discussed in the abstract. This chapter has brought empirical examples to show that peasants, elites and political leaders have all been guilty of infringing upon the rights of others and abusing public trust and property. Indications are that what Uganda needs is not more political rhetoric about the virtues of socialism or capitalism or the virtues of one group of people over another. Uganda needs, above all, a leader to help build institutions that will develop the country as well as ensure the protection of the basic civil, legal, social and political rights of all. It is everyone's responsibility to care at all times and not only when it is convenient. People who have thrown bees and snakes at crowds of political opponents (Kiwanuka, 1979, p. 5) are hypocritical to turn around and talk about elections being rigged. While it is not difficult to find men of courage, threats by the public are not conducive to public spiritedness or free discussions. It is not going to be easy for honest Ugandans to stand up to evil, but that is what demands our immediate attention if we are to prevent discrimination, corruption, imprisonments and death from triumphing.

Notes

1. E. Kironde, quoted in Low, 1971a, p. 227.
2. Interview conducted 30 June 1974.
3. Hall, 18 April 1946, quoted in Worthington, 1949.
4. In the United States both on and off university campuses I am often approached by Americans who want to know why we Ugandans are denying the Baganda, in particular, and the southerners in general, the right to rule. Sometimes the statements imply that Bantu-speakers have a right to rule. Some of this reaches absurd points.

   A Ugandan working for a multi-national company in Washington, DC was in the habit of backbiting other Ugandans by claiming that except for his area the rest of Ugandans do not sleep in houses. This went on for three years until he talked to an American who had lived in Uganda for many years. He was publicly challenged to explain what he meant. He explained that: 'The rest of Uganda was underdeveloped economically and politically. Everyone wanted to work in Kampala instead of returning to their home areas.' The colonial policy of creating the 'cash crop', 'labour reserves', and 'soldier reserves' helped develop and underdevelop different parts Uganda. It is now a well-known fact that Acholi was a 'grain basket' that was stultified when large numbers of men made their careers in the army. With regards to the capital city, Kampala, most Ugandans feel that they helped build it through their labour and taxes and have as much right to live there as the host group of the Baganda. Other Ugandans have argued that the capital city should be moved elsewhere.
5. For analytical purposes it is important to distinguish between the benefits a public figure may have for a region or for a locality. Often the alleged ethnic benefits are limited to the local area from which a politician comes.

   One of the most tragic trends in recent years has been the tales being circulated that all Nilotic-speaking people were part of a conspiracy to perpetuate Obote's rule because they collectively benefited from it. This trend aims at counter-attacking those who claim that certain groups have dominated institutions through which one gets access to education, employment, and eventually power. One is reminded of discussions in the USA that the Affirmative Action Programmes designed to correct the historic imbalance in employment opportunities is reverse discrimination against the whites. There has been no room in this paper to discuss sexism as a critical variable in all Ugandan public service employment.
6. *The Persistent Pastoralists* is what Professor Peter Rigby calls his book which questions among other things the assumed superiority of the agriculturalists over the pastoralists. The pastoralists reject outsiders' perception of their societies and frankly the quality of life and political organizations should be the envy of all Africans. Patronizing them as tourist objects or dismissing them as backward reflects badly on non-pastoralists. The pastoralists rejected Westernization and were pushed to semi-arid areas.
7. Mamdani, 1976, pp. 182–3, notes that the rural violence of 1945 and 1949 was orchestrated by ambitious urban men and described by the editor of the *Uganda Herald* as the problem of the new African middle class being born.
8. Guns have been an integral part of Ugandan history. When they first arrived, Mutesa of Buganda tested out the new exotic machine by firing at some peasants. Indirect rule was always preceded by military pacification, whether one looks at the case of the defeat of Bunyoro or the activities of Semei Kakunguru in the Eastern Province. The chiefs, as mentioned previously, argued that the guns

would help them maintain law and order. Emin Pasha's displaced southern Sudanese soldiers whom he brought to Uganda to escape possible Mahdist revenge were borrowed by Captain Lugard for use by the British East Africa Company and eventually British rule in Uganda. There were 600 soldiers who, together with their families and dependants made up 9,000 Nubi.

In 1897 they mutinied and were officially disbanded and scattered in the main towns of Entebbe, Hoima and Bombo. One of their descendants, Idi Amin, was to resurrect the Nubi factor in the army. In 1979 fleeing Amin soldiers dropped guns along the route and these were used by some people against each other; in revenge or robberies.

The Nubi were an ethnic group that developed in Uganda. They were adaptable, but maintained their identity. They are often described by other Ugandans as 'black muslims' (as if Islam is not practised anywhere else in Africa) and Anya Nyas (a reference to the 1960s southern Sudanese freedom fighters). Both these are misidentities and reflect two grave problems in Uganda, that of ignorance about other groups and a tendency to reduce them to stereotypes. Unchecked ethnocentrism does not unite diverse groups: it is bad for Uganda.

9. Vigilantism in Uganda has often meant instant mob justice, so that in cases of car accidents drivers who are stupid enough to stop pay with their own lives, and suspected thieves are often beaten to death.

10. The 1900 Buganda Agreement created among other things an individualized land tenure system. Until 1927 the landlords, who were also chiefs, were entitled to tribute. It became necessary to protect the peasants from over-exploitation so that they would produce enough cash crops for the state. The result was the 1927 Busulu and Nvujo Act. This guaranteed occupier rights to the tenants as long as they paid a minimal annual rent. Landlords and peasant regularly sell occupier rights to tenants. The land in this case technically belongs to the landlord.

11. There is no doubt that spying was conducted among close friends and within ethnic groups. Most 'political' meetings were held in secret and the language used was coded. But there was always some betrayal. One can either claim the government to be omnipresent or that turncoats were common. Recently, a Ugandan claimed that nearly all the spying during the 1970s was done by the Nubi because they were multilingual. 'They attended meetings and then they went and betrayed the local people to the authorities.'

It needs to be pointed out that nearly all Ugandans can identify each other's name as belonging to specific ethnic groups. Since 1966 social groups became ethnically exclusive and one's name had to match the language one spoke. Thus, while the above statements appear to be attacking the Nubi specifically, they are in reality an attack on multilingualism in Uganda. All those easterners, and Banyarwanda who had settled in Buganda, and the northerners who worked in other parts of Uganda and had learned the local languages to facilitate communication are being negatively branded.

At a Ugandan workshop held in April 1986 at Minary Conference Center, Dartmouth College, USA, Otieno Odhiambo, a Kenyan historian, pointed out that the Ugandan elites have more inter-ethnic contacts through languages and marriages than any other group in Africa. This is a virtue that must not be abandoned as we retreat into the dark ages.

12. Unsolicited remarks from a poor Kampala resident made on 11 July 1971. This is not an isolated view. One has to see how soldiers treat members of the elite at road-blocks to appreciate it. For example one has to wonder whether a search for arms necessitates the throwing of books onto wet ground. Since the 1970s the Ugandan army has recruited *bayaye*, i.e. the ignorant, rough and tough urban and rural lumpen militariat in Uganda. We can agree with Karl Marx that the deterioration of peasant agriculture had produced 'an unemployed surplus

population for which there is no place either on land or in the towns, and which accordingly reaches out for state offices or joins the army'. Marx recognized them as an opportunistic group seeking to enrich itself. Fanon saw them as a declassed, depolitized group attracted to bourgeois ideology but ambivalent to bourgeois norms and values.

13. Kiwanuka, 1979, pp. 178–9.

FIFTEEN
Uganda and southern Sudan:
peripheral politics and neighbour relations
Peter Woodward

INTRODUCTION

It will come as no surprise in a discussion of Ugandan politics to
begin with references to the periphery, for there are two senses at
least in which it has become integral to an understanding of the
country, especially under the Amin regime. These are geographical
and social. The 'geographical' here relates particularly to West Nile,
but also to the north in general, for the whole region had suffered
from the impact of uneven development, and in the colonial period
had become marginalized in political and economic terms. The
'social' periphery relates to the Nubis and the Muslims in Ugandan
society, who comprised marginal groups scattered in various
locations around the country. There are many suggestions in the
literature on Uganda that the marginality of these regions and
groups was not simply an objective reality, but increasingly a
subjective force. Similarly southern Sudan as a whole experienced a
process of peripheralisation within what was also essentially a
colonially built state, under Turco-Egyptian, Mahdist, and finally
British rule, which was to flower into a self-conscious movement
seeking redress after independence.

Yet core–periphery relations within African countries do not
necessarily explain either the full character or the dynamics of the
conflicts to which such relations may give rise. There is also the
international dimension, which relates to both neighbour states for,
as indicated, peripheries are often geographically located near
borders, and neighbours thus become involved, and also to the
wider international environment as well. Peripheries may invite
intervention, both out of sympathy with the peripheral condition,
and also because the periphery may provide an avenue of attack on
the core, for whatever reason. Indeed if one sees at least some world
politics in core–periphery terms, then the African states as a whole
may be seen as the international periphery, thus placing their
internal peripheries on the 'periphery of the periphery'. Perhaps

some great power involvements in Africa do resemble that relationship, possibly the French support for Biafra or Soviet and later US support for guerrillas in Angola, but in the case of Uganda wider international intervention is less clearly core–periphery, especially the roles played by Israel and Libya. But that is to jump ahead.

At the level of neighbour relations, and indeed neighbours as part of the wider international system, a case has already been made for viewing the politics of post-independence Uganda very much in international and regional terms, notably by Mahmoud Mamdani, as the title of his book, *Imperialism and Fascism in Uganda* (1983), indicates. But relations between neighbouring states in Africa are not explained only by imperialism. Indeed 'imperialism' as the sole explanation of such a significant relationship as the peripheral areas of northern Uganda and southern Sudan have had, can become tortuous in the extreme. I have suggested elsewhere that instead it may be possible to discern a number of dimensions that are relevant to the understanding of the generally neglected subject of relations between states in Africa: borders, economic relations, shared political instability, domestic politics and involvement of neighbours, and relations with the core of the international community (Woodward, 1984). Although in the past there had been adjustment of the borders of southern Sudan, and although Amin made great play of claiming the territory of a number of Uganda's neighbours, borders did not in fact become of great significance in the post-independence years. Nor did economic relations, which are of such importance for students of 'imperialism', not least because of the lack of development on the two sides of the border and the fact that such change as did occur largely involved peripheralization, especially labour migration, within the respective domestic economic arenas. But the other three issues are of relevance. In particular the contribution of core–periphery relations to the growth of political instability can cause a spill-over in the form of refugees into neighbouring states that may effect not only relations between those states but also developments within them. It is a short step from there to some form and level of involvement in the affairs of neighbouring states, though in the case of southern Sudan and Uganda it was never as overt as Tanzania's invasion of Uganda. While the involvement of the wider international community is largely a matter of the pursuit of particular interests that may seek to capitalize on the opportunities provided by domestic instability, the use of that opportunity may involve not only the use of peripheral areas and groups within a particular state, but also the mobilization of a neighbouring country or part thereof, illustrating again the potential importance of the 'periphery of the periphery.'

Before proceeding further a note of modesty with regard to sources is required. Material on post-independence Uganda is always open to argument, as is also the case in southern Sudan, and unlike the authors of other papers I have not undertaken field work in either area. Much of what follows is therefore drawn from interviews, books, articles and unpublished theses, and aims to suggest the outline of an emerging topic rather than providing a definitive account of a subject that has not been specifically focused on hitherto.

SOUTHERN SUDAN'S CIVIL WAR AND UGANDA 1962–71

In one way the surprise should not be that one makes connections between northern Uganda and southern Sudan, but that they were ever disconnected in the first place. Clearly there are a number of ethnic ties, such as amongst the Bari and Bari-related groups, that traverse the border, and it is the existence of the border itself – as almost always in Africa only a result of imperial activity in the region – that is the oddity. Indeed from an ethnic standpoint the existence of cross-border links and a certain capacity for fluidity in identity between the two countries is extremely understandable, bearing in mind that peoples on either side of the border often have closer links with each other than with other peoples with whom they share 'nationhood'. It is not only that Acholi in northern Uganda have more obvious ties with Acholi in southern Sudan than with Baganda in Buganda, but that many of the peoples of Equatoria have closer ties with northern Uganda than even their fellow southern Sudanese, especially the Nilotics of Upper Nile. One official Sudanese report of 1965 comments, 'These tribes consider their domain to extend along both parts of the borders. The Acholi of Equatoria have some of their tribesmen under the administrative control of the Acholi district of north-east Uganda.'[1] Similarly historical experience, especially in that apparently important phase in the nineteenth century when Turco-Egyptian imperialism penetrated that region of the Upper Nile, had a similar impact on either side of what is now the border, contrasting with other areas of both countries. The slave-raiding from Khartoum largely bypassed the great Nilotic communities – the Nuer, Dinka and Shilluk – and concentrated further south along what is now the border area and Bahr al Ghazal. And when Mahdism overthrew the Turco-Egyptian rulers, Emin Pasha and his men were to forge the extraordinary Nubi community in the same area, with further devastating effects on local ethnic groups.

British imperialism of course set all that apart, but did so nonetheless on a basis of shared experience: the peripheralisation of northern Uganda and southern Sudan within the new states in which the peoples of those regions then found themselves. Thus, even before independence there were shared experiences and some ties, and links were to grow closer in the subsequent years.

In southern Sudan the civil war was well under way even before independence was attained in Uganda. The south had been only marginally involved in the political process by which Sudan became the first British-ruled territory in Africa to attain independence. That process owed more to Middle Eastern politics, and especially to the worsening relations between Britain and Egypt, than it did to the wind of change in Africa (Woodward, 1979). But even that omission had had its price, with the outburst of anti-northern sentiment that surrounded the southern mutiny of August 1955. Though sustained civil war was not in fact set in train by these events (contrary to the oft-cited description of it as a 17-year war from 1955 to 1972) it did have the effect of leaving a legacy of bitterness from the outset that boded ill for the future.

That certainly proved the case when the new parliament in Khartoum did nothing effective to fulfil the pledge given on independence to examine new constitutional arrangements for the south. And worse was to come when Abboudi's military regime, which came to power in 1958, decided to reverse the British isolation of the south by a policy of enforced Islamization. This was particularly resisted by the numerically tiny southern intelligentsia from whom the first political leaders in the region were drawn. The first of these left the south for Uganda as early as 1960, where the British colonial authorities, somewhat embarrassed by their presence, decided to assign them to different towns in order to avoid a concentration of political opposition to the Sudan government. John Howell gives the example of Father Saturnino Lohure, a former MP, who was sent to Kampala, while Joseph Oduho was placed in Kitgum and Ferdinand Adyang, an ex-minister, in Gulu (Howell, 1978a and b). Resistance was to spread, especially into schools and amongst junior officials and others of the 'salariat' who bore the brunt of the intrusive policies of Sudan's military rulers. By 1962 the outbursts of violent resistance were becoming sustained and a steady trickle of refugees, mainly from Equatoria, found their way into Uganda, where SANU, the Sudan African National Union, was established. At first their number was small, 4000 by 1963 and the total was up to 7000 in 1964. But in 1966 it rose sharply. The October Revolution in Sudan in 1965 had raised hopes of peace, but when the Round Table Conference failed and Muhammed Mahjoub's government was installed, the army became very repressive and the refugee figure rose to 44,000. With the civil war continuing unabated it rose to 74,000 by 1969, the largest concentration of southern Sudanese in any one country (there were a further 100,000 spread between Ethiopia, Zaire and the Central African Republic).

The refugees were of different kinds and in different situations. The number of political leaders in Uganda grew, and they tended to accumulate groups of dependents around them. Lacking organizational strength and being easily prone to external penetration (indeed often seeking to become dependent on it for resources), they were prone to factionalism, and by 1969 Uganda was the main centre 'with at least five movements claiming to represent southern secessionist movements (Howell, 1978a, pp. 255). In addition to the professional politicians and others of the southern intelligentsia, there were many students who sought to continue their education at schools and colleges in Uganda. Some southerners also became involved in petty trading. The people of the rural areas, who sought refuge not only from the Sudan army but sometimes also from the Anya Nya guerrilla forces, tended either to remain in the bush on the Ugandan side of the border or resort to the official refugee camps that had been established. (One informant claimed that refugees from Equatoria were not made to register or take Sudanese passports, unlike those from Bahr al Ghazal and Upper Nile.)

It was largely the presence of these refugees that developed and sustained the links with the Anya Nya inside southern Sudan. The actual connections between the political leaders and the guerrilla groups tended to vary, and certainly the structure of authority was often difficult to establish or maintain. Nevertheless there were links, and they helped both in sustaining the guerrillas and later in the peace process. Amongst those who responded, for very different reasons, were representatives of the international community working in Uganda. As Ali Mazrui somewhat tartly puts it:

> Many of the religious groups which poured money from the Western world into the southern movement were as much influenced by anti-communism as by any solidarity with Christians. At least one distinguished academic at Makerere from the Western world found it appropriate and compatible with his job at Makerere to involve himself financially and materially not only in the welfare aspects of the resistance movement of the south, but also in the military aspects of that movement. Small committees or cabals of Western intellectuals within Uganda, partly influenced by liberal concerns, partly inspired by Christian solidarity, and partly animated by the fear of communism in Africa, conspired in the corridors to play their part in the southern separatist movement (Mazrui, 1975, p. 106).

However, the Western intellectuals were not alone, for the Israeli military mission in Uganda also took a growing interest, especially after the Arab–Israeli war of 1967. Israel launched a diplomatic offensive designed to isolate Arab North Africa from the sub-Saharan black states and her propaganda was helped by secretly supplying the Christian African southern Sudanese against their Arab Muslim oppressors; at the same time tying down a large part of the third largest army in the Arab world.[2] From 1969 they began to supply arms regularly, particularly to Joseph Lagu, who was thus helped in giving the Anya Nya, and indeed the southern movement as a whole, a degree of military and political unity that had been conspicuously lacking hitherto. (Ironically it was a vital factor in making possible the negotiated peace settlement achieved at Addis Ababa in 1972.)

However, officially the Uganda government was less inclined to be encouraging. It has already been seen that the British colonial authorities were reluctant to encourage political activity from Uganda, while after independence the new Prime Minister, Milton Obote, appeared to wish to keep broadly in line with the strictures of the newly formed OAU concerning non-involvement in the internal affairs of other African states. Nevertheless there was a good deal of leakage of support, both from refugees and the external backers, though it was checked in 1966 when Muhammed Mahjoub, Sudan's new Prime Minister, made a tour of East Africa to promote his 'good neighbour' policy. There were joint activities of the two armies along the border against the Anya Nya; refugees were moved back from the border and told not to involve themselves in political activities; and Father Lohure was killed, apparently while in the hands of the Uganda army, when on a mission to investigate the extent of the crackdown among the refugees. But by 1968 this attitude had eased, partly apparently as a result of pressures from church groups and the Israelis, but partly too as a result of the sympathies of the southerners' fifth column within the Ugandan state, especially the army.

A good deal had already been published on the whole question of the ethnic composition of the Uganda army, and the changes that took place in it. Ali Mazrui was one of the first to draw attention to the recruitment of northern Ugandans and the possible implications. Much has also been made of Idi Amin Dada as soldier, Kakwa from West Nile, and Nubi. Whatever the motives, it does appear that Amin was very prominent amongst those in the army and government who felt a certain sympathy, and perhaps even some form of affinity with the southern Sudanese guerrillas, and who sought to encourage Obote to disregard his agreement with Muhammed Mahjoub and turn a blind eye to the help the Anya Nya were receiving from Uganda. Indeed Amin appears to have gone further, personally assisting the Anya Nya and the Israeli military mission, and even going into southern Sudan himself. After 1969, when a new radical regime came to power in Khartoum, Obote again gave orders to Amin to stop such activities, but it has been suggested that these orders were disregarded. It was to be an ominous connection in view of the dramatic changes that were about to take place in both southern Sudan and Uganda and appear to have had some links with each other.

But before that point is reached a brief recapitulation is appropriate. The conflict in southern Sudan had all the hallmarks of a peripheral response to attempted domination by the core. While many factors, including economic exploitation, were involved, it was perceived primarily as a political problem on both sides. The government in Khartoum saw it overwhelmingly as the aftermath of Britain's policy of isolating the south; the region's own political leaders were more inclined to point to the failure of adequate incorporation into the political system at independence. The movement was particularly strong in Equatoria, the main province for recruitment into the intelligentsia, and it was to Uganda in particular that refugees fled. Most guerrilla movements in North-East Africa do have some kind of connection with refugee camps and supply bases in neighbouring states, indeed the regular pattern is for dicontent to give rise to repression, followed by refugees and then guerrilla warfare turning into a self-sustaining cycle. Since rebellion is frequently on the periphery – northern Chad, northern and eastern Ethiopia – where cross-border links may exist, the cycle of conflict is relatively easily developed, and becomes the major factor in relations between the neighbouring states involved.

It is also common for political exiles to seek international support, and on occasions core states with an international objective – most frequently in Africa a strategic objective – may become involved. In this case Israel had an understandable motive and became the main source of arms to the Anya Nya. What was more unusual was the extent to which certain leading figures in the state were involved in this relationship, in this case most notably Idi Amin.

THE TRANSFORMATION: SUDAN ENTERS UGANDAN AFFAIRS
Coups are always occasions for accusation and counter-accusation and the Amin coup of 1971 has certainly had its share of conflicting interpretation. Nevertheless whatever one may make of the structural explanations preferred in terms of class and/or major political alliances, two points recur in several accounts. One is that Amin appears to have had his own immediate motives for taking some

kind of action; and the second is that in his action he was in close contact with the Israeli military delegation, and especially its leader, Colonel Bar Lev (Mamdani, 1983, p. 29; Martin, 1974, p. 38).

Obote's growing estrangement from Amin, and the latter's expectation of some kind of confrontation during or after Obote's visit to the Commonwealth Conference in Singapore has been well documented, but particular interest here is on the immediate grounds on which Obote might have wished to make a move. In David Martin's biography of Amin it is suggested that there were three specific charges that were being levelled, two of which related to the southern Sudan. One was that in spite of the growing improvement in relations between the two radicalizing governments in Khartoum and Kampala, Amin had disregarded orders to discontinue his involvement with the Anya Nya. This had become very clear with the trial of the German mercenary Steiner in Khartoum, following his arrest by the Ugandan authorities as he left the Southern Sudan. The second was that a large sum of money had been misappropriated by Amin, and it was possible that some of it had been used to help the Anya Nya. (The third allegation concerned the killing of Brigadier Okoya and his wife.)

As for the Israeli connection, the suggested motive also involves not only the southern Sudan, but strategic questions of North-East Africa. Not only did the growing rapprochement between Khartoum and Kampala threaten Anya Nya links with Uganda, but with the more radical direction being taken by Obote, and the close relations already being established between Egypt and the new radical leaders in Sudan and Libya, a major shift in the strategic picture of North-East Africa might be in the making. It has been alleged that not only Israeli military personnel, but also Britain's MI6 may have been involved. If so, it probably had more to do with these strategic questions than the oft-cited bad blood between Obote and Prime Minister Edward Heath. (It is certainly not inconceivable that this was so: British security appears to have assisted President Numeiri of Sudan against his would-be Communist usurpers in July 1971, and Britain made a determined and successful effort to win him for the West.)

Matters did not end with Amin's coup, but were to become even more Byzantine and tortuous. Amin had not come to power without a struggle, and many of Obote's supporters fled, including a number of Langi and Acholi troops from Obote's home area of East Nile. They went into southern Sudan, where the Sudan army helped them to reorganize, and prepare a force of about 1,000 men for a pro-Obote invasion. Obote himself visited the camp, and had his headquarters in a house in Khartoum North given him by Numeiri.

Numeiri and Amin were thus in comparable situations. Neither was very securely in power, and for both men there was a significant threat posed by forces that they were supporting against each other – Obote's force in southern Sudan, and the Anya Nya in the same region – neither of which could be destroyed militarily by the governments they threatened.

There is evidence to suggest that Numeiri and Amin, both of whom had an innate instinct for survival (they have even survived their respective downfalls quite comfortably), came to the same conclusion and that deals were struck. Numeiri expelled Obote and his men who left for Tanzania, from where an invasion was more difficult than from southern Sudan; while Amin decided to get rid of the Israeli military mission. This move had also been associated with the refusal of Britain and Israel to supply the arms he requested, as well as to offers of aid he had received instead from Libya, but witnesses have also stated that an understanding along the above lines was established. The loss by the Anya Nya of military support from Israel, and restrictions on their links with Uganda, in turn put pressure on them. Numeiri had already opened contacts with them, and in January 1972 the Addis Ababa agreement ended the civil war. A close student of this whole process, John Howell, remarks, 'I would therefore suggest that the mutual interests of Numeiri and Amin were instrumental firstly in removing the Obote threat from northern Uganda; secondly in persuading part of the Anya Nya leadership to reach a settlement; and thirdly in hastening the expulsion of the Israelis from Uganda' (Howell, 1978a, p. 293). Numeiri and Amin could sleep a little easier in their beds.

Clearly this was relations with a neighbour at its most important (the Addis Ababa agreement also involved understandings about Sudanese–Ethiopian relations), but it also shifted the whole discussion of core–periphery relations within the two countries. The southern Sudan became for ten years more politically incorporated as well as attaining regional autonomy. But for Uganda it was to mark the start of a process that brought the periphery to power, and that periphery had strong connections with the southern Sudan.

THE QUIET YEARS, 1972–9

From the standpoint of Sudan–Uganda relations, the years of Amin's power, which were so turbulent within Uganda, were for the most part relatively quiet. The primary reason, of course, was that politically the peripheries had acquired new positions within their respective states. Southern Sudanese politicians now became more at home in Khartoum than Kampala, while Amin and his henchmen abused Uganda.

The analysis of this latter phenomenon is not within my capacity, nor is it part of my purpose, except to suggest that in the whole issue of the Nubis and the Ugandan army, the southern Sudan is not necessarily forgotten. One indication of this is found in the recruitment for the Uganda army from the south that had occurred before the coup of 1971, but appeared also to continue thereafter, especially with the demobilisation of the Anya Nya following the Addis Ababa Agreement in the following year. David Martin gives a figure of 500 southern Sudanese in the army when Amin took power, and he estimates that a further 1000 were recruited even before the Addis Ababa settlement. Avirgan and Honey claim that in the following years thousands more were recruited from the 'rural poor' from Zaire and southern Sudan, with the State Research Bureau sending trucks over the borders at night dropping off recruits for the Uganda army. By the end they claim, 'It was a foreign occupation army', comprising they say 50 per cent southern Sudanese and Nubis, 26 per cent from Zaire and only 24 per cent Ugandans.[3] These suspiciously high and precise figures may well be disputed, but they do raise the problem of identity that others have also discussed (Jorgensen, 1981, p. 307; Hansen, 1977). Holger Bernt Hansen has labelled the Nubis, and would presumably also regard the southern Sudanese, as 'mercenaries', for which he has been accused of denying the former their Uganda birthright. But it is precisely this question of identity that may once more indicate a southern Sudan connection and link Uganda's Nubis and southern Sudanese. The Nubis did after all initially identify themselves in 1948 as the Sudanese East African Association, and Barry Wanji, still their fullest and best informed discussant, refers to other peoples in Uganda regarding them as 'aliens'.[4] This sense of cultural isolation is vividly spelled out not only by Wanji, but also by Dennis Pain (1975), and what emerges clearly is not merely the sense of difference but of superiority and cruelty which derived from the historical experiences in which this unique community was born. Some have explained Amin's regime in terms of its increasingly narrow base, and a violence born of fear, but if the cultural component is also significant then it suggests that both features did not simply happen, but were in part innate in the core of the community.

The possibility of a specific outlook towards Sudan, as well as recruitment from there, may appear to be far-fetched, but something of this kind could also be adduced from certain tendencies that became mentioned more often, if to my knowledge nowhere written down, even before Amin's downfall. From 1977 stories began to circulate about various figures from the Amin regime starting to build houses and acquire land in Equatoria, partly in the event of trouble in Uganda, but also because, whether Nubi or mercenary, that was the area to which they felt drawn. At first it was only a trickle, but with the Tanzanian-led invasion it was to turn into a flood. Moreover, it was noticeable that it was to the southern Sudan and Zaire, rather than for instance towards the eastern border with Kenya, that Amin's tattered army retreated.

AFTER AMIN

In all it was claimed that at Amin's downfall around 130,000 people fled Uganda for the southern Sudan from a variety of backgrounds. Some were from communities that had apparently become virtually synonymous with support for Amin. Scopas Dima was quoted as saying, 'If you had a Moslem name you died, if you were from the Lugbara, Madi, Alur and Kakwa tribes you died. If you were from the Sudan you died.'[5] In addition to these elements identified with Amin – particular tribes, Nubis/Muslims and Sudanese – there were a further 2000 people of very varied origins such as Rwandese and Yemenis.

The refugees' material conditions were as varied as their backgrounds. The early arrivals, some of whom had already established their positions in the southern Sudan, were certainly well-equipped. Mustafa Idrisi, former Vice-President, had a large house in Yei, which, with three wives, thirty-seven children and a staff that even included a public relations officer, he needed. He also brought 11 tractors with which to start farming, and soon began trading as well. Appropriately, Juma Oris, most recently Minister of Animal Resources, arrived with 3000 head of livestock; and in all some 25,000 cattle crossed the border. Within three months 400 vehicles were registered at Nimule on the border, and military equipment of all kinds also poured across.

Once in Sudan some refugees settled with relatives or built their own houses and found work. Houses with corrugated iron roofs sprang up all along the 46-mile road from Kaya to Yei. While some went into business, like Brigadier Hassan Marele, who had been astute enough to leave before Amin fell and was soon being described as a 'mini-millionaire', others found work with the refugee agencies, which catered for the less fortunate; and one presumably mellifluous man, who had presided over the press corps in Uganda, became an announcer on Radio Juba.[6]

Such an influx of people, some with rarely seen wealth, and others with nothing, could not but have a social and economic impact. Around Kaya on the Uganda–Zaire–Sudan border a bizarre trading centre of great ingenuity and scope grew up – a true testament to the currently fashionable economic theories of market forces as well as to the historians' claims for the existence of long-distance trading networks in pre-colonial Africa. Other effects, however, were more damaging, especially the ready availability of large numbers of weapons, including many automatic rifles, which were to contribute much to the growing lawlessness of large areas of Equatoria, especially on the east bank.

However, the influx of refugees was not to be a once and for all affair, but instead rose and fell, largely depending on developments within Uganda. By the end of 1971 those described as refugees numbered only 35,000, but a year later it was 74,000 and early in 1981 was put at 84,000. This was attributed mainly to troubles in West Nile caused first during the elections, and later to the 'invasion' in which Hassan Marele played a leading part. Violence in 1983 and 1984 again drove up the figure to 200,000, and the problem persists at the time of writing.

Yet in spite of this, the impact on Sudan–Uganda relations was relatively slight, and generally less significant either than that made by the refugees from southern Sudan in Uganda in the 1960s, or of the refugees from Ethiopia on Sudan's relations with that country. True, immediately after Amin fell there were strong feelings in Uganda about the ease with which Sudan gave refugee status. At the Arusha Conference of 1979 an irate Ugandan representative charged that, 'These people who have fled from Uganda to Sudan are not refugees, they are Sudanese citizens returning home after massacring Ugandans'; adding, 'There are perhaps only 5000 genuine Ugandan refugees in Sudan.' To which the Sudanese lawyer, Natalie Olwak, gave the interesting reply, 'Many of these people left Sudan more than one hundred years ago and settled in Uganda. So Uganda has no right to call them Sudanese. It is Uganda who is refusing to acknowledge its own citizens and declaring these people stateless.'[7] But relations between the two countries subsequently improved, which may have been related to two aspects of the politics of southern Sudan. First the issue of re-division, in which Numeiri after much uncertainty finally came down on the side of re-dividing the Southern Region established at Addis Ababa in 1972. The reasons for the rise of this issue and its outcome are of less significance here than the fact that Joseph Lagu, at one time the leader of the re-division campaign, was supported by amongst others the more wealthy and prominent of those who had crossed the border at Amin's downfall. Perhaps for them their position in Equatoria was such that they too had acquired an active political interest in the outcome of this hotly contested issue.[8] A second and related reason was that the re-opening of civil war in the southern

Sudan, in which re-division was one of the issues, developed in Upper Nile and Bahr al Ghazal, and indeed incited considerable resistance to the Sudan Peoples Liberation Army (SPLA) in Equatoria. (It is one of the several differences between the present conflict and the earlier one that at present it is being fought in the area not predominantly involved last time, and in consequence it is to the Ethiopian border that southern Sudanese refugees have predominantly fled, many to become involved in SPLA operations from there.)

CONCLUSION

The relevance of core–periphery relations to inter-state relations between Uganda and Sudan has thus tended to decline in recent years (though it has been growing in Sudan–Ethiopian relations), but it may be far from finished. The wide shifts of power that have recurred within Uganda and the southern Sudan in the years since their independence could well move in further unpredictable ways in the future likely to give rise to fresh periods of important inter-state relations. Indeed it may be hard to exaggerate the potential importance of neighbour-state relations for Uganda, for if there was a significant southern Sudanese input into the establishment and maintenance of the Amin regime, then how much greater was the role of Tanzania in his overthrow. It almost appeared to be not Ugandans who were involved one way or the other in his downfall, but Tanzania on one side and the 'mercenaries' (including the ill-fated Libyan contingent) on the other side.

Yet discussion of the two peripheries in the context not only of recent history, but also the indigenous cross-border ties alluded to earlier, raises the possibility of the formation of a regional identity straddling the border, which itself may be traversed when it becomes necessary or desirable so to do. Economically the growth of the market at Kaya illustrates this well, but politically so too does a comment from one of those who left Uganda in 1979. He remarked that he did not feel himself to be a 'refugee' or a 'returnee' but conceded that 'ridiculous colonial borders have at least afforded us somewhere to flee.'[9]

The possibility of some embryonic cross-border identity is not purely a matter of conjecture. Writing in the 1970s Ali Mazrui was able to point to those in Uganda who were talking of 'uniting the Nilotic people of Uganda with those of Sudan and creating a state separate from both Uganda and the Sudan' (Mazrui, 1978, p. 45). And that dream was carried on, particularly by some of those who fled Uganda for Equatoria following Amin's downfall. Some of them became noted for their strength of support for re-division of the Southern Region, and were actively behind Joseph Lagu when he first backed the idea. More recently the line taken has been support for the Equatorian state, involving the re-drawing of the Uganda–Sudan–Zaire borders in order to accommodate the new state. It is not only ideology that gives the idea appeal, but apparently also the prospect of the job opportunities that will proliferate if it should ever come to pass.

However, such thought are highly speculative and at present the continuing instability in both countries continues to affect the other. In July 1985:

> A week before Obote's downfall, the coup leader, General Basilio Okello, convened a secret meeting in the Sudanese border town of Nimule. At the meeting were leaders of the UNRF (Uganda National Rescue Front) and Amin's former defence minister, a leader of the Madi people who make up two-fifths of the Ugandan refugee population in Sudan. A deal was struck, and several thousand members of Amin's old army returned from Sudan to Uganda, where they were deployed in support of the new government and against Museveni's troops (Crisp, 1986, pp. 77–8).

And when this move failed, and Okello too fell, many of these recent recruits returned to Sudan once more. Now it was reportedly the turn of the Sudan government to seek their mercenary services as the SPLA decided to attack Equatoria again, both to hinder the elections of April 1986 and to strengthen its position in the proposed peace talks. That alleged recruitment may have been the reason for attacks in the summer of 1986 launched by the SPLA on the Ugandan refugee camps, apparently in an attempt to drive them out of Sudan. At present these cross-border migrants appear less the shapers of the events in southern Sudan or Uganda than their victims, with the initiatives coming from the SPLA and the NRA respectively, neither of which has a significant cross-border dimension. But such is the turbulent history of both regions that further significant change may not be far away, and with it a return of the importance of cross-border influences.

Notes

1. Report of the Joint Commission for Repatriation of Refugees July 1965. Quoted in Karadawi, 1972, p. 41.
2. Sudan did contribute forces to the garrisoning of the Egyptian front. (Her forces had been too slow to contribute to the Six-Day War.)

3. Avirgan, T and Honey, M., 1982, p.7 (Doubt has been cast on these figures however).

4. A. Wanji, *The Nubi Community : An Islamic Social Structure in East Africa*, Makerere University, Sociology Working Paper, No. 115. An informant who was a refugee in Uganda told me that Nubis also recalled their southern tribes – Madi, Bari, even one Shilluk family and some from Nigeria.

5. *Sudanow*, July 1979.

6. *ibid.*

7. *ibid.*

8. Some of those from Uganda became prominent political figures in their own right, e.g. George Lomoro who had fled Uganda during Amin's years following a company collapse and who became Commissioner for Eastern Equatoria, and the writer Taban Lo Liyong, who was in the People's Regional Assembly. Support for the former Uganda Muslims in Equatoria has also come from the backers of certain of the new Islamic movements which have operated in recent years such as *Dawlat al-Islamiyya*.

9. *Africa Contemporary Record*, 12, 1979–80, p. B111.

SIXTEEN

Refugees in and from Uganda in the post-colonial period

Louise Pirouet

By the time Uganda became independent on 9 October 1962 it was already host to over 100,000 refugees from the Congo (Zaire), Rwanda and Sudan. By the time Obote fell from power in mid-1985, the total number of refugees in Uganda was little changed, but from being primarily a host country, Uganda had become primarily an exporter of refugees, some three times that number having fled to neighbouring countries and beyond. A study of refugees in and from Uganda must take into account four categories of displaced persons, and must raise major questions about the change that has taken place.

The four categories of persons that must be considered are, first, those already mentioned who fled to Uganda from Congo, Rwanda and Sudan; secondly, ethnic groups evicted by successive post-colonial governments; thirdly, Ugandans who fled the country; and lastly, those displaced within the country. We must consider why there were relatively few refugees during the Amin period as compared with what followed; why the numbers fleeing the country increased so sharply after 1980; and the extent to which people have been displaced within the country, and why. It will be argued that the number of refugees leaving a country is an indication of the type as well as the extent of perceived danger.

Refugees were not the only immigrants in Uganda in 1962. Other groups of immigrants were Banyarwanda (the largest group), Kenyans, Nubians and Asians. The Banyarwanda and Kenyans (the latter mainly Luo from the overpopulated areas of western Kenya) were often employed as labourers or domestic servants, though some were self-employed. The Nubians were descendants of Sudanese, mainly from the southern Sudan, who had been brought into the country at the end of the nineteenth century as troops, and had settled. Most of them were found in the army or were petty traders. The Asians, by contrast, were largely a successful business class. Uganda, relatively rich, and with plenty of land for its population of under 7 million in 1962, was attractive to many who found themselves economically squeezed in neighbouring countries. There were no border controls between the three East African territories, and immigration from Rwanda was generally welcomed by the colonial authorities (Jorgensen, 1981, pp. 112–13; Clay, 1984, pp. 9–15). The Asians' commercial dominance made them the object of hostile envy, and the Nubians remained a group apart, but ethnic affinities enabled the Kenyans and the Banyarwanda to find acceptance as long as the economic climate was favourable, as did refugees from Rwanda, Congo and Sudan. Few Ugandans were found outside their own country: neither 'push' nor 'pull' factors encouraged them to emigrate.

The Banyarwanda labour migrants who came to Uganda in the colonial era were mainly Hutu who had become increasingly dominated and exploited by the Tutsi ruling majority, partly as a result of Belgian policies (Linden, 1977). They migrated to escape labour dues and to find money for tax, and mostly found work in agriculture in Buganda. They had little contact with those Tutsi who had migrated at the turn of the century and who lived as pastoralists among the closely related Bahima of Ankole. In 1959 the Hutu in Rwanda rose against the Tutsi, and in the years that followed thousands of Tutsi fled from a series of massacres, 80,000 of them reaching Uganda with many of their cattle. They were placed in settlements in southern Ankole and later in Toro. A small number found their way into secondary and higher education. During the Amin period increasing numbers moved out of the settlements, which were becoming overcrowded. Voluntary agencies and the UN High Commission for Refugees (UNHCR) assisted them to settle initially, and gave some continuing help, especially for school fees, but by the end of the 1970s they had become largely self-supporting (Clay, 1984, pp. 9–17).

The first refugees from the Congo arrived in mid-1960, and they continued to filter over the border during the next four or five years. There were fewer of them than of the Banyarwanda, around 33,000 (*Africa Research*, no. 8, 1967), and they were not placed in settlements but were self-settled (ICARA II, p. 188). As a result, their presence has never been very noticeable, and they appear to have been partly absorbed into the population at large. Many found work on the Madhvani Sugar Estates (Jorgensen, 1981, p. 305).

The first southern Sudanese refugees arrived at the very end of 1960, but the main influx was later, in 1964 and 1965, and the number grew steadily until 1972. The strife in Sudan was sometimes presented in ethnic and religious terms: in fact it was a complex mix of uneven development, inadequate representation of the south in the independence government, and cultural, political and economic aggression by the north (Scherf, 1971 and Chapter 15 in this volume). By 1972 the UNHCR had registered 75,000 Sudanese refugees in Uganda, but one informed guesstimate put the real number at 178,000 (Morrison, 1971, p. 20). As with the Rwandans, there were ethnic ties between many of the Sudanese and some of the peoples of northern Uganda. Some of the refugees lived in settlements – there was a huge and unsatisfactory settlement at Nakapiripirit, an arid area of Karamoja where farming was not very successful because of periodic drought – but many were self-settled, especially at Kigumba in Bunyoro on the Tsetse Consolidation Belt, and in Acholi and West Nile where there was easy access across the border whenever a lull in hostilities permitted. The main guerrilla bases were at Kajo Kaji and in the Imatong Hills. Proportionately rather more Sudanese than Banyarwanda found their way into secondary and higher education in Uganda. They found employment in both the public and private sectors, and after 1971 some enlisted in the Uganda army.

Uganda's policy towards the war in Sudan underwent a change after Numeiri came to power in 1969. Prior to that, Uganda had been extremely cool towards the Sudan government, and the ethnic element in the struggle inclined Uganda towards tacit support for the southerners and the refugees. Numeiri, however, seized power, and Obote moved towards ending his tolerance of the Anya Nya resistance movement. Amin's seizure of power at first made things easier for the southern Sudanese, as he openly supported them, but he was persuaded by Libya to shift his support: the Anya Nya's chief arms supplier was Israel, and the Sudan civil war was in danger of becoming a second front in the Arab–Israeli conflict. By this time, however, moves towards peace were already under way (Pirouet, 1976). Most Sudanese refugees returned home when the war ended in 1972, but 6000 who had land around Kigumba were among those who remained. How many others remained is unclear: Jorgensen says fewer than 6000 altogether (1981, p. 329, note 136), O'Ballance (1977) says 31,000 (p. 147), and the Sudan government asked the first International Conference on Assistance to Refugees in Africa (ICARA I) for assistance in resettling 60,000 people who had returned in 1979 and 1980 (ICARA I, p. 73). Sudanese in Uganda had become endangered because of the involvement of some of them with Amin's regime.

Until 1982 Uganda's policy towards refugees was for the most part generous and humane. The UNHCR and the voluntary agencies were unhampered in their work, and refugees were admitted to all grades of education, and were able to find employment. Selected secondary schools were enlarged, with international money, in order to admit them. Nevertheless they sometimes felt insecure, and they suffered some discrimination. Matters worsened for the Sudanese as time went on, partly because the economic climate was less favourable, and partly because of Uganda's changed policy towards Sudan. Even so, the Anya Nya were able to receive supplies through Uganda fairly continuously. Only when an agreement to end the civil war was imminent was pressure put on some refugees, apparently in an attempt to pre-empt the peace settlement. Sudanese government officials were allowed to visit refugee camps and to see university students, and persuade them to return, a move that caused anger and dismay. None of the refugees were willing to leave at this juncture (Pirouet, 1976, pp. 131–2).

Uganda still claimed to host 120,000 refugees in late 1983 (ICARA II, p. 186). Of these, 32,000 were Zaireans, 1000 were Ethiopians, Kenyans and Sudanese, and the remainder were Rwandans. The last mentioned lived in rural settlements, whilst the others were self-settled.

The second category of displaced persons whom we have to consider consists of ethnic groups that have been expelled from the country under successive governments. By the late 1960s urban unemployment was becoming a problem, and in 1970 Obote expelled some 33,000 Kenyans (Jorgensen, 1981, p. 286). *Target*, published by the National Christian Council of Kenya, called them 'Africa's newest refugees'. The Uganda government justified the expulsions by saying that the Kenyans had no work permits: most had arrived long before work permits were required. Not all Kenyans were expelled: those who were deemed useful remained, and others remained because they had become assimilated and were not noticed. Relations between Kenya and Uganda were considerably soured by these expulsions: had those expelled been Kikuyu, perhaps the Kenyan reaction might have been stronger, but most were Luo from western Kenya.

The expulsion of 50,000 Asians by Amin in 1972 was administered far more harshly, included people with Ugandan citizenship, and caused an international furore, largely because so many of them went to Western Europe and North America. Animosity towards the Asians, who controlled large sections of the economy, had been building up for years, and few Ugandans objected to Amin's action, even if they had misgivings about the way the expulsions were carried out. There were honourable exceptions to the general approval, and when Amin turned on citizen Asians, stronger objections were raised. Equally few foresaw the damage this would do to the economy. To a section of the European community, mostly aid personnel (missionaries, teachers and others), backed by a grouping of the voluntary agencies in Britain, must go much of the credit for ensuring the safety of most of the Asians, and achieving what measure of order there was. The UNHCR's spectacular bluff in designating temples as UN territory when the deadline arrived before the last few hundred could be air-lifted out possibly saved several hundred lives. The Asians themselves behaved with dignity and restraint (Humphrey and Ward, 1974, pp. 36–46).

The eviction and displacement of a larger number of Banyarwanda, including some 40,000 people who claimed Uganda citizenship, and 31,000 people registered with the UNHCR as refugees, caused barely a ripple on the international scene by comparison. This was no doubt because, unlike the expelled Asians, they did not come to Europe, and the problem was confined to a remote area of East Africa more or less inaccessible to journalists. The reasons for the evictions were complex, and were both political and economic. The economic reasons related to land. The larger areas over which the Banyarwanda pastoralists grazed their cattle, both within and beyond the limits of the settlements, aroused the envy of the growing population of Ankole, as did the cattle that they possessed. When the Banyarwanda were forced out, the land was quickly taken by Banyankole, who also enriched themselves by seizing cattle and other possessions of the Banyarwanda. The political reasons are more difficult to summarize. For two main reasons the Banyarwanda seemed suspect to the Uganda People's Congress (UPC), the party that came to power in 1980. First, the Banyarwanda were mostly Catholics, and Catholics were identified with the opposition Democratic Party (DP). They first came under suspicion for this reason in 1969 (Clay, 1984, p. 28). The elections that returned UPC and Obote to power in December 1980 were characterized by malpractice (Final Report of the COG, *passim*), and Obote and the new government turned on the DP and other opposition groups early in 1981. By this time the Banyarwanda were doubly suspect. Because they had felt threatened by Obote during his first term of office, they had to some extent welcomed Amin's coup, and some of them had actively supported him, as a result of which all were branded. Clay suggests that there is evidence to indicate that the Banyarwanda were no more involved with Amin than were other ethnic groups (p. 34). Secondly, the Banyarwanda who were evicted were those in Ankole, the home of Museveni, leader of a major section of the armed resistance to Obote during his second presidency. Museveni is a Muhima, and the Bahima are ethnically related to the Tutsi of Rwanda, and they were therefore held guilty by association (Clay, 1984, pp. 28–34; see also *Oxfam Bulletin*, 1 November 1982 and Chapter 11 above).

There is good reason to believe that the evictions were planned over a long period, and that they were carried out at the instigation of central government. Threats and inflammatory speeches had been made by Obote himself and others (Clay, 1984, p. 33). By May 1982 the UNHCR Representative, Tom Unwin, was taking action to try and prevent all Banyarwanda refugees being forced back into the settlements. Local factionalism within the UPC in Ankole was the main cause, and one side in the dispute saw the possibility of rewarding its followers with lands and goods confiscated from the Banyarwanda. UPC Youth Wingers and other party officials actually enforced the displacement (Clay, 1984, pp. 7–8; MRG Report, p. 11). Obote was out of the country at the time, but eventually he issued a statement on 29 October, apparently designed to mollify international concern. He concluded by saying,

> I want to assure the Chairman, Councillors, Ugandans, and the rest of the world that there was no government approval, scheme or decision for persons of Rwandese origin to be uprooted from amidst the Ugandan population. I also want to assure all the rest of the country as well as the world, that the government of Uganda will not pursue such policy.

But no practical steps were taken to reverse the policy. Moreover the deployment of the Special Force leaves no doubt that the evictions had the approval of the President's Office. A week after the President's statement, the chairman of the Mbarara District Council addressed a meeting of councillors, county and sub-county chiefs. He told his hearers,

> I summoned you to inform you that the battle to collect and return the refugees to their places is over, and to thank you for the work you have done ... What remains now is to scrutinise refugees that might have stayed behind and rid villages of refugees ... I am glad to tell you that our exercise was perfomed perfectly well even if there were sporadic incidents which did not please us, e.g. our two youths and one policeman were killed ... This is not negligible. The good thing is that we won the battle through the blood of our friends above. Let us observe a minute of silence in their remembrance[1] ... Go and preach the gospel and inform the people that we have won the battle. Let them follow as we know our destination and we have already started seeing sunshine there ... I am warning everyone to avoid the property of the Banyarwanda ... Be patient and the District Council will determine a way for you to share these properties ... To dispel all rumours and loose talk, the President's speech from the start to

the end does not anywhere state that refugees and aliens should return to the lands they occupied.

As a result of these evictions, between 75,000 and 80,000 people were displaced. Some 45,000 fled to Rwanda, 5000 of whom were trapped on the border when it was closed by Rwandan authorities. They remained at Merama Hill, unable either to return to Uganda or to be admitted to Rwanda, and received some help from the Anglican Diocese of Kigezi. Of those who reached Rwanda, the Rwandan government claimed that most were Ugandan citizens, being Banyarwanda born in Uganda, or Bahima. In spite of international pressure, Obote's government refused to have them back except in exchange for all the Rwandan refugees then in Uganda (*Africa Confidential*, 16 January 1985). In October 1985, after Obote's fall, the two governments co-operated in repatriating these people. The exercise caused yet further hardship, and their condition is still unclear. Those of the Banyarwanda who had fled to Uganda as refugees feared to go back to Rwanda when evicted, and crowded into the refugee settlements, whose boundaries were pushed back by those who carried out the evictions. They were later moved to Kyaka, having lost most of their possessions. There they faced an acute shortage of water (*Refugees*, 11, pp. 10–11), and for the third time they had to try and make a new start in life (the second time was after the 1979 invasion of Uganda when the areas the refugees occupied suffered severely, being in the direct line of march of the Tanzanian and Ugandan troops). In December 1983 the Banyarwanda living in Rakai District were displaced and harassed. The district commissioner of Rakai, who was married to a Munyarwanda, refused to follow the suggestion made by the DC of Mbarara for removing the Banyarwanda, but his assistant carried out the evictions. The DP Member of Parliament for Rakai, Mr Luke Kazinja, protested openly, and subsequently disappeared (Clay, 1984, p. 8).

Uganda had thus rid herself of many of those people whom she could identify as aliens (the Nubians fled north after the fall of Amin). The Banyarwanda refugees remaining in Uganda felt doubly insecure.

We next have to consider those Ugandans who have sought refuge outside the country. In 1966 Obote used force against the Baganda when they defied the central government and attempted to secede. A small number of Baganda left the country, many of them going to Britain, and did not return until after the Amin coup. The best known of those exiles was Kabaka Mutesa, who died in Britain. After the Amin coup there was a further exodus. Obote himself was in Singapore when the coup took place, and was unable to return to Uganda. He and a group of supporters lived in exile in Dar es Salaam throughout the Amin period. A steady trickle of people went across the border to Kenya, but given the brutality of the Ugandan regime, the trickle might seem fairly small, only increasing to a large flow after the murder of Archbishop Janani Luwum in February 1977. The Archbishop, along with two senior members of government, was accused of involvement in an Acholi plot to overthrow the government, and after their murder a large number of Acholi, especially those in and around Kampala, felt themselves endangered, not primarily as individuals, but because they were Acholi.

Acholi were not the only Ugandans to flee at this juncture, but others who did so fled because they perceived themselves to be endangered as individuals. These included, for example, the son and daughter-in-law of Kampala's chief traffic policeman, who had refused to draw a map showing the traffic accident that the government claimed had killed the three men. There was alleged to be a death-list of Acholi; at any rate, Kenyan immigration officials accepted that Acholi were endangered whether or not they could prove themselves to be individually threatened. This was one of the few points during the Amin period when a group was endangered in this way (outside the army, that is).

The refugee population in Nairobi was made up of individuals and some family groups representative of most parts of Uganda. A high proportion of those who reached Nairobi were so-called urban refugees. Not even Muslims were safe from the violence: of the hundred people listed by Henry Kyemba as victims of Amin in *State of Blood* (1977), seven were Muslims, and there were a few Muslims among the refugees who reached Nairobi, though understandably they were somewhat afraid to declare themselves (for the general situation of Ugandan refugees in Kenya see Pirouet, 1979 and *Refugees*, November 1985, pp. 14–15).

Did the relative fewness of refugees indicate that the violence under Amin has been exaggerated? Some incidents were certainly exaggerated by the Western media, who seemed willing to publish anything about Amin provided it was sufficiently horrifying. Two alleged massacres that did not take place were those at Karuma Falls soon after the coup, and that at Makerere in 1976 (Langlands, 1977, p. 18; Amnesty International, 1978, p. 25). Nevertheless Amnesty International considered that 'up to 300,000 people may have died' in the eight years of Amin's rule. J.J. Jorgensen considers that such a figure is far too high, and suggests a total of between 28,000 and 50,000, including 'ordinary civilian crimes' at a rate of 2000 to 2500 per year. His main reason for believing the total number of killings to be as low as this is that so few people fled the country. 'If so many died,' he asks, 'why did so few flee?' He notes that a far lower rate of killings led to tens of thousands fleeing from the southern Sudan and Rwanda. The refugee totals he gives for Kenya are much too low (many refugees were unable to get recognition from the Kenyan authorities, and only heads of families were counted in the official totals), but nevertheless the number of refugees from Amin's Uganda in no way matches the size of the exodus from either Rwanda or Sudan, as he notes. Jorgensen believes that the totals have been exaggerated as a result of treating peaks of violence as averages.

However, it is contended here that the higher totals that have been suggested cannot easily be dismissed. Some attention must be paid to the population statistics, and an explanation found for the fall in the rate of population increase during the 1970s (World Bank, 1984, Table 19, p. 254). During the 1960s the annual rate of increase was 3 per cent, and this was expected to rise to 3.3 per cent in the 1970s, instead of which it fell to 2.7 per cent.[2] This translates into a shortfall of 420,000, if the annual rate of increase had remained at 3 per cent, and 850,000 if it had risen to 3.3 per cent as expected. During these years life expectancy rose and infant mortality fell, though less than almost anywhere else in Africa (World Bank, 1984, Table 32, p. 262). Since the slowing down in the rate of increase certainly cannot be explained by successful population control programmes, some other explanation must be found. Of course it is not suggested that the shortfall represents the number of killings: one person killed may represent more than one in the final shortfall since s/he is unable to reproduce. The violence of these years must surely account for some part of the otherwise unexplained slowing down in the rate of increase, and the census data make the suggestion that up to 300,000 people may have been killed begin to look less unlikely.

After Amin's overthrow there was a dramatic rise in the number of people fleeing Uganda. New elements in the situation explain this rise, and also throw light on why there were not more who fled from Amin's Uganda in spite of its horrors. The first was the growth of armed resistance to Obote and the UPC government. In attempting to crush this, undisciplined soldiers were permitted to take reprisals against the civilian population, and this in turn fuelled the resistance movements. The second was that groups as well as individuals were endangered. We have already noticed that during the Amin period, as soon as the Acholi saw themselves endangered as a group, the number of refugees rose. We will survey briefly the groups affected.

The first group to flee after the fall of Amin were the remnants of his army, Nubians and others, who crossed the border into Sudan.

The Sudan was hesitant to grant them refugee status, and Uganda claimed that they were returning Sudanese. They continued to behave in the lawless fashion to which they had become accustomed, and were unco-operative with the UNHCR. The Sudanese authorities had to take strong measures against them (Rogge, 1985, pp. 54–5, 77–8, 81, 112–13, 116).

The next group of refugees were the people of West Nile, which saw by far the largest exodus. The area as a whole is a stronghold of the Democratic Party, which, with its Roman Catholic links, is the major opposition party to the UPC. The northern part of West Nile, inhabited by the Kakwa, was Amin's power base. After the ousting of Godfrey Binaisa as President in mid-1980, the Uganda National Liberation Army (UNLA) took over from the Tanzanian troops who had previously been stationed there, and who, in spite of petty pilfering, were well-behaved by comparison with the UNLA troops, who were bent on revenge. UPC electioneering was disrupted by armed resistance in August 1980, and this gave the army its excuse. In the last few months of 1980, 30,000 people took refuge in the southern Sudan (ICARA I, p. 72), and over 100,000 in Haut-Zaire (ICARA I, p. 99). The registration of voters in West Nile ceased, and among the irregularities noted by the Commonwealth Observer Group who monitored the election was the eventual return of unopposed UPC members for this area (COG Final Report, pp. 11–15). A year later there were reported to be 300,000 refugees in Zaire and another 50,000 in Sudan: some 70 per cent of the population of the area had fled. 'We thank God that Zaire and Sudan were so near,' wrote a missionary working in Arua, 'otherwise the slaughter might have been far greater than it was' (Dr Ted Williams, 4.9.1981, in *Uganda Church Association Newsletter*, November 1981, p. 7). As it was, the number killed was estimated variously at between 5000 and 30,000 (MRG Report, p. 9). One of the best-documented massacres took place at Ombachi Catholic Mission in June 1981 (*Catholic Herald*, 3 July 1981; *Guardian*, 6 July 1981). The International Committee of the Red Cross publicized this massacre and was expelled from Uganda as a result (MRG Report, p. 9). The largest exodus to Sudan occurred in 1982–3, when a total of 200,000 in UNHCR settlements was reached, and perhaps as many as 100,000 others were self-settled. (*Sudanow*, August 1982, p. 5; *Sunday Times*, 31 October 1982; *Refugees*, December 1983, p. 43; *Africa Confidential*, 2 November 1983, p. 4).

There was large-scale spontaneous repatriation from Zaire as the southern part of West Nile became more peaceful, and harassment by the Zairean army increased (S. and P. Maclure, 16.5.1982, in *Uganda Church Association Newsletter*, November 1982, p. 17), but by mid-1984 some 63,000 still remained, 57,000 of whom were in UNHCR settlements (ICARA II, pp. 225–28). As the northern part of West Nile was still the scene of insurgency, very few refugees returned from Sudan. In mid-1983 the UNHCR began a voluntary repatriation scheme for refugees in both Zaire and Sudan who wanted to return to Uganda, but on 18 June 1984 a prominent returnee, Al Hajji Jabiri, was murdered by UNLA soliders, and the UNHCR suspended the scheme (*Refugees*, September 1984, p.17). Although the scheme was eventually restarted, the number asking for repatriation from Sudan slowed to a trickle, and the UNHCR did not find it worth running a convoy every month. By May 1985 25,000 people had returned from Zaire under this scheme, and 3000 from Sudan, leaving 28,000 in Zaire and 250,000 in Sudan (Crisp, 1984b, pp. 10–23; *Refugees*, May 1985, p. 7). The methods of persuasion used to encourage refugees to return has been the subject of much debate and criticism (Crisp, 1986).

The reasons for the large-scale exodus from West Nile are clear. First, there was armed resistance, and the UNLA swept through the area driving out the civilian population along with the guerrillas. 'Reports of atrocities committed by the UNLA in the north abound, and it is now generally accepted that one of its objectives was to clear the West Nile region completely of its population, thereby eliminating once and for all support for Amin'; such was the view of a researcher into the refugee problems of Sudan (Rogge, 1985, p. 113). In fact the guerrilla movements distanced themselves from Amin and from his supporters who fled in 1979, as Rogge elsewhere admits, and as Dr Harrell-Bond has made clear (Harrell-Bond, 25 October 1982, cyclostyled letter). The fact that military action was indiscriminate is evidenced by the fact that there were UPC members *and officials* among the refugees in Sudan (Harrell-Bond, personal communication, 25 October 1982).

The other area of Uganda that saw massive insurgency was the Luwero triangle in Buganda, where Museveni's National Resistance Army (NRA) was based. The Baganda have always been opposed to Obote and the UPC, and dreaded his return to power. This area experienced much of what West Nile experienced, but its inhabitants were unable to flee. Not only was there no international boundary anywhere near them, but also the UNLA surrounded the area and penned the people up into camps in a counter-insurgency operation. According to some diplomatic sources, the Uganda government knew that this would be attended by heavy civilian casualties and cause an international outcry. The government nevertheless decided to go ahead, presumably in the belief that the insurgency could be defeated. Apart from the fact that the UNLA entirely failed to defeat the guerrillas, things turned out much as the government had predicted. Thousands of civilians died, not only as a result of massacre or being caught in cross-fire, but also because of the forced cessation of normal life, including food production. The figure of 300,000 dead, which was widely bandied about in the British press, stems ultimately from a report to the Uganda Government by the International Committee of the Red Cross, which had been permitted to run a tracing service in the area, and which allegedly said that between a third and a half of the population could not be accounted for. The USA led the international outcry (*Washington Post*, 5 August 1984; Abrams, 1984, see also *Le Monde*, 20 June 1984; Crisp, 1984a; ICRC Review, 1984).

A consideration of the Luwero triangle brings us to the fourth category of displaced persons, those who were internally displaced. In this case the displacement was first a forcible uprooting from their villages by the UNLA, to be followed by their forcible dispersal from those same camps when they were closed about a year later. By this time the people were reluctant to leave: their homes had been destroyed, and the camps had become something of a haven during the daylight hours when aid agency staff were present and provided some measure of protection. The Uganda government claimed that the population was depleted because people had been removed and relocated in safer areas elsewhere in the country. Whilst individuals and family groups had certainly been able to escape and had taken refuge with their friends and relatives outside Luwero, or had fled abroad, observers failed to find any evidence of major resettlement. The same scorched-earth policies were carried out in the Luwero triangle as had been employed in West Nile, and had the area been close to an international boundary, so that the population could not be hemmed in, no doubt there would have been a massive refugee exodus from Luwero, and less loss of life. The type of violence used in West Nile and Luwero is the kind that can normally be expected to result in large outflows of refugees. It was not a type of violence that occurred during the Amin period.

If we examine the types of violence and oppression, and the effect they had on refugee flows, we find the following:
(1) Intra-army violence. This has been endemic since 1971. In the Amin period there were massacres of Lango and Acholi soldiers and, later on, rivalries between different groups of troops from West Nile resulted in bloodshed. Intra-army violence increased in 1985, and was partly responsible for Obote's overthrow in July. This type of violence produced very few refugees, though there were some army and air force officers among those who fled to Nairobi during the Amin period (ICJ, 1977, pp. 28–9, 32–4, 55–8).

(2) Army indiscipline has characterized Uganda since the attempted assassination of Obote in 1969 (indeed, it goes back earlier, to the mutinies in 1964). Travellers have regularly been robbed at road-blocks, cars have been stolen at gunpoint, and soldiers have carried out burglaries on homes both in the towns and in the countryside. Sometimes such attacks have led to injuries or murder, and the survivors have fled the country. There is evidence of both soldiers and police holding people to ransom in barracks and police stations, and when the victim has been bought out by family or friends, s/he may well deem it wise to leave Uganda. Soldiers have also been willing to pay off old scores for people with grudges, on receipt of a suitable payment, of course, and again, the family of the victim may flee the country (ICJ, *passim*; Amnesty, 1978, 1985).

(3) Political repression has taken two forms. Under the Public Order and Security Act (1967) a person may be detained without trial if it is considered that he 'has conducted, is conducting, is about to conduct himself so as to be dangerous to peace and good order of Uganda; has acted, is acting, is about to act in a manner prejudicial to the defence or security of Uganda' (quoted from a detention order). Such an order should bear the Public Seal and be signed by the Minister of Internal Affairs. The order from which this is quoted is a poorly duplicated piece of paper, with the detainee's name misspelt, and the signature consists of a mark thus: ∝). During Obote's two presidencies considerable numbers of people were detained without trial, some of whom were released. After release, some did not feel it safe to remain in Uganda, and went to Kenya, Europe or North America. Their families occasionally accompanied them (Amnesty International, 1985; *Munnansi* listed names of detainees when possible). Since 1971 political opposition was also dealt with more summarily, and people who opposed the regime were murdered or have 'disappeared'. The Public Order and Security Act was little used by Amin. His more brutal methods were also used during Obote's second presidency. Relatives of political opponents who have been murdered or 'disappeared' often fled the country, believing themselves to be endangered, particularly if they were in a position to point out those responsible (Amnesty International, *Annual Reports*, 1972–85).

(4) We next come to the type of violence that produced large migrations of refugees from Sudan, Zaire, Rwanda and Uganda. This was directed against ethnic groups, and was what the Western media like to describe as 'tribalism'. But 'tribalism' is

never simply a matter of ethnicity: underdevelopment, unequal development, and hence politics and ideology are ingredients of all such 'tribal' conflicts. When an ethnic group finds itself the object of pogroms (as with the Tutsi of Rwanda), or when an area becomes a theatre of insurgency or civil war (as in Sudan and Uganda), then a mass exodus of the civilian population may take place. Governments like to blame such refugee movements on the insurgency, which begs the question of why the insurgency erupted in the first place.

(5) Finally we must mention the forcible evictions that have characterized Uganda's post-colonial history, when Kenyans, Asians and Banyarwanda have in turn been expelled from the country or been displaced within it. These evictions have occurred in each of the three main presidencies of the post-colonial years.

The main reason, therefore, for the huge increase in the number of refugees fleeing from Uganda under Obote's second presidency has been the existence of armed resistance, and the extreme measures used against it. Whether this state of near civil war could have been avoided if the elections had been properly carried out is open to debate. At any rate, Africa's only experience of an ousted president returning to power proved disastrous, and the refugees generated since 1979 placed a burden on most of Uganda's neighbours.

Two major questions remain to be raised, though it is not intended to answer either of them. The first is, in view of the ferocity of the Amin period, why did it take so long for any coherent resistance to emerge? Yoweri Museveni led the Front for National Salvation, and a group of guerrillas was trained in Tanzania under Obote's leadership, but it was minuscule, and activity within Uganda was very restricted (MRG Report, p. 6). During Obote's second presidency, Museveni's NRA was a large and very successful movement. Museveni, from south-western Uganda, was ideologically motivated, but his movement gathered strength from among the disaffected Baganda, who joined his resistance for reasons of their own.

The final question that must be raised concerns the effect on development of the displacements of people that are here described. It is most usual to discuss refugees and development in the context of the host country, and to consider how an influx of refugees affects that country's development. This emphasis results from the immediate problems raised by the need for refugees to be fed and otherwise provided for. The effect of population loss of development may be just as serious. The loss of urban refugees is the loss of qualified people in whose education and training much has been invested. Sudan lost a generation of students from the south in the 1960s, for instance, when the repression following the school strikes resulted in most of the students fleeing (Albino, 1970, pp. 46–7). Uganda lost many of its doctors in the 1970s: in 1960 there was one doctor to every 15,050 persons; by 1980 there was one to every 26,810 persons (World Bank, 1984, Table 24, p. 264). Only five countries in Africa suffered a deterioration in the doctor–patient ratio, and Uganda's was one of the worst.[3] The Asian exodus had a dramatic effect on the Uganda economy, sparking off massive inflation, as well as wreaking havoc on the country's industry and commerce. But large-scale rural outflows also have a severe effect. One only has to look at the budgets for rehabilitating returnees proposed to ICARA II to grasp something of the massive cost involved. And, of course, if there is insurgency, a large proportion of the national income has to be diverted to countering it, instead of being available for development.

Notes

1. 'On 15 September 1982, two UPC Youth Wingers and a policeman were shot dead in Mbarara District. Local UPC officials announced that they had been killed whilst investigating instances of cattle-theft by Banyarwanda herdsmen, but other reports suggest that it was the Youth Wingers themselves who had been discovered stealing cows, and that they had died in the gun-battle that followed' (MRG Report, p. 11).
   The DP statement on the incident accepts the latter version of the story: 'On 15.9.82 armed Youth Wingers accompanied by a policeman invaded Rakai district and stole many head of cattle ... The victims of the theft reported the incident to the authorites. As the 'invaders' had not reported their presence or their purpose to the authorities they were taken to be criminals and a deployment of security personnel pursued them. A confrontation and shoot-out between the 'invaders' and the security personnel occurred at Rwangabo ... It is during the shoot-out that the three Ugandans (2 Youth Wingers and the 'escort' policeman) were killed ... One of the youths killed was a relation of a Minister of State in the Government. It is after this incident that the decisions to drive out the Rwandan refugees from their homes in Mbarara district was put into operation...' (Clay, 1984, p. 52). *Exile*, 1, p.4 also refers to these murders, but whilst this incident may have precipitated the evictions, it did not cause them.
2. The 1969 census figure was 9,548,847 and the provisional figure for the 1980 census was 12,636,179. These censuses are thought to be reasonably reliable. The provisional 1969 total was adjusted c. 20,000 upwards, and the 1980 provisional figure is likely to be of the same degree of accuracy. I am grateful to Dr Cherry Gertzel for drawing my attention to the *World Development Report*, and to Professor Bryan Langlands for looking up the census figures for me. Four other African countries experienced a slowing down in the rate of population increase: Ethiopia, Zimbabwe (both of which suffered civil war – the fall was 4 per cent from the previous decade in each case); Togo (where emigration is a possible explanation); and Niger (a fall of 1 per cent). Uganda was one of only ten African countries which carried out a full census in both years.
3. The other countries were Malawi, Mozambique, Zimbabwe and Morocco.

SEVENTEEN
The Uganda crisis and the national question

Martin Doornbos

Is Uganda about to see a return of peace and social rehabilitation instead of new cycles of political confrontation and violence? Will the country be able to restore its national unity and integrity or will it yet face the prospect of fragmentation? Does the NRA takeover in early 1986 signify a historical and strategic turning point or could it be only a passing phase?

Against the background of years of disruption and trauma these questions are now raised with renewed urgency and anticipation. Yet to many observers of Ugandan politics a way out of the stalemate has for long seemed remote indeed. In recent years Uganda's politics has come to be marked by diminishing expectations. As new rounds of confrontations shaping the country's future have followed each other, both at conference tables and in the field, each time their outcome has been anticipated in many quarters with lessened confidence and increased scepticism. Could it still make a difference? Commonplace attitudes have come to view the course of Ugandan politics as a downward spiral: retrogressing from one missed opportunity to another. It seemingly succeeded in reaching new depths of hostility, destruction and self-destruction at each interval. Increasingly, the question has become whether any conceivable settlement could disrupt this commonplace perspective.

Thus for years Uganda's paradox appeared only too familiar: in few situations would there have been more widely shared affirmation of the urgency to re-create political stability and social justice, yet few instances would have manifested sharper divergences and conflicts as to what and whose priorities ought to be followed towards achieving this. Thus, a spectre of unfulfilled expectations surrounded the stalemate between contending parties.

In recent years several moments have at first seemed to offer a promise of change and rehabilitation. First, of course, there was the ousting of Idi Amin in 1979, desired by many factions and parties but seriously delayed as a result of mutual conflicts and suspicion. The moment of relief and expectation at Amin's overthrow was short-lived, though, and soon became dampened by renewed rivalries and political dispute. As factional struggles along familiar lines of petty politics appeared to resume their course, the installation and demise of the Lule and Binaisa governments were marked by heightening fatigue and increased pessimism. Obote's subsequent return to power, anticipated with mixed feelings as it was, nonetheless gave rise to some renewed expectation, among at least some quarters, that perhaps it might re-establish a power base from which political stability might be extended. 'If only order could be restored, then ...' was more or less. how the argument ran. Economically, things did not turn out too badly (Kasfir, 1985 and Chapter 11 above), but in political terms the failure proved more dismal than even the most gloomy forecast could have anticipated. Obote, who had been a master at playing off ethnic and other factions against each other, now found that his skills in this respect acted as a boomerang. In a context marked by aggravated distrust, internal strife along ethno-religious, party, and intra-military lines escalated to virtually unprecedented heights. There was a widespread conviction that the elections held in 1980 to regularize the political basis of government had been rigged by Obote's UPC to ensure its recapture of power. All too strongly, it seems, had Obote come to believe that as he had been illegally removed by Amin, he was personally entitled to a restoration of his position at the collapse of the Amin regime engineered by Tanzania's intervention. And as a matter of fact, the Tanzanians did put their money on him.

With reference to Obote's second regime, the International Commission of Jurists came to quote a figure of 300,000 as victims of oppression, army and police brutality, and ethno-political conflict, identical indeed to the number of casualties attributed earlier to Amin by Amnesty International. Increasingly, controlled and uncontrolled terror had become a dominant feature of political life. Once more, therefore, there was a sense of relief when Obote was ousted in 1985. The overthrow itself had come as a byproduct of narrowly ethnic intra-army hostility between Acholi and Langi, exacerbated by Obote's manoeuvres in favour of the Langi. The Acholi-led Okello coup was staged as a pre-emptive measure in this connection, just as years earlier (1971) Amin's coup had sought to pre-empt Obote's plans to reduce his position of power within the army.

During 1985 symptoms of political disintegration multiplied rapidly. A wide assortment of political groups and coalitions each had their different 'project'. Militarily, the scene had become fragmented into an array of alternative armed power bases, the most important of which were the increasingly Acholi-dominated 'official' Uganda Army, the ex-Amin forces, and Museveni's National Resistance Army. Underscoring how much the pursuit of power had become an end in itself, the 'official' army of Basilio Okello did not shy away from entering into an unholy alliance with the ex-Amin troops they had earlier been persecuting when it was evident that the NRA had become a serious challenge to their power. Only the NRA leadership seemed fairly clear as to what should be its next steps. Inevitably, in many quarters questions as to what *should* happen next were shifting into what *might* happen. More generally, hopes for improved prospects tended to mix with anticipations of worse to come. 'If only ...' became a matter of wishful thinking as much as of political argument.

DOMINANT THEMES

It is instructive to look back at the trajectory of Ugandan politics since independence, which might well be viewed in terms of a succession of 'if only' arguments, each based on a particular and dominant interpretation of what appeared to be the key axis of political cleavage and conflict at the time and of what seemed to be required to overcome it. Basically, one could distinguish some four or five more or less distinct waves of interpretation (Doornbos, 1978). Essentially, each of these themes raised the national question from a different perspective, or rather put forward different national questions and answers. First, no matter how remote from realities it may now appear in retrospect, a good deal of thought around the time of independence was based on the premise that if only 'traditional–modern' dichotomies and cleav-ages could be reconciled, then things would augur well for Uganda's political destiny. The main issue, as perceived by observers as well as participants at the time, was how to make viable provisions for the incorporation of traditional institutions, especially the kingship of Buganda and the smaller kingdoms, within the structures of a modern nation-state. However, as the sources and nature of conflict soon seemed to be shifting, during the next several years 'if only' arguments likewise acquired a new contents: by the mid-1960s, ethnically based dispute – ranging from micro intra-district to macro Bantu–Nilotic levels – seemed to have become highly pervasive in the Ugandan political arena. Thus interpretations converged next on the conclusion that if only ethnic conflict could be overcome, the Uganda would be in better position to achieve its national integration. Only a few observers paused to ask whether it was ethnicity *per se* or other forces that had triggered off the observed conflicts. Again, however, towards the end of the 1960s a new premise suggested itself: if only the class basis of politics could be resolved, then there would be better prospects for genuine national development. The Common Man's Charter, at the political level, and neo-Marxist approaches at the conceptual level, posed the centrality of class and class conflict where previous themes had been silent about this.

Amin's armed intervention in 1971 put an abrupt end to all these lines of thought, while at the same time beginning to generate a new kind of hypothesis: if only the military could be ousted and civilian rule restored, then the country at last would find its true basis for national reconciliation, etc. The record of what subsequently evolved, however, is fresh enough in the memory. Basically, from 1971 till the present internal strife in many respects has been particularly severe in Uganda, causing the national question to be articulated and echoed in a whole range of dimensions. In the end, with diminishing expectations, 'if only' arguments came to include, or even to concentrate on, calls for at least a 'clean' military, which in turn, it was hoped, would help recreate basic 'order'. As it happened, with the NRA slowly extending its control over southern Uganda, confirmation was increasingly received that it did in fact live up to its reputation of constituting a reasonably disciplined, non-looting, non-harassing people's army. In south-western Uganda, it was reported to be popularly experienced as a liberation force, or indeed as a kind of blessing in disguise.

'If only' assumptions in politics have a peculiar quality. They can imply a mobilizing element, conducive at least in the short run to orientate thinking towards alternative national strategies. But in the Ugandan case many or most of the conceivable 'if onlys' were somehow advanced and exploited within a relatively short span of years. In the process the stock of such arguments soon got exhausted: as basic political trust and relationships were progressively being eroded, each next cycle could only succeed in arousing diminishing credibility. Successive traumatic experiences, especially with the politics of the gun, accumulated into such depths of political cynicism that virtually any group or project could expect to be met with *a priori* disbelief, and with the chance of new waves of political confrontation. The question then becomes which national project can still be worth that. If Uganda after 1986 will be able to break out of this circle and stalemate, it will be no minor achievement.

STARTING FROM SCRATCH?

Uganda's current condition may be likened to a 'starting from scratch' predicament, applicable here to a whole nation. It is not exactly the first time that the country finds itself in this condition. At the end of the Amin regime much the same kind of situation had presented itself. It could well be argued, in fact, that Uganda's predicament has since only been perpetuated and aggravated, producing a sort of continuing zero-sum situation.

Generally speaking, it is in relatively rare instances only that one may encounter situations of similarly gross political havoc in the wake of some major confrontation or calamity and the traumatic experience that goes with it. It is different from liberation, coups, elections *per se*. Its physical illustration might be one of uncounted casualties and pervasive debris, and in fact, one of the first things it may require is clearing the minimum necessary to enable the most immediate, pressing needs to be attended to. That, necessarily, is conveyed in any notion of 'starting from scratch'. Beyond the actual physical disaster one would find actual evidence of the following: a) a significant diminution in resources and resource capacity; b) a significant change, diminution and 'disrupting' in public decision-making capacity; and c) a destruction of pre-existing social ties, a breakdown in value systems and difficulties in the viability of non-local exchange systems (Schaffer, unpublished note).

First things first. But what things are first things? Dazzled still from the final explosions of disaster, people may be trying to reorientate themselves in what suddenly appears a strange silence or interlude, trying to formulate answers to questions as simple as 'what now?' What questions indeed should be asked first? There might be 'how to' questions, presuming basic goals are clear enough and given, though even these would probably involve an exercise of greater magnitude than the usual in sizing up and implementing what will be required by way of reconstruction, restoration, returning to 'normal'. But the 'what new' may well demand more qualitative reappraisals, concerning the *kind* of start, and the *kind* of direction, that should be chosen. 'From scratch', after all, suggests that once the immediate debris has been removed, there will be a clean slate to start from. This would not restrict one to the extrapolation of pre-existing designs or structures, but may present one with a rare chance to strike out in novel directions, even the kind-of-direction-one-had-always-wanted-to-go had it not been for the accumulated past acting as 'constraint'.

Notwithstanding the misery that may have given rise to them, there has often been something euphoric about the notion of fresh starts; such moments tend to raise expectations of enlarged scope and promise. Whether this applies to Uganda still is a moot question. But it should be plain that often there has been not so much a fresh *start* as at best a fresh *slate*, and that the fresh slates that perhaps appeared to offer new room for manoeuvre or for choice among alternative courses, have been extremely rare historically. When, then, can fresh slates be expected to serve as liberating charters, releasing rather than restraining energies towards reconstruction?

The basic question in regard to the notion of 'starting from scratch' is, of course, is it *conceivable* and *possible* to strike out in ways that are not in some sense derived from the past? No matter how disorienting the present may be, and thus to appear suggestive of a 'new' situation of sorts, what real chances are there of a move away from historically given divisions or strategies?

Experience so far is not too promising. Uganda, together with Kampuchea, Nicaragua immediately after Somoza, and famine-stricken Ethiopia, has come to be regarded among some of the most extreme 'scratch' cases imaginable. After years of unprecedented obliteration of the very fabric of society, even basic relief stagnated at times due to bitter persistence of political enmities. Again, notwithstanding the sigh of relief which the country enjoyed at the ousting of Idi Amin, pre-existing divisions had resumed their course as if these horrendous years had been merely an interruption, or as if no lesson was learnt. To the contrary, it appeared as if the Amin years had been a learning period. Revenge took a heavy toll and mutual distrust perpetuated the stalemate. In turn, fear for revenge at least in the north led to preparations for an expected final reckoning.

What must be recognized, though, is that where the social, economic and political scene is largely in havoc, few survivors will be ready to start from blank slates. To anticipate differently may be to expect the heroic or the impossible. The bitterness of trauma tends to enhance, rather than to diminish, determinations to fulfil sworn pledges, frustrated goals or simply to hold on to positions of power. Prolongation and intensification of previous hostility, exacerbating a kind of involution of political options, may thus be as probable an outcome as their sublimation or reconciliation, as again the Ugandan case has illustrated over the past several years.

It is useful, therefore, to consider such 'starting from scratch' moments more closely and see what they imply. Do they allow fresh starts, at all? What is the room for manoeuvre? What are the options, what the chances of a process of perpetuated stagnation? If the government apparatus itself is in disarray and as yet unable to confront key issues, are there not, rather, chances of political fragmentation or even of a gradual dismantling of the state? In that event, what new socio-economic patterns might be emerging, and what power configurations would be likely to shape up? Alternatively, with a basic shift in the power balance, what new chances are there for national reconstruction, or for at least new answers to the national question? And at what price?

THE NATIONAL QUESTION

Along with Ethiopia, Sudan, and Chad, Uganda is one of the countries of Africa with regard to which the 'national question' has come to be posed in its most basic form, that is, referring increasingly to the viability of Uganda as a 'national' political entity. The redefinition of the 'national question' which this has implied in the case of Uganda is no less than dramatic and may well constitute the most significant and enduring change resulting from the rifts that arose and deepened during the Amin and Obote episodes. Basically, during the 1960s and even well into the 1970s, national integration perspectives (irrespective of whether they were based on modernization notions, or emphasized the bridging of either ethnic or class gaps) had generally been anticipating the progressive incorporation of various social categories and ethno-political sub-units within the context of the post-colonial Ugandan state. The premise of national integration as an empirical process as well as a constant point of reference had in fact been underlying each of the 'if only' themes that were successively articulated in Uganda. In the 1980s, however, the 'national question' has been acquiring a different and more complex content, concerned less with the *how* of national integration, but with *what* basis there is for it. How realistic will it be to continue to conceive of Uganda as a viable national unit? What conditions are required for its fulfilment? What are the limitations? What the alternatives?

Posing these questions is in no way to deny the urgency of calls for reason today to all conflicting parties to bury their differences (and preferable their arms) and to be prepared jointly to make a fresh start. Earlier, the initiative for the Moshi meeting at the termination of Amin's regime, where all the various groups opposed to his dictatorship came together to formulate a joint plan of action under the umbrella of the Uganda National Liberation Front, was an excellent precursor in this regard. At the same time, it should be realized that such calls have their limitations and to some extent are likely to remain illusory. The scope for fresh starts, as noted, is extremely thin generally and quite problematic still in the concrete case of Uganda today.

But it is equally important to confront these questions from a longer-term perspective, no matter which policy conclusions might finally be drawn from such an exercise. National boundaries are widely viewed as sacrosanct, which is an important principle indeed in the face of possible external designs and interventions. Yet as not a few examples in European and world history illustrate, boundaries are apt to be transformed over time with changing circumstances. Denmark and Norway, like Holland and Belgium, are only two out of a number of cases that once formed a single state. As growing internal contradictions and mutual incompatibilities led to aggravating irritation and tension, in these two cases the partners reconciled themselves to a divorce, which as it happened, in the end probably allowed them a coexistence on friendlier terms than their earlier unison had seemed to make possible. Today, Belgium itself is slowly but steadily breaking up into two parts, a Flemish and a Walloon nation. The process is a complex one, manifesting itself over several decades, and is generated by a combination of factors: differential economic transformation, socio-political emancipation, and cultural revival. Disappointing as it may at first appear step by step to see two partners wind up their relationship, they deserve credit if they have the courage to face the potential prospect of deepening divergences and separation and accordingly manage to take rational measures towards reconstructing their contractual bonds on a new basis.

Thus also in the Ugandan case, as the possibilities of fragmentation have been getting closer, it will be important to treat this not as a taboo topic but in any event to consider its potential implications more closely. In fact, the relative (political) cost of 'disintegration' – to the centre as well as to the regions concerned – might be assessed and contrasted with the cost of maintaining national 'integration', that is, of continued efforts to maintain the post-colonial framework as a basis for development.

Concretely, what ties the various regions of Uganda – east, west, north, south – together is principally a common centre (though not centrally located), and a common political-administrative framework. In turn, there is the common but competitive interest in capturing a share of the resources that the centre controls. Economically, there are very few integrative complementarities between the regions, particularly north–south, unless one would consider as such a certain risk-spreading through reliance on more than the dominant cash crop: cotton in the north, coffee in the south. On the other hand, precisely one dimension of inter-regional competition is focused on the differential way in which the centre determines how it will draw revenue from these two main export crops. The annual fixing of producer prices for coffee and cotton has thus always been keenly anticipated by peasants in the north and south, and by necessity constitutes one of the key policy choices of the Ugandan state: is the state going to extract relatively more heavily from the north or from the south to acquire the resources it requires for its own upkeep? What difference will a southern-dominated or northern-dominated government make in this respect?

No matter in what direction the balance might go, however, from the side of the centre or the state system as such the matter may be posed rather differently. The centre clearly will have a stronger interest in having access to two or more resource poles it can exploit, no matter in how biased a way this may be, than it appears to be of interest to each of the producing regions to be tied to the others within a common framework. Again, at present there are few complementarities that would provide a different basis. One implication of this though is that questions about the preservation (or dissolution for that matter) of national unity and the corresponding state frameworks generally will be of more immediate concern to those social strata that are more directly associated with the state system – e.g. through employment, contractual relations or patronage – than they are for the majority of peasants in any of the regions. In that sense there is clearly a differential class interest in the concern with national unity.

By implication, however, the crisis of the Ugandan state will also have hit harder at some of the people who economically were fully dependent on it than at sections of the peasantry who still had access to land for food crops. Subsistence in various parts of the country was acquiring a fresh meaning, and to some extent indeed provided a protective shield to many peasants vis-à-vis the demanding and increasingly capricious state, precisely as they succeeded in remaining 'uncaptured' (Hyden, 1980, 1986). By implication, to many of them the state increasingly became of limited relevance. Still, relative food security hardly extended to physical security. Many peasants were not spared the cruelty and harassments of marauding soldiers, who could confiscate their supplies or make it impossible to work on their land.

In the process, the state itself was becoming increasingly 'militarized', that is, in a political context marked by vagaries about the immediate future, control and 'occupation' of the central state institutions was sought not so much out of a determination to initiate any alternative national policies, but because they constituted a highly strategic bulwark in the continuing power game with opponent groups. As noted above, both Amin's and Okello's seizures of power had had such pre-emptive strategic functions. By implication, though, the effectiveness of central institutions for policy purposes could only get further impaired and reduced, and without intervention this process of deterioration might conceivably have advanced to a point where central state institutions would have become fairly irrelevant from a point of view of public policy. Theoretically, at least, the dwindling state might then more easily have been dispensed with.

More immediately, it would have accelerated a certain contraction of spheres of political action, leaving increased room to local and regional centres of power. Already, the experience with road-blocks marking distinct areas of control tended to accentuate such tendencies towards contraction. In due course, they might have come to constitute the protective barriers behind which, perhaps, novel kinds of mini-states or polities might have been emerging. There has been the Rwenzururu case as one possible forerunner, for example, experimenting with a grass-roots administrative technology for no less than 20 years (Doornbos, 1970). Irrespective of its long-run likelihood or possible merits, one thing to note within this speculative scenario is that at least it would have begun to relate government and politics much more close to rural people generally. As it happens, failure to achieve this has widely been cited as one of the root problems of the crisis of the African post-colonial state.

THE NORTH–SOUTH RELATIONSHIP

It hardly needs further emphasizing in the present context, that in social, cultural and linguistic terms the differences and contrasts between the various Ugandan regions, but again especially between north and south, are vast indeed. Though many African countries incorporate significant cultural and ethnic diversity, in the Ugandan case this is particularly pronounced. Less clear than sometimes assumed, however, are the political implications of such diversity. Ethnic or cultural differences as such do not necessarily lead to social or political confrontation. Whether conflict will be infused with a dimension of ethnic hostility, will basically depend on the way and extent to which ethnicity is being (or has become) manipulated for political or economic ends. Once politicized, however, the ethnic dimension may come to represent quite a forceful element precisely because of the collective emotive processes that are thus being generated.

In Uganda the ethnic factor clearly has been aroused to an extremely critical level for over two decades now; so much so that it can hardly be expected to readily let itself be obliterated – even if, as presently appears to be the case, a deliberate effort is made by the new regime *not* to play the game of ethnic politics. At this juncture, therefore, pleas for national reconciliation alone can still hardly avoid being read as expressions of wishful thinking: 'If only, etc...' If left to itself, the ethnic factor thus must certainly be expected to articulate itself in novel forms of expression. In fact, if it were not for the bitter animosity that culminated between Acholi and Langi within the Ugandan army between 1981 and 1985, one might hypothesize that in the years ahead one could witness more explicit revivals of the dream of a Luo nation as a defensive reaction, just as at earlier points Buganda had reasserted itself as a candidate for separation when it feared imminent domination from the north. As the point of gravity has now shifted to the south a revival of the latter claim is less likely, but recent years of internal warfare have undoubtedly also raised Baganda, Bantu and southern ethnic political consciousness.

One of the most delicate tasks of the new regime will be how to handle this new consciousness and the regained political confidence that forms part of it. Consciousness of nationalism and regionalism can work out as either a relatively positive and constructive force or as progressively a narrowing and destructive one, depending essentially on the stimuli it receives. It is precisely at junctures such as the present one in Uganda that one may be witnessing the process of choice of direction of such collective moods. The best that could happen would be the emergence of a 'clean slate' kind of Uganda identity, the worst would be the fostering of superiority and revenge feelings in the south vis-à-vis the north.

In the short run the chances of Uganda actually breaking up into several rival armed camps, potentially evolving into two or more de facto mini-states, seems to have diminished with the collapse of the Okello-led Acholi resistance and the NRA extending its presence into the north. Nonetheless, the country has been very close to a spiral of fragmentation, which with a different handling of the immediate confrontations might well have accelerated on its course. Needless to say, much of the explosive material piled up, especially under the north–south relationship, though provisionally defused, is very much present still and will take a long period of very careful handling to prevent it from being mobilized once again.

Besides, the Ugandan case is not an isolated example. Within the African inter-state system one case of potential fragmentation is fairly readily contained. The role of and significance of the OAU Charter are well known in this regard. However, problems not unlike those of Uganda have been manifest also in neighbouring Sudan, Ethiopia, Chad and to some extent in Somalia. In some instances, the question may well be posed whether one can still speak of a state in a Weberian sense, as opposed to the OAU definition (Buijtenhuis, 1984). As it happens, the countries concerned form a more or less continuous region, which in time to come might possibly allow for novel alliances of political movements across the official interstate boundaries (See Chapter 15 in this volume.) Conceivably, some of the latter in the decades to come might be receding to more formal lines of demarcation, while new *de facto* boundaries could become more prominent. E.E. Evans-Pritchard's distinction between 'states' and 'stateless societies', both endowed with governmental function but differently, might then re-assert itself with a fresh meaning. What, in that case, would the African map be looking like in say 50 years from now?

At least as important in a longer-term perspective, however; the formation in Uganda of a NRA-led government during the first months of 1986, and the steady expansion of NRA-control throughout the country may be considered to signify a historic transition in two major respects: one, for the first time in post-colonial Africa a popularly based guerrilla movement has demonstrated the practical possibility of overthrowing one of the notorious and illegitimate military regimes that had become so characteristic for the continent. Second, for the first time in post-colonial Uganda the power balance shifted in favour of the south; that is, a mainly southern-recruited armed force came to provide the basis for government power and has thus ended the feeling of people in Buganda and elsewhere in the south of being subejcted to an occupation force from the north. Together, these two transitions are likely to have a major impact on the future trajectory of the Ugandan state and politics, potentially giving it a significantly different direction as well as greater stability.

As is well known, the Amin and Obote regimes had basically maintained their sway over the economically more important south on the basis of army support, which had been overwhelmingly recruited from the north. This happened *per definition*, as it concerned – not without irony – a legacy of the colonial regime that had sought to create a power balance, divide and rule model, through concentrating military and police recruitment on Acholi, Lango and West Nile in the north, away from the economic, educational and administrative central region of the country.

Now that this key political resource has been taken away from the north, further developments on this front will be of crucial importance. In the longer run, one question is what will be the reaction of the north, or rather of different groups from Acholiland, Lango country and West Nile, which in recent years have become profoundly divided amongst each other. In fact divisions and mutual hostilitites here within and outside the Ugandan army no doubt constituted one major underlying factor facilitating the NRA victory. Now that the latter has become a fact, what long-term chances will there be of their eventual reconciliation and the redefinition of a 'common northern interest'? Are there likely to be efforts to recapture part of the lost resource base, e.g. by renewed pressures for special recruitment into the armed forces? Are there chances of an underground option, or alternatively of armed operations from bases in Southern Sudan or Zaire? At least as important, however, is what will be the south's and especially the new centre's position, concretized partly in new recruitment policies for the armed forces, partly in other policy measures that the new internal balance of power enables it to initiate. What, in short, will the south *do* with the combination of military, political and economic power that it now has gained, for the first time since independence?

Though not without hazard, one might speculate that if the post-Amin and post-Obote process of political disintegration had come to its ultimate conclusion, namely, a falling apart into several regional monopolies of power and political control, in the long run this might possibly have provided an alternative suitable point of departure for reconciliation and negotiated reunification. Thus, paradoxically, due to its demonstrated power advantage the NRA government now faces the more difficult task of having to lay down and impose a framework which otherwise might possibly have come about through more voluntary association. Though such a process would by no means have been easy and its outcome far from certain, the longer-term mortgage of a southern-imposed settlement should not be underestimated.

The role and position of Buganda, as defined by its elite strata, as always present special problems. Earlier its very centrality militated against its ambitions for a separatist option. At that time, if it had instead constituted a distinct region away from the political centre it might have represented a ready-made candidate for separate state-hood. Today, one might assume decreased interests in any separate status for Buganda, as influential political and economic strata perceive the advantages of a renewed primacy of Buganda, and the south generally, as a region dominant within Uganda. This will probably prove true whether or not a restoration of kingship in Buganda is again considered. A central location will be advantageous from any such hegemonic perspective, whereas it poses problems to any alternative scenario including the option of a division.

One final irony in this connection, is that in the relative stability of the early 1960s one had seen the formal tabling of motions for Buganda's independence plus indeed the actual secession of Rwenzururu. In contrast, while the collapse of the Ugandan state had never seemed so imminent as it was to become in 1985, there were no voices yet publicly favouring an exit option for any other region.

KEY QUESTIONS

As for the future, again, much will depend on the way in which some of the underlying conflicts and grievances are handled: will NRA forces succeed in maintaining lasting control throughout the north *and* inspire a renewed sense of trust and rehabilitation in West Nile, Acholi, Lango? Will the Museveni government manage to infuse its policies with a reasonable doses of equity – regionally, sector-wise, and in terms of urban–rural equations – while nonetheless avoiding a resumption of the politics of petty trade-offs which had so often been advanced as a substitute? Will one achieve a way of balancing the centre and granting a fair amount of autonomy to regions and districts while retaining a flexible form of co-ordination? What new conception, and content, of the role and position of the state will be evolving under NRA control? And lastly, in what direction will the NRA, mindful no doubt of Kalecki's admonitions addressed to 'intermediate regimes' (Kalecki, 1972), be specifying its political plans and ideology beyond the all-embracing populist ticket with which it made its political entry?

However heavy the legacies of the past, it is in several of these respects that the first steps taken, 'from scratch' so to speak, will prove to be of decisive importance in the search for new political openings, or indeed for new answers to the national question.

PART FIVE
POLITICAL PERSPECTIVES

EIGHTEEN
Islam under Idi Amin: a case of déjà vu?

John A. Rowe

INTRODUCTION

If one inclines toward anecdotal interpretations of great events, the decision to Islamize Uganda came to Idi Amin as a celestial communication, by way of the miracle of a violent and unseasonal thunderstorm while the general was at Mecca performing the *haj* (Gwyn, 1977, p. 176). On the other hand, there are observers of Amin's behaviour who view the shower of Libyan money and material aid as being more decisive. In any case, there is no question that after a visit to Gadaffi in February 1972 Amin suddenly rediscovered his nominal Islamic antecedents and began to emphasize the Islamic character of his regime. The previously influential Israeli expatriate community in Uganda (accused by Obote of having a hand in the 1971 coup) were promptly expelled, and Uganda's foreign policy described a 180 degree turn to a pan-Arab, pro-Palestinian stance. While still in Tripoli, Amin had allegedly – and quite imaginatively – spoken of Uganda (with its 5.6 per cent Muslim population) as an Islamic nation.[1] Was this a wishful expression of future intentions, or merely Amin's habitual carelessness with facts? Whatever the general's policy – if indeed he had one – the Muslims of Uganda were quick to welcome their elevation of a position of respect, visibility, relative privilege and – within the restricted limits imposed by Amin's self-destructive strategy of 'economic war' – new opportunities to acquire property and business.

Reasonably enough, many Ugandans among the Christian majority grew apprehensive at these signs of resurgent Islam. They noted Amin's reintroduction of Islamic courts for Muslims, the establishment of a Uganda Muslim Supreme Council, the ominous banning of a number of smaller Christian sects (Seventh Day Adventists, Salvation Army, etc.). Even more alarming were the contrived 'disappearances' of such prominent figures as Benedicto Kiwanuka (former Prime Minister and leader of the Democratic Party) and

Father Kiggundu (editor of the popular Roman Catholic news-paper, *Munno*), as well as other Christians. Was this evidence of the beginnings of a brutal jihad against Christianity?[2] The murder of Protestant Archbishop Luwum in February 1977 and the flight into exile of Bishop Kivengere added fuel to this belief. The response of Uganda's Christians was a revival of faith despite or because of Amin's perceived hostility. Churches filled to overflowing with people standing in the doorways and peering in windows. The stage seemed set for a clash between Islam and Christianity, with inevitable martyrdoms reminiscent of events in Uganda almost a century earlier.

In the 1880s and 1890s religious-political parties of Christians and Muslims had fought in the name of almighty God to establish the ascendancy of true religion in the Buganda kingdom. At once a number of parallels between the nineteenth-century struggle and the situation in the 1970s suggest themselves:

(1) The continued existence of religious-political parties (like the Roman Catholic sponsored DP and the largely Protestant UPC).
(2) A Muslim ruler established by military coup (Kabaka Kalema was the Idi Amin of 1888).
(3) External alliance and dependence on foreign supplies essential for the continuation of the regime in a period of economic hardship (the Sultan of Zanzibar playing Gadaffi's role in providing foreign aid to a fellow Muslim).
(4) A minority Islamic government able to maintain its dominance over a vast non-Muslim population because of its command of modern arms (the muskets and gunpowder of 1888).
(5) A force of Nubian mercenaries[3] able to dictate the balance of power (Emin Pasha's Sudanese garrison introduced into Uganda by Lugard in 1892 were the forefathers of many of Amin's troops in 1971).

History does not necessarily repeat itself, but as Professor Ajayi pointed out in 1965 at Dar es Salaam, many historical themes continued intact through the brief colonial era to reappear after independence in Africa.[4] The presence of historical parallels and probable existence of continuities suggest that a careful examination of the nineteenth-century Islamic revolution may well be of value in understanding events of the 1970s.

THE NINETEENTH-CENTURY ISLAMIC REVOLUTION IN BUGANDA
The history of Islam in the late nineteenth-century in Buganda is reasonably well documented from a small corpus of written and oral sources.[5] It was introduced by Muslim traders from the coast whose

attitudes resemble those of the famous Dyula of West Africa in an earlier period. That is, they were interested in trade rather than proselytization, but by the example of their religious practice, and above all the magic of literacy, they often sparked an interest among the people where they settled. So it was in Buganda, and as in the case of Songhay, once a ruler evinced an interest in Islam, conversion might proceed 'from the top downward'.

In the Buganda kingdom, a young Kabaka (king) Mutesa (1856–84) invited traders at the court to read the Qur'an and to speak of such wonders as bodily resurrection. Mutesa was already impressed with the exotic goods brought by the Muslims, particularly guns and gunpowder, though the manufactured cotton cloth (*kaniki*) from India was initially rejected as being damp and smelly. Mutesa learned to read the Qur'an in Arabic, and later on conversed in that language with European explorers from Egypt. Soon his enthusiasm for the new religion led him to construct a mosque and to signal the Friday prayers by running a flag up a newly constructed mast. The Kabaka's interest was echoed by his chiefs, who in any case owed their positions to him and dared not raise objection. In particular, the young men in training at court (*bagalagala*, king's pages) were quick to receive lessons in the new religion. In 1867 Mutesa observed the Ramadhan fast, and continued to do so annually for the next decade. He commanded his subjects to do likewise and required everyone to substitute the Islamic greeting 'Salaam alaikum' (peace be unto you) for the traditional 'Wasuze otyanno' (how have you been?).

After several years the Kabaka discovered that the assurances of his flattering chiefs were false: the nation was not at one with its monarch in obedience to Islam. Inspectors were sent into the countryside to check on the correct observance of the new edicts, but they found the people ignorant and confused. Many did not greet with 'Salaam alaikum'; mosques were hard to find; some people misunderstood the use of stones (on which to stand while washing the feet during ritual ablutions before prayer) and poured water over the stones while praying to them. The angry Kabaka ordered a massive purge of the so-called *bakaffiri* (unbelievers) and many were killed. It appeared that the creation of an Islamic state was at hand, but appearances, as we know, can be deceptive.

Scholars have, of course, been intrigued by the question of how the prominent Baganda, led by their king, could so quickly accept an alien belief system. David Apter coined the term 'instrumentalism' to describe the apparent utilitarian approach of the Baganda to ideas that might advance their interests. He, and others, observed that the Buganda state was staffed by a highly competitive crowd of office-seekers who seized on anything that could promote their careers.[6] But what of the Kabaka? Surely he was aware that – as in other African states – traditional religion (*lubaale*) and kingship were closely intertwined? It has been suggested that traditional religion was weak, or that the king sought to make it so to increase his own power. But it is unnecessary to cast about for reasons why the king turned his back on his people's belief system, because he did nothing of the kind. Even while observing Ramadhan, praying in the Friday mosque, and studying the holy Qur'an, Kabaka Mutesa continued to observe the new moon ceremonies, consult the priest of *lubaale*, and honour the departed spirits of the former kings. And he rejected circumcision, for the sacral kingship of the Baganda required a physically unflawed monarch and there was a prohibition against shedding royal blood. (When necessary, rival royals were starved to death by the king's order, never directly executed.) So it appears that Mutesa was adding Allah to the hierarchy of Buganda's gods.[7] If the Muslim traders understood this, they diplomatically kept their mouths shut.

Eventually, however, a collision occurred as the sincere and intense beliefs of the Kabaka's young men (*bagalagala*), who *were* circumcised, clashed with their loyalty to the Kabaka. They refused to eat the meat he provided, saying it was 'unclean' because he himself was not a true circumcised Muslim. For this act of high treason the young Muslim converts were burnt at the stake, but not before their disconcerted king gave them numerous opportunities to recant. The martyrdom of these true believers has served as an inspiration to Uganda Muslims ever since. Kabaka Mutesa died still enthralled with Islamic theology but he never completely converted. Instead, he invited rival Christian missionaries to teach their own versions of the one-book religion and to bring literacy to an increasing number of converts. The king insisted, however, that these rival groups of believers competed for his shifting favours, thus ensuring that none grew strong enough to threaten the throne.[8]

'Après moi le déluge' – famous words in history that might well be applied to Buganda. Mutesa's successor, Mwanga, became Kabaka in 1884 and four short years later he was overthrown by a revolution engineered largely by Muslim converts armed with guns. Mwanga began well enough by persecuting the Christian Baganda when their loyalty to him seemed suspect, but he then made the mistake of abandoning his father's policy of setting the religious factions at each other in competition for royal favour. Instead, he allowed both Christian and Muslim converts to form well-organized regiments; he gave them guns and set them against the older chiefs whom he had inherited from his father's government. Mwanga intended thus to acquire greater personal power at the expense of the 'old guard', but he belatedly discovered that the loyalty of the new regiments was less to him than to their new religions. Both Christian and Muslim converts gradually came to believe that some form of theocracy was the only government possible for true believers. But would it be a Christian establishment or an Islamic state?

The Muslims were stronger and better organized. It was they who engineered the coup that toppled Mwanga;[9] a coup initially as quick and relatively bloodless as was Amin's in January 1971. But, as in the latter case, more blood was soon to flow. They expelled the Christians and eventually elected a new Kabaka, Kalema, who accepted circumcision and took the Qur'anic name Nuhu (Noah). Unlike Mutesa, Nuhu Kalema made himself a model Muslim ruler, or so the Muslim chroniclers would have us believe. The brief period of his regime, before he died of smallpox in 1890, is regarded by modern Ganda Muslims rather like the 'Camelot' myth of John F. Kennedy in America. It was a golden age, albeit one of struggle and sacrifice, but a time of hope and confidence, of life under *dar al Islam*, before being cut short by tragedy. Jealous Muslims set about attempting to convert the entire country. Traditional shrines were burnt and impatience led to an attempt at forced conversion of the masses, as Muslim scholars readily admit today.[10]

A steady supply of arms, gunpowder, and imported goods was introduced into the country from Zanzibar, whose Muslim ruler engaged in frequent diplomatic correspondence with his coreligionist Kabaka Kalema. The Muslims realized their supply line was vital, both to provide the goods to reward loyal followers (swords, robes, ornate prayer rugs), and the military means to keep their restive population quiescent and the Christians at bay. (Compare this with Amin's Russian arms via Libya, and the famous Stansted 'whisky run' of luxury goods flown in to keep the troops happy and loyal. Incidentally, the route followed by Obote's ill-timed counter-attack from Tanzania in 1972 was almost identical to that followed by the Christian exiles in their own counter-attack of 1889. (Instead of a disguised commercial DC-6 to land troops at Entebbe, the Christians attempted successfully to put their men ashore by boat from the lake.)[11]

The Christian campaign cut the Muslim supply line, destroying the Arab dhows with their vital cargo of gunpowder in what might be called the first 'Entebbe raid'. Facing a two-pronged assault by gun-armed Christians and spear-wielding traditionalists, the Muslim troops retreated northward into exile (as in 1979). Later, when they were offered a small section in a kingdom governed by

Christians, the Muslims agonized before accepting. One leading chief committed suicide rather than bend the knee to an infidel ruler. Eventually the disgruntled Muslims attempted a countercoup in 1893. Their aim was the restoration of a legitimate Islamic state under a Muslim ruler. They sang songs denigrating the Christian establishment as pig-eaters and vowed that no unclean meat would ever pass their lips.[12] In this 1893 coup attempt, the Muslim Baganda hoped to enlist the aid of a new factor on the scene: Nubian mercenary troops from the southern Sudan whom the British had enlisted as a coercive force both more convenient and less expensive than Sikhs or sepoys from India. These Nubians[13] were notoriously ill-disciplined and independent, but they were formidable fighters and were foreign to the Uganda scene. The British regarded them as 'good material': a kind of martial race, like the Gurkhas of Nepal. But they were Muslims, and the Muslim Baganda thought they might be subverted in the name of Islam.

In the event, the 1893 coup failed, as the Nubians, despite deep suspicion on the part of their British commanding officer (he disarmed one garrison), remained loyal to their paymasters and routed their coreligionists.[14] It was an important omen for the future. The Nubians had discovered that they were the military arbiters in Uganda. It is not surprising, therefore, to find that barely four years later they mutinied against harsh British discipline and delays in receiving promised pay and equipment. Once again the spectre of militant Islam threatened the Christian establishment in Uganda, but again the Muslim Baganda and the northern Nubians failed to join forces. Ethnic differences seemed too strong to be overcome by shared belief in Islam, a principle that would reappear in the 1970s. The mutineers were eventually dispersed and driven from the Uganda Protectorate in 1899.

Thus the Muslims of Buganda entered the twentieth century as a thrice defeated party, relegated to a small and poor province (Butambala) within Buganda. There they were left remote and largely isolated from the cultural influences affecting the rest of the country. They preserved their heritage, cherished their memory of Kalema's 'Camelot', read their Qur'ans and looked to the hereafter to right the wrongs of this earth. Education was limited to a few mosques or itinerant Qur'anic readers. Except on the northern fringe of Uganda, no Islamic scholars appeared on the scene for at least two decades and when the first Ganda Muslim made the *haj* to Mecca, the ideas he gained abroad only served to split the local Muslims into two factions (the Juma–Zukuli controversy).[15] The jobs that came with Western education and literacy in English were denied the Qur'anic schooled Muslim youth. They became the butchers and taxi drivers of Uganda. Only in 1940, with the foundation of the Uganda Muslim Educational Association, did the Muslim community begin the process of trying to catch up, but their effort was very late and always too little in terms of school places available. Ganda Muslims were looked down upon by everyone else, and their 'strange' manner of dress (turbans or tarbushes) and their discounted religion made them seem foreign. In 1962 I was told more than once that allegedly most of the thieves in Uganda were Muslims because they were not countrymen to the rest of the population and therefore had no moral prohibition about robbing non-Muslims. The expression 'si Muganda – ye Musiramu' (s/he's not a Muganda – s/he's a Muslim) was also familiar. Thus the advent of Idi Amin with his claim to being a true son of Islam brought an immediate response from a community whose members felt they had suffered too long.

THE TWO STREAMS OF ISLAM IN UGANDA

Another community whose members had the right to feel disadvantaged in Uganda were the Nubians.[16] After the failure of the mutiny of 1897–9, the British were slow to restore confidence in the Nubians, but the advantages of cheap, ready-made coercive agents still had a strong appeal. Many British officials seemed to feel that with proper officers and strong, paternal leadership the Nubians could be loyal and effective fighting men. The King's African Rifles was formed, and barracked in strategic posts across the country. Around these barrack towns – Bombo, Jinja, Gulu – settled large communities of Nubians, who steadfastly preserved their own sense of identity. They dressed distinctively, maintained strong kinship ties with others in distant military posts, spoke a 'Nubi' dialect of Arabic. If the Ganda Muslims were sometimes regarded as foreigners, there was no question about the Nubians. They regarded themselves as a nation apart, and the British colonial government, which had to employ them against internal as well as external opponents, was pleased to keep it so.

Like the Ganda Muslims, the Nubians lacked Western education, and even some fellow Muslims regarded their syncretic brand of Islam, with its emphasis on magic and sorcery, as suspect. Though a number of Nubian youth followed their fathers into the family KAR company or battalion there were too few places, and an increasing number of Nubians drifted into jobs as drivers and nightwatchmen. (In the mid-1970s one of Amin's most trusted lieutenants, Malyamungu, was a former gatekeeper at Nyanza Textiles; another officer, Major Juma Aiga, had been a taxi driver at the time of the 1971 coup. Certainly a large proportion of the Military Council had not been in uniform when Uganda achieved independence in 1962.)[17]

Not only were the Nubians ethnically and culturally remote from the general African populace, they were also significantly removed from many of their fellow Muslims. In addition to the all-important ethnic and language differences, there was variety in the practice of Islam. Apart from the scattered and self-contained Nubian garrisons, Uganda had two centres of Islam separated by considerable distance. [18] In the north, the Alur and Kakwa of the remote West Nile Province followed the Malikite school of Islamic law (as did the Nubians – more or less), having been converted by Malikite Muslims from North Africa. In the south, the Muslims of Buganda, Busoga and Ankole rooted their orientation in the brief *dar al Islam* of Kabaka Kalema, which was Shafi'ite, having come from Shafi'ite Muslim traders of coastal East Africa and Zanzibar. Normally such theological distinctions are not important, but they were reinforced by identification with different mosques and styles of public prayer, different historical origins and traditions, and everyday spoken language that might be unintelligible from one group to another, lack of kinship ties and sheer physical separation by vast distances. Between the northern Muslim centre at Arua with its five large mosques, and Kampala with its many mosques and magnificent Kibuli complex, stretched the non-Muslim territories of the Acholi, Langi and Banyoro, all people who had fought long and hard against the Muslims in the nineteenth century and who were not quick to change their attitudes.

The physical distance from Kampala to Arua was reinforced by cultural distance. Southern Muslims were led by the sophisticated Prince Badru Kakungulu of the royal house of Buganda. Not only did he share little fellow-feeling for the non-Ganda, non-royal northerners, it was said that he never once visited the Arua centre during a half century of his leadership. In 1965 President Obote further complicated the picture by attempting to split the Muslim community – especially the southerners – and diminish the role of the Ganda Prince Kakungulu. Obote created the National Association for the Advancement of Muslims (NAAM) closely associated with his Uganda People's Congress (UPC) party, to wean away those who might otherwise follow the Ganda Kabaka Yekka (KY) party. Thus in 1971 when Idi Amin ousted Obote, the Muslims of Uganda were a divided group who shared only two traits: they were members of the same world religion in a 94 per cent non-Muslim country; and they were tired of being an economically and socially depressed group, and were keen to make up for lost time.

THE AMIN ERA: AN ISLAMIC STATE?

Certainly the status and prospects of Muslims improved spec-
tacularly during the early years of Amin's rule.[19] Symbolic of this
transformation were the frequent direct flights between Entebbe
and Mecca, as increasing numbers of Ugandans joined the new 'jet
set' elite who had made the *haj*. Muslims moved into important
positions in government, university and business. Amin created the
Supreme Muslim Council, an unwieldy body of 300 members whose
role was never well defined. In the rush to grab businesses following
the Asian expulsion, it was a prerequisite to be a Muslim if one
hoped to obtain anything at all. Non-Muslims became quite wary of
their Muslim colleagues, wondering what important or dangerous
connections they might have. At a time when most private construction ground to a halt due to material shortages, the new houses
of the Muslim elite could be seen going up on Kibuli hill, site of the
great mosque. From the point of view of Christians it all looked
ominous, particularly as their bombastic new President, Field
Marshal Doctor al-Hajji Idi Amin Dada, VC, DSO, MC, etc., made
public claims to his Libyan and Arab sponsors of the primacy of
Islam in Uganda and its place among the Islamic nations of the
world.

From the point of view of Uganda's Muslims, however, these
claims could be irrelevant, embarrassing or downright dangerous. It
was irrelevant for the Muslims in the military who appeared
uninterested in the conversion of the country. Their main concern
was survival and promotion amidst the shifting uncertainties of
barrack-room politics. With Amin leading the military council,
publicly berating its officers, making speeches to the troops in which
he directly encouraged them to spy on their officers – in those
circumstances no captain or colonel who hoped to survive (and
many did not survive) could afford much attention to the national
proselytization of Islam. No one was safe. Finally even Amin's
reliable Vice-President, General Mustafa Adrisi, suffered an
arranged auto accident and was hustled off to an Egyptian hospital.
In any case, many of the officers were illiterate, even in Arabic, and
had minimal acquaintance with theology.

Non-military Muslims feared the military almost as much as
anyone else. In an era of food and fuel shortages, and trigger-happy
patrols by the Public Safety Unit and the State Research Bureau,[20]
their attention was on more immediate goals than the ultimate
establishment of an Islamic state. The Muslim shaykhs may well
have harboured aspirations in that direction, but for them Idi Amin
was hardly the model Muslim leader that the legendary Kabaka
Nuhu Kalema had been. Amin was a notorious drinker, married

275

outside the mosque when it suited him, dismissed the learned shaykh who headed the Supreme Muslim Council, dismissed the Muslim Minister of Education (replacing him with a Christian), and to the fury of the shaykhs carried out public executions during the Ramadhan observances.[21] Money donated for the construction of Islamic institutions – hospitals, a university, a national mosque – vanished. For years the only evidence of the massive Saudi contribution to build the Kampala Hill Mosque was a big pile of sand on the spot where Amin had made a typically bombastic dedication speech.

It seems unlikely from the available evidence that Idi Amin's Islamization proclamations, despite the reaction aroused among Christians, were anything more than a crude propaganda exercise intended to ensure continuing supplies and cash from the Libyans and Saudis.[22] But even that could appear dangerous to some Muslim Ugandans, who became apprehensive of an anti-Muslim backlash should the Amin regime collapse. In the event, after the Tanzanian invasion of 1978–9 and the flight of the Nubian troops into exile, there were reports of civilian Muslims being assassinated in Ankole. But the political struggle to fill the vacuum in Kampala soon diverted attention. When President Lule was deposed in June 1979 after only two months in office, the Muslim leaders were promised not only protection but a share of the spoils if they would support the new Binaisa clique.[23] Afterward, any lingering grievances against Muslims were apparently submerged in the general political turmoil, economic crisis, and physical insecurity as everyone, regardless of religious adherence, sought (to use a common expression in Uganda) 'to survive'.

CONCLUSION

A number of parallels have been suggested between events of the 1880s and 1970s, among them:

(1) A Muslim military coup, followed by continuing struggle.

(2) A minority regime dependent upon its command of modern weaponry.

(3) External alliance with an Islamic state to ensure aid necessary to prop up the regime.

(4) Court politics involving constant intrigue and shifting favouritism.

(5) Violence.

There are also significant continuities from the pre-colonial era:

(1) Religious-political allegiances.

(2) The presence of a foreign mercenary coercive force.

(3) Divisions within the Muslim ranks.

(4) A Muslim sense of historical grievance.

Among these continuities perhaps the most important is the final one: a long-term sense of victimization by Muslims as a marginal group. Through historical accident and religious bigotry (reinforced by colonial attitudes), the Muslims of Uganda had been denied a reasonable share of economic and educational opportunity; worse than that, for more than two generations they had been regarded as 'Untermenschen', a kind of sub-species of Ugandan.

Other continuities and parallels no doubt exist and can equally be employed in analysing what happened, and why, in Uganda in the 1970s. But for the Muslim minority, who may have anticipated that their years of deprivation were at an end, it is regrettable that they were forced to pin their hopes on a leader like Idi Amin. For his Islamization policy seems to me to have been a sham, as hollow as the empty walls and pile of scaffolding that mark the great Kampala Hill Mosque, still not built ten years after its cornerstone ceremony. In many ways this ragged silhouette on the Kampala skyline is the appropriate symbol and monument to Amin's Uganda.

Notes

1. Uganda Census of 1959. Estimated numbers of Muslims in Uganda have been the subject of much controversy. Kasozi, n.d.(a), argues that Muslim numbers have always been undercounted in colonial Uganda, and that there were large-scale conversions during the early years of the Amin presidency. This was particularly the case after the Uganda Muslim Supreme Council inherited property of expelled Muslim Asians that had been registered under their religious organizations: 'The Supreme Council by 1973 became the richest landlord in the country.' Not surprisingly, he goes on (p. 19) to say that 'The year 1973/74 was a year of success for very many people converted to Islam in Uganda'. Kasozi estimates (p. 4) that 10–20 per cent of the country were Muslims, and that later on 'Sample censuses of Muslims we conducted in March 1980 at the Uganda Muslim Supreme Council of 100 sample villages or settlements gave the figure of 15 per cent' (p. 42 note 10c). Oded, 1974, pp. 315–16, speaks of increased conversion to Islam under Amin, but does not offer any estimate of his own except to suggest that the 'three million' claimed by the Chief Qadi may be somewhat exaggerated. Pirouet, 1980, p. 26, note 1 refutes these claims and point out that the Asian exodus deprived Uganda of a substantial number of Muslims. Pirouet, 1976, p. 141, argues that the decisive issue in Amin's turn toward Libya and Islam was not money but the resolution of the southern Sudan conflict, in which he played a role. This put him at odds with the Israelis, leading to their expulsion and Amin's realigned foreign policy. See also Pain, 1975, pp. 177–92; Smith, 1980, pp. 90–1.
2. Many published accounts describe arrests and deaths, or disappearances, of Amin's victims. The most comprehensive is IJC (International Commission of Jurists), 1977; several books were produced in the later 1970s emphasizing

Amin's persecution of the Christian Church, among them: Woodling and Barnett, 1980; Sempangi, 1979; Kivengere, 1977. Also Bakaitwako, 1981. See in addition, *US Policy Toward Uganda*, US House of Representatives, Hearing Before the Sub-Committee on Africa of the Committee on Foreign Affairs, 26 April 1979, p. 16 where Deputy Assistant Secretary of State for African Affairs, Mr Keeley described Amin as 'a militant Muslim in a basically Christian country'. Mazrui, 1977a, refutes the militant Islam analytical model.

3. For the origins of the term 'Nubi' see Woodward, 1978, p. 155 note 11. The Nubian background is treated in Soghayroun, 1981, Chapters 1–2; Mazrui, 1977b, pp. 22–4.

4. Ajayi, 1965.

5. Rowe, 1966, for a discussion of sources in Luganda; also Rowe, 1969, pp. 217–19. More recent studies of Islam in Uganda are: Oded, 1974; Kakungulu and Kasozi, 1977; King et al., 1973. A typical early Muslim view is Sekimwanyi, n.d.; see also Kasozi, 1974.

6. Apter, 1961, Low, 1971, Chapter 1.

7. Rowe, 1966, Chapter 2; on Ganda traditional religion see Kyewalyanga, 1976; and Kagwa, 1905, a somewhat careless translation of which can be found in Edel, 1934.

8. Rowe, 1966, Chapter 4; contemporary accounts by the Protestant CMS mission-aries and Roman Catholic White Fathers provide abundant evidence, for example: Pearson to Felkin, 1 June 1880, CMS Archives G3A6/01; diary entries, juillet 1880 in *Chronique des Missionaires d'Afrique*, a White Fathers publication for internal use.

9. Twaddle, 1972b, pp. 54-72; Wright, 1971, pp. 39-66. Excellent primary sources exist, among them H. Mukasa, *Simudda Nyuma*, Vol. II *Ebiro bya Mwanga* (memoirs), and B. Mayanja, *Ebyafayo ebyentala za Kabaka Mwanga, Kiwewa ne Kalema*, 1937, as well as Kagwa's *Basekabaka* and oral accounts.

10. Kataregga, 1977, p. 10. See also Kakungulu and Kasozi, 1977, pp. 32– 42.

11. Mayanja, *Ebyafayo ebyentalo*; H. Mukasa, 'Simudda Nyuma, Vol. III' unpublished manuscript in Makerere University Library; Gray, 1950.

12. Wright, 1971, pp. 131–58.

13. For a fascinating analysis of the role of Nubians, the marginality of Islam and its political importance in the post-independence era see Constantin, 1981. Michael Twaddle brought this essay to my attention after I had completed this paper.

14. Macdonald 'Memorandum on Selim Bey, 22 June 1893' Outward A3/1-2, 1893-94, Entebbe Secretariat Archives; and Soghayroun, 1981, pp. 56–79.

15. Sekimwanyi, n.d.; King et al., 1973, pp. 15–16; Welbourn, 1965, p. 8; Kasozi, n.d.(b), pp. 6–9.

16. On the Nubian community in Uganda there is not as yet a great deal of information. For example, see Kokole, 1985; Kasfir, 1976, p. 220; Hansen, 1977, pp. 79, 108–110. The best account that I have been able to locate are Pain, 1975; and Wanji, n.d.

17. Kyemba, 1977, pp. 45, 49. Also Mazrui, 1975, pp. 127–146; Jorgensen, 1981, pp. 276–9.

18. King et al., Chapter 3; Jorgensen, 1981, p. 321, note 8; Kasizi, 1976.

19. Interviews in Nairobi, July-August 1976, with a number of frequent visitors from Uganda, some recent exiles, others 'colgating' to buy supplies unavailable in Kampala. Also interview with several Muslims in Kampala, June 1979. See also Oded, 1974, pp. 312–5; Mamdani, 1983, pp. 56–7.

20. *Ibid*. See also report of B.W. Langlands commission of inquiry: 'Makerere Murders, 1976: Progress of the Commission of Inquiry into Makerere University Affairs, March-August 1976', January 1977, cyclostyled; and Pirouet, 1980, p. 18 cited above.

21. Kiwanuka, 1979, p. 79; Woodling and Barnett, 1980, p. 58; Smith, 1980, p. 177; Kasozi, n.d.(a), pp. 21–2.
22. This is the view of Gwyn, 1977, and of Mazrui in his 'Afterword' to the same book, pp. 215–23, where he goes on to make a stronger case against the Muslim–Christian conflict as a significant factor in Amin's policies. See also Hansen, 1977, for another interesting discussion of ethnicity and religion; also Nayenga, 1974, p. 136 for comment.
23. Personal experience: I was in the appropriate office in Kampala in June 1979 when the phone call from Nile Mansions came through. See also Kasozi, n.d.(a).

NINETEEN
Political transitions since Idi Amin:
a study in political pathology
Dan Mudoola

After the abortive invasion of Uganda by pro-Obote exiles in 1972, Milton Obote was politically silent for some seven years. It was not until January 1979 that Obote appealed to the Uganda army to stage an uprising against Idi Amin.[1] This no doubt was also in the interests of his Tanzanian hosts, who were out to mobilize their resources to expel Amin's troops from their territory. The Tanzanian government had allowed Ugandan exiles to form a 'Kikoosi Maalum' (special unit) to fight side by side with the Tanzanian army. When the Tanzanian/Ugandan troops were poised at the gates of Kampala, a 'Unity Conference' was called in Moshi where deliberations resulted in the formation of the Uganda National Liberation Front, headed by Yusufu Lule. The apparent objective of the UNLF was to form a united front of all 'democratic forces'[2] to fill the political vacuum that would be left after the overthrow of Amin. Although, as events were to prove, the UNLF's political feet were made of clay, overnight an organization was formed that appeared to be very powerful. There was a convergence of forces favouring the formation of the short-lived UNLF. The Tanzanian authorities saw an urgent need to sponsor an organization that would fill the political vacuum after the Amin defeat. In any case, even when anti-Amin troops were outside the gates of Kampala, Tanzanian soldiers were not officially in Uganda: it was Ugandan anti-Amin liberation forces. Whatever one might think of the Tanzanian physical presence in Kampala, an all-Ugandan political body would help legitimize the Tanzanian presence. In purely physical military terms Tanzania could have entered Kampala and 'proclaimed' a new Ugandan leader. But this would have been bad politics and would, most probably, have alienated forces within Uganda as well as outside, forces that Tanzania could not afford to alienate at this time in a war that was so expensive for her.

The obvious candidate for a purely Tanzanian solution would have been Obote. But before his fall in 1971 Obote had made enemies within and outside Uganda. Internationally he had not been on the best of terms with Britain nor, by proxy, with the United States either. The Kenyans were also obsessed with fears of 'socialist encirclement' by Tanzania, Ethiopia and Somalia. Since the Kenyans knew Obote was a good friend of Tanzania and had a 'socialist' past, he was not an acceptable candidate to them. The Kenyan authorities were reported to have indicated that 'installation' of Obote by Tanzania would be considered an 'unfriendly act.'[3] Within Uganda, Tanzanian and Ugandan troops were marching through Baganda country, which, geopolitically and strategically, was very vital to the defeat of Idi Amin. Baganda were receiving the liberation forces with open arms and helping them to flush out remnants of the Amin forces, but there was no telling what their reaction would have been if they had learnt that they were helping blaze the trail for the one man whose political past they hated. Tanzania, then, could not afford to bog down her drive to Kampala and, therefore, prolong the war.

The UNLF was acceptable to Tanzania in order to fill the political vacuum in Uganda and help to regularize the political situation there. The Tanzanian authorities had sponsored the Moshi Conference and were reported to have even paid airfares for some key individuals to come and attend as special delegates.[4] To the UNLF leadership, Obote was a 'finished man'. And yet, the UNLF leadership turned out to be its own greatest enemy in the sense that, all along, in its apparent search for power, its priorities were wrong. Immediately on the formal assumption of power, the UNLF leaders seriously believed they had power, when in reality power was too elusively diffused within Uganda. Such meaningful power as there was lay in Dar es Salaam, and yet the UNLF leadership acted, in power terms, as if Dar es Salaam did not exist. For the UNLF or, more precisely, those who constituted an anti-Obote front in the UNLF to survive, they should at least have momentarily closed their ranks and sought the active support of the Tanzanians to help restore law and order in Kampala.[5] Instead, they lost sight of who their real 'enemy' was, took actions that alienated their actual or potential allies, and committed acts that amounted to political cannibalism. Without a single effective coercive force to fall back on, Lule made reckless pronouncements that earned him the wrath of friend and foe alike. He talked of disarming the newly constituted Uganda National Liberation Army and bringing in an external force to replace the Tanzanians. The threat of disarming the UNLA, the core of which was pro-Obote, left the UNLA sulky. Of course, the Tanzanians also feared they would be cheated of their victory.

As pointed out earlier, basically the UNLF was an anti-Obote front. In the initial struggles after the liberation from Amin they appear not to have regarded Obote and the UPC as serious factors to be reckoned with. Whatever may have been the political ineptitude of Yusufu Lule, his removal within two months of his assumption of 'power' only served to strengthen the hands of the anti-UNLF elements, the most significant of whom were Obote and the UPC. The removal of Lule alienated virtually all the politically and strategically important Buganda region, which otherwise would have been an effective force against Obote. Perhaps the anti-Obote forces' failure to strengthen and consolidate themselves vis-à-vis the UPC may be attributed to conflicting political goals within the UNLF, and to a sense of idealism that did not take into account the realities of Ugandan politics. Apart from their common front against Obote, the UNLF did not have much in common. It was made up of groups that lacked a common political programme. While some groups sought to have the UNLF as an umbrella, others (especially the Democratic Party, or the old traditionalist groups) sought to dissolve the UNLF, form their own parties and fight for national elections separately. Some factions, haunted by Uganda's political ills, which they attributed to the 'politics of conspiracy, tribalism and religion', sought to abolish the very social bases of politics and in the process ended up by not nurturing the very socio-political forces that could have provided them with some power bases. One could say that those in the UNLF who were against the politics of tribe, religion and 'conspiracy' preached against such forces precisely because they had none of them to manipulate to their own political advantage. The most ardent advocates of the 'politics of compatriotism',[6] namely Dan Nabudere, Yash Tandon, Edward Rugumayo, and Omwony-Ojok had no social bases of political significance. In the manner of 'popular democracies', they sought a 'popular front of democratic forces'. But in the tradition of Bolsheviks, Mao's United Front or Ho Chi Minh's National Liberation Front, such 'fronts' only succeed in a situation where the front is woven around an ideologically cohesive political party with a military arm, a properly defined programme and goals, and where there is also a clearly defined enemy. In the Ugandan case, while an enemy could always be found, the 'compatriots' had no core party, no reliable military arm, no defined programme or goals around which they could have woven 'popular democratic forces'.

The UPC, although initially in a minority in the UNLF, was about the only group that knew what it wanted, and had more than an idea about how to get it. Its leaders wanted power, and worked out ways of getting it. They sought to unite with forces over issues that undermined the UNLF. When the National Consultative Council sought to remove Lule, the UPC and other anti-Obote factions shook hands[7] and removed him, but the real victors in this were the pro-Obote forces. By the removal of Lule they had antagonized most Baganda, who were the potential allies of the anti-Obote group. The UPC remained both outside and inside the UNLF: outside, in the sense that a UNLF not dominated by them was not acceptable, and the UPC leader had only given very qualified support to the formation of the UNLF. Until the formation of the UNLF, the UPC leadership regarded themselves as the legitimate government. The UPC was 'within', in the sense that its members belonged to strategic organs of the UNLF, especially the Military Commission. This placed them in a position to support any issue or issues that undermined the UNLF as a durable governing front.

Lule's successor, Godfrey Binaisa, by default strengthened the UPC, dismissing Museveni as Minister of Defence. Here one should note that factional politics were rampant in the fledgling national army. The dismissal of Museveni removed a force that could have neutralized the pro-Obote faction in the army. The Obote group then proceeded to purge the pro-Museveni elements. With the confidence of a sleepwalker, and without any effective coercive force to back him up, Binaisa dismissed Oyite-Ojok, the Chief of Staff. Of course, that was more than the Obote supporters could take, because Oyite-Ojok was Obote's man. The Military Commission, a predominantly pro-Obote organ by now, staged a coup d'état and presented the rump of the UNLF with a fait accompli. This coup was well timed, for the UNLF leaders who would probably have rallied the National Consultative Council against the coup were in Arusha holding 'consultations' with President Nyerere. The Military Commission announced that there would be elections to be contested by all political parties, and that there were no objections to Obote's own return to Uganda.

In terms of his subsequent ascendancy, Obote's return was well timed. He had a number of advantages that provided a launching pad for his second bid for power. As earlier pointed out, other than his supporters in the UNLF, whose basic role was to destabilize it, Obote kept his distance from the UNLF and such apparent support as he had given it was grudging and he could not, therefore, be identified with its failures. His return was supported by the Military Commission or, more precisely, by the strong men in the Military Commission, who provided him with logistical and material support and security. While earlier on Nyerere may not have been too enthusiastic about Obote's return, this time Obote had more than tacit blessing from the Tanzanian authorities.[8] Although he still had formidable opponents in the Democratic Party and other parties that mushroomed on the eve of the December 1980 elections,

Yusufu Lule and Godfrey Binaisa had been neutralized and the Baganda were 'under control', thanks to the Military Commission.

Obote chose to return not by way of Entebbe International Airport, in Baganda country, but by way of Bushenyi in Ankole. Not that his supporters feared for his security on the way from Entebbe to Kampala, but his choice of Bushenyi was more than symbolic politically. He clearly knew who his opponents were. By landing at Bushenyi he was reviving his strategy of encircling Buganda, a strategy that had effectively worked on the eve of Ugandan Independence 25 years before.

With the formation of the UPC in 1960, a party that had been formed to 'contain' Buganda, Buganda was encircled by two major parties, the Democratic Party and the Uganda Peoples' Congress. With this encirclement, Buganda's options had been somewhat limited: she had to join the UPC to defeat the DP or vice-versa; or go it alone and press for independence on her own terms. The option of joining the DP was anathema to the Protestant establishment at Mengo. The option of going it alone, for all the bravado of Baganda leaders, was out because Buganda just did not have the resources to effect this. Even if she had had the resources, encircled, and without the sympathies of, and material assistance from, the retreating British colonial power, she just could not have got away with it. To defeat the Democratic Party, and in return for concessions from the UPC and the colonial power, Buganda 'broke out' of encirclement by forging an alliance with the UPC: the famous UPC–KY alliance.

But the politics of 1980 were different from those of 1961–2. A lot more had happened to alienate the Baganda from Obote in the meantime. The Baganda had 'lost' their 'Lost Counties' to Bunyoro, which was the immediate cause for the break-up of the alliance in 1964. Obote had had a physical showdown in 1966 with Sir Edward Mutesa, the Kabaka of Buganda, who subsequently fled and died in exile. Thereafter Buganda, until Obote's overthrow in 1971, had been more or less under military occupation. The Baganda had, therefore, no cause in 1980 to exchange smiles with a leader who had destroyed their Kabakaship. Obote knew very well there was no way he could win over the Baganda in his second bid for power. He therefore opted for the strategy of encirclement that had so effectively worked in the early 1960s. The Bushenyi landing, therefore, was a symbolic invitation to the non-Baganda to march on Kampala – a 'Drang nach Kampala'. For the moment, it was in Obote's interest to keep the 'Buganda Question' alive. The kind of reception he was given was a measure of the extent of support from the Military Commission.

It is relevant to round off the account of Obote's second coming by discussing Tanzania's attitude towards the power struggles in post-1979 Uganda and the extent to which these attitudes contributed to Obote's ascendancy. Tanzania's attitudes were determined by Tanzania's basic interests, insofar as we can discern them vis-à-vis the Ugandan imbroglio. This is worth emphasizing because anti-Obote groups and critics of Tanzanian policies in Uganda have tended to argue that Nyerere had worked out a ready timetable for the installation of Obote. This is too neat an interpretation of events, and credits Nyerere with political ingenuity that, for all his admitted political acumen, he may not necessarily deserve. It is our view that if there was such a timetable, it was written out through the behaviour of the Ugandan leadership and all that Nyerere did was to interpret the timetable and relate it to concrete Tanzanian interests as he perceived them.

What were Tanzania's basic interests in Uganda? The first arose when Amin occupied Tanzanian territory in October 1978 and Tanzania mobilized her resources, initially to repel the invader; the second emerged on the eve (and after) the fall of Kampala and Amin's final defeat. In the first phase, the basic interest was relatively modest: namely to mobilize resources to dislodge Amin from occupied territory. At this stage, Amin's strength could not be determined, nor was Tanzania in a position to determine whether she had resources to go beyond this. With the expulsion of Amin's troops, however, the march on to Masaka and Mbarara, and with the road to Kampala open, Tanzania regarded the fall of Amin as merely a matter of time, and became more concerned over who would replace him. However, until the fall of Masaka and Mbarara, Tanzania took care not to internationalize the conflict and insisted that beyond the Tanzania–Uganda borders it was Ugandans who were fighting Idi Amin.

On the eve of the fall of Kampala, Tanzania, while seeking not to get bogged down in Uganda, was basically interested both in seeking secure borders with Uganda and having a regime established there friendly to Tanzania and opposed to the return of Idi Amin. Hence Tanzania's material sponsorship of the Moshi Unity Conference, which gave birth to the UNLF.

The fall of Lule and Binaisa, as we have already indicated, was not dictated from Tanzania. Lule had fallen because he was not acceptable to the power-brokers within the UNLF; Binaisa, because he did not have the abilities to time the removal of his opponents. True, both were not too popular with the Tanzanian authorities, but had neatly played into Tanzanian hands by creating conditions for their own removal by Ugandans. One may argue that Tanzania – to borrow an adage attributed to that seasoned diplomat, Talleyrand – intervened in support of one party by *not* intervening. In the early stages of the Ugandan struggle for power after 1979, the Tanzanian army was the only cohesive instrument available for use. But, most probably, active intervention in support of Lule and Binaisa would have bogged Tanzania further down in the Ugandan quagmire. A pro-Lule intervention would have entailed a confrontation with the power-brokers in the UNLF, and its possible dissolution, and would have meant disarming the Uganda National Liberation Army. A pro-Binaisa intervention would have meant a confrontation with the Military Commission and its by now relatively organized pro-Obote UNLA. All of this would have been too expensive and, in any case, would not have served Tanzanian interests.

Obote and the UPC had infiltrated the UNLF, divided and isolated their opponents, built a power-base wihin the UNLA and used the state machine, by August 1980, under the control of the Military Commission, to consolidate themselves. For all the controversy surrounding the December 1980 elections, even if the Democratic Pary *had* come into power after them, such was the balance of forces in real terms that it would have needed Tanzania to deploy her forces to disarm the pro-Obote UNLA and rebuild a new army favourable to a Democratic Party government. Insofar as the Tanzanian attitude contributed to the re-emergence of Obote, we can then say that Tanzania, disillusioned with Lule and Binaisa, and fearful of further expensive entanglements in Uganda, displayed an attitude that was fully taken advantage of by the pro-Obote forces in *their* struggle for power.

THE POST-1980 UGANDA PEOPLE'S CONGRESS

The Uganda People's Congress was not very different from the UPC of the early 1960s.[9] Then it was a loose federation of notables with varying bases of support from different areas. As we have already noted, its basic raison d'être had been to encircle and contain Buganda, defeat the Democratic Party, and succeed to the colonial mantle. This raison d'être was enough to bring in groups with sometimes conflicting ideologies and interests. Under its umbrella there were traditionalists, socialists, and republicans. Like other Ugandan parties, the UPC, for all its rhetoric of nationalism and radicalism, had ethnic and religious bases. While the Democratic Party was popularly identified with the Catholics who made a bid to challenge the Protestant establishment, the UPC was generaly identified with Protestants.[10]

Two years after independence, the party was riddled with factions, which, in their bid for power, vied for support from factions within the army. In this struggle for power, Obote won with the support of the army. But, for the party as a whole, the Obote victory had the negative effect of paralysing it as an effective organ for peacefully resolving conflict since effective power lay elsewhere, in the army. The party ceased to be any longer a vehicle for winning power, but as a means for legitimizing political courses of action introduced by Obote.

While the old notables of the 1960s had disappeared by 1980 through natural causes, political casualties, or through defections, the party again had emerged as a federation of aspiring notables with varying bases of support from their respective areas. Thus, in this regard the party had the image of the early 1960s. It is hard at this stage to determine the extent of its religious base outside Buganda since the struggle for power after the war against Amin brought together politically strange bedfellows: the Baganda power-brokers and the Democratic Party. The ethnic base, however, and the apparent success of Obote's encirclement strategy were evidenced by the fact that the UPC won most of its seats outside Buganda and Busoga.

In real power terms, however, the contest between the two major parties did not determine which party assumed power. For all the talk about free and fair elections at the time, and irrespective of the results, the issue of who the rulers would be had been effectively resolved by the assumption of power by the Military Commission, whose sympathies were clear, as evidenced by Muwanga's behaviour in the course of announcing the results.[11] If the power issue had been resolved before the UPC came formally into power, what, then, was the role of the UPC and what was the function of the December 1980 elections? Membership of the UPC was the means by which power-holders could tell, at least, vaguely, who their 'friends' were; the means by which they could determine who should be allocated or denied resources; the means by which they could mobilize support to legitimize particular courses of action decided on by the UPC leadership; and one of the means by which the power-holders could get some semblance of international respectability. While the ordinary members of the party keenly realized where in reality power lay, membership was the means by which they could legitimize their demands and have access to resources and probably domesticate the power-holders themselves.

For all the apparent strength of the UPC after the elections, it is worth noting that in the early days after the war against Amin, UPC strength could only be measured in terms of UPC activists' organizational abilities to undermine the UNLF's effectiveness, its growing influence within the army, and Obote's towering shadow over events in Uganda. The party, however, faced problems of leadership. We have noted that at Moshi the UPC did not come out well and that initially they were in a minority in the UNLF organs. The leadership had been depleted by death though natural causes, Amin's ruthlessness, and through defections to other parties. The paucity of leadership may also be attributed to the fact that the Kampala area, which was a strategic region, was intensely hostile to the UPC, and to the fact that until the UNLF disintegrated through the infiltration activities of the UPC and the political ineptitude of its leaders, it had enjoyed a wide degree of legitimacy. But with the advent of the Military Commission, it had access to a variety of material resources and, above all, the coercive instruments were available to protect its harassed members. The leadership ranks were filled partly because the situation was sufficiently reassuring for the leadership underground to come into the open, and partly because of opportunistic calculations on the part of the aspiring leadership that the UPC was surely on its way to power.

This initial paucity of members was in some sense a blessing in disguise for the party, for a new generation of leaders came up to fill its ranks. After the 1980 election the party leadership was mostly made up from former party 'youth-wingers' of the 1960s, relatively young men, especially graduates of Makerere University in the late 1960s and early 1970s, and former activists in the National Union of Students in Uganda (NUSU), a *de facto* affiliate of the UPC.[12]

Organizationally, the UPC appeared at its best when seeking to win elections, as evidenced by its pre-independence and December 1980 campaigns, but at its worst when in power. It did not quite succeed in building an effective administrative machine from the top to the grassroots for the day-to-day running of its affairs. True, before the 1971 coup, on paper there was an administrative machine, and after the 1979 war there were attempts to build one, but its effectiveness had yet to be tested. This organizational state of affairs may be attributed to the tendency on the part of the party leadership to drift into government after elections; the patron–client nature of the party; and to the fact that fundamental power conflicts at critical times had been resolved outside the party.

The tendency to drift into government is evidenced after the April 1962 and December 1980 elections. After the two elections some of the party's ablest leaders, in organizational terms, sought government posts.[13] All the way from the top to bottom there were no full-time party officials. This inevitably deprived the party of organizational talent and even created instances where incumbents held dual government-party posts: the party was not given the organizational attention it needed. One may argue that the establishment of a bureaucratic machine with a party based on patron–client relations may be a contradiction in terms, because there is the danger of a bureaucratized party machine generating its own power base that may threaten the power bases of the patrons as well as the interests of the clients. The UPC leadership, especially Obote, has always been wary of a strong party machine. There would probably have been serious rationale for strengthening organizational machinery in the party if there had been fundamental commitment on the part of the leadership to regard the party as a legitimate organ for resolving fundamental power issues within the party. But evidence from the past did not quite suggest so. As we have noted, the Obote faction resolved the power struggle by using the army in 1966 and, after the anti-Amin war, the UPC went to the elections fully confident of the support of the Military Commission. Thus, in a situation where the party simply serves as a means of access to governmental posts, patrons fear their political bases might be undermined. Moreover, where the party was not regarded as the major arena for resolution of fundamental conflicts there were no incentives to have the party institutionalized.

THE OPPOSITION: DEMOCRATIC PARTY

In the wake of the December 1980 elections a number of parties appeared on the scene to oppose the UPC, the most formidable of which was the Democratic Party. This was the same party that was, as we have noted, its bitterest opponent in the 1960s. The post-1979 DP attracted into its ranks the old DP members, Baganda, and old UPC members who for various reasons were disillusioned with the UPC. The basic raison d'être of the DP was to defeat the UPC; certainly this was the basic objective of its new members. In a bid to break out of the UPC encirclement, Baganda joined it en masse. Purely in terms of electoral politics, the DP constituted a very formidable opposition. Before the 'crossings' it constituted numerically a very powerful opposition in Parliament. Five years after the formation of the UPC government in 1980 the DP continued to survive, it had its MPs, a press through which it criticized the government, its president continued to openly attack the government and, generally, in spite of all the odds, it had a political visibility of its own.[14] How do we account for the survival of the Democratic Party to this time? The survival may be attributed to three factors: ironically, the balance of forces in favour of the UPC; an effort to maintain good external public relations; and to the very limited resources available in the political system.

We have pointed out that the issue of who was to govern Uganda had been resolved – at least for the time being – by the coup d'état of the Military Commission in mid-1980. Supported by the military, the UPC already had the balance of forces in its favour. Confident of army support, it had worked out rules of the game that favoured its continuation in power.[15] Under these circumstances, the governing party was in no hurry to legislate against the DP or harass it out of existence. Of course, the UPC did not see the DP as an alternative government under rules of a game clearly favourable to the UPC. Here the UPC may have calculated that at this stage it would have been too expensive, in a situation of very limited resources, to seek a head-on confrontation with the DP, given that party's strong socio-political bases in the Catholic Church and Buganda. Already the government had on its hands the problems of post-war reconstruction as well as fighting the guerrillas under Museveni. It was good politics to fight only a limited number of enemies at any one time. Linked with this effort to stabilize the situation at home was a desire to maintain good external public relations. The governing party, in need of aid to assist its reconstruction efforts, could hardly afford to keep Uganda 'in the news' by overtly harassing the opposition, for this would have antagonized liberal forces abroad and other aid-giving agencies. It was therefore good international politics to allow the Democratic Party 'to breathe'.

In the normal course of events, one would have thought that to strengthen itself the UPC leadership would have sought massive 'crossings' by DP members into the UPC. Officially 'crossing' was encouraged but in the rural areas, the writer has come to learn, the mid and grass-roots level leadership was not too enthusiastic about welcoming new members.[16] In a situation where joining a governing party was regarded as a means of access to resources, there would not have been enough resources to go around if the party had been flooded with 'newcomers'.

There were also other limitations to DP activity during the second UPC period of power in Uganda. In circumstances in which the ruling party determined the rules of the political game, in which it did not see the opposition as an alternative government, and in which resources were not so readily available to the opposition to sustain itself, any other party was quite likely to 'wither away'. If the UPC continued to manipulate the balance of forces favourable to itself, other groups could however challenge it by extra-legal means and this in turn provoked the UPC into using coercive measures against the opposition. And in this, eventually, all the other calculated political subtleties for keeping the DP down were to go overboard.

THE UGANDA NATIONAL LIBERATION ARMY

Since 1966, when Obote unleashed the army against Sir Edward Mutesa, it had been a critical factor in Ugandan politics. Part of the

Ugandan tragedy is that the post-colonial Ugandan army was built up and expanded in response to the secessionist Rwenzuru movement, disturbances in the 'Lost Counties', the cattle raids in Karamoja, and spillover effects of the disturbances in the Congo (now Zaire) and the Sudan, and the Buganda 'Question', at the time of independence. It is worth noting that four battalions were established in the epicentres of domestic trouble spots: Toro, Mubende, Moroto, and Lubiri, and the Ugandan post-colonial leadership came to regard the military as an instrument for maintenance of law and order within the state, and later as an instrument of domestic policy.[17] As domestic problems became more serious, the army became increasingly visible, the leadership pampered it with status and material rewards and this in turn generated within it a sense of psychological self-importance and politico-functional indispensability, especially as regards those groups that successfully sought its support in successive political power struggles.

Political problems increased when factions within the ruling party, unable to resolve their conflicts peacefully, vied for support from groups within the military, which was itself riddled with factions reflecting civilian strife. The Obote-Amin faction within the army gained the upper hand. It had a successful showdown with the Baganda, and silenced UPC anti-Obote factions. But even after the apparent physical solution of the Buganda 'Question' in 1966, civilian struggles continued to be carried over into the military, with various factions seeking to establish hegemony over each other. The Obote–Amin quarrel was the logical conclusion to this strife, culminating in the January 1971 coup.

After 1979, Ugandan leaders were highly ambivalent towards the military. With the defeat of Amin's army, there was some chance for reconsideration of the role of the army in the newly 'liberated' country. On the one hand the military was seen as the most effective instrument in the removal of Idi Amin and as a critical factor in the ensuing power struggles; on the other, Ugandan leaders saw the army as a monster that had to be domesticated somehow. Seen as a liberating instrument, the new-army-in-the-making enjoyed a honeymoon period with leaders and civilians alike. Seen as a critical factor in ensuing power struggles, the military was an object of ingratiating attention from various political groups. Hence such labels as 'Museveni's', 'Obote's' and 'Mwanga's soldiers' were freely bandied about. The critical role of the military in the unfolding power struggles of this period was clearly evidenced by the fact that Lule and Binaisa, who did not gain backing by the military, did not survive.

The post-1979 Ugandan leaders' attitudes towards the military as a liberating instrument and as a critical factor in the power game, and then as a monster that had to be domesticated, were of course highly contradictory. Factional vying for support within the military inevitably implied a sense of political helplessness, and dependency on the military, and therefore a lack of institutionalized means of domesticating it. Under the UNLF, steps were taken in an apparent effort to subordinate the military to civilian control. The general thinking among some of the UNLF leadership was that a future Ugandan military monster could only be prevented from arising if efforts were made to strengthen the UNLF as an organization by proportional ethnic representation in the new army, by having a literate army with an educated officer corps, and by representation of the military in UNLF organs and parliament.

The tentative steps or ideas to domesticate the new army generated hostility from various political forces. The apparent assumption behind strengthening the UNLF vis-à-vis the military was that the army could be neutralized politically if there was a civilian political organization. But, of course, as we have seen, factions within the UNLF had little in common beyond the common UNLF label. Proportional ethnic representation was Lule's idea.[18] This proposal earned him bitter attacks from those groups whose numerical strength would have been weakened within the army thereby. His opponents were quick to point out that, since Buganda and the southern areas of Uganda are numerically predominant, these two areas would have had a greater numerical advantage and this was a blatant way of one group establishing its own hegemony over the army. Opponents of Lule went so far as to revive the doctrine of 'ethno-functionalism', the most outstanding advocates of which had been Gasper Oda and Felix Onama in the 1960s. Simply stated, the doctrine advocated that particular ethnic groups endowed physically and historically to perform specific functions, should be left to perform them. While Oda subscribed to the principle of evenly spreading recruitment in the Uganda army,

> ... there is one thing which should be taken into consideration, that not all tribes, not only in this country but also throughout the world, are born warriors or warlike people. Some tribes are warlike people, and others are intellectuals, and are not prepared to face warlike people.[19]

For Onama, the Minister of Defence in the 1960s, it was the manifest destiny of northern people to defend Uganda, since

> ... thousands of northerners died in the two world wars to defend

Uganda against Nazism and Fascism and if the young ...
generation or their children who have grown up in the North
would like to follow in the footsteps of their fathers, nobody is
going to stop me recruiting them into the army ... In the colonial
times some tribes believed that the life of a soldier was a very low
job unfit for people from certain tribes and that is why you find in
the army the Northerners ... Because people think there is no war
and these young men wear a very smart uniform, they want their
weaklings from certain tribes also to wear this uniform.[20]

The area that would have been most adversely affected, if Lule's
ideas had ben implemented, would have been the north generally
and Acholi and Lango specifically. And this inevitably would have
entailed a change in the balance of power in the army to the
disadvantage of the north, Langi and Acholi in particular.

The search for a literate army and an educated officer corps after
1979 was a response to the low levels of literacy and education in
Amin's army and its officer corps respectively, to which some
Ugandan leaders partly attributed the bestiality of Amin's army. Of
course, opposition to this proposal, muted as it was, was based on
particularistic political considerations. Political groups making a
rush for support within the army and seeking to establish their bases
within it, could not have had education and general literacy as
important criteria, particularly if they considered them political
disadvantages. Certainly, Lule quickly earned the hostility of the
core of the UNLA who had marched from the Uganda–Tanzania
border. They saw the educational criterion as a ruse to have them
disarmed: the educational and literacy criteria would again have
placed the south, especially Buganda, at a greater advantage over
the north.

The UNLF leaders at Moshi saw that they had to come to grips
with reality by recognizing the UNLA-in-the-making as an interest
group. Not only would interests peculiar to the military be taken
care of by military representatives, but military representation
would also enable the military to participate in the decision-making
processes in top civilian political institutions. At the Moshi Conference it was decided to establish a Military Commission as an organ
of the National Executive Committee and to have ten members
representing the military in the National Consultative Council. A
system of political commissars and political education officers would
help inculcate values into the military that could sustain subordina-
tion of the military to the supreme civilian authority.

It may not have occurred to the Moshi statesmen that in a highly
fragmented political system, military representation, political commissars and political education are no panacea. These mechanisms

for control may be successful in revolutionary situations where a revolutionary party has a cohesive leadership with properly defined programmes, and such a party has the political upper hand. But such conditions did not prevail in Uganda after 1979. In a fragmented political system, military representatives cannot be insulated from civilian political strife, which will certainly be reflected in the military. In the factional power struggles that ensued, we have seen that the military representatives identified themselves with factions or parties. As we have also seen, it was clear where the sympathies of the Military Commission lay. Establishment of a system of political commissars assumes core political values to which political actors or the system as a whole subscribe and which they seek to be inculcated. No such core of political values existed in Uganda after 1979. The appointment of the 'first' political commissar, 'Major' Katabarwa, was regarded by Brigadier Oyite-Ojok as a joke.

That efforts to domesticate the Ugandan military failed was illustrated by the assumption of power by the Military Commission in 1980, whose political sympathies (as we have seen) lay with the UPC. The military thus demonstrated that it still had the veto power to determine which political rulers it preferred.

THE PATHOLOGY OF UGANDAN POLITICS

Ugandan politics between 1962 and 1986 are a case study in institutional pathology, characterized by an ideologically fragmented elite unable or incapable of working out viable political formulas to neutralize local conflicts, and by socio-political forces completely out of joint. Ugandan politics were soured because of this, not so much because the underlying socio-economic infrastructure was fragile. When Uganda had her first political upheavals in 1966, and later in 1971, the country had a strong, agriculturally based economy in relation to her neighbours. Ironically, a country like Tanzania, with a relatively fragile socio-economic base, established relatively viable political institutions after independence. Indeed, as we have argued elsewhere (Mudoola, 1983), the principal problem for Tanzania has not been lack of institutions, but over-institutionalization.

We attribute institutional fragility in Uganda to a highly fragmented political elite operating in a socio-political framework that is out of joint. Ugandan political elites have not worked out a basic consensus to resolve political conflicts short of physical force. In Uganda, force is not a state monopoly in the Weberian sense, but a means by which the political forces seek to establish their hegemony over other competing political forces. Of course, to say that the political elite is fragmented begs the question. While Ugandan elites reflect various political traditions – monarchism, liberalism, republicanism, and so on – they have not outgrown the local social forces they purport to represent. Ugandan elites have worked out political formulas not as means through which conflicts can be resolved for the ultimate good of the political system as a whole, but as tactical weapons for taking care of interests peculiar to themselves or the social forces they purport to represent.

This is not to say that constitutional formulas should not be vehicles for interests, but the peculiarity of Ugandan politics lies in the fact that the political elites only adhere to political formulas as long as they serve immediate interests. If political actors feel disadvantaged through these formulas, and if they are strong enough to operate outside them, they are only too ready to do so and thereby imperil the overall political rules of the game in Uganda.

The period between 1962 and 1966 was one of relative peace, not necessarily because the leaders were committed to the 'politics of reconciliation'[21] but because none of the leaders and the forces they represented felt strong enough to question the constitutional arrangement decided at the time of independence. The major antagonists – the Obote supporters, the anti-Obote group within the UPC and the Kabaka's supporters – discovered in the last two years of this period that their interests could not be taken care of by normal constitutional procedures. The anti-Obote group and the Kabaka's supporters therefore vied for support within the army. As we have noted, the physical showdown was resolved in favour of the Obote faction, which dictated its own rules in 1966. But the net effect of the new political formulas was to alienate Baganda and other groups, which initially legitimized the Amin coup of 1971. Amin was therefore not behaving eccentrically when he introduced rules only intelligible to himself and his cronies.

We have also pointed out that institutional pathology may be attributed to imbalance within the socio-political forces. This, in turn, may be attributed to the legacy of colonial institutional arrangements, and to the inequitable allocation of resources under colonial rule. As in other colonial situations, in Uganda institutional arrangements subordinated the colonial entity to the external metropolitan institutions, where ultimate colonial sovereignty lay. The central colonial government in Uganda was remote, in contrast to other colonial situations where the colonial presence was keenly felt through settlerdom, land alienation, and forced labour. In the Ugandan case, after the initial colonial conquest and the establishment of regular administration and a certain socio-economic infrastructure, the role of the colonial government was that of arbiter in inter- and intra-ethnic disputes. It only intervened directly whenever its power appeared to be undermined by local interests. Through the 1900 Agreement, Buganda was given some meaningful degree of autonomy, and so were the other areas of the Uganda Protectorate through the 1949 African Local Government Ordinance. These local power centres provided meaningful arenas for political participation. Conflicting socio-political forces only sought arbitration and such instances are many: the Buganda–Bunyoro historic conflict over the 'Lost Counties'; the Bamba–Bakonjo bid to secede from the Toro Kingdom; the Bahima–Bairu conflicts in Ankole; and boundary disputes of other ethnic groups that found themselves contained within the same administrative boundaries. The most notable occasions when the colonial power had earlier intervened was during the 1945 and 1949 riots, and when Sir Andrew Cohen exiled the Kabaka of Buganda from Uganda in 1953.

The basic point here is that the earlier colonial situation did not provide a setting in which central political institutions could in future generate the loyalties of politically significant social forces to create bases for viable central institutions enjoying a wide degree of acceptability. Besides the alien character and remoteness of the central British colonial institutions, the drawing up of the internal political-administrative boundaries coincided with more or less culturally (and, in some cases, politically) homogeneous groups. These politico-administrative boundaries acquired political distinctness, a fact commented on in the Wallis Report, and behind which socio-political forces defined their interests. It has been argued by Tarsis Kabwegyere (1974), Samwiri Karugire (1980), and Grace Ibingira (1973) that these politico-administrative arrangements in no way gave meaningful power to the African kings or chiefs of the Uganda Protectorate; that 'Indirect Rule' was direct rule, and that British colonial sovereignty was in no way impaired or undermined (Kabwegyere, 1974; Karugire, 1980; and Ibingira, 1973). This argument is however tautological, for the very logic of the British colonial presence meant that sovereignty, the ultimate power to make politically binding decisions, lay with the colonial power. For us these politico-administrative arrangements are significant insofar as they had important consequences for the political behaviour of Ugandans during and after colonial rule. Through these politico-administrative arrangements, political elites and the socio-political forces they represented in Uganda perceived, defined and advanced their interests. There was the growth of power-centres in local areas that provided arenas for political action relating to allocation of resources, at the finally fatal extreme expense of the growth of legitimate central political institutions.

On the eve of independence the country therefore embraced varying political entities. Although under the same colonial sovereign these had different political traditions nurtured before and after the establishment of British colonialism. These traditions were to provide bases for conflicting political attitudes that were to have negative consequences for the Ugandan political system as a whole. Ugandan political culture on the eve of independence was therefore a hotch-potch of authoritarianism, liberalism, traditionalism, and republicanism. This is not to say that there are no viable political systems with heterogeneous political traditions. The Ugandan political dilemma lies in the fact that the Ugandan political elite liberally subscribes to this hotch-potch of traditions, and there are no residual political values common to them all that are strong enough to sustain the system short of overt coercion. That, in essence, was the pathology of Ugandan politics, at least up to January 1986.

Notes

1. *Daily News* (Tanzania), 15 January 1979.
2. According to Nabudere (1980, p. 334), there were 'twenty two organizations and groups' in Moshi.
3. Communication from a Tanzanian official, who asked to remain anonymous.
4. *ibid*.
5. At a talk given by Omwony Ojok to Ugandans at the University of Dar es Salaam, the author asked a question related to the problems of law and order in Kampala and Omwony Ojok retorted, '*Whose law and order?*'
6. 'Compatriot' was an epithet coined apparently to reflect the 'umbrella' politics of the UNLF. Given a choice, the 'Gang of Four' would have preferred 'Comrade'.
7. Interview with Massette-Kuya, a UPC stalwart. According to him, Dan Nabudere approached him seeking support for the revival of Lule. 'I immediately embraced him!', says Massette-Kuya.
8. At the time of the Moshi Conference and immediately after the installation of the Lule government, Nyerere was reported to have discouraged Obote from going to Moshi and returning to Kampala. Given the delicate political situation in Kampala, Nyerere may have considered his friend a political liability. On his return to the country in 1980 however, the Tanzanians provided Obote with a plane and a high-ranking entourage.
9. On the UPC in the 1960s, see Mujaju, 1976a; and Satyamurthy, 1978.
10. On the religious factor in Uganda politics, see Welbourn, 1965; Mudoola, 1978; and Mujaju, 1976b.
11. When election results were being announced, the DP reacted with jubilation, assuming that they had won. Paulo Muwanga however announced that polling results would be handed over to the Military Commission, and issued a decree providing for terms of imprisonment for anyone who talked about election results.

12. Officially, NUSU was supposed to embrace all youths in Uganda, irrespective of party affiliation.
13. Only once has the party had a full-time Secretary-General, John Kakonge, but immediately after independence Kakonge joined the government and held dual posts until his removal in 1964. Since then there has never been a full-time Secretary-General of the UPC.
14. The party was most visible in Kampala, where it still has its headquarters, but in the countryside the UPC middle level leaders' visibility was sometimes extremely tenuous.
15. All this in spite of the rhetoric about the multi-party system. The Opposition insisted on revision of electoral laws, some aspects of which had loopholes allowing rigging, but as long as these were to the advantage of the governing UPC, the prospects for reform remained very slim, indeed.
16. Information based on interviews with UPC officials in Busoga.
17. This attitude was very well reflected by the leaders both in government and opposition during parliamentary debates on security in the country: see Uganda parliamentary debates, Hansard, especially on the 'State of Emergency' in Buganda and Toro.
18. *Uganda Times*, 17 April 1979. See Lule's address to the nation on a new Uganda army.
19. Proceedings of the Uganda Parliament, Hansard 1963-64, Vol. 35, pp. 3135–36.
20. *ibid*, p. 3205.
21. Professor Ali A. Mazrui broadly categorizes Ugandan politics of the early and mid-1960s as more of 'reconciliation' and 'violent constitutionalism' without going into how, and why, the politics of 'reconciliation' degenerated into the politics of 'violent constitutionalism'.

TWENTY
External and internal factors in Uganda's continuing crisis

Dani Wadada Nabudere

The crisis that has engulfed Uganda today can only be understood if its root causes are clearly understood. In this short chapter we try to bring out the basic roots of the crisis and to indicate some approaches as to how it can be resolved. In this we emphasize that the only force that can resolve this broadening and widening crisis is the people of Uganda themselves, and for this reason we denounce the interference of foreign powers in the affairs of Uganda.

To be sure, this interference based on the acquisition of economic interests by foreigners on the Uganda soil is the very factor that constitute the roots of the crisis. It is a well-recorded fact that the future of those societies that were shaped into what is today called 'Uganda' was the result of contention and rivalry between four European powers who were engaged in cut-throat competition to acquire colonies. Britain and Germany were among those four European powers, with France and Belgium being the others.

Although Uganda formally regained her political independence in 1962 – a very important victory for the people of Uganda – Britain in particular, and to some extent Germany, have continued to exert pressure in Uganda in order to create new agencies for the safeguarding of their global interests in our country. Those continued interests of Britain in Uganda became a hindrance both to the consolidation of Uganda's independence and to a strengthening of the democratic rights of the people of Uganda to determine the affairs of their country through regular elections. Indeed, in order to safeguard these interests, Britain manoeuvred itself, by using the well-dusted policy of 'divide and rule', to install a government that compromised these fundamental rights of the people of Uganda, namely the first Obote government from 1962.

The fact that the people of Uganda were being excluded from the discussions and resolution of factional fights that were taking place already prepared the ground for military intervention. The army had of course no business intervening in this process. Nevertheless its very intervention strengthened the forces of dictatorship that had already arisen and of which the army itself had been part.

From then onwards, any sign of opposition was dealt with in a summary fashion; execution. The Amin regime from 1971, with British and Israeli support, had abrogated all those democratic organizations that the Obote regime had also abrogated under emergency rule. Even the pseudo-parliament, which had existed to give 'democratic respectability' to the civilian dictatorship of Obote, was also dissolved, so that the only institutions that remained in the country were private companies, parastatal bodies, the churches and co-operatives to market the cash crops.

The eight years of Amin's murderous regime therefore constituted a record of intrigue by foreign interests in our Motherland for which the Ugandan people paid dearly, not only in 'cash' but also in blood. The support given by Libya to pay for the regime's expenses above what the Uganda worker and peasant could afford, only added to this international intrigue, in which the Soviet Union was also involved (through proxy powers such as the German Democratic Republic and other Eastern European countries) to assist the fascist regime. It is this fact that strengthened the regime's hand and made it even more aggressive in spreading its murderous activities outside its borders, preparing the ground for the Uganda–Tanzania War.

THE 1978–9 WAR AND THE RISE OF THE UGANDA NATIONAL LIBERATION FRONT (UNLF)

The Uganda–Tanzania War exposed not only the aggressive intentions of this foreign-inspired and foreign-supported regime, it also exposed the organizational weaknesses of the Ugandan people. During the ten years of the civilian dictatorship under Obote, all democratic organizations were harassed, their leaders detained and their existence finally declared illegal in the emergency measures that the regime adopted between 1966 and 1971. Amin had given a further seal to this outlawing of political parties and other democratic organizations in his decrees which abrogated even the right to life itself.

In these circumstances the people of Uganda found themselves too disorganized to be able to organize a co-ordinated resistance. Added to this, Obote used his eight years of exile to frustrate all efforts at forming a national front of resistance, because of his desire to continue to dominate the political scene in Uganda. He resisted all proposals for a broad democratic unity of all national forces opposed to the fascist dictatorship. At the same time he presided over the disintegration of those of his own political forces that had followed him into exile. From his comfortable Tanzanian-state-paid villa at Msasani, Dar es Salaam, he played his politics of deceit and duplicity and created ethnic and religious divisions among his men in the camps who had been in the Uganda army, with the result that when Amin attacked Tanzania his band of former soldiers were not in a position to enter the war as a united force.

Thus it required a Tanzanian intervention to fight Amin's army for Obote and other military factions of Uganda to talk about integrating their forces under Tanzanian laws and command. All that had happened in all the twenty years of Obote's leadership as a politician was a weakening of Ugandan democratic organization to the point where we had to accept foreign mobilization and organization of Ugandans to fight the regime. In this Obote wanted the Tanzanian army to organize, recruit, train and fight a war to go and reinstate him as President of Uganda 'to start where he left' in 1971!

These hopes of Obote were somehow dashed, at least temporarily, when a group of Ugandans insisted on forming a broadly based national democratic front to unite the people of Uganda *politically* to prepare the ground for the restoration of democracy in the country. When the people of Tanzania publicly expressed hostility at the idea of using the Tanzanian army to re-install Obote in power, Nyerere found that he had to accept the efforts of this group of Ugandans to organize a front. For Ugandans who wanted to get the second-best situation out of this rather unsatisfactory state of affairs, such a front at least offered them an opportunity of dialogue to find a formula that would form the basis of a post-Amin transitional administration.

This was the background to the formation of the UNLF in Moshi in March 1979, one month before Kampala fell to the Tanzanian forces. The hurried formation of a government out of this conglomeration of political groups to take over post-Amin Uganda expressed the dilemma of Ugandans: to be 'liberated' by a foreign force and yet pretend to be in control. But the dilemma had to be faced and the best had to be made of any favourable leeway to advance the democratic cause, unsatisfactory as it was.

The 'exclusion' of Milton Obote from the Moshi Conference has been a matter that Obote has played on to explain his hostility to its outcome. Yet there can be no doubt that his 'exclusion' was an act of advice to him by his friend and supporter, Julius Nyerere. The organizers of the conference invited all political leaders, including Milton Obote, and the UPC representative at the conference and other supporters of Obote in fact came with this letter of invitation to Obote as their credentials for admission. It is Nyerere who told Obote not to go to the Moshi Conference, because in his opinion his presence would have frustrated the formation of such a front. Obote knows that no one on earth would have prevented him from attending the Moshi Conference, if the Tanzanians were in favour of his attending it. Yet he has persisted in telling these lies in order to justify not only his hostility to the UNLF interim administration that was preparing the country for an early democratic election in the planning of which all political opinions were to be involved, but also his manoeuvres to weaken it from inside and finally to stage a *coup d'état* against it in May 1980. Not until he had achieved this objective did he return to Uganda under the pretence of a 'liberator', which became the platform for rigging the elections of December 1980.

THE ELECTION FRAUD AND THE SECOND OBOTE DICTATORSHIP

The overthrow of the UNLF interim administration by the Oyite-Muwanga military clique in the UNLA, with the connivance and support of the Museveni military faction in the UNLA, signalled the first step towards dictatorship. The Tanzanian support to this military junta that took power was decisive. Tanzania in the end did what had been feared right from the beginning: it imposed its will on the people of Uganda by manipulating the political situation. This it finally did, and it has as a result soiled its hands with the blood that continues to flow in Uganda today.

Nyerere's role in helping Obote to regain power through a rigged election was also decisive. He was central in convincing the Democratic Party to co-operate with the junta by assuring them that the election would be free and fair. He also manoeuvred to obtain a Commonwealth team of observers to give an approving stamp to the election fraud, and in this the British came in. Britain was also decisive in convincing the DP of the 'foolproof' election mechanism that it was providing, backed by the observer group. The election fraud that followed in the wake of a violent repression of the other parties to the election is no longer disputed by any sensible person except the hardcore supporters of the regime.

Yet this fraud is the very basis upon which foreign powers based their support for the regime. The first again was Britain. It is well known that during the period of the military junta, Obote negotiated with the British to give him support on the basis of promises. Immediately after the election fraud, Britain was the first country again to recognize the regime by sending in an assistant minister of foreign affairs, Richard Luce, in March 1981 to seal an agreement with the UPC-Obote regime. Among the promises made and accepted by the British government as conditions of its support were that the regime would guarantee British investments, return or compensate British businesses that were taken over by the Amin regime (including Asian properties) and also give permission to

Ugandan Asians to return to Uganda. On the foreign side, the regime agreed to co-operate with the British at the UN, particularly at the Security Council where Uganda had secured a two-year term. In return the British government agreed to give the regime political and diplomatic support, give it 'aid' and convince other EEC members to give it support. It also agreed to sponsor, together with the World Bank, a donors' conference in Paris of a consortium of bankers and businessmen to finance Uganda's 'Recovery Programme'. Later, the British Prime Minister, Mrs Thatcher, convinced the Americans to back up the regime and support IMF 'standby' loans.

In the same frame appeared a German element. The Christian Democratic Union (CDU) in Germany had given aid and support to the DP through a foundation. At this crucial moment in the history of Uganda, when the opposition should have come out to refuse to give consent to election fraud that had been committed against it, the CDU played a significant role in convincing the DP to accept the dictatorship on the premise that since Obote had taken power and since he had offered to 'respect' a 'multi-party system', the DP should respect and work 'within the democratic process'.

This position was revealed to the author of this chapter by one Dr Heusch, a CDU member of the Bundestag, and chairman of the foreign economic co-operation committee of the West German Parliament. He also happened to be either a member of the board of, or chairman of the foundation that had relations with the DP in Uganda. In these positions he went to Uganda to observe the 1980 elections in Uganda and during a ten-day stay in the country he formed a firm opinion that the election that had been concluded in December, was, to put it in his words, 'unfree, unfair and invalid'. Yet despite this fact, Dr Heusch explained to the present writer in his office in Neusse that he, in consultation with other Western interests in Kampala, agreed that the best policy to take was for the West to deal with the Obote government. This advice was communicated to Dr Paul Ssemogere, the DP leader, at a time when the DP Council was of the overwhelming opinion that it should not accept the fraudulent results and should instead boycott the Parliament. The pressures exerted at this time in the DP by these foreign interests became the *determining factor* not only in changing the position of the DP, but also in pressuring their acceptance of dictatorship in the country.

Indeed, as it has turned out, the acceptance by the DP of this 'advice' became a crucial factor in giving the regime the *legitimacy* it needed to consolidate the dictatorship, a fact that made its diplomatic task much easier against the democratic forces. This same interference by the German foundation later became the basis of still further legitimation of the regime, when the CDU and other European democratic parties held an international conference in Kampala in October 1984 to mark the 'return' of Uganda to democracy!

It can then be seen how foreign interests clearly came out as the main perpetrators of dictatorship in Uganda. The regime obtained support from these interests in order to wage a war of extermination against the Ugandan people. The suffering that this brought about became in turn the basis for further support to the regime when it was argued again that in order to alleviate this suffering 'humanitarian' assistance must be extended to the regime.

The imperialists – the British in the forefront – believed that as long as the regime held the gun to the heads of the people of Uganda, a form of coercion that they could reinforce with their military assistance, they could use the economic carrot ('humanitarian assistance' is the bogy phrase) to convince the people of Uganda that opposition to the dictatorship would be of no avail, and that it would be in their own interest to accept the dictatorship if their economic and social situation was to improve. The pumping in of millions of dollars in 'aid' by the World Bank, the IMF, the EEC, the British and Germans has however gone down the drain, for instead of 'recovery' and reconstruction, devastation in all parts of the country has been the real *development*.

This violent devastation of the country is in fact the very result of government repression in order to rule the country. To blame 'bandits' for the devastation is in fact to put the cart before the horse. The regime had no basis to blame anybody for being 'bandit' when its very existence in government came into being by use of banditry against the democratic process that denied the people of Uganda their democratic rights. In coming to the aid of the regime, the Western powers and Eastern bloc countries therefore started from a position that was counter-productive even to their own interests. It was the shock of realization that the effort was counter-productive that increasingly brought the US government to reassess is position and seek the best way out.

The spread in the devastation of the country was linked to the fact that the regime lacked sufficient political support from the population to be able (even in those areas in which it claimed to have support) to mobilize the population to combat problems such as, for example, 'cattle rustling'. We say this because it was claimed that this was the problem in Ankole and Karamoja. In both cases the regime claimed that it had overwhelming support from those areas in the last 'election'. But contrary to these claims, the way the regime responded to the 'cattle rustling' in Ankole was to attack the homes of the ethnic Rwandese whom the regime in fact knew to be supporters of the opposition parties. They instructed their youth wingers to attack, rob and set on fire houses owned by these ethnic Rwandese who had settled in Uganda. Thousands upon thousands of these people were forced to flee their homeland to become refugees in neighbouring Rwanda from where they had fled in the first place to seek refuge in Uganda. Many Uganda citizens who were accused of 'looking like' Banyarwanda, ethnic Hima, were also made to flee their homeland to become refugees in Rwanda and later in Tanzania. To be allowed to return they were required to 'prove' that they were Ugandans, when all their properties including documentary evidence had been destroyed during the attacks.

The same treatment had in fact been meted out to the people of West Nile. There, whole populations of the two districts of Arua and Moyo were forced into exile in southern Sudan and Zaire for no other reason than that the regime suspected them to be 'supporters of Amin'. Since October 1980 they have tried to return to their homelands, and yet each time they were beaten back by the regime's genocidal army. There was no question here of the need to 'prove' citizenship. When the UNHCR tried to test the regime's sincerity about the alleged 'amnesty' for these innocent ordinary Ugandans to return home, which the regime had been orchestrating in foreign countries as proof of its having returned the area to 'normalcy', a prominent chief who had fled to Zaire returned under this UNHCR inducement. He ended up being killed at a police station by soldiers, who beat him to death, having been hauled by them from the police cells where he had been kept for his 'own protection'.

What then happened in Karamoja should not surprise anyone, because here too it was alleged that the Karamojong had to be 'disciplined' for engaging in 'cattle rustling', a phenomenon that has been recurrent in this area for years; yet this time the regime used more violence than had ever been used by the colonialists and even the Amin regime put together. The picture that emerges is one of a widening and broadening crisis that the regime and its foreign backers found increasingly difficult to control.

OBOTE'S SECOND OVERTHROW AND THE NEW CRISIS

It was in these circumstances that the second regime of Milton Obote was overthrown by his 'Liberation Army' on 27 July 1985. A month earlier, the British-based Amnesty International had issued a condemnatory report based on direct evidence of the victims of torture and various forms of repression. This listed a number of serious violations of human rights in the country by the regime.

Faced with this evidence the British government – the main supporter of the regime – at first tried to hedge but in the end agreed to lodge a protest with the Uganda government in which it threatened to withdraw 'aid' unless the human rights record were improved in the country.

Events did not, however, wait for the regime to 'improve' its record, for internal contradictions within the regime itself (including the party and army) had built up in the meantime to the point where open confrontation between the different factions erupted. The Vice-President, Paulo Muwanga, was known to be opposed to Obote and to be working with an Acholi faction in the army to overthrow the regime he had helped bring into power. Among the dissidents in the army were the Army Commander, Major-General Tito Okello, and the Commander of the Northern Regiment, Bazilio Olara Okello (no relative). The reason given by them was that the regime had created disunity in the country, causing civil strife that the army was finding it difficult to contain.

Faced with the reality that they could not win the war against the various armed groups that had emerged in opposition to the regime, the Tito faction of the UNLA linked up – through Paulo Muwanga – with the main resistance group fighting around Kampala – the NRA – with a view to finding a common position to bring about the downfall of the Obote regime. The NRA itself had come to the conclusion that it could not overthrow Obote on its own and hold power for any length of time. The two groups therefore saw reason to work out joint plans to topple Obote. The NRA leader, Yoweri Museveni, realizing Obote's days were numbered, left the country to obtain support outside. But events moved very fast and the UNLA – on its own – moved to topple Obote's regime.

Finding itself with the baby in its hands, the Tito faction then made contact with the NRA to share the loot of power that it had grabbed. At first Museveni, responding from Stockholm, reacted with enthusiasm, expressing the NRA's willingness to co-operate with the new regime. He did not impose any conditions, apparently because he took it for granted that they would share power equally. But military dictatorship knows no 'equal' representation of power and the Okellos in Kampala moved fast to consolidate themselves by bringing together the four political parties that had taken part in the rigged 1980 elections to join its cabinet, which it set up under the former Vice-President, Paulo Muwanga, who had succeeded in making himself an indispensable power-broker.

Muwanga swiftly put together a cabinet comprised of the four parties, and in the meantime the army set up what it called a Military Council, with Tito Okello as its chairman and Head of State, and one

Captain Toko – formerly chief of the air force under the army of Idi Amin – as vice-chairman. Toko had been sacked by Amin from the army and Amin had sent him out of the country to become director-general of the East African Airways. Later he was appointed chairman of the Uganda Airlines. He was generally respected, but it is clear that he was appointed in an attempt to woo the former Amin army into the UNLA and redress the situation in West Nile where the UNLA had committed genocide against the population during Obote's second regime as revenge for having supported the Amin regime.

This move clearly indicated a strategy: the creation by the Tito-Bazilio UNLA of an alliance with the former army under Idi Amin, in order to strengthen itself against the guerrillas of the NRA in case they became stubborn and refused to co-operate, particularly as the UNLA did not wish to share power with the NRA on an equal basis. Very soon the former Chief of Staff of the Amin army, Brigadier Lumago – who had been exiled in the southern Sudan and Zaïre – appeared in Kampala with some of his army officers. He held a press conference with the support of Bazilio Okello, the man who actually staged the coup and who had now become the Chief of Defence Staff. Lumago demanded the return of all exiles, 'including Idi Amin'! Soon companies of the former army of Amin poured in from the north-west under the command of General Onzi; Onzi called himself the Leader of the Uganda National Rescue Front (UNRF), a force that had been fighting in the north-west against the UNLA. They were incorporated into the army and given ranks.

In the meantime the NRA demanded a share of power with the UNLA on the basis of parity. This was not outrightly rejected, but efforts were made to stall while appointments to the cabinet continued to be made. Furthermore, the new regime made contact with other armed groups that had not been very active and entered into 'talks' with them, and 'agreement' was soon reached with them. Soon they were also being used to denounce the other resistance group, the NRA.

The NRA's position also began to harden. It now insisted that the UNLA had committed crimes in the past and that they were the main cause of instability in Uganda. It also condemned the return to the army of former Amin soldiers, and played on it in a populist way. Their statements sounded hollow in many quarters; while they were prepared to share power with the murderous army of Milton Obote they were not prepared to do so with the equally murderous Amin army. In this connection it was observed in some quarters that Museveni himself had signed a co-operation agreement in Tripoli with the former leader of the UNRF, Moses Ali, who was formerly in the Amin army. So the issues began to become confused.

Tanzania's reaction at first to the events in Uganda was to support Paulo Muwanga in forming a government. Nyerere had begun to entertain this possibility even before Obote was overthrown. In fact it was reported that while in Scandinavia on his visit in May 1985, he met Museveni and tried to work out this kind of alliance with Muwanga. Indeed Museveni's first reaction to Muwanga after the coup was positive, saying Muwanga had worked for 'unity' during the Obote regime. This clearly referred to Muwanga's role in linking them up to the UNLA to co-operate in toppling Obote.

But soon after Muwanga's appointment as Prime Minister there was an outcry against him from different organizations. He was accused of having rigged the elections in order to bring Obote to power. He could not be trusted to organize another election that would be fair and free in the 12 months promised by the new junta. At this point the NRA also began to object to Muwanga, although it had not done so on his appointment. But, embarrassed by the reaction, the junta now decided to terminate Muwanga's appointment 'with immediate effect'. At this point the NRA pointed out that the removal of Muwanga was not of any significance because it was not their major demand. They demanded not only a fifty–fifty share in the Military Council, but also to be consulted on all appointments so far made. When talks opened in Nairobi, it was therefore clear that no agreement was possible between the militarists on both sides.

Indeed the holding of the Nairobi 'peace talks' was a way of avoiding the holding of a Round Table Conference (RTC), which had been demanded by almost all the organizations, both internal and external. This demand was symbolized in the consistent position that the Cardinal of the Catholic Church in Uganda had taken during the entire second period of Obote's rule. He had demanded such a conference in a neutral country attended by all parties and groups, including those fighting the regime. The NRA had given lukewarm support to such a conference, and throughout the four years it never spelt out a position on the issue. When Obote fell, it mentioned the idea only peripherally. Its main concern was first to settle 'security' matters with the junta before it could entertain the idea of an RTC. This naturally weakened the democratic demand for such a conference. The NRA now concentrated on the military issue of sharing power with the junta of the same army it had been fighting, to the exclusion of other democratic forces. It did not occur to its leaders – or, if it did, they brushed it aside – that the sharing of such power between the two armies undermined the very rationale for an RTC.

The other political parties and groups that were in the meantime incorporated into the junta and its cabinet also now kept quiet on the issue of the conference. Indeed the Democratic Party – which was the main *political* force behind the junta – now stated that if such a conference was to be held it should be held *'inside* Uganda'. This in turn weakened the Cardinal's demand. Very soon the DP leader became part of the junta's delegation to hold 'peace' talks with the NRA *outside* Uganda! Opportunism and philistinism had over-powered most 'democratic' leaders in the country. This of course not only strengthened the junta in avoiding the RTC, but also strength-ened the NRA in its own militarist demands for a two-sided conference between the UNLA and the NRA as the 'main fighting forces'.

With these developments it became clear that the issue in the country was not how democracy would be restored to the people of Uganda, but *which* one of the militarist groups would become hegemonic and be in a position to impose its own rule on Ugandans. The political leaders were being incorporated one by one on the side of one of the militarist groups vying for power. The situation had moved so fast that even the Cardinal was being co-opted onto the side of the junta's delegation at the Nairobi talks. His proposal for an RTC was receding in the background in the meantime.

While these manoeuvres were going on, the two sides to the conflict were busy preparing the country for another round of civil war. The UNLA continued its routine activity of looting, murdering and raping in the country. Indeed, they spent the first three days of their 'liberation' looting the whole of Kampala. The other army, the NRA, was also, while talking peace, busy moving into military barracks and looting weapons from them, clearly to strengthen itself for another civil war. The NRA crowned this activity by carrying out the biggest bank robbery in the country's history at Kabale, south-western Uganda, where it raided a Bank of Uganda branch and robbed some 4,000,000,000 shillings, equivalent to US$ 700,000. The NRA leader explained on the BBC that this was not robbery but 'confiscation of property in the hands of the regime to feed our people'. It did not occur to them that they were robbing the savings of the very 'people' they were 'fighting' to 'liberate'!

It was in this atmosphere that the first outbreak of fighting took place on 12 September between the UNLA and the NRA in which the NRA suffered for the first time a major defeat at Mbarara with the bulk of their men on the mission being wiped out, incidentally by the UNRF units which came in from Sudan and West Nile. With their test of blood, it was clear this would raise the morale of these troops to pursue NRA fighters, thus moving the conflict into a full-blown civil war that could transform Uganda into a country of warlords ruling along ethnic and regionalist lines. The country was definitely drifting in this direction because the militarists would not give the people a final say in their affairs.

THE CRISIS OF DEVELOPMENT IN UGANDA

It is clear that Uganda's economic and social development has been seriously affected by the prevalance of dictatorships in the country. In earlier years Uganda had been looked upon as one of the most vigorous economies based on peasant production. It had a well-developed intellectual force in the civil service; and a middle class was beginning to emerge on the land and in the commercial sector, although still dominated by the Asian middle class, which was servicing the British monopolies. In fact this picture obscured the fact that this whole structure was erected upon the super-exploitation of the peasant producer and the worker who had emerged with the colonial economy. This super-exploitation had enabled the British colonial state to dispense with British grants-in-aid as far back as 1915.

The neo-colonial state inherited the tax structure as well as continuing the colonial economy. Export taxes continued to rise over time as the state's expenditure continued to rise, with the result that by 1977 – at the height of Amin's dictatorship – the state was taking as much as 70 per cent of the peasants' earnings in the world market as compared with 18 per cent imposed by the colonial state.

It should be observed that as the economic crisis heightened in the world market – expressed in declining terms of trade and stabilization programmes of the IMF – so also the political crisis was heightened, requiring the neocolonial state to revert to openly dictatorial and brutal methods of ruling the people. The defence budgets increased so much that it could be said that peasant and worker exploitation was the other side of the coin of dictatorship. This had become so sharp that by the time of Obote's fall the peasant was being paid only 15 per cent of every US\$ he earned on the world market for his coffee, with the state taking 85 per cent. In these circumstances, the crisis in the country was a crisis of the neocolonial plunder of Uganda's resources, and dictatorship was a result of it and not the cause.

This final result was achieved through the IMF-imposed policies that the Obote regime was bound to accept, faced as it was with the revolt in the country. While this was praised as helping Uganda to implement its own 'Recovery Programme', in fact the stabilization measures imposed by the IMF contributed to the increased exploitation not only of the peasant and worker, but also of the middle class, which was increasingly wiped out. The harshness of these neo-colonial policies was indeed the expression of the crisis of development in the country, and indeed of the crisis of the entire political system.

Such crisis can only be overcome if the people unite to oppose the newly created dictatorship. This can be done on the basis of a general programme of the people to oppose the neocolonial exploitation and plunder of their resources and labour. It also means continuing to oppose militarist manoeuvres to impose a civil war in the country and to insist on peace. Already the masses have formed a movement for peace. Also businessmen and university lecturers have formed another movement called the Uganda Peace Movement. The people are tired of being preyed upon by warring factions of militarists, each claiming to be fighting to 'liberate' the people. The people want peace so that they can attend to their social and economic needs in a peaceful atmosphere and strengthen their democratic organizations to struggle for their economic and social rights.

EPILOGUE

The analysis above is borne out by recent events in Uganda. The Nairobi 'Peace Talks' produced a 'Peace Agreement' in Nairobi on 17 December 1985 but, as predicted, none of the parties had in fact any intention of implementing it. What had happened was that these talks were used by each side to consolidate itself in order to defeat the other side. As indeed happened this was the result. The NRA resumed its military push and the government of the Okellos fell on 26 January 1986, almost six months to the day after their military takeover.

Several months after the fall of the Military Council, the new government in Kampala is still trying to bring the situation to a consolidation. The four parties that had been part of the Okello military government also joined the NRM military government in what was said to be a 'broadly based freedom fighters' government'.

But it is clear that the government is not united in any way since the aim of the NRM is to consolidate itself under the powers it has gained through the military control of the country. It is quite clear that the other parties in the government are pursuing a 'wait and see' strategy while they work underground to strengthen themselves, taking advantage of every mistake the NRM is making.

In their own efforts to consolidate their dictatorship the NRM started by imposing restrictions on the other political parties, including the right to issue press statements and to hold political rallies. This muzzling of the press has already created divisions within the government. The DP is known to be pressing for an early election and a return to a multi-party arrangement. The UPC is already involved in arming its supporters to destabilize the new government and the new government has indeed declared that Obote is planning a come-back through an organization called FOBA (Force Obote Back Again). It has started to arrest large numbers of UPC supporters, particularly in the Busoga areas. The former Kabaka Yekka forces are also known to be reorganizing and are demanding that Ronnie Mutebi should be made the Kabaka of Buganda. This is known to have support within the NRA itself.

On the military side, the NRM has tried to consolidate its army, and there is no talk any more of recruiting and training a 'national army'. The UFM has gone along with this arrangement if only to get its soldiers recruited within the NRA, hoping to make a point of their advantage later on. The defeated remnants of the UNLA have also been recruited within the NRA and many are seen also as 'liberators', along with the NRA soldiers. The FEDEMU have, however, refused to join the NRA and are arguing that they will remain an independent force until the whole issue of the national army is resolved. They still carry their weapons. In the north-east of the country, the security situation is still unclear, as many people remain under arms. And this is made worse by the activities of the UNRF and the elements of the UNLA who are still moving freely in the West Nile and Acholi areas.

All this goes to show that the political conflict in the country is not resolved. The so-called 'broadly based government' is in fact another cover for a new military dictatorship. The avoidance of a Round Table Conference by the NRM – just like the other regimes did – is creating a situation of no return, so that although the parties in the government claim to be working together, yet it is clear to all of them that a conflict is inevitable. The defeat of the UNLA – although welcome in parts of the north – is nevertheless a political issue that could develop into an ethnic one. Many weapons distributed by Basilio Okello to his supporters in Acholi still remain unaccounted for.

In these circumstances, it becomes clear that the only way to avoid another conflict in the country is to create an atmosphere of dialogue between the various political forces on the essential issues of how to maintain the unity and integrity of the country. This must be supplemented by genuine talks and dialogue by all the democratic organizations about crucial issues affecting the future of the country. These are: the interim government, the creation of a truly national army, the constitution punishing those guilty of crime, the setting up of electoral machinery, fundamental freedoms, political parties, etc. Unless this is done conflict is inevitable.

TWENTY ONE
Museveni's Uganda: notes towards an analysis

Michael Twaddle

Just before you reach Entebbe and turn off for the international airport, there is an armed post at which travellers' bags and papers are scrutinized. It is an obvious place for an armed post, astride a narrow isthmus of land between two arms of Lake Victoria and commanding the entry to Entebbe town. In 1981 my baggage and passport had been checked at this place by troops supporting Milton Obote's second presidency. Now, in September 1986, my baggage was being checked by one of Yoweri Museveni's boy-soldiers with all the seasoned obsessiveness of the warrior minus-eleven-plus.[1] Even more startling than the youthfulness of this soldier, however, was the story I heard from the driver of the vehicle in which I had travelled from Entebbe airport, while waiting to be checked at Katabi. For overlooking this particular roadblock on the Entebbe–Kampala road, on the top of a ridge of banana plantations to the side, was a blockhouse and several other buildings from which various other NRA soldiers were emerging and walking towards us.

'A barracks?', I asked the driver.

'Yes, and down there was a prison in which I nearly died'. He pointed to a small building with just one large room into which, he claimed, he had been herded along with 180 others. Space in this small building had been so limited, and the other prisoners so numerous, that it had been quite impossible for him to stand upright during the daytime or to lie out flat upon the floor in order to sleep at night. Only the death a few days after his detention in that terrible place of Oyite-Ojok, Milton Obote's military commander, had saved his life in his view, along with protests by the Roman Catholic Cardinal and a certain American diplomat.

Why had he been detained in that terrible place?

Because as a young Muganda he had been suspected of being a guerrilla, and Oyite-Ojok had ordered that nobody suspected of guerrilla activity should be released until positively cleared of all suspicion.

Had he been a guerrilla fighting against Obote?

Not to start with, but being rounded up and detained in such conditions without reason immediately made him into one; and thereafter he fought as a guerrilla with the National Resistance Army of Yoweri Museveni against Obote. At that time, the driver continued, 'everybody in Buganda turned against Obote' because Obote's people 'were killing us everywhere'. By comparison, NRA soldiers 'were disciplined'.

Some NRA soldiers appeared to be remarkably young, I commented.

'They are far better than previous regimes' troops', the driver replied.

Subsequently it became clear that many other people around Entebbe and Kampala had had similar experiences during the period of Milton Obote's second presidency. Within the notorious Luwero triangle of territory immediately north-west of Kampala the *New Vision* newspaper reported in September 1986 that 'hundreds of thousands' had died under Obote's most recent regime, and local smallholders were setting up memorials to dead relatives so that the sheer extent of the slaughter there should not be forgotten. These, the newspaper reported, 'often take the form of skulls mounted on poles or laid out on tables'.[2] I did not myself visit the Luwero triangle, but there is description enough of the devastation visited upon the area during Obote's second regime in Uganda in other accounts for at least some idea of their horrors to be appreciated.[3] A Swedish aid official who did visit the Luwero triangle during my visit to Uganda in later 1986 told me that, in the section of it which he visited, the local Church of Uganda pastor had reported that out of an earlier population of approaching 6000 families only 500 now had survivors living there. Obote's soldiers had looted widely, even removing window frames and roofing materials; previously cultivated land had mostly reverted to bush, and it was exceedingly difficult for an outsider to detect where roads had run formerly. Amidst such devastation, it was difficult to know where to begin in the task of rehabilitation. But, clearly, those memorial tables and poles, with human skulls mounted upon them, indicated that 'rehabilitation' was now being viewed at least in the Luwero triangle as a moral matter as well as a material concern. So, too, was it in other parts of Uganda in September 1986. There, too, it was widely felt that in future all soldiers' behaviour should be closely controlled, in order to prevent such outrages against humanity ever recurring.

Indeed, by now it was clear that there were definite strains of moral utopianism politically at work in Uganda. A sense of moral outrage and hope was embedded in many statements published in the newspapers. It was widely expressed in private conversation. It was also deeply embedded in plans for future political, economic and social change issued by the Democratic Party and monarchist groups in Buganda, and lay at the very heart of the Museveni government's own plans for national reconstruction. Here, indeed, seemed one of the most attractive aspects of Uganda to the visitor: concern that atrocities which had occurred under both the Amin and second Obote governments, and then recurred unter the short-lived military administration of the Okellos during the second half of 1985, should not continue. Also immensely attractive was the concern that in future pressure should be brought to bear continually upon the National Resistance Army to ensure that it too behaved itself properly and did not become like the Uganda National Liberation Army, which had initially liberated Ugandans from Idi Amin in 1978–9 to widespread applause, but within a few months had deteriorated into a mafia of marauding gangs looting and killing the wider population.

But how was all this to be achieved? Utopia, by definition, is nowhere on earth. Moral outrage is also a poor long-term substitute for analysis of actual causes and effects, however important it may be in implementing whatever action is decided upon in the short term. Economically, the condition of the country seemed even more devastated than five years before, and its smallholder farmers every bit as 'uncaptured' as Goran Hyden's peasants in Tanzania (Hyden, 1980). Inflation, too, the driver of the vehicle from Entebbe airport remarked, was worse than ever. Yet he did not seem overly concerned. Museveni's government had many more educated people as ministers than immediately preceding governments, and 'the professors' in it would rescue the country from disaster.

Will they? Here the basic document for the foreign analyst as well as for Ugandans themselves to ponder is clearly the '10-point programme of the NRM'. This was born in the course of the war against Obote's second government and reissued several times during 1986. It is a document which expresses moral outrage, analysis of the causes of Uganda's discontents since independence, and utopian aspiration, in roughly equal proportions. Together, these form a heady programmatic cocktail.

The first 'point' in the cocktail concerns democracy; or rather the democracy for which NRA guerrillas fought so tenaciously from initially a very weak base for five years. This democracy is distinguished in the document from the kind practised by successive post-independence governments in Uganda, before as well as after the tyrannical years of Idi Amin. That sort of democracy was marred by 'sectarianism, a repressive style in dealing with the masses and a conspiratorial approach in dealing with political colleagues and opponents' (p. 2). The essence of true democracy lies in three other things. First, there is parliamentary democracy based upon regular, 'clean' elections; democracy which is 'free of corruption and manipulation of the population'. Secondly, there is the democracy of the grassroots, of the sort that NRA guerrillas themselves established in the Luwero triangle and other areas of core support during their war against Obote's second government. Thirdly, there is economic democracy; 'a reasonable standard of living for all the people of Uganda' (p. 6). From the language of the '10-point programme' itself, as well as from the first actions of Yoweri Museveni's government upon coming to power in the centre of the country in January 1986, it is clear that, while all three kinds of democracy are highly desirable in Uganda, it is the second which the Museveni government is concerned to establish first. There are doubtless several reasons for this.

The guerrilla struggle against Milton Obote's second government was precipitated by the bitterly disputed manner in which that particular government came to power. This was through the general election of December 1980, which returned Obote's Uganda People's Congress (UPC) to power after both the eight-year tyranny of Idi Amin – which had overthrown Obote's first government in January 1971 – and the successive post-Amin governments of 1979–80 led by Yusufu Lule, Godfrey Binaisa, and Paulo Muwanga's military commission. The campaign preceding the December 1980 election was a very violent one. It was also one which may be described very accurately as having been characterized by 'sectarianism, a repressive style in dealing with the masses and a conspiratorial approach in dealing with political ... opponents', if not also 'colleagues', in the words of the 10-point programme's subsequent condemnation of Ugandan parliamentary politicking. This was especially the case as regards counting of votes. Obote's ally, Paulo Muwanga, was in charge of this and halted announcement of results at the very moment they appeared to be going in favour of the Democratic Party (DP) rather than the UPC; Muwanga's final announcement of a close UPC victory over the DP therefore had more than a hint of manipulation about it. That, at any rate, was the widespread reaction in non-UPC circles in Uganda to Muwanga's declaration that Obote was the victor in the December 1980 general election.[4]

Yoweri Museveni had led the smaller UPM (Uganda Patriotic Movement) in this election, but the UPM had only won one seat on Muwanga's recount; Museveni himself not even winning a seat. Early in 1981 both Museveni and Lule and their followers took to the bush to fight against Obote's return to power. By January 1986 their armed struggle had proved successful. Not only had their guerrilla activity helped to bring Obote's second government to an end in July 1985, but it led directly in January 1986 to Museveni becoming president of the country (Lule had died shortly before and Lule's successor, Samson Kisekka, became prime minister). Museveni's new government therefore replaced the short-lived military dictatorship of the two Generals Basileo and Tito Okello (both from Acholiland). This took over control of Uganda from Obote in July 1985.

One problem facing Museveni's government in January 1986 was what to do with national political parties like the DP. Arguably, the Democratic Party had been even more a casualty of the controversial general election of December 1980 than Museveni's UPM, because it had enjoyed greater popular backing throughout Uganda at the time. It still retained widespread support, if not now by any means universal backing, because of its leaders' active collaboration with the Okellos' dictatorship. What was to be done with the DP, let alone the UPC? By September 1986, the Museveni government's answer had been threefold. One part of it had been to offer DP leaders comparable cabinet positions to their earlier offices under the Okellos. Another was to delay fresh national parliamentary elections for four years. Yet another was, as already indicated, to build up democracy at the grassroots through local resistance committees throughout Uganda.

This last policy was not merely Machiavellian in intent. The '10-point programme of the NRM' makes clear (p. 6) that peoples' committees established 'at the village, muluka, gombolola, saza and district level' were to perform a multiplicity of separate functions. Their members could

> deal with law-breakers in co-operation with the chiefs and police, take part in discussing local development projects with government officials ... above all be political forums to discuss relevant issues concerning the whole of the country and act as forums against the corruption and misuse of office by the chief government officials – medical and veterinary, market officers, headmasters, police men, soldiers etc. They would be channels of communication between the top and the bottom ... also take part in screening applicants to join the national army, police and prisons in order to avoid anti-social elements worming [sic] their way into these institutions as has been the case in the past.

'In fact', the 10-point programme continues,

> we had already implemented this system before the enemy –

Obote – disrupted the life of the population in the liberated zones.
We had committees at the village, muluka, and zone (several
gombololas) levels in the following gombololas: Makulabita,
Semuto, Kapeeka, Nakaseke, Kikamulo, Ngoma, Kikandwa,
Bukomero, Kiboga, Bukwiri, Kasanda, Busunju, Sekanyonyi,
Kakiri, Masuliita, Gombe, Wakiso, Nyimbwa, Migyera, Kalungi,
Wampiti, Wabusana, Kirobwe, and Wabinyonyi. Through these
committees the people could criticise anything they disapproved of
e.g. NRA soldiers misbehaving...

In other words, the resistance committees that Yoweri Museveni's
government attempted to establish throughout Uganda in 1986
were modelled upon ones developed during the guerrilla war
against Obote's second government in areas like the Luwero
triangle. Initially, they had been an important part of the wider
Maoist strategy of building up popular support for the anti-Obote
cause amongst the small farmers of southern and western Uganda,
amongst whom of necessity guerrilla fighters would have to 'swim' if
they were to prove successful. But, as the guerrilla struggle itself
developed, NRA activities also clearly became increasingly enam-
oured of local resistance committes as *democratic* institutions. Here
their utility was clearly considerable in countering what the 10-point
programme characterizes as a 'local elite, pandering to the various
schemes of the unprincipled factions of the national elite, ...
manipulating the population on behalf of the latter with bribes,
misinformation ... ignorance'. Moreover, the utility of local resistance committees in this respect was not complicated by ideological
differences which, within the NRM/NRA coalition at national level,
were potentially politically lethal.

For, in origin, Museveni's government was not one movement but
several. At the time of its takeover of the Kampala–Entebbe region
at the beginning of 1986, its behaviour was openly opportunistic in
incorporating both at cabinet level and in its armed forces a number
of smaller guerrilla groupings as well as the larger and older
Democratic Party. But, before its seizure of the central area of the
country, the NRA itself had been divided into two separate
movements fighting against Obote – three even, if one also counts
the Uganda National Rescue Front (UNRF) made up of ex-Amin
soldiers from the West Nile area of northern Uganda, with which
both Museveni's followers and Lule's guerrillas were aligned at one
stage of the armed struggle against Obote's second government.

Yusufu Lule had been president of Uganda immediately after
Amin's overthrow in 1979. Museveni had been important too in
removing Amin from power, a prominent figure in the Uganda
National Liberation Front, and leader of one of the smaller parties

contesting the notorious general election of December 1980. During the ensuing bush war against Obote, the national Resistance Army (NRA) was established as an alliance between fighters from Museveni's UPM on the one hand, and associates of Yusufu Lule – many of whom had doubtless voted for the DP in the 1980 election – on the other. Geographically, many of Museveni's guerrillas came from Western Uganda; Lule's associates were overwhelmingly from Buganda. Ideologically, too, there were differences between these two sets of anti-Obote activists. These differences seem clear from public pronouncements made by NRM leaders during their first year of power. For, while NRA/NRM activists such as Commander Katirima might stress the necessity for socialist reconstruction and the need for continual vigilance against an 'imperialism' which appeared to be just another name for international capitalism,[5] other prominent figures within the ruling coalition were saying rather different things. Samson Kisekka, the new prime minister, for example delivered speeches stressing the importance of 'self-reliance' in terms more familiar to students of that *other* political tendency in post-colonial black Africa, the rise of the post-independence national bourgeoisie.[6]

In mimeographed notes prepared for use at the NRM School of Political Education at Wakiso in late 1986, these internal ideological differences are rather glossed over. The 'allies' of the new regime are identified as being not only 'The peasants who currently constitute more than 90 per cent of our total population ... oppressed in that they are poor, ignorant and diseased', but also 'The middle class (small richmen): – These are also allies' *and* the 'National capitalists and all potential capitalists ... since they need to be saved from foreign domination'.[7] In the '10-point programme of the NRM', no separate internal groupings within the National Resistance Movement are alluded to. Instead the importance of 'an independent integrated, self-sustaining national economy' is stressed, in which 'the aspirations of ... many groups' would be accommodated as the tenth 'point'. Also advocated here is 'an economic strategy of mixed economy which means allowing the majority of economic activities to be carried out by private entrepreneurs'. Only certain 'crucial sectors' are to be handled directly by the state. These are 'import-export licensing ... commercial banking ... the Central Bank [and] ... certain basic industries like iron and steel as well as the construction of the physical infrastructure (education, health etc)'. The resultant mixed economy is explicitly defended as being one designed to 'combine the best of both worlds', capitalist as well as socialist.[8]

The 10-point programme also implicitly unites Ugandan peasants and capitalists in common defence against international financial institutions such as the International Monetary Fund. The IMF, in fact, is openly condemned at the very beginning of the programme because of its support for economic policies implemented during Obote's second period of power in Uganda: 'None of the concoctions of people like Obote can work in spite of the 'advice' from the top-brass of the IMF' (p. 2). This opposition to IMF advice is morally understandable, in the circumstances of the bush war against Obote during the early 1980s. Technically certain aspects of IMF advice proffered to the second Obote government also seem, in retrospect, to be open to criticism, as will be suggested later. But totally to repudiate all IMF assistance in the rehabilitation of the Ugandan economy will surely be difficult. Nonetheless, before any further remarks are made about IMF/World Bank structural adjustment policies – and their relevance to Museveni's Uganda as well as Obote's second government – we must first review briefly the 10-point programme's other 'points'.

The second point stresses security. 'Obote and Amin must have by now killed over 800,000 Ugandans between them over the past 22 years of so called independence', the programme here asserts, indicating amongst other things its date of composition during the bush war. Nonetheless:

> As soon as NRM takes government, not only will the state inspired violence disappear, but so will even criminal violence. Given democracy at the local level, a politicized army and police and absence of corruption at the top as well as interaction with the people, even criminal violence can disappear. Thereby, security of persons will be restored and so will security of legitimately earned property (p. 8).

Though armed crime can by no means be said to have disappeared yet from the country, by general agreement Museveni's Uganda has seen a dramatic improvement in security. This is certainly the case for occupants of the southern and western parts of the country, which all suffered grievously in this respect under the earlier governments of both Milton Obote and Idi Amin. But, concerning northern Uganda, the situation is less clear. Some early omens read encouragingly,[9] others less so.[10]

This brings us to the 10-point programme's third point: the need for national unity and the 'elimination of all forms of sectarianism'.

> The politics of Uganda at independence was unabashedly sectarian: DP mainly for catholics, UPC mainly for protestants

outside Buganda and KY [the Kabaka Yekka or 'king alone' movement] for protestants in Buganda. In the army there were opportunistic factions and manipulations of the day: Bantu versus Nilotics in 1966 (where the Bantu included the Itesot[s] who do not speak a Bantu language and where the Nilotics included the West Nilers most of whom do not speak Nilotic languages). In 1970, the West Nilers versus Acholis and Langi; then as Amin's rule progressed, moslems versus christians; after the downfall of Amin, the reintroduction of the DP and UPC, having undergone some fresh permutations of sectarianism; and Obote, following the elections, trying to erect a new alliance of Acholis, Langis and Itesot[s] against the 'enemies' – principally Baganda and Banyankole (pp. 8–9).

As a fighting document developed during armed struggle, the NRM programme here seems more concerned to attack such 'sectarianism' than to suggest any positive antidote to it other than the desirability of unsectarian behaviour. However, the NRA policy of releasing – rather than killing – captured Acholi and Langi soldiers during the bush war is quoted as an example of unsectarian behaviour. 'Going back to their colleagues after treatment (for the wounded), the prisoners of war we released have caused pandemonium in Obote's army' (p. 10). The implication is that this may be taken as a model for future NRA behaviour too.

The fourth point stresses the importance of defending national independence against attack by outsiders. Here Museveni's own experience of office in the quick succession of post-Amin UNLF governments is briefly alluded to in a further moral condemnation of political corruption at that time:

> We were also proposing to deal with Canada for the purchase of buffalo transports for the army, with Britain for the purchase of military radio communication sets and with Italy for the Agusta Bell helicopters. They all seemed ready to do business on mutually favourable terms. In fact they looked to be flabbergasted by the corruption of those good-for-nothing traitors who made deals unfavourable to their country in exchange for money put on personal secret accounts in Switzerland ... Our conclusion was that, provided the national leadership is clear in its own mind, budgets its resources frugally, identifies the fulcrum-like points in the economy and evolves overall politics that are in consonance with the actual dynamics of the situation ... Uganda with its good soil and climate, dynamic people with a tradition of relative civilisation can easly overcome its difficulties and deal with countries of divergent social systems (p. 13).

These remarks are straightforward enough, but they by no means unequivocally support the document's earlier attack upon international capitalism in general and the IMF in particular. Instead a certain flexibility regarding economic policy in future enters the 10-point programme at this stage.

The fifth point in it underlines the need for 'an independent, integrated and self-sustaining national economy'. Here Museveni's years as a liberal arts student at the University of Dar es Salaam ten to fifteen years before are probably built upon in elaborating plans to reverse what he characterizes as 'the 'development of the underdevelopment' to use one scholar's words' (p. 14). To reverse dependence and 'parasitism', agriculture needs to be diversified away from 'the present narrow confines of just producing requirements for external markets', encourage import-substitution industries, develop agroindustrial plants as well as heavy industries 'where feasible'. The 10-point programme here further develops the argument that 'sectarianism' is the product of too many aspirants seeking too few jobs in an excessively 'narrow economy'. And here we are provided with some revealing asides on 'sectarianism' too.

For example, in Ankole district during the period of British protectorate rule, the document remarks that there were here only 55 sub-county chiefships, 10 county chiefships, and the offices of chief minister, treasurer, head of civil service and chief magistrate, in a population of just over half a million. These were the only high-level jobs for which local people were qualified to compete:

> This accounted for much of the sectarianism in the politics of Ankole as the various factions of the elite tried to use the population as bases in their unprincipled struggle for jobs ... Proof that the whole struggle was for jobs is ... that when the Bairu-Protestant clique took power in 1963, it soon split up again between the *Nkomba* and the *Mufunguro* factions. Another good example is that the Bahima chiefs, though in power from 1900 to 1946 did absolutely nothing for the Bahima population ... forced by the adverse economic situation created by the colonial situation (tsetse flies, unplanned cultivation), lack of education and their own ignorance (and consequence arrogance) to disperse from their home-land to many other parts of Uganda (p. 20).

In Buganda, on the other hand, Protestant chiefs monopolized power throughout the Britsh period. Eventually 'Catholic elite elements' there fought for justice – a clear reference to the founding of the DP. But it was only justice for themselves, not the ordinary people. 'If you talk of 'justice' for the masses, the DP leaders accuse you of communism'. The solution? 'If the economy, however, was expansive, interest in state office would somewhat decline' (p. 20).

But before this can be done – and this is the programme's sixth point – social services require rehabilitaion, particularly in war-ravaged areas. 'As far as the overwhelming majority of the people are concerned, there is no clean water, hygienic housing, literacy, adequate level of calorie or protein intake, doctors available to treat people etc. etc.' (p. 21). There is also ' the abysmal ignorance of the people' – most obvious in attitudes towards disease and misfortune encountered in areas like the Luwero triangle during the bush war, but also evident in a whole range of other activities. These range from brick-making ('requires a lot of labour which ... could be easily solved through mobilising communal labour') to literacy-teaching ('there are enough form 6, form 4, and primary 7 leavers to wipe out illiteracy in Uganda'), all of which require attention.

The seventh point emphasizes the need to end 'corruption – particularly bribery and misuse of office to serve personal interests ... once and for all' (p. 23).

The eigth concerns 'Redressing errors' adversely affecting particular groups of Ugandans, three especially:

(a) people that have been displaced from their lands by illegal land-grabbers or erroneously conceived development projects; (b) the long suffering Karamojong people; (c) the salaried people that have been impoverished by the inflation of the 70s and 80s.

Concerning the first category, 'An outstanding example are the 15,000 people with tens of thousands of cattle that have been thrown out of Nshaara by the [second] UPC regime in order to make the area a game reserve' – and there were victims from similar gazettings of new game areas in many other areas. The Karamojong required more watering holes ('International aid agencies could help in this respect', p. 24). And as for salary earners, 'The real solution for inflation is production in order to create abundance and lower prices. Salary rises can, however, assist in the short term' (p. 24).

Ninthly, 'Co-operation with other African countries in defending human and democratic rights of our brothers in other parts of Africa' is stressed (pp. 25–8).

Thus far the '10-point programme of the NRM' has been treated with far greater seriousness than the '18 points', which Idi Amin issued upon his toppling of Obote's first government, would command from any observer of the country's politics nowadays. This is done advisedly. It is not done because the NRM's accession to power in January 1986 can really be viewed as representing 'a change of government under armed popular pressure ... never before achieved in Africa', in comparison with which Amin's seizure of power appears to have been just another African army coup (Brittain, 1986, p. 51). On the contrary, the toppling of Obote by

Amin in 1971 was also an event greeted with much initial euphoria, at least in southern Uganda – and we misunderstand the NRM if we ignore its essential nature as *an army* – albeit a highly disciplined and puritanical one compared with Amin's troops' fatally fragmented structure of command and sense of morale.[11] No, the main reason for treating the '10-point programme of the NRM' more seriously than Amin's '18 points' is basically threefold. It was much longer in the making during the bush war against Obote's second government as a guide for future action. It is revealing as an indication of both Museveni's own thinking and that of his most immediate reference group, the left-leaning Bahima intelligentsia of post-independence Uganda; indeed, several of the published versions of it are copyrighted in Museveni's own name. And, thirdly, it is a document to which each member of Museveni's government has been required to swear allegiance. It is therefore an important political document in its own right.

How has it fared as a guide to action since the NRM's seizure of power in January 1986?

The Democratic Party issued a 15-page commentary on it after Museveni's government was sworn in. In this the DP formally welcomed 'the change that took place on 25.1.86', but criticized the NRM's suspension of party political activity. The charge of sectarianism, the DP rejected utterly. 'In the 1980 general elections, in spite of massive rigging and the disenfranchment of northern Uganda, DP still emerged as the only party with divergent tribal and religious representation in parliament' (para 29) – an obvious reference to Museveni's UPM, just as the next para (30) was a clear attack upon current NRM policy – 'DP is totally opposed to any design aiming at dividing ... either on tribal or religious or political or any other sectarian grounds'. 'The main problem in Uganda,' the DP asserted, 'and the principal cause of our suffering has been the denial of the democratic process and of respect of the democratic verdict to the people of this country (para 12)'.

It is only when people like those in West Nile cannot speak through their political parties that they will fall easy preys to the self-imposed leadership of warlords some of whom might even belong to former discredited regimes ... To speak for them will be self-styled leaders calling themselves Northern Consultative Group, or Fighting Groups, Bakaka ba Buganda etc. These groups emerge to fill the vacuum created by the suspension of political parties. Our view is that political parties are the most viable and democratically-minded groups with which the Government should work to solve seemingly intractable problems like the Kingdom issue, the West Nile issue, the accommodation in the mainstream of political life of groups like FUNA, UNRF, UFM, FEDEMU etc (para 36).

There should therefore be only a 2-year interval before a new general election would be held – not four, as the NRM was proposing.[12]

As the DP issued these comments during 1986, the Museveni government was hastening to instal local resistance committees in each additional area it conquered in eastern and northern Uganda. In structure these quickly came to resemble a pyramid. A myriad of resistance committees at village or *muluka* level provided delegates to ones at higher levels in an interlocking succession of indirect elections until, at direct level, the NRM's own administration was reached. Here district administrators now provided a link with the old provincial administration of earlier regimes. At national level, Museveni's cabinet ministers coexisted somewhat uneasily with leading army officers. Somewhat uneasily because NRA commanders were still frequently involved in military operations in northern Uganda and, whereas around Kampala life was more peaceful, they were concerned to keep NRA soldiers under much tighter discipline than earlier post-independence regimes' troops. This led them on occasion to dispense summary justice and to take other actions which completely bypassed cabinet ministers. An interim legislature was also introduced during 1986, known as the National Resistance Council (NRC). But this seems to have met only intermittently, because most of the NRM representatives on it from amongst the original 26-odd NRA fighters who started the bush war against Obote's second government, were themselves still fighting for the new government on the northern border.

Therein, indeed, lay the new government's most serious problem. By the close of 1986 armed opposition in Karamoja seems largely to have been contained.[13] West Nile also seems to have been quietened for the moment by the incorporation of the former UNRF leader, Moses Ali, within the Museveni government at deputy minister level.[14] Armed opposition seemed really serious now only in Acholiland. But there the conflict did not appear to be just a military one. For, as the allegations of the Anglican Bishop Ogwal on the BBC African Service in February 1987 indicated,[15] there is a very real danger of atrocities being committed there comparable in scale to the earlier ones in Luwero under Obote's second government if the war in Acholiland is not brought to a speedy end. Clearly the basic danger here is that the still predominantly southern and Bantu-speaking soldiery of the NRA in this situation might well get out of hand. Other dangers also arise from any continuing war in

Acholiland. As long as trucks and petrol have to be diverted in substantial quantities to support military operations in the north, there is a severe economic price to be paid in transport facilities diverted from taking the country's coffee and cotton exports to railhead – exports needed urgently to improve governmental cash flow.

But in Buganda, in September 1986 and into 1987, there have been additional threats to the character of the new order. These have been posed by the political energies and ambitions that have been released as a result of the overthrow of the second Obote government and the succeeding Okellos' dictatorship. For in Buganda it is not only the Democratic Party that has been circulating alternative political plans to those of the '10-point programme of the NRM'. Baganda monarchists have also been busy at utopian and moralistic political work.

Indeed, in September 1986 a group of Baganda were actually brought to court in Kampala by the Museveni government accused of planning to overthrow it and to revive the kingdom of Buganda by force.[16] The Buganda kingdom had been dismantled during Obote's first presidency, but following the overthrow of the Okellos' government many Baganda started agitating widely for the revival of the Ganda monarchy. Some of this agitation took the form of letters in the newspapers simply demanding restoration of the *status quo ante* 1966, other kinds expressed themselves in political meetings of various kinds throughout the geographical area of the old kingdom – in which, of course, the principal government offices of the whole country also happen to be situated. It is still not clear whether or not the Kirimuttu conspiracy of September 1986 was especially serious, or whether the two Baganda members of Museveni's cabinet to whom Kirimuttu documents were copied even received any documents, let alone had anything to do with the alleged conspiracy. What is abundantly clear, however, is that the constitutional status of Buganda and its symbolic head, the last king or *Kabaka's* son and heir, Ronald Mutebi, remain thorny problems for the Museveni government to resolve.

The victory of the NRM in the bush war against first Obote's second government, and then against the immediately following Okellos' dictatorship, was clearly made possible in part by active and widespread Baganda support. It also created a certain ideological as well as ethnic imbalance in the inner circles of the resultant Museveni government: between the more conservative Baganda leaders on one side, as against generally more socialist members of the NRM from western Uganda on the other. This westerner/ Baganda alliance may have been crucial in ensuring military success against Obote, but its very success left unfinished business as regards Buganda. In September 1986 Buganda was clearly in ferment regarding its future, and the new government was being bombarded with memoranda on this subject on every front.

Basically, there were two kinds of memorandum presented. One simply requested that the kingdom be restored and its properties transferred back to the rightful heir, Ronald Mutebi, who happened to be revisiting Uganda at the time (he has since returned to Britain for further studies). This was a demand made both by individual letterwriters from places like Mukono or Mubende, and by the princes' clan of the former kingdom. It was a demand that, if actually acted upon, would have led directly, or later, to the coronation of Prince Mutebi as the restored king of Buganda, and to a possible re-run of the constitutional battle between Mutebi's father and Milton Obote during the 1960s, this time between Mutebi and Museveni. On the other hand, however, were the clan leaders of Buganda to whom Mutebi was principally 'head of the clans' or *Ssaabataka* and there were other petitions presented which treated him as this. This was a status that the Museveni government itself seemed happy to accept in September 1986, because Mutebi had supported the National Resistance Moverment during its five-year bush war against Obote's second government, and Mutebi behaved with extreme circumspection in accepting recognition only as *Ssaabataka* at this time. However, the Kirimuttu affair put one question-mark against the acceptability of Mutebi to the Museveni government even as *Ssaabataka* – all the supposed Kirimuttu conspirators were themselves apparently Baganda clan leaders, albeit very lowly ones. By the end of the year, too, the Museveni government's earlier willingness to accept Mutebi even as *Ssaabataka* appeared open to doubt in view of the relish with which *New Vision* newspaper reported the decayed condition of his palace at Bamunanika.[17]

It is easy for an outsider to underestimate the strength of feeling over this vital matter. Indeed, I myself grossly underrated it in September 1986. A staff-member from Makerere University happened to be standing beside me just below the southern end of Namirembe Cathedral in the centre of Kampala and, like me, looking southwards towards Lake Victoria. I remarked to this person on how beautiful the view was. It is a spectacular view, but my remark provoked the immediate response – which I *should* have anticipated, but did not – that this was a most unhappy sight which underlined the continuing misery of all true Baganda. It was not necessary for me to request any further explanation. We were both looking southwards, not only towards Lake Victoria but directly down upon what remained of the last Ganda king's palace. Mutebi's father had been driven away from that palace by Obote's military commander, Idi Amin, twenty years before, and since that time the palace had been devastated. Instinctively, as an academic observer of Uganda since independence, I had assumed that any Makerere lecturer would realize that tribal kings were things of the past. Clearly, I had been extremely misguided in assuming this.

One other thing also seems clear about the political action of ethnicity in Uganda today. Despite its evident distaste for ethnic coalition-building by earlier post-independence regimes in Uganda, the NRM is itself the product of an ethnic counter-coalition formed during the bush war against Obote's second government – between Baganda and non-Ganda (but still similarly Bantu-speaking) allies from the western areas of Uganda. In its current political practice, too, the opposition of the NRM to religiously based 'sectarianism' in earlier district as well as national politics in Uganda, also itself mirrors the very thing objected to. For its condemnations of earlier regimes' corrupt and divisive practices are drenched in a secularized puritanism which clearly owes as much to the NRM leaders' own education in Christian mission schools as to their further education in Marxism or 'underdevelopment theory' at various institutions of further education in East Africa and elsewhere. Both Obote's and Amin's ethnically allied mafias might be rightly accused by the NRM of earlier malpractice, political and otherwise. But the very purita-nism of the Museveni government's own attitudes towards modern manners and money in Uganda would appear to be based on the predominantly missionary character of most of its members' earlier education, as well as on a markedly restricted social base.

This is made clear by the '10-point programme of the NRM' itself, particularly what it says about Museveni's principal reference group, the Bahima intelligentsia. For clearly behind Museveni's alliance with this particular constituency lie a number of crucial interactions with social, economic and political developments in Ankole district at the end of the British colonial period and at the start of the post-independence era. The marginalization of the Bahima intelligentsia seems to have taken place as it did, at least in part, because the religious 'sectarianism' that became politically incarnate in the form of the Democratic Party at this time in Ankole district was of the Protestant as well as the Catholic variety: hence, incidentally, the all-embracing character of the anti-clericalism that characterizes so much NRM political rhetoric nowadays. For, as one of the quotations already made from the '10-point programme' indicates, it was political manipulation by 'the Bairu [that is, non-Bahima or non-cattle-keeping clans in Ankole district] – Protestant clique' that adversely affected the career opportunities of Bahima of Museveni's acquaintance there shortly after independence from Britain. 'Uncontrolled economic developments' and the gazetting of large areas of land as game parks under the second Obote government also further marginalized this Bahima intelligentsia, as the same document makes clear too. This naturally increased Bahima support for the NRM when it took to the bush to fight against those considered to be responsible for these developments. Nonetheless, it would be misleading to describe Yoweri Museveni as a conscious manipulator of ethnicity. It is rather that in the circumstances of Obote's second presidency it was impossible for a successful opposition movement to attract popular support in Uganda in any other way.

At any rate, the '10-point programme of the NRM' here does help to clear up one of the basic ethnic classificatory puzzles of Uganda during the earlier 1980s: why the principal ethnic divide of political importance in the country at that time appeared to be basically between Bantu-speaking southerners and non-Bantu-speaking northerners. It was not just that there was political manipulation of one of the basic linguistic divisions of Uganda from above, as it were, by a minister in the second Obote government such as Paulo Muwanga, interacting with these basic divisions or simply trying to make sense of them (Twaddle, 1983a, pp. 162–3). It was that there was also a much more complex set of interactions taking place, which involved political manipulation from below by Museveni's associates too. Or, rather, not so much political manipulation of Uganda's internal cultural and linguistic cleavages by these associates of Museveni, as the imposition upon these cleavages of their own mental map of them. And, as the '10-point programme of the NRM' makes clear, this mental map of the politicial and economic miseries of Obote's second presidency did not just develop out of a vacuum. Nor did it develop out of any one particular person's mind, or out of even twenty-six or twenty-seven persons' political ambitions. Rather it arose out of the social and economic frustrations of an already marginalized Bahima intelligentsia. For, during the earlier 1980s, this marginalized Bahima intelligentsia appears to have been rendered still more desperate regarding its future by changes imposed upon it by a national government which was unusually beholden to a whole host of international agencies ranging from the World Wildlife Fund to the International Monetary Fund.

In September 1986 there was a widespread feeling throughout elite circles in Uganda that Obote's espousal of IMF/World Bank policies in their entirety 'had not worked'. Most obviously, they had not worked in the sense of enabling Obote himself to remain in power. Indeed, in the short term the increased real prices paid to farmers, reduction of subsidies, floating of the Ugandan shilling and other policies of economic liberalization implemented by Obote on IMF/World Bank advice most probably increased rather than reduced social immiseration, especially in the urban areas, and this immiseration soon worked through into still wider popular resentment against his government in southern Uganda. Still wider popular resentment; because Obote's second government was already generally regarded as only having acquired office as a result of a gigantic fraud, namely, through the 'dishonest' general election of December 1980 (Twaddle, 1983a). Technically, too, there were problems with the implementation of IMF/World Bank-supported structural adjustment policies of the sort suggested by Ajit Singh for neighbouring Tanzania: 'with respect to the parallel market [i.e. black market] for foreign exchange, the primary determinant in this market is the desire of a section of the business community and other rich Tanzanians to repatriate some of their wealth abroad ... not by the underlying health of the economy or current account considerations' (Singh, 1986, p. 106). Singh also points out that, in the short term, the provision of transport for cash crops and inputs like fertilizers and water 'is likely to have a far greater quantitative effect on export crop production than any price incentive resulting from a devaluation' (ibid., p. 107). With reference to Obote's second presidency, all that requires altering is 'likely' to 'actually'.

Not that IMF/World Bank personnel themselves do not have alternative explanations for the failure of their adjustment policies to work in Uganda. As was clear from the comments of those of their personnel at the Roskilde conference – and as argued in Chapter 7 of this volume – the very large percentage increases in public sector workers' salaries implemented by the second Obote government in 1984 were considered to have substantially undermined the anti-inflationary effect of the other adjustment policies it implemented upon their advice. In addition, guerrilla warfare made efficient marketing of agricultural produce in the fertile south-western crescent of the country virtually impossible. In these circumstances, it was not considered surprising that IMF/World Bank policies proved unsuccessful under Obote's second government.

On the NRM side, not only were *all* policies aimed at economic liberalization during the earlier 1980s automatically suspect simply because the second Obote government was implementing them, but more radical activists like Comrade Asiimwe have since stated that all Western financial institutions are suspect on theoretical grounds as 'imperialistic'. Further caution in NRM circles has doubtless been induced by the example of Obote's overthrow shortly after he had started implementing IMF/World Bank policies: and the inevitable resulting fear lest policies only recently contributing to the over-throw of one Ugandan government might cause undue difficulty for another if adopted too speedily. However, this was not the most widely expressed reason in Uganda in September 1986 for objecting to any over-rapid readoption of IMF/World Bank-supported adjust-ment policies in the first year of the Museveni government. This was essentially moralistic rather than pragmatic in character. It was a sense that international financial institutions had contributed greatly to the corruption so visibly accompanying Obote's second government in Uganda and still persisting. *That* was what was most widely considered to have brought Obote finally down, and *that* was what was still very widely objected to.

Stories of corruption in the civil service provided a seemingly never-ending source of copy for *New Vision*, the principal NRM newspaper, in September 1986. Museveni's government itself also constantly stressed the need to punish civil servants who continue to err in this respect. But the thought that civil servants should be rewarded with reasonable salaries, in order to avoid the necessity for 'corruption' – simply in order to be able to purchase on the black market sufficient for themselves and their families to eat – was not accorded very much space in ministers' speeches or in the news-papers. Yet, as we have seen, there is a clear reference in the '10-point programme of the NRM' to the difficulties caused to all salaried workers by inflation during the period of Obote's second government. Clearly, inflation had not been finally curbed by that particular government, even with the benefit of structural adjust-ment. Prices of basic foods for all urban dwellers continued to spiral out of sight of civil servants' salaries to an even greater extent than under Idi Amin's regime, before as well as after the 1984 civil servants' pay increases. To be sure, increasing insecurity at this time hardly helped structural adjustment, but what was the *cause* of that insecurity? As Chango Machyo has pointed out, in eastern Uganda local people blamed 'a particular region' or 'individuals in positions of leadership' as the principal causes of their current discontents (Machyo, 1985, p. 45). But once Obote had been again overthrown, and the insecurity attending the immediately succeeding Okellos' regime had given way to the new NRM coalition, there was great stress in government pronouncements that civil servants who had played the black market in order to supplement salaries severely reduced by runaway inflation were moral reprobates. Punishment was what they deserved, and would get.

In fact, insofar as its economic difficulties are more than a result of the adverse international terms of trade affecting all third world countries, what is needed most of all in the economic sphere in Uganda is surely better control of inflation, and more efficient production of both food and export crops. But how are these things to be obtained? Surely not just by punishing erring civil servants. Not just by introducing a new currency either, if IMF/World Bank advice is substantially ignored as regards paying the small farmers of Uganda a realistic percentage of world prices for their cash crops and a realistic exchange rate is not adopted. Here, to be sure, there are difficult short-term problems for any new government fighting a protracted war in northern Uganda with an army it is concerned to control more effectively than its immediate post-independence predecessors. Soldiers need to be paid as well as civil servants, otherwise in the short term they can cause even more havoc. Soldiers also require uniforms and footwear, which also must be paid for. And if these *have* to be paid for because there is a war still persisting in northern Uganda, it is understandable why the Museveni government should have procrastinated over agreeing to a policy of devaluation with the international financial institutions. In the short term, keeping the Ugandan shilling artificially high *did* enable the Museveni government to acquire boots and capes and other equipment for NRA troops more cheaply than otherwise would have been the case. In the longer term, however, keeping exchange rates for the Ugandan shilling with foreign currencies at artificially high levels is surely suicidal as regards any effective counter-inflation policy.

Here three other points also need to be made. In September 1986 the feeling was widespread in Uganda that structural adjustment policies 'had not worked' additionally because, so it was widely said, the Ugandan commercial class behaved according to the rules of Ugandan economics rather than those of the International Monetary Fund. This view was justified in various ways. One was that, if earlier IMF-based devaluations were any guide to future economic behaviour in Uganda, black marketeers would simply raise the *magendo* rate above whatever rate was fixed by government. It was also said that neither the international exchange rate nor the prices paid in Ugandan shillings to Ugandan smallholders for their produce were the most important 'choke points' economically: trucks, and other infrastructural improvements were the most urgently needed things to get Uganda's export crops to railhead. (Here Ugandans clearly agreed implicitly with points made for Tanzania by Singh.) Another point made frequently in September 1986 concerned the present Ugandan commercial class's capacity to sabotage any internationally agreed economic recovery programme.

This was especially emphasized by the Ugandan bishop who took pity on a Britisher walking in the midday sun and remarked to me, just as his driver plunged the vehicle in which we were by now both travelling into a large pothole, that most trouble came from people who plunged the country into instability – of the political sort, that is. Unfortunately the subsequent course of this particular journey proved too unsteady for further discussion. But his basic point was surely an impeccably obvious one. One precondition for any durable economic growth in Uganda is political stability. Nonetheless, the point could hardly have been emphasized in a more dramatic manner.

The bishop was perhaps also partly making two further points. He would surely have agreed with the substance of what Deryck Belshaw says in this volume about the importance of microeconomic factors in Uganda as well as macroeconomic ones. And here, political instability and conflict apart, the Ugandan commercial class created in part upon the expulsion by Idi Amin in 1972 of the Asian business community from the country surely represents one of the most important microeconomic developments in the country since independence. Besides building itself up upon the remnants of departing Asians' businesses and shops, this *mafutamingi* stratum – as it is popularly known in Uganda – was also strengthened by land laws passed during Amin's time that made leasehold purchases of property both easier and more enduring, and by their much more extensive participation in the hitherto Asian-controlled import-export trade (Green, 1981; Kasfir, 1984). Nelson Kasfir's contribution to this volume considers this as well as other aspects of class formation with special respect to two areas of Ankole in western Uganda. But two personal cameos from eastern Uganda also spring immediately to mind here. One is the memory of the elderly bank clerk who changed some of my British pounds into Ugandan shillings at Mbale in September 1986. If only I had arrived just a few weeks before Professor Mulema's budget had raised the cost of the Ugandan shilling to foreigners, he commented, I could have obtained nearly three times as many shillings for my pounds. But, as the bank clerk also remarked, it remained to be seen whether Professor Mulema's budget would also apply to the black market. His implication was clear, and indeed forms the centrepiece of a second memory of Uganda in September 1986: at the still-mushrooming mud-and-wattle settlement at Malaba on the border with Kenya, where on the bridge over the Malaba river between the two countries' customs' posts a multitude of moneychangers waved wads of Ugandan shillings in their thousands; some being offered at ten times the official Ugandan rate of exchange for Kenyan shillings, some at twenty times or more. The parallel economy was still clearly thriving.

Since September 1986, a new Ugandan currency has been introduced, and a partial loan agreement arranged with the International Monetary Fund covering national debts inherited from the second Obote governement. But it remains to be seen whether the Museveni government can effectively triumph over the *mafutamingi* stratum in the also inherited parallel economy; or whether, with the NRM's clearly growing preference for non-monetary, barter deals with non-aligned countries in the Caribbean and the Middle East as well as elsewhere in Africa, *mafutamingi* become still more central economically in the country.

This brings us to a third point, whose significance is by no means confined to Uganda but seems particularly important there. What makes political instability so subversive of local economic life in so many African countries nowadays is the fragility and volatility of the post-independence state, its simultaneous omnipotence and weakness. The Ugandan state decides upon the currency, fixes official exchange rates, makes many other rules for commercial life, determines taxes, and collects customs. As such, its economic importance in Uganda is all-embracing. However it is not yet powerful enough throughout the country to impose its decisions widely and effectively. It is only strong enough to punish particular individuals when the people protest. To be sure, the NRM itself is evidence enough, at the level of guerrilla insurgency in southern and westen Uganda, that the people's protest against the second Obote government was strong enough to ensure its overthrow and eventual replacement by a more popular government. But whether the NRM's improving and puritanical 10-point programme for the development of a self-sustaining economy can be implemented successfully in Uganda remains to be seen.

It depends upon so many unknowns. Future relations with immediately neighbouring states, especially Kenya, Sudan and Tanzania, are one critical unknown. The continuing internal coherence of the NRM as a political coalition is clearly another. Yet another is the continuing *impasse* in the international credit system regarding Third World debts. But probably most important of all as regards Uganda, and least amenable to prediction, is how long armed resistance may continue against Museveni's government. For the moment the omens for the present Ugandan government's success seem generally favourable. However, the basic problem remains. What one initially small group of puritanical and highly motivated guerrilla fighters could successfully achieve in one area of Uganda in the earlier 1980s, another *might* be able to repeat in another part of the country at some later date – if popular protest in that part of the country against 'a particular region' or person or persons, also grows to critical proportions.

Notes

1. This visit to Uganda and East Africa was supported financially by the Hayter Fund of London University. On problems of children as a consequence of political violence in Uganda, see Dodge and Raundalen, 1987.
2. *New Vision*, 26 September 1987.
3. For example, Richard Hall in *The Observer* (London), 2 February 1986; *Le Monde* (Paris), 5 February 1986; *The Times* (London), 11 February 1986. The present editor of *New Vision*, William Pike, was one of the first to document the atrocities in Luwero during the bush war itself.
4. Besides my account in Twaddle, 1983a, see my further discussion in Twaddle, 1983b.
5. For example 'Cadres have eyes opened', *New Vision*, 15 August 1986.
6. The classic statement is still Fanon, 1967.
7. I am indebted to Hugh Dinwiddy for loaning me his copy of these notes.
8. NRM Publications, Kampala, 1986 (1st 1986 edition, copyrighted by Yoweri Museveni).
9. For example, *Africa Confidential*, 4 February 1987; 'War for Karamoja', *New African* (London) February 1987, by Mike Kidon-Unyang, himself a Karamojong.
10. Vision, 13 February 1987 ('Bishop attacks NRA'); *Le Monde*, 4 March 1987.
11. See further, Twaddle, 1972a. (The argument also ignores the earlier success of Frolinat in Chad, where another guerrilla movement successfully seized power.)
12. DP, 'Proposals for interim government programme', mimeo, Kampala, 1987: again I am indebted to Hugh Dinwiddy for facilitating access.
13. See Kidon-Unyang, 'War for Karamoja' (cited in note 9 above); Cathy Watson in *New Vision*, 4 November 1986.
14. e.g. *New Vision*, 9 December 1986 ('Moses Ali hands over flag').
15. See note 10 above.
16. *New Vision*, 2 September 1986 ('Monarchist group 'Kirimuttu' exposed by NRA'). The name comes from the Ganda proverb *Ekiri mu ttu: kimanyibwa nnyiniryo* ('What is in the little parcel: is known to its owner').
17. *New Vision*, 9 December 1986. However, by mid-1987 these doubts seemed drowned in the immense enthusiasm with which Ganda descent groups demonstrated their respect for *Ssaabataka* Mutebi by organizing an inter-clan football league at Nakivubo Stadium in Kampala – leading to a revival of such intra-Ganda insults as 'You are a Dog' to the losing Dog Clan side.

TWENTY TWO
Is Africa decaying? The view from Uganda

Ali A. Mazrui[1]

Uganda was the cradle of my academic career and, but for the politics of the situation, would have been my permanent home. But politics did intervene. When I returned for the first time after Idi Amin's fall in 1979, among the things that moved me most were not the elements that had changed, but the things that had remained the same. Even just driving from the airport at Entebbe to Kampala and looking at the countryside, the impact was of a very beautiful country. I suddenly discovered my eyes were filling up. They were filling up because it looked so unchanged, so beautiful. It was the triumph of nature over politics. When I was later with Ugandan friends, I witnessed how they laughed at their misfortunes. This was the triumph of laughter over a tragedy. It was a tremendous experience.

My mission at this symposium is to discuss the African situation as a context of the Ugandan predicament. Are Uganda's crises of development unique, or are they really part of a continental phenomenon that we are witnessing in the post-colonial age? A major factor to bear in mind is what I call 'The War of Cultures in the African Continent'. It is as if the ancestors were angry, and have rejected the post-colonial deals of our elites. African culture is fighting back, and the combat takes the form of sabotaging the existing order. There is a kind of a curse of the ancestor upon our political and economic institutions, our new-fangled machinery for law enforcement, our artificial educational institutions, and in general, upon the entire spectrum of post-colonial political, social, and economic arrangements.

The war of cultures also takes the form of decay. Hence the question I have posed: 'Is Africa decaying?'

Africa is certainly in crisis. Governments are unstable, economies are under strain, infrastructures are decaying. Why? The emergencies may all be a consequence of 'dis-modernization' – a reversal of the 'Westernization' processes initiated by the colonial experience.

We are confronted with the contradictions of 'Westernization without modernity.' Africa has Western-style armies that stage military coups, Western-style police forces that are failing in law-enforcement, Western-style bureaucracies that are increasingly corrupt, and Western-style agricultural plans that are deficient and often unproductive. What has gone wrong?

It certainly looks as if the whole post-colonial euphoria about 'modernization' has been a mere illusion of modernity, a mirage of progress, a facade of advancement. The reality behind the face is grim and devastating. Africa is bleeding; Africa is starving. The reasons lie in a hundred years of colonial history and a thousand years of Africa culture.

Some modernization has taken place in Africa under European rule and tutelage. Schools have been established, roads built, railway systems constructed, police forces inaugurated, and modern armies recruited. We define modernization as innovative change based on more advanced knowledge and leading to wider social horizons. We define development as modernization minus dependency, the promotion of innovative change and the broadening of social horizons without excessive reliance on others.

But even the degree of dependent modernization that Africa had achieved under colonial rule is in the process of being reversed. Africa is indeed in the process of decay or social decomposition. Instead of African economies growing, they show signs of shrinking. Instead of Africa's per capita production expanding, it betrays a tendency to diminish. Instead of greater experience leading to greater efficiency, Africa's experience paradoxically seems to result in decreasing competence. Latest estimates shows that 30 of the hungriest nations of the world are in Africa. The World Food Council estimates that population in the African continent may be growing at three or four times the rate of growth in food production. And the threat of famine in Africa will persist well into the twenty-first century.

Let us look at the evidence of dis-modernization, the evidence of reversal and decay. Uganda in the first quarter century of independence has to be seen in those terms.

INFRASTRUCTURE: THE RUST AND THE DUST

One of the more obvious areas of Africa's decay is the infrastructure, the system of roads, railways and other broadly supportive facilities and utilities.

The roads of Africa have been taking a terrific beating – miles and miles of potholes in some parts of the continent. There is a Ugandan joke about a bad Ugandan road – 'When you see a man driving in a straight line along Kampala road, he must be drunk!' Well, this joke is equally applicable to many other roads throughout the continent. In Ghana the main artery between north and south is the road from Accra to Tamale. The road is fundamental to the nation and yet it is in large parts in utter disrepair, for mile after mile. It tells us a lot about the state of communications in Africa. It tells us a lot about the African condition. It was Julius Nyerere, founder President of Tanzania, who once said that while the great powers are trying to get to the moon, we are trying to get to the village. Well, the great powers have been to the moon and back, and are now even communicating with the stars. In Africa, however, we are still trying to reach the village. What's more, the village is getting even more remote, receding with worsening communications even further into the distance.

Railway systems are also in difficulty in different parts of the continent, with reduced access to foreign exchange for the purchase of spare parts. This also applies to lorries and buses, many without tyres or spare parts, languishing by the roadside.

As for telephone systems in Africa, they are in part the usual contradictions of dependency. It is easier to place a call to the Western world from an African country than to place a call to a neighbouring African country. Sometimes it's easier to telephone Michigan in the US from Mombasa, Kenya, than to telephone Thika, another part of Kenya.

But as compared to other African countries, Kenya is in fact among the better endowed in telephone systems. There are countries where a telephone call, even to the Western world, has to be booked days in advance. And in places like Ghana many telephones have gone silent in the last ten to fifteen years. In other words, the telephones has become more of a luxury, and the number of those that work has shrunk considerably. This is quite apart from endemic corruption affecting long-distance phone calls in places like Zaire. Telephone operators have to be bribed when one is booking a call.

Apart from the decaying infrastructure, the whole system of production in Africa that is up against severe constraints. Certainly the problem of foreign exchange and spare parts has made many an African machine grind to a standstill. Dependency upon the West has not made matters easier.

In Pwalugu, Ghana, I followed the story of a tomato factory which management had tried to make self-reliant, but soon discovered that it was up against the hazards of the international market in technology. At first the deal was with Yugoslavia. The Yugoslavs installed the equipment for manufacturing cans or tins for the tomatoes. For reasons that are unclear, the Yugoslavs were not able to complete the job. The Ghanaians then turned to the Italians, who had in fact manufactured the machinery in the first place, but left the installation to Yugoslavs. The Italians, however, for reasons of their own, wanted to sell the Ghanaians new equipment and new spare parts, but the Ghanaians are still eager to make the right size of tin for their tomatoes, an optimum size for Ghana, but they are unable to do so. Equipment for making the tins is available, unused because the installation was never completed. What is more the Ghanaians still have to import the tins for their tomatoes from outside after all.

At Maluka in Zaire I witnesed a dead steel mill, cobwebs all over it. The mill was built hundreds of miles away from Zairean sources of iron ore, and hundreds of other miles away from the port that imported foreign ore. In other words, there was no logic to the location or the goals and purposes of the steel mill.

While our ancient kings built palaces and pyramids, our modern presidents erect steel mills and hydroelectric dams. These latter structures are the new temples of the gods of technology. Why do I call them temples? Because like temples they are built in faith rather than through rational calculation. President Mobutu Sese Seko once said that he had built the steel mill at Maluka and the Inga-Shaba hydroelectric dam as an investment in tomorrow for the sake of tomorrow. But what about today? The steel mill was silent and unproductive; and even when it is productive it is only at 10 per cent capacity.

But the most serious problem of production in Africa concerns agriculture. Part of the problem has arisen because of inadequate returns for farmers and a disproportionate use of resources by bureaucracies of marketing boards. In a country like Nigeria agriculture was, in a sense, murdered by oil wealth. In a brief honeymoon of petro-power, Nigerians made a lot of money from the oil and diverted skills away from cultivation and basic production to wheeling and dealing in the temporarily oil-rich Nigeria. In spite of slogans like 'the green revolution' under President Shehu Shagari, Nigerian agriculture was mortally maimed by the petro-bonanza.

Related to this issue is the whole crisis of the cash economy in Africa. Money in some African societies is a relatively recent phenomenon. Traditionally some of these societies dealt in barter and other forms of exchange, though West Africa had devised ways of using money or its equivalent in shells centuries before the British pound or the French franc penetrated the African continent.

But in much of the rest of Africa exchange of goods in kind was more common than currency. And now this new entity called money is under stress, and is earning for itself considerable distrust among the ordinary people of the continent. The value of the money seems unpredictable, and sometimes changes very rapidly at the behest of such incomprehensible foreign institutions as the International Monetary Fund (IMF) with its 'conditionalities'. Quite often, several devaluations rapidly follow each other.

There are also occasions when governments suddenly decide to change the face of the currencies almost overnight. Old bills are recalled at short notice, in exchange for new bills and notes. Sometimes only two weeks are given as notice for the exchange. Beyond those two weeks the old notes become totally valueless, and sometimes dangerous to possess due to government regulations against them. People in rural areas who might have saved the old notes for years suddenly discover that what they hid under their mattresses is no longer legal tender and is to all intents and purposes garbage. This new institution of money is therefore under a cloud of suspicion and distrust. Some rural people have returned to the ancient system of barter in their dealings with each other. And many are looking for alternative ways of saving outside the cash economy, alternative methods of insuring for the future.

Also in the process of decay is Africa's schooling system. Teachers are getting disprofessionalized in their commitment to teaching. They are often underpaid, and in some countries not paid at all for months on end. The teachers have to look for moonlighting opportunities, opportunities that give them an additional livelihood alongside teaching. In Africa, the sense of vocation in education is under severe strain.

Foreign exchange constraints also result in decaying libraries, with old books published years previously and falling apart, with no new books to replace them on the shelves. The bookshops are also relatively empty because of the tightening controls over foreign purchases and modest levels of publishing within the national boundaries.

There has also been declining support for African universities. And in those countries where money has declined in value enormously, professors have to look for additional jobs, ranging from taxi driving to farming, as a method of augmenting their resources.

At Navrongo in rural Ghana I witnessed the slow death of a village school. The desks that broke were not replaced. Those that remain are carefully stored away during vacation-time. Some of the walls are beginning to crumble, the hinges coming off doors and windows, the desks fewer every year because more legs have dropped off.

And yet that was not the worst of it. Africa is quite familiar with schools without walls, classrooms in the open. Teaching can go on without desks, learning can take place without walls. However, teaching without teaching materials is a different situation. The whole term had taken place at this school without the basics of writing, without paper, without pens. Someone complained, 'Why not write to the head of state?' Someone else retorted, 'Write? With what?'

There was more at stake in that school than a dying classroom. I was perhaps witnessing the slow death of an alien civilization. There before me was perhaps the gradual death of Western culture as we have known it in Africa.

CRIME, PUNISHMENT, AND COMPENSATION

Yet another example of decay and 'dis-modernization' is the whole general area of law enforcement in Africa. As in most of the rest of the world, crime in Africa has been growing. But unlike the rest of the world the law-enforcement machinery in Africa seems to be crumbling. In many African countries the police is getting more corrupt rather than less, the judiciary is getting more politicized and sometimes dis-professionalized, the prisons are not only over-crowded but often falling apart, the legislative system is getting less predictable and sometimes militarized in the form of decrees, the citizens are getting more confused as to what is the law. They are also getting less and less secure in person and property. Law and order is falling apart not only in the wider society, but also within the law enforcement machinery itself.

Again, much of this law enforcement machinery came with the Western impact upon Africa. Before European colonization there were alternative forms of law enforcement in operation. These were partly Islamic in those areas that had become Islamized. In the rest of Africa there were other indigenous traditional methods of protecting the innocent in society.

In indigenous terms, the protection of the innocent was precisely the main focus of law enforcement, rather than the punishment of the guilty *per se*. Arising out of this emphasis in indigenous methods of law enforcement came the victim-focus in law enforcement rather than the villain-focus. When a crime was committed it was more fundamental to have the victim's family compensated than to have the villain or culprit punished.

In some traditional African societies the principle of compensation permeated the entire area of morality as well as law. Adultery with another man's wife could result in the guilty man being forced to compensate the aggrieved husband for the violation of conjugal rights.

I remember when I was a child the very different case of a young man who was working for my family as a domestic help. One of my aunts sent him to a shop nearby to buy salt and coconuts. It had been raining. On his way back from the shop the young man passed an electric lamp post. It turned out that there was a live wire, and the young man touched it. In the wetness of the occasion the young man was electrocuted immediately. His family had to come to our family to negotiate compensation. We provided a suitable recompense and prayed for the departed soul of the unfortunate youth.

The coming of Western systems of law enforcement played havoc with African systems of compensation, especially in the field of Western criminal law. There was a sudden and decisive shift from focus on the victim of a crime to focus on the suspect or culprit. The new infrastructure of law enforcement demanded prison houses for violators of the law without adequate machinery for compensating victims of crime. And even when fines were imposed in a criminal case, the money went to the state and not to the victim. Compensation as a principle became almost irrelevant in criminal justice under Western law.

Under Western stimulation, Africa's law enforcement also shifted from emphasis on shame to emphasis on guilt. Shame is a subjective state of mind that implies a state of unease and internal anxiety about something that has gone wrong. Guilt, especially in Western terms, is an objective condition that can be ascertained by laws of evidence and that can be measured in terms of degrees. In other words, shame is primarily subjective, whereas guilt in Western judicial systems is supposed to be objective.

Second, shame is a condition that is sensitive to the disapprobation of the wider society. A single individual's shame is shared by his immediate and extended family, and sometimes by the whole village. Shame in African terms is a principle of wide social accountability, as well as being intrinsically subjective.

Guilt, in Western terms, is a principle of individual culpability. The Western system of law enforcement seeks to establish guilt rather than to arouse a sense of shame; it makes the defendant face a judge and jury but does not require him to face the family of his victim. The system of ascertaining guilt insists on the personal accountability of the individual violator; a system of arousing shame makes crime a matter of family concern and of collective social responsibility.

The Western system of law enforcement substituted prison sentences for negotiations about compensation. It also substituted guilt ascertainment for shame arousal. Thirdly, it substituted strict personal accountability by the culprit for collective family and social responsibility for violations committed by a member of the group.

It would not have mattered if the new system had worked. It could then have been asserted that the new and 'modern' method of law enforcement – consisting of judges wearing wigs, policemen wearing uniforms, and the prisoners behind barbed wire – had rescued Africa from a life of violence, destruction and basic criminality. But of course what has happened is the reverse. The new system, like many other 'modern' institutions, has simply not been working. The substitution of cage for the villain to replace compensation for the victim, the insistence on objective guilt as against subjective shame, the focus on personal individual accountability as against collective responsibility, all these have resulted not only in escalating violence and criminality, especially in African cities, but also in the relentless decay of the police, judiciary, legal system and prison structures.

In the face of this social and legal disintegration, unfortunately almost no African country is returning to the basic principles of indigenous and traditional modes of norm fulfilment. The two most popular approaches towards dealing with rising crime have been either to make the Western method of punishment even more severe or, in the case of Muslim Africa, to return to Islamic law (the Shari'a). In the field of crime, both Western and Islamic law are disproportionately villain-focused rather than victim-focused, predicated on personal accountability rather than social collective responsibility. However, it is arguable that Islamic law is more conscious of the imperative of shame as against guilt than Western law has managed to be in the modern period.

Desperate African governments seeking to control crime waves in their societies often forget the distinction between severity of punishment and certainty of punishment. Almost all desperate African govenments assume that making the punishment more severe is what is needed in the face of disintegration, and forget the option of making punishment more certain. If there is a death penalty for a particular crime, but only a 10 per cent chance that the criminal would be apprehended, this could be less of a deterrent than a life imprisonment with a 60 per cent chance of the criminal being apprehended. In many African countries the likelihood of arrest and imprisonment are quite low, not simply because police forces are small, but also because they are quite often corrupt, and their systems of detection and investigation are rudimentary and relatively backward. So African governments do in fact have a choice between making their systems of investigation and detection more efficient and the police force less corrupt, on the one side, and making the punishment for crimes more and more severe on the other. Of course the latter appears cheaper, easier and seemingly quicker. Thus the easy option is adopted, very often with capital punishment for more and more crimes. A number of African countries, including Nigeria and Kenya, have experimented with the death penalty for robbery with violence. There have been occasions when Nigeria has actually routinized executions of thieves, robbers, and drug-traffickers, every second Saturday, in public.

The system of executions in public is in fact a perversion of the African principle of shame. It is true that many African societies use the device of shaming the culprit, but quite often in front of the victim's relatives as well as the culprit's own extended family. The idea was not to execute in front of television cameras for the entertainment of an impersonal public. Yet the latter strategy of public executions before television cameras has been precisely what some military regimes in Africa, including Muhammed Buhari's government in Nigeria, have experimented with in a desperate bid to control rising lawlessness.

COLONIALISM AS AN EPISODE

There is a case for regarding the European impact as a whole as no more than an episode in millennia of African history. This episodic school of evaluating colonialism has two main versions. One version insists that Africa could have entered the world economy and the international state system without being colonized by Europe. After all, Japan is now a major power in the world economy and has at times been a major figure in the international state system without having undergone the agonies of European colonization and imperialism.

Related to this is the argument that modern science and technology were in any case destined to convert the whole world into a global village. Twentieth-century science and technology had become too expansionist and all-embracing to have left Africa untouched. If this body of expertise could reach the moon without colonizing it, why could it not have reached Africa without subjugating it?

What follows from all this is the conclusion that European colonization of Africa was not the only way Africa might have entered into the global system of the twentieth century. Africa could have made such an entry without suffering either the agonies of the slave trade, or the exploitation of colonialism, or the humiliation of European racism.

The second version of the episodic school asserts that the European impact on Africa has been shallow rather than deep, transient rather than long-lasting, a mere episode in Africa's history rather than a drama of epic proportions, a brief interlude rather than a fundamental turning point.

It is against this background that there emerges a crisis of viability for Western civilization in Africa. Is that civilization under siege? Is

Africa reclaiming its own? Is Westernism losing ground to the forces of re-indigenization?

First is the shallowness of the kind of capitalism transferred to Africa. Western consumption patterns were transferred more effectively than Western productive techniques, Western tastes acquired more quickly than Western skills, the profit motive adopted without the efficient calculus of entrepreneurship, and capitalist greed internalized sooner than capitalist discipline.

All this is quite apart from the anomaly of urbanization without industrialization. In the history of the Western world the growth of cities occurred partly in response to fundamental changes in production. Urbanization followed in the wake of either an agrarian transformation or an industrial revolution. But in the history of Africa urbanization has been under way without accompanying growth of productive capacity. In some African countries there is indeed a kind of revolution, but it is a revolution in urbanization rather than in industrialization, a revolution in expanding numbers of people squeezed into limited space, rather than a transformation in method and skill of economic output.

These processes have made capitalism in Africa, such as it is, lopsided and basically shallow. This is a case of capitalism in decay.

But alongside this phenomenon is the post-colonial state in Africa, which is also quite often in the process of decaying. The African state since independence has been subject to two competing pressures: the push toward militarization and the pull towards privatization. In the capitalist Western world state ownership is regarded as an alternative or even the opposite of private ownership. The privatization of the steel industry in England, for example, is an alternative to state ownership and state control.

In post-colonial Africa, on the other hand, the question arises whether the state itself can indeed be privatized or become privately owned. Is there a new echo in Africa of Louis XIV's notorious dictum: 'I am the state'?

There is indeed an echo of a sort, but with distinctive African variations. What must be remembered simultaneously is that the pressures of privatization in Africa are accompanied by pressures towards militarization. The pull towards privatization is partly a legacy of greed in the Shylock tradition. The push towards militarism, on the other hand, is a legacy of naked power in the tradition of Shaka. Africa, in other words, is caught up between Shylock and Shaka, between greed and naked power, and the decay of the post-colonial state is one consequence of that dialectic.

In Nigeria between 1979 and 1984 the two tendencies of privatization and militarization appeared to be alternatives. Under

345

civilian rule from 1979 privatization gathered momentum. The resources of the nation were, to all intents and purposes, deemed to be the private hunting ground of those in power and their supporters. Lucrative contracts for trade or construction were handed out on the basis of particularist considerations. Foreign exchange was privately allocated and arbitrarily distributed. Millions of dollars and naira disappeared into the private holdings and accounts of key figures abroad.

This rampant privatization of the state's resources seemed to have set the stage for the state's militarization. Nigeria's armed forces – restive for a variety of reasons – found additional grounds for impatience with the civilian politicians. On 31 December 1983, the soldiers once again intervened and took over power. The push towards militarization had triumphed over the pull towards privatization of the Nigerian state. The soldiers justified their intervention on the basis of ending the private pillage of the country's resources. The action of the soldiers seemed calculated to arrest the decay of both the Nigerian economy and the Nigerian state.

THE PRIVATE STATE: THREE VERSIONS

Although in this particular phase of Nigeria's history the two pressures (privatization versus militarization) appeared to be alternatives, in much of the 1970s when the soldiers were in power, they tended to reinforce each other. The soldiers were themselves inclined to raid the coffers of the state, though not quite on the same scale as the civilians did from 1979 to 1983.

Three forms of the privatized state appear on the political landscape of Africa: dynastic, ethnic and anarchic tendencies of privatization. Again, these are not necessarily mutually exclusive categories, though their characteristics are often quite distinctive.

The case of Nigeria from 1979 to 1983 was primarily anarchic, though with some ethnic features. The state's resources went into private hands partly because there was no effective control. President Shehu Shagari might himself have been personally 'clean', but he did not seem inclined or able to check or control the process of privatization. This almost complete lack of economic control in Nigeria in those four years was what made the economic processes primarily anarchic in character. It is also what made Nigeria's capitalism in that period particularly prone to decay.

But there were ethnic attributes as well in the situation, mainly because the base of Shagari's party (the National Party of Nigeria) was, in the final analysis, Hausa-Fulani, though by no means exclusively so. Many Hausa and Fulani belonged to rival parties, and the NPN's support was in fact much broader and more national than that of any other single party. The privatization of Nigeria's resources did have ethnic boundaries, but fundamentally the 'pillage' was anarchic.

A clearer case of combined ethnic and anarchic privatization was Idi Amin's Uganda. On the one hand, the moral order in the society had collapsed and both state and the economy were in serious decay. This was the basic anarchic condition into which Idi Amin had plunged Uganda.

On the other hand, there was little doubt that the Kakwa and the Nubi enjoyed a disproportionate share of the resources of the state and the opportunities of the economy. To that extent, the privatization was in part a diversion of resources from public ownership and control to narrow ethnic possession.

But the Amin case was not merely a manifestation of ethno-anarchic privatization. It was also combined with the militarization of the state. Contradictory trends were discernible in a somewhat complex phenonenon.

Some of the evidence seemed to suggest that in a technologically underdeveloped society in the twentieth centry ultimate power resided not in those who controlled the means of production but in those who controlled the means of destruction. The Asian community in Uganda, the new black bourgeoisie and some of the more prosperous farmers controlled a substantial part of the means of production. But it was Uganda's lumpen militariat, the rough and ready military recruits, who captured the state and proceeded to privatize it. The means of production were not modern enough to serve as levers on the power of the state, nor were they complex enough to produce countervailing social groups like effective trade unions. The military was more than just 'the first among equals', as the military-industrial complex tends to be in more technologically developed countries. The military factor in Amin's Uganda was almost overwhelming in the political arena. The balance of political supremacy was on the side of the instruments of destruction, rather than the side of the means of production. The soldiers in control of the state could then proceed to dispossess the existing planters and petty bourgeoisie of Uganda. What was already private changed hands. What President Milton Obote's first administration had put under public ownership a couple of years previously was re-privatized, partly on an ethnic basis. The forces of both political and economic decay, once unleashed, seemed difficult to check.

But that very ethnic privatization of the resources of the state in Uganda revealed another historical contradiction. It revealed how societies that were themselves stateless in the precolonial era could then inherit the post-colonial state. The Kakwa – Idi Amin's 'tribe' –

were stateless in precolonial times and were in an area that now constituted part of eastern Zaire, part of southern Sudan and part of northern Uganda. Their traditional institutions were not centralized enough, nor politically distinctive enough, to add up to what we normally mean by 'the state'.

On the other hand, precolonial centralized societies like Buganda and Bunyoro were indigenous and authentic states. The colonial period under the British helped to demilitarize the Baganda and the Banyoro with licensing laws for guns and through new forms of socialization, acculturation and Western education. Modern schools and cash crops diverted the new elite of Buganda and Bunyoro away from the warrior tradition and towards white collar jobs and the new money economy. The people of these precolonial states lost the military foundations of what had once made them states.

In contrast, some of those societies which in precolonial times had been basically stateless now became recruiting grounds for the new colonial army. In Uganda the Nilotic 'tribes' of the north were regarded by the British as particularly suitable for recruitment into the King's African Rifles. The very fact that these 'tribes' had not been centralized states when the British first arrived had made them less dangerous to the new colonial order. And so – while the Baganda and the Banyoro were getting demilitarized and losing their warrior tradition – the Acholi, Langi and the Kakwa among other northern Ugandans underwent militarization of a new and modern kind. They were being absorbed into the colonial security forces, with guns rather than spears. This change was destined to have enormous consequences for the future of Uganda.

By the time the British were leaving Uganda, the armed forces of the newly independent country were disproportionately Nilotic in composition. Although all the Nilotic 'tribes' in Uganda together add up to only a small minority of the population, the stage was already set for a Nilotic supremacy in at least the first few decades of post-colonial Uganda. This Nilotic power prevailed under Milton Obote, under Idi Amin and under Tito Okello. Different wings of the Nilotic presence, different sectors of the northern configuration of Ugandans, ruled Uganda during the two periods and continued to do so. But on the whole, it was still a case of precolonial stateless societies inheriting the post-colonial state. After all the Langi (Obote's 'tribe'), the Kakwa (Amin's 'tribe'), and the Acholi (Okello's 'tribe') were all fundamentally stateless in their pre-colonial incarnations. It was their militarization during British colonial rule that prepared them – quite unwittingly – to inherit the post-colonial state. The whole European experience had played havoc with the different traditions of Africa, casting old groups into new roles, and 'mis-casting' decentralized people into centralizing functions. This whole cultural disruption had a lot to do with the decay of the post-colonial state in countries like Uganda.

Under Idi Amin especially, that post-colonial inheritance became substantially privatized in both ethnic and anarchic ways. The second Obote administration since Amin's overthrow and Yoweri Museveni's government have substantially reduced the scale of the privatization of the state's resources, although the push towards militarization remains strong. So indeed have tendencies towards political anarchy and violence, which still remain considerable, long after Amin's departure. The Ugandan state even under Museveni still shows signs of partial decomposition.

Uganda is by no means the only case in Africa where members of pre-colonial stateless societies have inherited the post-colonial state. In Ghana under Jerry Rawlings we find a comparable case. The most complex pre-colonial state of Ghana – the confederal empire of asante – was basically demilitarized during the British rule in ways similar to those of colonial Buganda and Bunyoro. Under Jerry Rawlings the Ashanti by the 1980s were overshadowed by the Ewe, who had been basically stateless when the British, the Germans and the French began to carve up their land nearly four generations earlier. Jerry Rawlings is in part a symbol of the colonial militariza-tion of the Ewe in preparation for inheriting the post-colonial state, partly at the expense of those who had once created the Asante confederal state well before European intrusion.

Mobutu Sese Seko in Zaire lies in the same contradictory tradition of precolonial statelessness inheriting the post-colonial state. Mobutu does not come from one of the great kingdoms of precolonial Zaire. He does not come from among the Bakongo, Baluba or Balunda. Mobutu comes from the far less centralized equatorial area of Northern Zaire, along the fringes with the forest. Zaire, like Uganda, has had its lumpen militariat, inherited from the colonial period – and Mobutu symbolizes that heritage.

Today the language of that lumpen militariat – Lingala – is triumphant in the capital city, Kinshasa, alongside French as the official language of the state. Of the accepted national languages of Zaire – Kikongo, Chiluba, Kiswahili and Lingala – only Lingala is completely 'stateless' in its origins, unassociated with either city-kingdoms or indigenous empires. It is the language of those who were particularly disadvantaged by the colonial experience. However, precisely because they had fewer alternative oppor-tunities during the colonial period, many entered the armed forces, hardly realizing that they were thereby acquiring credentials for inheriting the post-colonial state. Then once that inheritance by the

Lingala-speakers was consolidated, the state in Zaire began to be privatized.

But is this privatization of the state in Zaire basically anarchic and ethnic, as it was in Amin's Uganda? Or does it reveal different characteristics?

In the earlier years of Mobutu's rule, the 'model' seemed similar to what later became Idi Amin's style. Zaire betrayed a considerable tendency towards anarchy, combined with a tendency towards ethnic solidarity and nepotism. Ethnicity and anarchy reinforced each other. And the 'raiding' of the state's resources followed both tendencies.

But there has since developed in the Zairean state a third tendency, the dynastic trend. This is a distinct form of privatization, crystallizing into a kind of 'royal family' with special prerogatives and perquisites. It is a neo-monarchical tendency.

In addition to the privatization of the state's economic resources, and the personlization of the state's power, there is now also a personification of the state's sacred symbols. A personality cult goes to the extent of sacralizing the top man and royalizing his family. The rulers' immediate political supporters evolve into a kind of aristocracy, complete with social ostentation, conspicuous consumption, and sometimes the equivalent of aristocratic titles.

Mobuto Sese Seko has not gone to the extent of ex-'Emperor' Bokassa with his neo-Napoleonic coronation in the Central African Empire (now once again a Republic). But the dynastic tendency is definitely evident in Mobutu's state, echoing in its own way Louis XIV's dictum 'I am the state'! The state in Zaire is thus privatized not just economically (by appropriating its resources), not just politically (by personalizing its power) but also symbolically (by personifying its sacredness). Yet while the glitter of royalty continues in mineral-rich Zaire, both the state and the economy endure the insidious effects of decay.

On the more positive side of his policies, President Mobutu Sese Seko has made the principle of authenticity the central doctrine of his national commitment. By 'authenticity' Mobutu means the pursuit of life-styles and tenets compatible with Zaire's indigenous and ancestral heritage. In short, authenticity is the ambition to recapture some of the original spirit and substance of Africa's own civilizations.

There was a time when Mobutu had a confrontation with the Roman Catholic Church over the issue of Christian names. If Christianity was a universal religion, why could not African names be recognized as Christian names? Why did every African baby have to be baptized with a Euro/Hebraic name? President Mobutu actually recalled virtually all Zairean passports that used European or Hebraic names for indigenous Zairean citizens. He himself deleted the name Josef by which he had been known since his childhood, and he emerged as Mobutu Sese Seko Kuku Ngbendu Wa Zabanga.

Mobutu also decided that the Catholic Church, its schools and related institutions had become too much of a state within a state in Zaire. Strong measures were taken to put denominational schools under state control. Likewise, religious youth organizations were suppressed. In February 1973 similar measures were taken against 31 religious newspapers and periodicals, as well as the Roman Catholic television and radio services. For a while the Bishops of Zaire were forbidden to meet at all (Hastings, 1979, pp. 191–2).

Relations with the Church later improved, and Pope John Paul even managed to visit Zaire, the largest Catholic country in Africa. But the Church's powers in the country seem to have been permanently reduced for reasons that included the pursuit of 'authenticity'.

But Mobutu's most effective realization of authenticity lay not in his explicit cultural policies, nor in his rhetoric and eloquence on behalf of African culture, but in his mismanagement of Zaire's economy and his privatization of the Zairean state. By helping to damage and even destroy some of the inherited institutions of the colonial order, Mobutu was inadvertently carrying out patriotic cultural sabotage. By reducing modernization and Westernization to a farce, Mobutu was helping indigenous culture to reassert itself after the masssive cultural onslaught of the colonial era. As the roads decayed, and factories ground to a standstill, Zaireans began to turn increasingly to older and more traditional ways of earning a living, of surviving. The drift from the countryside to the cities has been partially reduced as unemployment and squalor in city slums dimmed the glitter and glamour of Kinshasa, Kisangani and Lubumbashi.

Also seriously damaged was that Western invention, paper money. The currency, named after the country, Zaire, had rather rapidly fallen in value. At times, including 1983, one needed a substantial bag of money in order to pay for a meal in a restaurant in Kinshasa. Mountains of paper money were exchanged for trivia. Thus, faith in the cash economy was substantially undermined in important sectors of Zairean society.

Africans in the countryside are beginning to revert to older forms of exchange, including barter. And many are also beginning to explore alternative forms of saving. Sometimes in confusion they saved the bigger currency bills, apparently on the mistaken assumption that the larger bills would retain their value longer. At its worst this habit can cause an acute shortage of denominations, since these are taken out of circulation by nervous villagers seeking to protect themselves. What this particular habit illustrates is the relative newness of the cash economy in many parts of Africa, the relative shallowness of the impact of that economy, and the nervous decline of faith in it in large sections of the population of Africa.

UGANDA: TOO LITTLE GOVERNMENT OR TOO MUCH?

One interesting paradox of the Ugandan situation is that it has indeed tended quite often since 1971 to display both tyranny (too much government) and anarchy (too little government) at the same time. Both centralized violence and decentralized violence. At the time when we were campaigning against Idi Amin, and were trying to consider the possibility of ostracizing him, I had to give testimony before Congressional committees in the United States about imposing sanctions on Amin's Uganda. I raised precisely that issue. When you have overthrown the tyrant you still have the issue of anarchy to deal with. The instrument of sanctions seems to be, at best, a cure for the tyranny. One still has to prepare to cure the society of the anarchy. Because a kind of moral collapse had taken place in Uganda: the lights had gone out, important areas of restraint had been weakened. And just as in New York City when power collapsed, people looted, because it was an opportunity, moral power in Uganda also had, to some extent, collapsed. The restraints, which operated before 1971, were under severe strain.

In 1978, I also suggested to the American Congress that they should make a sanctions package: one set of sanctions against South Africa and one set of sanctions against Idi Amin. Because to act just against Idi Amin was a cheap way of doing it. However, the United States Congress was not ready at that time for such ideas.

I then carried out the discussion about tyranny and anarchy once with Paulo Muwanga while he was still in exile. The discussion was conducted across radio waves. The BBC had organized a debate on Uganda after the murder of Archbishop Luwum. Muwanga was in London, and the last British High Commissioner to Uganda was also in London. There was the last US Ambassador to Uganda in New York. There was a representative of the All-Africa Conference of Churches in Nairobi. Finally, there was myself in Ann Arbor, Michigan. The BBC had connected three continents in a discussion on the radio.

Idi Amin was still in power. Uganda had just witnessed the murder of Archbishop Luwum. My concern at that time was the same. Everybody was talking about the tyrant. I suggested that more people had died in the second half of the Amin years as a result of anarchy than as a result of tyranny. Many of the killings were not orchestrated orders from the top. Soldiers perpetrated them in night clubs, at road-blocks, in the villages. Yet the cases due to anarchy were not of conspicuous political significance. They were cases of a basic moral collapse among those who wielded weapons.

And yet we were not, as yet, thinking at all about how to deal with the society's moral collapse. We kept on thinking about how to deal with bad governments. At some stage one has to begin to worry about alternative ideas for the self-discipline of the country. Those alternative ideas were not even on the agenda in many cases.

In the radio discussion Paulo Muwanga was hostile and unreceptive to my suggestion that more people had been killed by anarchy than by tyranny in the second half of the Amin years. He was angry because he thought this was a kind of apology for Idi Amin. Muwanga was so angry that his ire lasted right up to the time when he was in power in Uganda. When I arrived in December 1980 and went to see President Obote, Muwanga was also there. It was a very chilly reception. I thought it was the President's displeasure. But I later discovered that the chill was Muwanga's. He still believed that I had been an apologist for Idi Amin. Obote himself later changed his mind and asked me back to an atmosphere that was less chilly and more conducive to a five-hour conversation. So much for the political dimension, the dialectic between anarchy and tyranny.

THE DEMON OF DEPENDENCY

The second dialectic is between dependency and decay. These are twin evils in the economic domain. Unfortunately until now African countries that have tried to fight dependency have also deepened the tendency towards decay. Tanzania is one very good example: major efforts to transcend dependency have resulted in relatively accelerated decay without really reducing dependency. A country ends up with both evils. Nkrumah's Ghana may have embarked on a similar path to transcend dependency, although less clear-cut than Nyerere's Tanzania.

Those that opted for dependency, like Kenya and Côte d'Ivoire, have they succeeded in reducing at least the scale of decay? One embraces one evil and hopes that it will reduce the tendency in the other. Uganda under Idi Amin had more decay and less dependency, precisely because one was leading on to the other. The decline of the importance of cash crops within the economy; the increasing emphasis on food production because of the difficulties of the situation; the arrested pull towards urbanization because the cities were no longer quite as attractive as they used to be; the increased links between town and country (because, for example, professors and other urbanites needed to cultivate additional vegetables for themselves); the new emphasis on cultivating food-crops. All these trends added up to a reduction of dependency. But they were also the result of the decay of the infrastructure, of the capacity to export.

Uganda under Obote's second administration was probably more dependent than under Idi Amin. But was there less decay than under Idi Amin? Certainly there was a partial revival of cash crops with their dependency-consequences. There were reduced links between town and country, as compared with the Amin years, partly because part of the western countryside was no longer usable for cultivation. There were improved foreign exchange possibilities, which again helped to increase dependency, but hopefully arrested decay.

As for the overall reasons for these twin evils of dependency and decay, this writer has come to believe that the problem in Africa is not too much capitalism, rather there is too little of it. The West did not, repeat not, transmit its own structures. There is one thing worse than being made fully capitalist – being made a minimal capitalist. Western capitalism has certainly used Africa, but it did not create African capitalism. Many of the tendencies we associate with capitalism just don't exist. Only a partial transmission occurred. Western consumerism is transmitted, Western consumption patterns transferred, at least to the elite, but no Western production techniques came. As indicated earlier, Western tastes are transmitted, but not Western skills. Western materialism was transmitted, not Western rationality; capitalist greed was transmitted, not capitalist discipline; the profit motive was transmitted, not entrepreneurship. Western leisure habits are transmitted, but not Western work habits. Either by design or by accident, or both, a massive distortion occurred. There was no real capitalist socialization of Africa. Only a distorted transmission of precisely the elements of capitalism that were not productive reached Africa.

If one paraphrased Alexander Pope, the English poet, a little, one would say: 'A little capitalism is a dangerous thing. Drink deep or taste not the Western spring.' Even if you want, later on, to build socialism, this notion of too little capitalism is an impediment to the vision of building socialism. This level of minimalist capitalization is an impediment to the realization of the socialist dream. The structures of production, the class foundations of the socialism are glaringly absent. You impede the emergence of a local proletariat, and you have an elite rather than a bourgeoisie, a cultural aristocracy rather than an economic vanguard. All this grievance we have had about the capitalist presence in our midst is a mistake, because it isn't there. It is a capitalist mirage. The West has come and used us and then gone away. Western capitalism is triumphant, but African capitalism is almost non-existent.

Idi Amin played a game of 'I'll bring more capitalism'. He expelled the Asians, but this made no difference to the essential nature of Ugandan capitalist reality. Ugandans continued to have capitalist greed without capitalist discipline; they still had consumption under Idi Amin instead of production; we still have, at best, the profit and acquisitive motive without entrepreneurial skills. Idi Amin's effort to replace Indian duka-wallas with African duka-warriors did not work.

As demonstrated earlier, another aspect of the growth of capitalism in the West was urbanization. In tropical Africa, however, none of this happened. Africa has experienced urbanization without industrialization. Under Idi Amin in Uganda we had, for a while, this urbanization without industrialization. Later on even the urbanization itself stopped.

Obote while in exile in Tanzania discovered that efforts to escape dependency could lead to decay. Hence his move to the right in his second (post-Amin) incarnation. He wanted to strengthen capitalism too, but not in fundamentals. The problem we have had remained the same: too little capitalism creating excessive consumption and a diminished capacity to produce.

The dependency leads to need for aid in fairly fundamental ways. The other day I was looking once again at 'The White Man's Burden', Rudyard Kipling's poem of imperialism written in the last century. I wonder whether the message has really changed.

> Take up the white man's burden
> Send forth the best ye breed
> Go bind your sons to exile
> To serve your captives need ...
> The ports ye shall not enter
> The roads ye shall not tread
> Go make them with your living
> And mark them with your dead ...
> Then take up the white man's burden
> The savage wars of peace
> Fill full the mouth of famine
> And bid the sickness cease.

As long ago as the nineteenth century the message concerned our need for help. 'Take up the white man's burden/ The savage wars of peace,' we have to combat hunger and famine among these poor and uninstructed lot. 'Fill full the mouth of famine/ And bid the sickness cease.' It's still happening. The message was recurrent, 'Go and help them build the infrastructure.' 'The ports ye [white men] shall not enter/ The road ye shall not tread/ Go make them with your living/ And mark them with your dead.' So help them build the infrastructure.

Then, what is even more recurrent, these blacks are actually hungry and sick, 'So take up the white man's burden/ The savage wars of peace/ Fill full the mouth of famine/ And bid the sickness cease.' It was the first 'Live Aid' song. But did it all begin as 'A-song-for-a-penny-Sir' in Shakespearean terms? The trouble with singing for Africa's hungry is that while it is tremendously exciting as charity, it is painful to witness the hunger and sickness persisting generation after generation, a hundred years after Kipling's heyday.

Finally, briefly a discussion of the cultural alienation and cultural surrender. Sometimes one has to decide how much to borrow from the West. The Japanese asked themselves, 'Can we economically modernize without culturally Westernizing?' The Japanese after their Meiji restoration of 1868 said, 'Yes, we can economically modernize without culturally Westernizing. We just choose. We are going for Western technique, and we shall retain Japanese spirit.' The Turks after Mustafa Kemal Ataturk asked themselves, 'Can we economically modernize without culturally Westernizing?' The Turks gave a different answer from the Japanese. They said, 'No, you really must go the whole hog. You must culturally Westernize if you want to economically modernize.' So for the Turks, even the dress had to be Western, the cap had to be Western, the alphabet has to be Western, etc. The Turks changed more than what would normally be regarded as the necessary elements of economic transformation. 'We have to go Western culturally if we are to be effective in the modern, economic world.'

The trouble with Africa is that it has been, at best, culturally Westernizing without economically modernizing. In fact it is a third class apart. It moves in the direction of learning to use Western dress, Western manners, Western languages, Western religious denominations, Western alcoholic drinks. But not much of Western skills, Western techniques. Because these are the foundations, the questions do arise: 'Is Westernization in Africa reversible?' 'Can Africa beat a retreat if what we are choosing are only these particular shallow elements?'

I think a partial reversal of Westernization is already under way. It has taken the forms I mentioned earlier; the schools as major instruments of Westernization are under strain and ceasing to be efficient transmitters of Western culture; the villages are being forced back into areas of self-reliance, because the wider national set-up is unproductive; the people losing faith in currencies not only because they are valueless, but also because they are susceptible to abrupt change altogether. The money and cash aspects of economic life, which in many African countries have come with colonialism, are themselves losing the sanctity they had. Africans are compelled to search for alternative ways of saving, for new protection, and insurance. Those aspects of Westernization are under partial reversal. As for the army, on one side the army's modern weapons are part of the Western impact. Africa accepted Western technology of destruction in a manner that has made it a major variable in the power equation. In many African countries it is in fact true that those in control of the means of destruction are more powerful than those in control of the means of production.

Perhaps the most unfortunate thing about the technology of destruction in Africa is that it is so totally alien that militarization has not resulted in industrialization. In the history of the West militarization very often helped industrialization since governments invested in technological research for military purposes, which they could not have done if it had not been security-oriented. There was, therefore, an interplay between research for the military and research for industry, the so-called military-industrial complex that US President Eisenhower once reminded his fellow Americans about.

Does the link between militarization and industrialization exist in Africa? No, Africans buy almost every cartridge, every bullet, every gun, often even the uniforms that our soldiers wear. In most African countries, militarization has had no impact of a developmental kind at all. Perhaps at least as bad as the marriage between the military and politics in Africa is the divorce between the military and development, between the military and production, between development and defence. The fact that militarization is so totally a consumptive experience (buying equipment from the outside) rather than a productive process is one of the unfortunate prices we have had to pay.

CONCLUSION

What then is the future? Personally I think that a partial reversal of Westernization is not bad. Africans of my ilk ought to be cut down to size. They have enjoyed disproportionate influence for too long. In any case most of us constitute a cultural elite, not an economic vanguard. Therefore we are less relevant to the transformation of our societies than we might be.

Secondly, I'm not unhappy that the ancestors are fighting back, that they are saying, 'Your pact of the post-colonial era is inappropriate and therefore we shall make sure your roads won't work, your trains won't move, your telephones won't ring, your schools won't educate, and your soldiers will take over power every so often. We pronounce a curse upon all your post-colonial arrangements until a new compact of African authenticity is devised.' I'm not unhappy about that curse.

I'm not unhappy about the expanding population of Africa either, because in a way it is also a ray of hope. Here is a continent with enormous areas of disease. The continent has one of the highest rates of infant mortality world-wide, one of the worst cases of starvation and famine. It also harbours some of the worst natural killers in terms of germs. And yet the same continent has one of the highest rate of population growth. Something must be right if in spite of all that excessive mortality Africans are still capable of reincarnating the next generation. I regard the population growth as one of the signs that all is not lost. Africa is not a shrinking continent, nor is it a dying population. The Queen may be dying, but because she is at the same time reincarnating herself, long live the Queen!

Amen.

Note

1. Plenary Keynote Address at the International Conference on 'Crises of Development in Uganda'. The general thesis of this Address is developed more fully in the author's book *The Africans: A Triple Heritage*, BBC Publications, London, and Little, Brown, New York, 1986.

Bibliography

Abrams, Elliott, 1984, Testimony of Elliott Abrams, Assistant Secretary of State, Bureau of Human Rights and Humanitarian Affairs: 'Human Rights Practices in Sudan, Ethiopia, Somalia and Uganda', before the Joint Hearings: Human Rights and African Affairs Subcommittees, United States Congress, 9 August 1984

Adesimi, A.A., 1970, 'An econometric study of the air-cured tobacco supply in Western Nigeria, 1945–64', *Nigerian Journal of Economic and Social Studies*, 12,3

Ajayi, J.F.Ade, 1965, 'The continuity of African institutions under colonialism', public lecture to the International Congress on African History, Dar es Salaam, 30 September 1965

Albino, Oliver, 1970, *The Sudan, a Southern Viewpoint*, London

Amnesty International, 1972–84, *Annual Reports*, London

Amnesty International, 1978, *Human Rights in Uganda: Report*, London, June 1978

Amnesty International, 1985, *Uganda: Evidence of Torture*, London, June 1985

Apter, D.E., 1961, *The Political Kingdom in Uganda*, Princeton

Avirgan, T. and Honey, M., 1982, *War in Uganda*, London

Bagunywa, A.M., 1980, *Critical Issues in African Education. A Case Study of Uganda*, Nairobi

Bakaitwako, E. Muhima, 1981, 'The fellowship of suffering; a theological interpretation of Christian suffering under Idi Amin', unpublished PhD thesis, Northwestern University

Ballard, J.A. (ed.), 1981, *Policy-Making in a New State: Papua New Guinea*, St Lucia

Barnhum, H.N. and Sabot, R.H., 1977, 'Eduation, employment possibilities and rural–urban migration in Tanzania', *Oxford Bulletin of Economics and Statistics*, 39, 2

Bates, Robert H., 1981, *Markets and States in Tropical Africa: The Political Basis of Agricultural Policies*, Berkeley and Los Angeles

Belshaw, D.G.R., and Livingstone, I., 1981, 'The rehabilitation of the Ugandan economy: major themes in agriculture and rural development policy', *Development Studies Discussion Paper*, no. 91, University of East Anglia, Norwich

Bibangambah, J.R., 1983, 'A mischievous attitude to African agriculture', *Food Policy*, November 1983

Bisika, D.J., 1985, 'Action programme and the future of food situation in Africa, specific measures for improving food production and distribution in Africa: The Malawi case', Paper presented at AAPAM Seventh Round Table, 1985, Accra, Ghana

Boserup, Esther, 1965, *The Conditions of Agricultural Growth: The Economics of Agrarian Change under Population Pressure*, Chicago

Brett, E.A., 1973, *Colonialism and Underdevelopment in East Africa: The Politics of Economic Change 1919–1939*, London

British Refugee Council, 1983, *Exile*, No. 1, January/February

Brittain, Victoria, 1986, 'The liberation of Kampala', *New Left Review*, 156

Brock, B., 1968, 'Customary land tenure, 'individualization' and agricultural development in Uganda', *East African Journal of Rural Development*, 1, 1

Buijtenhuijs, R., 1984, 'Is Tsjaad nog een Staat?', in *Aspecten van Staat en Maatschappij in Afrika: Recent Dutch and Belgian Research on the African State*, (ed. Wim van Binsbergen and Gerti Hesseling), Research Report No. 22, African Studies Centre, Leiden

Bibliography

Bunker, Stephen G., 1984, 'Agricultural and political change in the Ugandan economic crisis', *American Ethnologist*, 11

Byarugaba, F., n.d., 'Problems of famine eradication in Uganda', unpublished paper, Department of Political Science and Public Administration

Bushenyi District Council, 1981, *Minutes*

Bushenyi District Files, 1979–84

Campbell, Horace, 1975, *Four Essays on Neo-Colonialism in Uganda: The Military Dictatorship of Amin*, CNTU, Ontario

Castle Report, *Education in Uganda*, Report of the Uganda Education Commission, 1963

Churchill, Winston S., 1908, *My African Journey*, London

Clapham, W.B., Jr., 1981, *Human Ecosystems*, London

Clay, James W., 1984, *The Eviction of the Banyarwanda: The Story behind the Refugee Crisis in Southwest Uganda*, Cambridge, Mass.

Commonwealth Secretariat, 1979, *The Rehabilitation of the Economy of Uganda: A Report by a Commonwealth Team of Experts*, 2 Vols, London

Constantin, F., 1981, Minorité religieuse et luttes politiques dans l'espace ougandais', *Politique Africaine*, 1, 4

Crisp, Jeff, 1984a, 'National security, human rights and population displacements, Luwero district, Uganda, January–December 1983', *Review of African Political Economy*

Crisp, Jeff, 1984b, 'Voluntary repatriation programmes for African refugees: a critical examination', *Refugee Issues*, 1

Crisp, Jeff, 1986, 'Uganda refugees in Sudan and Zaire: the problem of repatriation', *African Affairs*, 85, 339,

Dak, O., 1968, 'A geographic analysis of the distribution of migrants in Uganda', Makerere University, Department of Geography, *Occasional Paper No. 11*, Kampala

Dodge, Cole P., and Raundalen, Magne (eds.), 1987, *War, Violence, and Children in Uganda*, Oslo

Dodge, Cole P., and Wiebe, P.D. (eds.), 1985, *Crisis in Uganda: The Breakdown of Health Services*, Oxford

Doornbos, Martin, 1970, 'Kumanyana and Rwenzururu: two responses to ethnic inequality', in *Protest and Power in Black Africa* (ed. Robert Rotberg and Ali Mazrui), New York

Doornbos, Martin, 1975, 'Land tenure and political conflict in Ankole, Uganda', *Journal of Developing Studies*, 12, 1

Doornbos, Martin, 1978, 'Faces and phases of Ugandan politics: changing perspectives of social structure and political conflict', *African Perspectives*, 1978/2

Doornbos, Martin and Lofchie, M., 1971, 'Ranching and scheming: a case study of the Ankole ranching scheme', in *The State of the Nations* (ed. M. Lofchie), Berkely and Los Angeles

Dunn, J. (ed.), 1978, *West African States, Failure and Promise*, Cambridge

Easton, D., 1957, 'An approach to an analysis of political systems', *World Politics*, April 1957

Edel, M. (ed.), 1934, *Customs of the Baganda*, New York

Eicher, C.K., 1982, 'Facing up to Africa's Food Crisis', *Foreign Affairs*, 61109

Elizabeth of Toro, 1983, *African Princess*, London

Evans-Pritchard, E.E., 1949, *The Sanusi of Cyrenaica*, Oxford

Fallers, L.A. (ed.), 1964, *The King's Men*, London

Fanon, Frantz, 1967, *The Wretched of the Earth*, London

Feistrizer, W.V. (ed.), 1975, *Cereal Seed Technology*, Rome

Fieldhouse, D.K., 1986, *Black Africa 1945–80: Economic Decolonization and Arrested Development*, London

Friedland, W.H., and Rosberg, C.G. (eds.), 1964, *African Socialism*, London

Friedrich, K., 1968, 'Coffee-banana holdings at Bukoba – the reasons for stagnation at a higher level', in *Smallholder Farming and Smallholder Development in Tanzania* (ed. Hans Ruthenberg), Munich

Fry, G., 1983, 'Succession of government in the post-colonial states of the South Pacific: new support for constitutionalism?', *Politics*, 18, 1

Furley, Oliver W. and Watson, T., *A History of Education in East Africa*, New York

360

Bibliography

Gertzel, C., 1980, 'Uganda after Amin: the continuing search for leadership and control', *African Affairs*, 79, 317

Glentworth, G., and Hancock, I., 1973, 'Obote and Amin: change and continuity in modern Ugandan politics', *African Affairs*, 72, 288

Goldsmith, A., 1985, 'The private sector and rural development: can agribusiness help the small farmer?', *World Development*, 13

Gray, J.M., 1950, 'The year of the three kings of Buganda', *Uganda Journal*, 14, 1

Green, R.H., 1981, 'Magendo in the political economy of Uganda: pathology, parallel system or dominant sub-mode of production?', *Institute of Development Studies Discussion Paper*, No. 164, Brighton

Gukiina, Peter M., 1972, *Uganda: A Case Study in African Political Development*, London

Gwyn, D., 1977, *Idi Amin: Death-Light of Africa*, London.

Hall, M.Y. and Belshaw, D.G.R., 1972, 'Agricultural systems and nutritional problems in Uganda', in *Nutrition and Food in an African Economy* (ed. by V.F. Amann, D.G.R. Belshaw and J.P. Stanfield), Vol. 1., Makerere University, Kampala

Hamilton, A.C., 1984, *Deforestation in Uganda*, Nairobi

Hansen, Holger Bernt, 1977, *Ethnicity and Military Rule in Uganda*, Uppsala

Hansen, Holger Bernt, 1984, *Mission, Church and State in a Colonial Setting: Uganda 1890–1925*, London

Harrell-Bond, B.E., 1986, *Imposing Aid: Emergency Assistance to Refugees*, Oxford

Harriss, J. and Moore, M.P., (eds.), 1984, *Development and the Rural–Urban Divide*, London

Hastings, Adrian, 1979, *A History of African Christianity, 1950–1975*, Cambridge

Heyneman, S.P., 1983, 'Education during a period of austerity: Uganda, 1971–81', *Comparative Education Review*, 27, 4

Hill, P., 1963, *The Migrant Cocoa-Farmers of Southern Ghana: A Study in Rural Capitalism*, Cambridge

Howell, John, 1978a, 'Political leadership and organization in the southern Sudan', unpublished PhD thesis, University of Reading.

Howell, John, 1978b, 'Horn of Africa: lessons from the Sudan conflict', *International Affairs*, 54, 3

Humphrey, D. and Ward, M., 1974, *Passports and Politics*, London

Hyden, Goran, 1980, *Beyond Ujamaa in Tanzania: Underdevelopment and an Uncaptured Peasantry*, London

Hyden, Goran, 1983, *No Shortcuts to Progress: African Development Management in Perspective*, London

Hyden, Goran, 1986, 'The anomaly of the African peasantry', *Development and Change*, 17, 3

Ibingira, G., 1973, *The Forging of an African Nation*, Kampala

ICARA I, 1981, UN High Commission for Refugees, International Conference on Assistance to Refugees in Africa, *The Refugee Situation in Africa: Assistance Measures Proposed*

ICARA II, 1984, *Summary of Needs: Report of the Secretary General*

ICJ (International Commission of Jurists), 1977, *Uganda and Human Rights*, Report of the ICJ to the United Nations, Geneva

Jeffries, R., 1978, 'Political radicalism in Africa: the 'second independence'', *African Affairs*, 77, pp. 335–46

Jorgensen, J.J., 1981, *Uganda, A Modern History*, London and New York

Kabwegyere, Tarsis, 1974, *The Politics of State Formation*, Nairobi

Kagwa, A., 1905, *Empisa za Baganda*, London

Kakooza-Semanda, G. and Schluter, M., 'An internationally reputable and just way to market Uganda's coffee', mimeo

Kakungulu, H.B. and Kasozi, A.B.K., 1977, *Abaasimba Obuyisiramu mu Uganda*, Kampala

Kalecki, M., 1972, *Essays in the Economic Growth of the Socialist and Micro-Economies*, Cambridge

Karadawi, A., 1972, 'Political refugees; a case study from the Sudan 1964–1972', unpublished MPhil thesis, University of Reading

Karugire, S., 1980, *A Political History of Uganda*, London and Nairobi

Kasfir, Nelson, 1984, 'The notion of an autonomous African peasantry', Proceedings of the Second *Mawazo* Workshop on the Agrarian Question in Developing Countries, Makerere

Bibliography

Kasfir, Nelson, 1985, 'Uganda's uncertain quest for recovery', *Current History*, April

Kasfir, Nelson, 1986, 'Are African peasants self-sufficient?', *Development and Change*, 17, 2

Kasozi, A.B.K., n.d.(a), 'The Uganda Muslim Supreme Council: an experiment in Muslim administrative centralization and institutionalization, 1922–1982', unpublished paper, University of Khartoum

Kasozi, A.B.K., n.d.(b), *Uganda: Dilemma of State Formation*, paper, Department of History, University of Khartoum

Kasozi, A.B.K., 1974, 'The spread of Islam in Uganda', unpublished PhD thesis, University of California, Santa Cruz

Kasozi, A.B.K., 1976, 'The process of Islamization in Uganda, 1854–1921', *Uganda Journal*, 38

Kasozi, A.B.K., 1979, *The Crisis of Secondary School Education in Uganda, 1960–1970*, Kampala

Kasozi, A.B.K., 1986, *The Spread of Islam in Uganda*, Nairobi

Kataregga, B., 1977, 'Islamic relations with African traditional religion and Christianity in Uganda in the 19th century', public lecture at the Libyan-Arab-Uganda Cultural Centre, 28 July 1977, reproduced in *Makerere Department of Religious Studies Occasional Research Papers*, Vol. 32, 298

Kavuma, Paulo, 1979, *Crisis in Buganda 1953–55*, London

King, Noel., *et al*, 1973, *Islam and the Confluence of Religions in Uganda*, Tallahassee, Florida

Kivengere, Bishop F., 1977, *I Love Idi Amin*, London

Kiwanuka, Semakula, 1979, *Amin and the Tragedy of Uganda*, London

Kokole, Oweri, 1985, 'The 'Nubians' of East Africa: Muslim club or African 'tribe'? The view from within', *Journal of the Institute of Muslim Minority Affairs*, 6, 2

Kyemba, Henry, 1977, *State of Blood: The Inside Story of Idi Amin's Reign of Terror*, London

Kyewalyanga, F.-X.S., 1976, *Traditional Religion, Custom and Christianity in Uganda: As Illustrated by the Ganda with some References to Other African Cultures*, Freiburg

Lal, Brij, 1983, 'The Fijian general election of 1982', *Journal of Pacific History*, 18, 1–2

Langlands, B., 1977, 'Students and politics in Uganda', *African Affairs*, 76, 302

Lawrence, P. and Livingstone, I., 1983, 'Agriculture in African economic development', in *Africa South of the Sahara, 1983–84*, London

Lenin, V.I., 1956, *The Development of Capitalism in Russia*, Moscow

Linden, Ian, 1977, *Church and Revolution in Rwanda*, Manchester and New York

Lipton, M., 1977, *Why Poor People Stay Poor*, London

Lirenso, A., 1983, 'State politics in production, marketing and pricing of food grains: the case of Ethiopia', *Africa Development*, 8, 1

Lofchie, M., 1972, 'Political and economic origins of African hunger', *Journal of Modern African Studies*, 13, 4

Low, D.A., 1957, *Religion and Society in Buganda 1875–1900*, East African Institute of Social Research, Kampala

Low, D.A., 1971a, *The Mind of Buganda. Documents of the Modern History of an African Kingdom*, London

Low, D.A., 1971b, *Buganda in Modern History*, London

Low, D.A., 1973, 'Uganda unhinged', *International Affairs*, 49, 3

Ludwig, H., 1968, 'Permanent farming in Ukara; the impact of land shortage on husbandry practices', in *Smallholder Farming and Smallholder Development in Tanzania* (ed. Hans Ruthenberg), Munich

Machyo, Chango, 1984, 'Communal land tenure and rural development', a paper presented to the second *Mawazo* workshop at Makerere University, February 10–12, 1984

Machyo, Chango, 1985, 'The World Bank, IMF and deepening misery in Uganda', *Mawazo*, 6, 1

Maclure, Seton and Maclure, Peggy, 1982, Letter of 16 May 1982 from Aruska, West Nile, printed in *Uganda Church Association Newsletter*, London, November 1982

Macpherson, M., 1964, *They Built for the Future: A Chronicle of Makerere University College 1922–1962*, Cambridge

Mafeje, Archie, 1973, 'Agrarian Revolution and the Land Question in Buganda' in *Dualism and Rural Development in East Africa*, Institute of Development Research, Denmark

Bibliography

Mair, L.D., 1934, *An African People in the Twentieth Century*, London

Mamdani, M., 1976, *Politics and Class Formation in Uganda*, London

Mamdani, M., 1983, *Imperialism and Fascism in Uganda*, Nairobi

Mamdani, M., 1984, 'Analysing the agrarian question: the case of a Buganda village', *Mawazo*, 5, 3

Mamdani, M., 1987, 'Peasants and democracy in Africa, *New Left Review*, 37, 156

Martin, David, 1974, *General Amin*, London

Marx, Karl, 1961, *The Eighteenth Brumaire of Louis Bonaparte*, Moscow

Maxwell, I.C.M., 1980, *Universities in Partnership*, Edinburgh

Mazrui, Ali A., 1975, *Soldiers and Kinsmen in Uganda: The Making of a Military Ethnocracy*, Beverly Hills and London

Mazrui, Ali A., 1975, 'The rise of the lumpen-militariat', in Mazrui, *Soldiers and Kinsmen in Uganda: The Making of a Military Ethnocracy*, Beverly Hills and London

Mazrui, Ali A., 1977a, 'Violence in Uganda: is it religious, ethnic or Lebanese?', *New African Development*, February/March 1977

Mazrui, Ali A., 1977b, 'Religious strangers in Uganda: from Emin Pasha to Amin Dada', *African Affairs*, 76, 302

Mazrui, Ali A., 1978, 'Ethnic tensions and political stratification in Uganda', in *Ethnicity in Modern Africa* (ed. Brian du Toit), Boulder, Colorado

McGregor, G.P., 1967, *King's College, Budo: The First Sixty Years*, London

Minority Rights Group, 1984, *Uganda and Sudan*, Report No. 66, London

Morrison, Godfrey, 1971, *The Southern Sudan and Eritrea*, Minority Rights Group, London, Report No. 5

Mudoola, Dan, 1978, 'Religion and politics in Uganda: the case of Busoga, 1900–1962', *African Affairs*, 77, 306

Mudoola, Dan, 1983, 'The pathology of institution-building, the Tanzanian case', Paper to the Organization for Social Science Research in Eastern Africa (OSSREA), Congress at Dire Dawa, Ethiopia, June 1983

Mujaju, Akiiki B., 1976a, 'The role of the UPC as a party in government', *Canadian Journal of African Studies*, 10, 3

Mujaju, Akiiki B., 1976b, 'The political crisis of Church institutions in Uganda', *African AFfairs*, 75, 298

Munannsi, English edition, 14 September 1984

Museveni, Yoweri, 1985; 2nd edn, 1986, *Selected Articles on the Uganda Resistance War*, Nairobi

Mutesa, Kabaka of Buganda, 1967, *The Desecration of My Kingdom*, London

Muwonge, J., 1978, 'Population growth and the enclosure movement in Ankole, Uganda', *Eastern Africa Journal of Rural Development*, 11, 1 and 2

Nabudere, Dan, 1977, *The Political Economy of Imperialism*, London

Nabudere, Dan., 1980, *Imperialism and Revolution in Uganda*, Dar es Salaam

Nayenga, Peter, 1974, 'Myths and realities of Idi Amin Dada's Uganda', *African Studies Review*, 22, 2

Ndegwa, P., 1985, *Africa's Development Crisis*, Nairobi and London

Nsibambi, Apolo, 1976, 'The politics of education in Uganda, 1964–70', *Uganda Journal*, 38

Nsibambi, Apolo, 1980, 'Some reflections on the Uganda Independence Constitution of 1962', *Uganda Journal*

Nsibambi, Apolo, 1981, 'From symbiosis to antagonism: the case of the relationship between the landlord and the tenant in the rural development of Uganda', in *Rural Rehabilitation and Development* (ed. Nsibambi and Katorobo), Proceedings of the Conference held at Makerere University, 14–18 September 1981, Vol. 1

Nsibambi, Apolo, 1984, 'Four research methods in one study: a case study of Uganda', seminar paper given in the Department of Political Science and Public Administration, 29 October 1984

Nsibambi, Apolo and Byarugaba, F., 1982, 'Problems of political and administrative participation in a semi-arid area of Uganda: a case study of Karamoja', *African Review*, 9

O'Ballance, Edgar, 1977, *The Secret War in the Sudan 1955–1972*, London

Obol-Ochola, James, 1971, 'The implications of the Common Man's Charter for existing land tenure institutions in Uganda', *East Africa Journal*, 8, 2

Odaet, C.F., 1985, 'Uganda: system of education', in *The International Encyclopaedia of Education* (ed. T. Husen and T.N. Postlethwaite), Vol. 9, Oxford

Bibliography

Oded, A., 1974, *Islam in Uganda: Islamization through a Centralized State in Pre-colonial Africa*, New York and Jerusalem

Opio-Odongo and Bibangambah, J.R., 1984, 'Food self-sufficiency in Sub-Saharan Africa: a case study in Uganda', Paper prepared for an international workshop on Food Self-sufficiency in Sub-Saharan Africa, held in Tanzania, 7–9 May 1984

Pain, D., 1975, 'The Nubians: their perceived stratification system and its relation to the Asian issue', in *Expulsion of a Minority: Essays on Ugandan Asians* (ed. Michael Twaddle), London

Pirouet, M.L., 1976, 'The achievement of peace in Sudan', *Journal of Eastern African Research and Development*, 6, 1

Pirouet, M.L., 1979, 'Urban refugees in Nairobi: small numbers, large problems', Paper for African Studies Association (UK) Conference, London

Pirouet, M.L., 1980, 'Religion in Uganda under Amin', *Journal of Religion in Africa*, 11, 1

Post, K., 1972, "Peasantization' and rural political movements in western Africa', *Archives Européenes de Sociologie*, 13, 2

Raeburn, J.R., 1959, 'Some economic aspects of African agriculture', *East African Economic Review*, January, 1959

Resnick, I.N. (ed.), 1968, *Tanzania: Revolution by Education*, Arusha

Richards, A.I. (ed.), 1954, *Economic Development and Tribal Change*, Cambridge

Roberts, A.D., 1962, 'The sub-imperialism of the Baganda', *Journal of African History*, 3, 3

Rogge, John R., 1985, *Too Many, Too Long: Sudan's Twenty-Year Refugee Dilemma*, New Jersey

Rowe, John A., 1966, 'Revolution in Buganda 1856–1900', unpublished PhD thesis, University of Wisconsin

Rowe, John A., 1969, 'Myth, memoir and moral admonition: Luganda historical writing, 1893–1969', *Uganda Journal*, 33, 1

Sathyamurthy, T.V., 1978, 'Social base of the Uganda People's Congress, 1958–70', *African Affairs*, 74, 297

Saul, J. and Woods, R., 1981, 'African peasantries', in *Political Economy of Africa: Selected Readings* (ed. D. Cohen and J. Daniel), London

Scherf, Theresa, 1971, 'The Sudan conflict and its history and development', World Council of Churches, Geneva, cyclostyled.

Sekimwanyi, Shoykh A.M., n.d., *Ebyafayo Ebitonotono ku Dini ye Kiyisiramu Okuyingira mu Buganda*, Kampala

Sempangi, K., 1979, *Reign of Terror: Reign of Love*

Sempebwa, E., 1977, 'Recent land reforms in Uganda', *Makerere Law Journal*, 1, 1

Singh, Ajit, 1986, 'The IMF-World Bank policy programme in Africa: a commentary', in *World Recession and the Food Crisis in Africa* (ed. Peter Lawrence), London

Smith, G.I., 1980, *Ghosts of Kampala*, London

Soghayroun, E., 1981, *The Muslim Factor in Uganda*, Khartoum

Southall, Aidan, 1975, 'General Amin and the coup', *Journal of Modern African Studies*, 18, 4

Southall, Aidan, 1980, 'Social disorganization in Uganda', *Journal of Modern Africa Studies*, 13, 1

Southwold, M., 1961, *Bureaucracy and Chiefship in Buganda*, East African Studies, Kampala

Stigand, C.H., 1914, *Administration in Tropical Africa*, London

Symonds, R., 1986, *Oxford and the Empire: The Last Lost Cause?* London

Tandon, Yash, 1978, 'The food question in East Africa: a partial case study of Tanzania', *Africa Quarterly*, 17, 4

Taylor, J.V., 1958, *The Growth of the Church in Buganda*, London

Turok, B., 1979, 'State capitalism: the role of parastatals in Zambia', *Africa Development*, 4

Twaddle, Michael, 1972a, 'The Amin coup', *Journal of Commonwealth Political Studies*, 10

Twaddle, Michael, 1972b, 'The Muslim Revolution in Buganda', *African Affairs*, 73, 282

Twaddle, Michael, 1978, 'Was the Democratic Party of Uganda a purely confessional party?', in *Christianity in Independent Africa* (ed. E. Fashole-Luke, R. Gray, A. Hastings and G. Tasie), London

Bibliography

Twaddle, Michael, 1983a, 'Ethnic politics and support for political parties in Uganda', in *Transfer and Transformation: Political Institutions in the New Commonwealth* (ed. P. Lyon and J. Manor), Leicester

Twaddle, Michael, 1983b, 'Political violence in Uganda', in *Political Violence* (ed. W.H. Morris-Jones), London, Institute of Commonwealth Studies, mimeo

Twaddle, Michael (ed.), 1975, *The Expulsion of a Minority: Essays on Uganda Asians*, London

Uganda Department of Lands and Surveys, 1980, 'Guidelines to a New Land Policy', cyclostyled, March

Uganda Government, 1965, *Report on Uganda Census of Agriculture*, Vol. 1, Entebbe

Uganda Government, 1966, *Work for Progress, Uganda's Second Five-Year Plan, 1966–71*, Entebbe

Uganda Government, 1967, Public Order and Security Act, 20 of 1967, Entebbe

Uganda Government, 1969, *Supplement to the Second Five-Year Plan*, Entebbe

Uganda Government, 1977, *The Land Reform Decree, 1975 (Simplified and Explained to the General Public)*, Entebbe

Uganda Government, 1982–, *Background to the Budget*, published annually, Government Printer, Entebbe

UNESCO, 1973, *Educational Development in Uganda in 1971/72*, prepared for the 34th Session of the International Conference on Education to be held in Geneva from 19–27 September, 1973. Compiled by the Uganda Commission for UNESCO, August 1973

UNESCO, 1975, *Educational Development in Uganda, 1973/75*, prepared for the 35th Session of the International Conference on Education in Geneva from 27 August – 4 September 1975. Compiled by the Uganda Commission for UNESCO, August 1975

UNESCO, 1983, *Uganda Education: Recovery and Reconstruction*, UNESCO, Paris

United States Congress, 1985, 99th Congress, First Session, *Country Reports on Human Rights Practices, 1984*, pp. 360–70, February 1985

Vincent, Joan, 1982, *Teso in Transformation: The Political Economy of Peasants and Class in Eastern Africa*, Berkeley and Los Angeles

Walker, D. and Erhlich, C., 1959, 'Stabilization and development policy in Uganda: an appraisal', *Kyklos*,

Wallace, T., 1981, 'The challenge of food: Nigeria's approach to agriculture, 1975–80, *Canadian Journal of African Studies*, 15, 2

Wallis, C., 1953, *Report on Inquiry into African Local Government in the Protectorate of Uganda*, Entebbe

Wanji, B.A., n.d., 'A preliminary post-graduate research paper on the Nubi of East Africa', *Sociology Working Paper*, 115, Makerere University

Warner, A., 1958, 'African students and the English background' *English Language Teaching*, 10

Watt, W.M., 1961, *Muhammed, Prophet and Statesman*, London

Welbourn, F.B., 1965, *Religion and Politics in Uganda 1952–1962*, Nairobi

Whyte, Michael A., 1977–8, 'Blocked development: an analysis of bureaucracy and social reproduction in Bunyole, Uganda', *Folk*, 19–20

Willetts, P., 1975, 'The politics of Uganda as a one-party state 1969–70', *African Affairs*, 74, 296

Wolfson, M., 1985, 'Population and poverty in sub-Saharan Africa' in *Crisis and Recovery in Sub-Saharan Africa* (ed. T. Rose), Paris

Woodling, D. and Barnett, R., 1980, *Uganda Holocaust*

Woodward, Peter, 1978, 'Ambiguous Amin', *African Affairs*, 77, 307

Woodward, Peter, 1979, *Condominium and Sudanese Nationalism*, London

Woodward, Peter, 1984, 'Relations between neighbouring states in North-East Africa', *Journal of Modern African Studies*, 22, 2

World Bank, 1962, *Report on Economic Development in Uganda*, Washington, DC

World Bank, 1982, *Uganda: Country Economic Memorandum*, Washington, DC

World Bank, 1984, *Uganda: Agricultural Sector Memorandum: The Challenge beyond Rehabilitation*, Washington, DC

World Bank, 1985, *Uganda: Progress towards Recovery and Prospects for Development*, Washington, DC

Worthington, E.B., 1949, *A Development Plan for Uganda: The 1948 Revision of the Plan*, Entebbe

Bibliography

Wrigley, Christopher, 1959, *Crops and Wealth in Uganda*, East African Studies, 17, Kampala,

Young, Crawford, 1982, *Ideology and Development in Africa*, New Haven

Young, C.E., 1983, 'The northern republics, 1960–1980', in *History of Central Africa*, 2 (ed. D. Birmingham and P.M. Martin), London

Zwanenberg, R.M.A. van and Anne King, 1975, *An Economic History of Kenya and Uganda 1800–1970*, London

Index

Index

Index

Index

Index